D1190776

The Ideology of *Kokugo*

The Ideology of *Kokugo*

Nationalizing Language in Modern Japan

Lee Yeounsuk

Translated by Maki Hirano Hubbard

University of Hawai'i Press

Honolulu

"*Kokugo*" to iu shiso
by Yeounsuk Lee
©1996 by Yeounsuk Lee
Originally published in Japanese in 1996 by Iwanami Shoten, Publishers, Tokyo.
This English-language edition published in 2010 by the University of Hawai'i Press,
Honolulu, by arrangement with the author c/o Iwanami Shoten, Publishers, Tokyo.
Translator's introduction ©2010 University of Hawai'i Press

15 14 13 12 11 10   6 5 4 3 2 1

Library of Congress Cataloging-in-Publication Data
Yi, Yon-suk.
  [Kokugo to iu shiso. English]
  The ideology of kokugo : nationalizing language in modern Japan / Lee Yeounsuk ;
translated by Maki Hirano Hubbard.
    p. cm.
  Includes bibliographical references and index.
 ISBN 978-0-8248-3305-3 (hard cover : alk. paper)
  1. Japanese language—Philosophy. 2. Language policy—Japan. I. Title.
  PL513.I513 2009
  495.6'01—dc22

                    2009029427

University of Hawai'i Press books are printed on acid-free
paper and meet the guidelines for permanence and
durability of the Council on Library Resources.

Designed by the University of Hawai'i Press production staff

Printed by Edwards Brothers, Inc.

Contents

Translator's Introduction

This is a translation of Lee Yeounsuk's 1996 book *Kokugo to iu shisō: Kindai Nihon no gengo ninshiki* (literally, *The Idea of Kokugo: Perceptions of Language in Modern Japan*). In this book Lee Yeounsuk powerfully demonstrates the political nature of language. She details the history of the construction of an ideology of "the Japanese language" through a careful and meticulous reexamination of primary source materials, many of which have been neglected by mainstream scholars. She begins by questioning the very possibility of such an entity as "the Japanese language" at the beginning of Japan's modernization—the notion of such a monolithic unity as "the Japanese language" did not exist in the early Meiji period.

Lee discusses how *kokugo* was created as a value-laden norm suitable for Japan as a modern nation-state, locking together a political community called a "nation" with a linguistic community that was assumed to share the same language throughout that nation. Focusing on the Ueda Kazutoshi–Hoshina Kōichi line of contributions to this history, she illustrates various efforts to overcome the state of linguistic disarray from the early Meiji period through the numerous debates and proposals for the reduction or abolition of Chinese characters, the unification of written and spoken languages, and the standardization of language and script.

In doing so, she also demonstrates the competition within the field of language studies as well as the shifting views between conservatives and reformists, all contributing to the search for a Japanese linguistic identity based on a tacitly shared premise. That shared premise was of "the unshakable homogeneity of the Japanese language," a premise born of the political climate of the time, including Japan's colonization of East Asian countries.

The Japanese Language before the Meiji Period

Before I continue, let me offer a brief historical overview of the Japanese language in order to situate Lee's own introductory chapter in the linguistic context of the time and also to help readers understand some terms that frequently appear in her discussion (these terms are boldfaced.)

There are some Chinese documents about Japan written in China as early as the third century, as well as ancient artifacts in Japan with Chinese inscriptions, all of which indicate that there was some communication between the two countries using Chinese language and characters. However, the Japanese language did not have a written form or its own orthography before the importation of Buddhism in the sixth century. Gradually, these writings in Chinese were modified to suit Japanese word order. Both the original Chinese texts (various documents, poetry, prose literature, etc.) and the Japanese texts that were written in Chinese word order were later generally called **kanbun**. The common practice was to read these texts according to Japanese word order and pronunciation together with the aid of diacritics, a method called **kanbun kundoku**.[1] While each Chinese character (later called **kanji**) was an ideogram, a semantic element, the Japanese also started to use the characters as phonetic symbols, approximating their original Chinese pronunciation and disregarding the semantic value, in order to write Japanese sentences and phrases. This method was extensively used in *Man'yōshū*, the earliest anthology of Japanese poetry, compiled in the late eighth century, and was called **Man'yō kana**.

It was from this *Man'yō kana* that **hiragana** was devised, through a running or cursive writing of the Chinese characters, in order to transcribe Japanese phonetic syllables. Another set of letters for the same set of phonetic syllables, **katakana**, was also devised by adopting certain parts of *Man'yō kana*, and was used as an aid to reading Chinese texts in Japanese word order. The word *kana*, in both *hiragana* (hira+kana, running *kana*) and *katakana* (partial *kana*) literally meant "temporary script" as opposed to *mana*, the true or authentic script, which was the Chinese characters—indicating that the Chinese characters, *kanji*, were the official script with prestige and authority, and *kana* was for unofficial or personal use. *Kana*, being phonetic symbols, allowed users to write their native language (**yamato kotoba**) freely, and by the late tenth century *kana* contributed to the production of a flourishing Japanese literature, including *The Tale of Genji* (early eleventh century). Texts written in this classical native language later became the model for **wabun**, the language inherited from premodern literature.

Nonetheless, *kanbun* continued to be the script for men of letters and power and maintained its official status into the early Meiji period. Public and official documents and academic essays were written in *kanbun*. At the same time, classical literature in *wabun* was considered to be a representation of a Japanese ethos and aesthetics, and became the object of **wagaku** or later **kokugaku** (studies of Japanese classics). The *kanbun* writing had been "Japanized" over time as **wa-kan konkōbun** (mixture of *wabun* and *kanbun kundoku*), which appeared after the thirteenth century. Men in the lower classes joined the *kanbun* users, creating an epistolary style called **sōrōbun**, with each sentence ending with the peculiar copula *sōrō*. Yet neither *wabun* nor *kanbun* (and its derivations) reflected the evolution or changes in the spoken language; hence, by the time of the Meiji period the written and spoken languages were extremely disparate. Furthermore, the Japanese spoken language itself had many variations in different regions that had been isolated from each other under the feudal domain system for hundreds of years, variations so different that they were often mutually unintelligible. After the Meiji Restoration, as Japan drove quickly towards modernization, the disparity between the written and spoken language as well as among the dialects was considered a hurdle to be cleared in order for Japan to emerge as a modern nation. The so-called *futsūbun* was devised in the Meiji period for common use, using the standard eclectic **bungo** (written language) in a *kanbun* style following the grammar of classical Japanese. Nonetheless, the authority of the deep-rooted conventions of the written language, whether of the *kanbun* or *wabun* tradition, continued, still associated with prestige and a sign of the educated classes.

Synopsis

This was the linguistic reality in Japan at the beginning of modernization, and as Lee explains in her introduction, this was what made Mori Arinori despair and seek to adopt English: with the chaotic state of the Japanese language, entangled with *kanbun* and *yamato kotoba,* Japan could not survive in the modern world. Countering Mori's fears, Baba Tatsui argued in defense of Japanese for its systematic organization, an argument that resulted in his writing in English a comprehensive book of Japanese grammar. It is interesting here that both Mori's and Baba's arguments were written in English, and most of Baba's other writings were also in English: at the beginning of Japan's modernization, for those intellectuals knowledgeable about Western language and culture, the conventions of the Japanese language were not suitable for expressing or discussing new ideas.

This was when the Meiji government promulgated a series of school orders, directed towards instituting a modern educational system in order to educate the general public. An infinite set of *kanji* was considered a hindrance for the promotion of public education as well as for the expanding public communication media. Starting with Maejima Hisoka's proposal for the abolition of *kanji,* there came voluminous debates about which script was appropriate for the new nation, including advocacy for the adoption of *rōmaji* (roman letters) by Nishi Amane or adoption of *hiragana* by Shimizu Usaburō, to name but a few.

The new wave of novelists, such as Futabatei Shimei and Yamada Bimyō, also began to explore the use of colloquial language in order to express creatively the new ideas and emotions they were experiencing during this time of great change, and they made significant contributions to the process of **gen-bun itchi**, the unification of written and spoken languages. Japan had officially declared its modern nationhood through the promulgation of the Great Japan Imperial Constitution (1889), and it was in this linguistic and political context that Ueda Kazutoshi returned from Europe, inspired by the Neogrammarians' new movement in the Western science of language. He was appointed professor of philology at Tokyo Imperial University in 1894, the same year Japan engaged in the first Sino-Japanese war. With the collaboration of the government, Ueda passionately argued for the need to standardize the Japanese language in order to establish it as the nation's language, **kokugo**, and he initiated the academic field of **kokugogaku**, to "theorize" *kokugo*. Ueda inspired many excellent scholars who followed his lead, including Hoshina Kōichi. Thus this creation of *kokugogaku* connected a pseudo-scienticism with a national identity—that is, it connected language scholarship and politics.

Within the framework of the aspirations of modernization (i.e., Westernization) and the practical needs for education and communication, Lee illustrates how Ueda tried to disentangle the Japanese language from its myriad attachments to traditional linguistic conventions in *wabun* or *kanbun*. She also shows how the movements towards *kokugo* were intensified by a desire to free the nation from Chinese traditions at the time of modern Japan's first war against—and victory over—another country.

Following successive victories in the Russo-Japanese War (1904) and World War I (1914–1918), however, the rising ultranationalism in the Empire of Japan turned against such language reform, and the ideas advocated by Hoshina, Ueda's loyal student, often became the targets of attack—even to the extent of intimidating the Ministry of Education, of which Hoshina was a member. Nonetheless, Lee shows how Hoshina persistently tried to carry out Ueda's ideals, unaffected by the fanatic climate of the times, even through World War II. Lee points out here that by that time *kokugo* was tied to Japan's **kokutai** (the national polity or identity) and the notion of Japanese race and blood, and that when Japan tried to "assimilate" the colonized into the Greater East Asia Co-prosperity Sphere through the imposition of *kokugo,* the self-contradiction of such an ideology became apparent.

Lee traces Hoshina's experience and observation of the problems in multi-lingual nations in Europe, which convinced him of the need to systematically standardize Japanese, oppress dialects in the **naichi** (homeland), and then to apply this method in order to assimilate the colonized in the **gaichi** (Japan's colonies). Facing difficulties in this policy of assimilation in spite of the government's enormous effort to enforce *kokugo* in the colonies, Hoshina offered his vision of **kokka-go**, a state language, but it was considered a distortion of the empire's *kokugo* and never received academic or political attention at that time—a time of conflict between modernity and conservatism, between modern linguistics and the Japanese tradition. In spite of his numerous writings and conspicuous but continuous devotion to Japanese language policy for fifty years, Hoshina has been, as Lee says, a scholar forgotten after the war, forgotten together with the ideological undercurrents of *kokugo* in that history.

As if revealing writings done in invisible ink, Lee shows how the principles of the Ueda-Hoshina line survived in language policy after the war until today, and how oblivious scholarship and politics can be to the connection of this language policy with the history of colonial language policies in general.

Significance of This Book

There were numerous studies before and after World War II about **kokugo kokuji mondai**, that is, issues of Japan's national language and script. Most of the books on *kokugogaku* published after the war paid very little attention to Japan's colonial language policy, nor did they discuss Hoshina's ideas until very recently. Hoshina isn't even to be found in the index of the 1,500-page *Nihongo hyakka daijiten* (An Encyclopaedia of the Japanese Language, 1990),[2] nor does its sixty-page chapter on language policy and education mention anything about Japan's language policy in the colonies.[3] In the fiftieth anniversary publication of *Kokugogaku no 50-nen* (Fifty Years of *Kokugo* Research) by Kokugo Gakkai (Association for Kokugogaku), his name is mentioned in only three lines in one article,[4] even though the title reminds us of Hoshina's *Kokugo mondai 50-nen* (Fifty Years of *Kokugo* Issues), and Hoshina was one of the founding members of the association and on its board from 1944 until the first publication of its journal in 1948.

As you will see, Lee's book, situated in the time of Japan's modernization, imperialism, and colonization, is also a critique of the scope of conventional research in the field of *kokugo*, which ignored or was oblivious to the political aspects of language policies. Research on Japanese language policy and linguistic ethnicity has advanced in the last few decades. Prior to Lee's work on these topics there was other research, by such as Toyoda (1964), Suzuki and Yokoyama (1984), and Tanaka (1978, 1981), as well as works by Lee's contemporaries such as Shi (1993), Oguma (1995), Kawamura (1994), Yasuda (1997b), and Koyasu (1994), but Lee is perhaps the first scholar to begin her inquiry by exploring Japan's linguistic consciousness at the dawn of its modernization. She does so by reexamining the public's long-held negative view of Mori Arinori, a view that had been firmly constructed and disseminated by authorities in the academic field of Japanese language study. The native speakers of Japanese today, as Lee also points out, take it for granted that they have always spoken or written "one" language, Japanese, and thus have neglected questions of linguistic identity. In fact, the discussion of linguistic identity has tended to take on a more nationalistic tone, particularly in the face of external challenges.

Lee urges us to pay attention to the linguistic consciousness underneath scholarship and language policies in order to understand the ideology of *kokugo* as an academic apparatus as well as a political concept. Her critical discussion of the construction of *kokugo* reveals a cultural nationalism, long nurtured in the general education system in Japan and overpowering academic traditions as well.

When first published at the end of 1996, Lee's book did not receive much recognition from traditional schools of Japanese linguistics or Japanese history. At the same time, as found on the Internet at that time, the book became a target of harsh attacks by the right wing—Lee actually received waves of hate letters for daring to write this book.

However, the timeliness and importance of the book are demonstrated by the very fact that it was published by Iwanami, Japan's most prestigious academic publisher, and the fact that it was awarded the 1997 Prize for Social Sciences and Humanities by the Suntory Foundation in the category of Literary and Art Criticism, a prize given to those who have made "original and distinguished accomplishments in research or criticism with a broad perspective on society and culture."[5]

Lee's work has inspired a great number of readers among a new generation of critical studies of Japan's modernity and was reprinted a scant four months after its initial publication. The book has been quoted in numerous recent research works in the field of sociolinguistics, cultural studies, and language education[6] and is listed in the syllabi in many university courses in Japan.

The Dualism of "the Japanese Language"

The English expression "the Japanese language" corresponds to the Japanese terms *nihongo* and *kokugo*. *Nihongo* is said to be a neutral term to objectively describe or name the Japanese language as one of the many languages of the world. It is also *nihongo* that is taught to "non-Japanese" as a second or foreign language, as opposed to *"kokugo,"* which is the language taught to Japanese people in Japanese schools.

Shibata Takeshi, in his 1976 "Sekai no naka no nihongo" (*Nihongo* in the World), explains that *kokugo* is the language symbolic of *kokka*, the nation-state; *kokugo* is expected to be the only language in that nation. Shibata notes that the word *kokugo* tends to point to the uniqueness of the Japanese language while the word *nihongo* points to its universality. He also writes that *kokugo* has the connotation of "our language" or "the language just for us" while *nihongo* does not have such a connotation, implying that *nihongo* is for "other" people (3–5). However, Shibata immediately contradicts himself on the following page: "The Japan nation *(nihon-koku)* only has *nihongo*. *Nihon-koku* is the country where only *nihongo* is understood . . . *Nihongo* is the language of *nihonjin* (the Japanese people)" (6). And then he defines *nihonjin* not as those who have Japanese nationality, but those who belong to the Yamato race *(Yamato minzoku)*, who speak only *nihongo* (7). Thus Shibata Takeshi, one of the most influential academic authorities in the mainstream of scholarship on the Japanese language, contributed to the popularization of the *nihonjinron* discourse.

In spite of the rise of critical research during the last three decades, however, such a discourse still incites public feelings, as seen, for example, in the fact that Haga Yasushi's book *Nihonjin rashisa no kōzō*, which contains comments like the one below, saw a second printing two months after its first publication:

> The principles of the membership of a nation *(minzoku)* are that its members share not only a language but also a "way of life," in both physical and psychological aspects; they share the same fate *(unmei)* in a history that is objectively recognizable; and they hold a subjective sense of unity with other members in the group. The [English] word "nation," which refers to *minzoku*, shares the etymology of "nature" or "native," and thus indicates its essential meaning as a group which *naturally* grows in the various milieu of peoples in the world. (2004, 23; emphasis added)

Such arguments have been the backbone of the deep-seated *nihonjinron* discourse and continue to be widely accepted by the general public in twenty-first-century Japan—even though we can easily recognize that such a "national membership" is a product of the imagination: the Japanese populace consists of people who speak different languages or dialects and live in communities that practice different ways of life (violating the first principle); many come from different countries or have different experiences of Japan's history (violating the second principle); and many are legally "Japanese" or "native Japanese speakers" but have more than one cultural or ethnic background (violating the third principle). Moreover, such a view fundamentally contradicts Japan's expressed commitment to "internationalization" in that it denies "nonmembers'" participation in or entry into the "cultural community" as well as the "linguistic community." If a person violates any of the principles above, he or she cannot be a member of the nation or *minzoku* Japan, thus nullifying the possibilities of Japanese language education or scholarship by "non-Japanese."[7]

As Sakai Naoki points out, however,

> As long as we consider "Japanese people," "Japanese language," and "Japanese culture" as the three inherent attributes of [Japanese society and as] a unity, we are not able to imagine any different way a society can exist. . . . Such a framework excludes the possibility that different languages or cultures could coexist in one person: it excludes a person who is Japanese but does not share the "Japanese culture," or who speaks Japanese but is not a Japanese [citizen]." (1996, 141)

Today, scholars of the younger generations are critical and cautious about the implications of the *nihonjinron* discourse. In the profession of language teaching in Japan, too, more and more teachers recognize the diversity of Japanese society, and some of them protest the use of the word *kokugo*. Dr. Lee once shared with me the following episode: In an elementary school in a part of Osaka that has a large population of Korean Japanese, a young teacher decided to change the subject name from *kokugo* to *nihongo*. His conviction was that the Japanese language spoken by Japanese people, regardless of their race or where they live, is *nihongo*, as one of the many languages of the world, and he was also sensitive to the painful memories of Korean people regarding *kokugo*. As soon as his change was discovered, however, the Ministry of Education clamped down on him and immediately gave strict orders to change the subject name back to *kokugo*.

Nonetheless, changes have taken place over the last decade. As the year 2004 opened, after much debate the Association for Kokugogaku changed its name to Association for Nihongogaku, and the name of its journal from *Kokugogaku* to *Nihongo no kenkyū* (Study of the Japanese Language).[8] In his statement for the inaugural issue of the renamed journal, Maeda Tomiyoshi, chairperson at that time, explained the rationale behind the changes as follows: the study of the Japanese language must respond to developments in actual practice, such as the fact that many universities had recently changed the name of their departments of *kokugo kokubun* (national language and literature) to that of *nihongo nihon-bungaku* (Japanese language and literature); the increasing demand to promote research on *nihongo* to support its teaching (to non-Japanese); and the increasing demand in a highly technological society for processing information in Japanese. "The journal with the new title is to respond to such new circumstances and looks forward into the future, but at the same time it will by no means disregard the rich achievements of *kokugogaku*. I expect the members of the association not to forget that the new research in *nihongo* today is a result of the long history of the previous research, and also ask them to review that history from new perspectives."[9]

I think that the works of Lee and her contemporaries contributed somehow to such new scholarly movements and changes in academic institutions. And I wonder whether such changes in universities will eventually spread to a lower-school curriculum that has traditionally been tightly controlled by the government.

Translating This Book

There are several reviews of this book in Japanese (e.g., Yasuda 1997a), but I have seen so far only one review in English, by Marshall Unger (2000). Unger commends Lee's book as an excellent history of Japan's dilemma: "if the essence of *kokugo* lay in how it arose *naturally* in the hearts of Japanese, how could one teach it *artificially* to non-Japanese?" (148; emphasis in original). At the same time, however, Unger seems to have found Lee's writing emotional and biased, and he questions her scholarly objectivity—the opposite of my impression. In fact, this criticism was one reason that motivated me to translate this book: the notion of "objectivity" has been a controversial question in academic circles, and I found Lee's writing very sober and substantial. Even if the reviewer perceives Lee's work to be biased, possibly because of her Korean nationality, it is nevertheless important for interested readers to hear a different story, especially those who are more likely used to the *nihonjinron* rhetoric in this and many other fields.

Another reason that I wanted to translate this book is more personal. Lee, a Korean speaker, wrote this book in Japanese, and I, a Japanese speaker, have translated it into English. Notions of hegemony of any kind, including linguistic, are often challenged by the simple appearance of a minority voice. I believe that Lee is making a significant statement by writing the book in Japanese rather than her own native language. She has challenged the long-held belief in the homogeneity of the Japanese language, and her writing in Japanese is her way of actually practicing "non-Japanese Japanese language," as she mentions in closing: "Whether or not the idea of *kokugo* will be transformed into the ideology of a 'state language' or 'Co-Prosperity language' will depend on how seriously we listen to the voices in this 'non-Japanese Japanese.'" Thus she leaves us with critical questions about the authenticity of the Japanese language, including the meaning of "native speakers," and so too implicitly cautions us that today's fascination with the "internationalization" of the Japanese language can be seen as a refashioning of the same process as Japan's linguistic colonization in the past.

As we "reimagine" the future of globalizing postmodern Japan, we are curious to see how the dualism of the language as *kokugo* and *nihongo* will be transformed. It will also be interesting to see if and how the move from *kokugo* to *nihongo* in academic circles will change or develop the ideology of *kokugo* and the linguistic consciousness of the Japanese people in both public and governmental sectors.

I hope, as a reader deeply moved and inspired by Lee's work, that I have been able to convey her superb scholarship and academic passion. I have also tried to offer my English-speaking colleagues as well as students access to current critical research on *kokugo* written in Japanese. The translation of this book will be of interest not only to linguists, but also to historians, anthropologists, political scientists, and scholars in the fields of education and cultural studies.

My translation could not have been completed without Marian Macdonald's patient and thoughtful support in proofreading and editing. I am also thankful to Smith College for the funding to make my translation and its publication possible.

I have provided annotations wherever they seemed appropriate, and a chronology of events for readers' convenience. Notes that gave sources only have been moved to the text, enclosed in parentheses.

Maki Hirano Hubbard
October 2008

Acknowledgments

Ueda Kazutoshi is mentioned in every discussion about *kokugo*. However, Hoshina Kōichi, who attempted to introduce the term and concept of *kokka-go* (a state language) into Japanese, deserves the same recognition.

Dr. Tanaka Katsuhiko, my graduate adviser at Hitotsubashi University, once told me that Dr. Kamei Takashi (who died last year) had always urged the development of scholarship on *kokugogaku* in its genuine sense separate from *nihongogaku*, that is, a field of research into various phenomena that have been discussed under the name of *kokugo*. He had hoped someone would recognize Hoshina's contributions.

I am not sure if I have been able to fulfill Dr. Kamei's wish, but believe that I came to understand Hoshina very well. I only wish I could have presented this book to Dr. Kamei.

The chapters below are revised versions of articles previously published as follows:

Introduction: "Mori Arinori to Baba Tatsui no nihongo-ron: 'Kokugo' izen no nihongo" (Views of Mori Arinori and Baba Tatsui—the Japanese Language before *Kokugo*), *Shisō,* September 1990.
Chapters 8 and 9: "Kokugogaku to Gengogaku" (*Kokugo* Studies and Linguistics), *Gendai shisō,* August 1994.
Chapters 11, 13, and 14: "Hoshina Kōichi to gengo seisaku" (Hoshina Kōichi and Language Policies), *Bungaku,* May 1989.
Chapter 12: "Dōka to wa nani ka" (What Is "Assimilation"?), *Gendai shisō,* June 1996.

Yeounsuk Lee
November 1996

The Ideology of *Kokugo*

Prologue

Language and the Imagined Community

Language is the most basic evidence of being human. Ordinary people speak their mother tongue without being conscious of what language they are speaking and without referring to the rules of the language as grammarians do. Moreover, even the recognition that they are speaking a particular "language" is itself alien to them. In that sense, the moment they are made aware that they are speaking a certain kind of language or a national language, a new history of their language begins—a history of alienation from it.

When the critical consciousness does not interfere, we simply speak without any notion of our mother tongue as a particular or an objectified "language." However, when we start seeking an authority or a principle in speaking, "language" becomes an entity that precedes and dominates the simple act of speaking. It is then no longer the case that the speaking creates language, but rather that a certain "language" is thought to exist somewhere and to be the concealed foundation of speaking. Only then can we define, without hesitation, language as merely a tool of communication, because before then language could not have been "a tool" that could be taken out of the extralinguistic context.

Although the definition of language as a tool of communication is not completely wrong, it falsifies by obscuring the nature of the historical process whereby a "language" is alienated from speaking. To imagine language as an entity separate from the act of speaking and to consider language as a neutral tool arbitrarily abstracted from its context are two sides of the same coin. By the same token, linguistic nationalism—which considers language the essence of an ethnic spirit—and linguistic instrumentalism—which regards language as only a neutral tool of communication—are linked in a new era of "language" of a highly ideological nature.

According to Benedict Anderson (1983), language is capable of creating an imagined community and thus constructing a special unity, because "the members of even the smallest nation will never know most of their fellow-members,

1

meet them, or even hear of them, yet in the minds of each lives the image of their communion" (15). Here, language is indeed the means for shared communion—it is the bread blessed by the Holy Spirit, and sometimes too it presides over the communion. For Anderson, this shared communion presupposes that the group owns one language in common. However, is it really and universally true that members of a society are always aware of the coownership of their language and find significant value in it? Anderson defines a "nation" not as a visible institution but as an imagined political community. Then linguistic identity, or the identity of a linguistic community, is as much a product of the imagination as is "national" identity: each member of the linguistic community believes that every member, even those whom they have never met or spoken with, speaks one and the same language. Such a sense of coownership of a language transcending experience is obviously a product of history, just as is a political community. It is when these two communities—that is, a political community called a "nation" and a linguistic community sharing the same "language"—are interlocked in the imagination that a clear image of what is called "a national language" is created.

An institution called "the national language" appeared during the French Revolution in order to support the modern nation-state: the French language, as *la langue nationale,* became the symbol of the nation's spiritual unity. However, even before the revolution, the sense of linguistic identity already existed as a truism, which had been manipulated by the Ordonnance de Villers-Cotterêts or Académie Française.[1] The revolutionaries were but the successors to this ready-made linguistic tradition. Such, however, is not always the case: a national language is not always the result of melding a national identity or national institution with a preexisting sense of linguistic identity or with the identity of a linguistic community. The birth of Japan's national language, *kokugo,* has quite a different background from that of France.

In modern Japan, it is not the case that *nihongo,* the Japanese language, provided the solid foundation for the construction of *kokugo,* the national language. Rather, we can almost say, it was only after the showy tower of *kokugo* was constructed that the foundation, the identity of the Japanese language, was hurriedly made up.

It is widely recognized today that *kokugo* implies an invented concept steeped in various ideologies. On the other hand, *nihongo* is considered as referring to a neutral and objective entity recognized as such in the field of linguistics. However, even such an unassuming concept as *nihongo* cannot exist outside of a certain framework of consciousness. Kamei Takashi (1971), for example, rightly points out the concealed problem in the concept of *nihongo:*

There is no longer an obvious answer to the question "What, then, is the Japanese language?" For language cannot exist for us as a uniform entity or as a real object without an act of abstraction (229). . . . If we were taught to accept the language in the *Man'yōshū*[2] and that of the twentieth century as being the same "Japanese language" in spite of their substantial differences, it is, to say the least, because of arbitrary decisions based on certain preconceptions, rather than the study of the language in a genuine sense. Such arbitrary decisions are derived from the preconception of a mystical and metaphysical absolute that transcends history. (232)

Kamei is questioning here a diachronic identity of language that is guaranteed by temporal continuity. Similarly, we can also question a synchronic identity of language: the concept of *kokugo* can exist only if all those who live in this political and social space called Japan believe that they are speaking the same Japanese language. In reality, language has numerous variations in different regions, classes, and styles. It is only because there is a consistent, common measure that we discern the variations, however disjointed they are. That is, the foundation of *kokugo* calls for the belief that there is a solid consistency in the language beyond the actual variations: the belief in the imagined homogeneity of *kokugo* is essential, relegating actual variations to secondary importance. Obviously, in order to institutionalize *kokugo*, these variants had to be extinguished politically through a standardization of the language. However, the nature of language itself does not allow complete homogeneity. Therefore, the establishment of *kokugo*, along with the actual policies of standardization, required the production of an *imaginaire*.

When we attempt to throw light on language consciousness in modern Japan, we tend to overlook the fact that the process of establishing *kokugo* coincided with the advent of studies verifying the homogeneity of the Japanese language itself. While important, such studies were but the unobtrusive foundations for the showy construction of *kokugo*. Moreover, "the homogeneity of the Japanese language" also depends on one's intangible sense about the language, and is taken for granted if one is not a keen and shrewd observer. As long as we assume the uniformity of the Japanese language unquestioningly, we will not be able to explain the mysterious power of the idea of *kokugo*. Therefore, we must first go back to the time before the establishment of *kokugo* and look into the thinking of those who were not at all certain about the existence of a "single Japanese language." I will do this in the introduction.

Linguistic modernity in Japan was triggered by the uncertainty about whether or not such a monolithic linguistic unity as "the Japanese language"

existed at all. We can say that *kokugo,* then, is the idea that was created to forcefully expel this uncertainty. *Kokugo* did not exist a priori: the idea of *kokugo* was
absent from early Meiji. The idea and institution were gradually constructed,
simultaneously with the process in which Japan was building itself as a modern
nation. My approach will be different from the usual discussion of the origin
of the concept of *kokugo,* which refers to the tradition of *kokugaku,* the study
of Japanese classics, founded by Motoori Norinaga. I interpret *kokugo* as a
peculiar manifestation of Japan's modernity, more specifically, Japan's linguistic
modernity, for the following reasons.

It is indeed the case that *kokugaku* clearly connected the "Japanese spirit"
and the Japanese language. However, the language that those scholars idealized was *yamato kotoba,* the ancient language of Yamato free from *karagokoro,*
"the Chinese mind," and was confined to ancient writings such as the *Kojiki.*[3] It
was neither *kokugo* nor even the Japanese language *(nihongo). Kokugo* was the
ultimate representation of the idea of connecting the Japanese language to the
Japanese spirit. Thus, schooling in *kokugo,* not *nihongo,* became the important
basis of every assimilation policy in Japan's colonies through World War II.
That is, the ideology of *kokugo* was part and parcel of Japan's colonialism. The
investigation of how this ideology of *kokugo* was constructed will shed light on
another source of Japan's colonialism. At the same time, we may find in the idea
of *kokugo* a clue to prove that Japan's colonization was not simply a by-product
of the establishment of modern Japan. Rather, it was deeply intrinsic to Japan's
modernity itself.

Kokugo lived on even after Japan surrendered its colonies. The defeat did not
mean the end of the ideology of *kokugo: kokugo,* which was once a part of the
ideological basis of colonization, did not die even after Japan lost its colonies.
The institution of *kokugo* envisioned by two important scholars—Ueda Kazutoshi, who was the first to draw a clear picture of *kokugo* in his lecture "Kokugo
to kokka *to"* (The National Language and the Nation-state), and his successor
Hoshina Kōichi—is far more relevant to the linguistic context of postwar Japan
than it was before the war. That is, in the history of the ideology of *kokugo* there
is no definitive break between prewar and postwar times.

Investigating first the context of early Meiji where *kokugo* initially made
its shadowy appearance, I focus on the lineage from Ueda to Hoshina. There
were, of course, other important people responsible for the ideology of *kokugo.*
However, I believe that the Ueda-Hoshina lineage has crucial significance for
understanding the ideology of *kokugo* in its linguistic nature in addition to
its political and ideological implications. The ideological history of language
tends to be relegated to histories of philosophy, politics, or literature. Because,
however, *kokugo* is primarily a linguistic ideology, it requires an analysis of its

linguistic nature. This book, therefore, attempts to demonstrate that the ideological history of language has its own autonomous outline and structure. I discuss *kokugo* from the viewpoint of the ideological history of language in relation to Japan's linguistic modernity. This discussion will render visible the ideo-historical foundation for Japan's colonialism as well as the "modernity" of the Japanese language itself.

Outline of This Book

The introduction argues that the Japanese language had not been perceived as an autonomous unity before the idea of *kokugo*. In part 1, "*Kokugo* Issues in Early Meiji," I discuss changes in the idea of *kokugo* through the fourth decade of Meiji. Chapters 1 and 2 explain the historical background of the problems in scripts and styles, which later became crucial for determining what *kokugo* was in reality. Chapter 3 traces the ideological background of the formation of the idea of *kokugo* during this period.

Part 2, "Ueda Kazutoshi and His Ideas about Language," focuses on the centrality of Ueda's thinking in the formation of the modern idea of *kokugo*. His criticism of traditional *kokugaku* and his acceptance of modern linguistics are outlined in chapter 4. Chapter 5 explains the basis of Ueda's idea of language, scrutinizing his well-known lecture "Kokugo to kokka to." Chapter 6 discusses Ueda's creation of the field of *kokugogaku* (the study of the Japanese national language) based on modern theories of linguistics from the West. This chapter also discusses how he justified the connection between *kokugogaku* and language policies represented in the implementation of a "standard language."

Parts 3 and 4 focus on contributions by Ueda's loyal student, Hoshina Kōichi. Part 3, "*Kokugogaku* and Linguistics," discusses the relation between the state of *kokugogaku* in modern Japan and the direction of the *kokugo* reform envisioned by Hoshina. Chapter 7 is a brief review of Hoshina as a *kokugogaku* scholar, and chapter 8 examines the debate between traditional *kokugogaku* and modern linguistics regarding their perspectives on the history of *kokugogaku*. Chapter 9 further shows how the intense conflict over the idea of *kokugo* between linguistics scholars and traditional *kokugogaku* scholars not only took place in academia but also directly reflected the conflicting views of conservatives and reformers on "*kokugo* issues." Yamada Yoshio and Tokieda Motoki join Hoshina as main characters in part 3.

Part 4, "Hoshina Kōichi and His Language Policies," is, in one sense, the core of this book. Loyally following Ueda's idea of *kokugo*, Hoshina was the leader of *kokugo* politics for about fifty years. I will discuss how Hoshina contributed, in his contemporary discourse, not only to the field of *kokugo* education in Japan but also to the *kokugo* politics of Japan's colonization. Chapter 10 outlines the concept of "standard Japanese" *(hyōjungo)*, and chapters 11, 13, and 14 show the true nature of Hoshina's ideas by analyzing his policy proposals for Korea, Manchuria, and the Greater East Asia Co-Prosperity Sphere, respectively. In between, chapter 12 explains the connection between the idea of assimilation and the language policies of modern Japan.

Introduction

The Japanese Language before *Kokugo*:
Views of Mori Arinori and Baba Tatsui

I-1. Mori Arinori's View of the Japanese Language

In debates about *kokugo* and its merits as the national language in post-Meiji Japan, one person never fails to be mentioned: Mori Arinori, the first minister of education for the Meiji government. He is remembered, however, not as a model devotee of *kokugo*, but as an unpardonable traitor to the nation's language.

When he was the chargé d'affaires for the United States, Mori proposed what was afterwards called "the abolition of the Japanese language" and "the adoption of English." He did so in the introduction to his book (written in English) *Education in Japan* (1873; Meiji 6), and also in a letter of May 21, 1872 (Meiji 5), to William Dwight Whitney, a distinguished linguist at Yale University. These writings never gained any support and became the target of criticism by scholars after his time: they either laughed at his proposal as an absurdity or attacked it as an outrageous opinion. However, these attacks and ridicule did not necessarily reflect an accurate understanding of Mori's assertions, as seen in the following passages:

> When he was the chargé d'affaires for the United States in early Meiji, Mori Arinori asserted that the Japanese language had too many defects to meet educational needs, and he sought the advice of Western scholars regarding his idea to *abolish kokugo completely and to adopt English as kokugo instead*. On hearing this, the scholars reacted negatively. For example, Whitney warned him that such a wild scheme would endanger the nation's foundation; some scholars, such as Sayce,[1] were scornful of such an audacious proposal, and others ignored it and did not respond. (Yamada 1935, 298; emphasis mine)

> Scholars of classics in the Edo era, while adoring the elegant classical language, despised the spoken language of their time as the vulgar language of the common people. Similarly, people in Meiji lamented the chaos of their own language and

script. . . . Some people worshipped Western languages and alphabets, and they dreamed of replacing *kokugo* with one of them. Takada Sanae and Tsubouchi Shōyō were among those people, but Mori Arinori's proposal for abandoning *kokugo* was the most famous. (Tokieda [1940] 1966, 157)

In a well-known episode, Whitney, an American linguist, reprimanded Mori Arinori for proposing to abolish the Japanese language and to replace it with English. It seems that Mori was not the only one in early Meiji who had such an idea. (Tokieda 1962, 40)

In early Meiji, Viscount Mori Arinori, who would later become the minister of education, was troubled by the extreme complexity and irregularity of the Japanese language. He was very concerned about the severe inadequacy of the language for effective education of the people, and was of the opinion that the use of English in education would be more advisable. (Hoshina 1936b, 11)

Among the scholars who encountered the superior civilizations of the West, there were some whose worship of the West went so far as to advocate the reform of *kokugo* by replacing it with a Western language. This phenomenon during the Meiji Restoration was the same as the phenomenon in the past when the Japanese quickly adopted into their official writings the language and characters of China together with its civilization. The phenomenon in Meiji is represented by the proposal for "the adoption of English" by Mori Arinori in Meiji 5, who was at that time chargé d'affaires for the United States. (Hirai 1948, 173)

Many of the thinkers and intellectuals of that time believed that Western civilization was the ultimate civilization, and that Japan's progress depended on her adaptation to it. Such belief drew them to Western phonetic alphabets and even led them to advocate the adoption of a Western language to reform *kokugo*. For example, in June of Meiji 5, Mori Arinori, chargé d'affaires for the United States and later the minister of education, sent W. D. Whitney, professor of linguistics at Yale University, a proposal *to reconstitute the Japanese language* (nihongo) *by replacing* kanbun, *Chinese writing, with English.* (Ōno 1983, 19; emphasis mine)

We must notice, however, something subtle and strange in these condemnations of Mori's proposals. Their lines of argument, which lack an accurate understanding of Mori's true intentions, conceal a fact that explains the Japanese people's sense of their language. First of all, each critic has different and ambiguous descriptions of Mori's intention. For example, Yamada Yoshio states that Mori wished to "abolish *kokugo* completely and adopt English as *kokugo*."

This sentence is puzzling. The only way to understand this sentence is to interpret the first *kokugo* as the actual Japanese language and the second *kokugo* as the "national language" or the "official language." Such an ambiguity shows that Yamada was very careless in his use of the word *kokugo*. Ōno's explanation is similarly ambiguous: to understand his words "reconstitute the Japanese language, *nihongo*, by replacing *kanbun* with English," we have to interpret "the Japanese language" not as the proper name of a language but as a common noun meaning "the language used in Japan."

I have no intention of quibbling with their words. I simply want to draw attention to the fact that no scholars after Mori's time accurately understood his contention because the people's sense of language in Mori's time was substantially different from that which was formed after Meiji. The concepts of *nihongo* and *kokugo*, though clearly defined today, were hardly discernible, as in a haze, within Mori's sense of language.

This subtle but important shift dropped out of scholars' concerns in the discussions about Mori. For them, Tokieda's sensational and sweeping summary was sufficient: Mori proposed to abolish the Japanese language and to replace it with English, but such an idea was rebuked by linguist Whitney. Without any further examination, this episode started to gain its own plausibility.

What, then, did Mori really mean to say? Let us first read the beginning of his famous letter to Whitney.[2]

> The spoken language of Japan being inadequate to the growing necessities of the people of that Empire, and too poor to be made, by a phonetic alphabet, sufficiently useful as a written language, the idea prevails among us that, if we would keep pace with the age, we must adopt a copious and expanding European language. (Mori 1872, 310)

Mori did say that it was inevitable for the Japanese as a "commercial nation" to adopt English "in view of our rapidly increasing intercourse with the world at large" (ibid.). However, he never mentioned abolishing the Japanese language. He continued:

> All the schools the Empire has had, for many centuries, have been Chinese; and, strange to state, we have had no schools or books in our own language for educational purposes. . . . Schools for the Japanese language are found to be greatly needed, and yet there are neither teachers nor books for them. The only course to be taken, to secure the desired end, is to start anew, by first turning the spoken language into a properly written form, based on a pure phonetic principle. (309–310)

Mori certainly advocated an "introduction of the English language into the Japanese Empire" (310), but it is an agenda at a completely different level from "the abolition of the Japanese language." He simply urged the need for English as what he called "commercial language." At the same time, Mori was calling for an institutionalization of teaching methods in Japanese, reforming the traditional *kanbun*-based method, even suggesting a romanization of the language. This proposal also is far from "the abolition of the Japanese language." If there is a comment of that sort in his writing, it is not in his letter to Whitney but rather in his introduction to *Education in Japan*. As pointed out by Ivan Hall, one of the commentators in *Mori Arinori zenshū* (Complete Works of Mori Arinori), in these two writings there is a subtle difference in Mori's idea about the treatment of the Japanese language (Hall 1972b, 94).

Mori's opinion about English, on the other hand, was consistent. His proposal for adopting English was motivated by extremely practical concerns. Mori wrote to Whitney that "if we do not adopt a language like that of the English, which is quite predominant in Asia, as well as elsewhere in the commercial world, the progress of Japanese civilization is evidently impossible" (Mori 1872, 301). He even went on to say in his introduction to *Education in Japan* that for Japan to obtain "the commercial power of the English-speaking race" was "a requisite of the maintenance of our independence in the community of nations as a commercial race." Such extreme rationalism by no means meant that Mori was a submissive worshipper of the English language. He alluded to "the absence of law, rule or order, based either on etymology or sound, in its orthography, and to the large number of irregular verbs," which would make it difficult "to introduce English into Japan." This led him to "propose to banish from the English language, for the use of the Japanese nation, all or most of the exceptions" (308). He suggested, for example, eliminating irregular conjugations such as "saw/seen" and "spoke/spoken," replacing them with "seed" and "speaked," respectively. He also suggested making the English spelling system consistent with pronunciation, such as "tho" instead of "though" and "bow" instead of "bough." This was Mori's theory of simplified English, which Hall explains as follows: "The content [of Mori's letter to Whitney] is almost a proposal to abolish English, rather than Japanese: Mori spends six out of the eight pages of the letter attacking English, not Japanese" (Hall 1972b, 94). The major bone of contention between Mori and Whitney was indeed English—that is, Mori's proposal of simplified English.

In response to Mori, Whitney maintained that Japan must adopt English as it was if Japan wished to absorb Western civilization. "Simplified English" would instead become "a barrier between the Japanese and English speaker of English" (Whitney 1872, 416). Whitney did say that education in the Japanese language, "the native language," was the indispensable element in Japan's social and cultural development. However, he also suggested that it would be necessary to romanize Japanese and "to open the language, as rapidly as circumstances allow, to enrichment from the stores of English" (422). Furthermore, he advised Mori to "let it [English] take in Japan the place so long occupied by the Chinese; let it become the learned tongue and the classical language" (421). That is, Whitney suggested the establishment of a *diglossia* of English and Japanese replacing that of *kanbun* and Japanese. As Hall pointed out, such a status for English corresponds to that of Latin in the Middle Ages or English in British colonies (Hall 1972a, 26). In sum, the episode of Whitney reprimanding Mori was mere gossip among intellectuals that disregarded the actual content of the exchange between Whitney and Mori.

Mori and Whitney had the same view about the influence of the Chinese language on Japanese. Whitney's opinion that "the influence of the Chinese language on the Japanese has always been a harmful and regrettable one, and that complete emancipation from it would be exceedingly advantageous to Japan" (Whitney 1872, 420) corresponds to Mori's statement in his introduction: "The style of the [Japanese] language is like the Chinese. In all our institutions of learning, the Chinese classics have been used. . . . Without the aid of the Chinese, our language has never been taught or used for any purpose of communication. This shows its poverty" (Mori 1873, 265–266). By "poverty," Mori did not mean only the limited geographical range where the Japanese language was used, but that Japanese could not be an autonomous language as long as it was dominated by "Chinese," that is, by Chinese characters *(kanji)*, words *(kango)*, and sentences *(kanbun)*. Here we can see that Mori was not a wild dreamer but one who had already zeroed in on the core of future problems in the Japanese language and writing system, *kokugo kokuji mondai*. By adopting simplified English, Mori wanted to expel from the Japanese language Chinese elements, which were the major hindrance to Japan's modernization, and ultimately to eliminate the Japanese language entirely because it was "a weak and uncertain medium of communication" (266).

However, did Mori actually advocate the "abolition of the Japanese language"? As seen above, he wrote not a single word about it in his letter to Whitney. It was only in the following passage in the introduction of his *Education in Japan* that Mori mentioned anything related to an abolition of the language:

The march of modern civilization in Japan has already reached the heart of the nation—the English language following it suppresses the use of both Japanese and Chinese. . . . Under the circumstances, our meagre language, which can never be of any use outside of our islands, is doomed to yield to the domination

of the English tongue, especially when the power of steam and electricity shall
have pervaded the land. Our intelligent race, eager in the pursuit of knowledge,
cannot depend upon a weak and uncertain medium of communication in its
endeavor to grasp the principal truths from the precious treasury of Western
science and art and religion. The laws of state can never be preserved in the language of Japan. All reasons suggest its disuse. (266)

Here we must pay attention to the end of the passage above: Mori said "the
language of Japan" and not "Japanese." In fact, in the beginning he said that
English "suppresses the use of both Japanese and Chinese." It was not, of course,
that he was worried about the fate of China, but that he was intensely concerned about Japan. He firmly believed that "the language of Japan" consisted
of a disorderly mixture of Japanese and Chinese. In other words, for Mori, Japanese, *nihongo*, was not the same as "the language of Japan."

Though Mori's "proposal for the abolition of the Japanese language" has
often been discussed, what should be of importance is not the rights and wrongs
of "abolition," but rather the definition of the concept of *nihongo*, the Japanese
language. Hall's comment is full of suggestions in this regard: "In both Mori's
and his opponents' writings on problems in *kokugo*, the words 'Japanese' and
'Chinese' [languages] appear frequently, but their meanings are rather complex. The readers must carefully think what they mean each time they are used"
(Hall 1972b, 95).

For example, the word "Japanese" in "the English language . . . suppresses
the use of both Japanese and Chinese" in the above comment from Mori should
be understood as *yamato kotoba*, which is free from elements of Chinese words
or styles. The word "Chinese" should be understood as *kanji* (Chinese characters), *kango* (Chinese words), and *kanbun* (Chinese phrases and sentences)
used in Japan. The concept of "Japanese" *(nihongo)* may be self-evident for us
today, but it was not at all clear for Mori Arinori. The most serious problem in
"the language of Japan" for Mori was the hopeless distance between the spoken
and written languages. In his letter to Whitney, Mori wrote of "the spoken language of Japan being inadequate to the growing necessities of the people of that
Empire, and too poor to be made, by a phonetic alphabet, sufficiently useful as
a written language" (Mori 1872, 310). Furthermore, "the written language now
in use in Japan, has little or no relation to the spoken language, but is mainly
hieroglyphie—a deranged Chinese, blended in Japanese, all the letters of which
are themselves of Chinese origin" (309).[3]

In Japan at that time, the state of the language, "the language of Japan," could
not possibly have been a single, uniform "Japanese." It was impossible for Mori
to envision a unified "Japanese" to overcome such a linguistic split. This is the

very point that later scholars missed in their critiques of Mori: their criticisms (except for Baba Tatsui's, discussed in the next section) were based on a view of "Japanese" that was already established in their time as *kokugo,* "the national language of Japan." For those outraged at Mori's intention to "abolish Japanese," "Japanese" was already in an unshakable position, while "the language of Japan" for Mori was still a floating concept. Furthermore, though "Japanese" later took more obvious shape as "the national language of Japan," it was like a collage of blurred pictures in Mori's time. Mori was not yet able to place the linguistic unity of "Japanese" on the same level as the political unity of the "Japanese Empire."

To recapitulate, though the belief that "the Japanese language" is an unmistakable unity is dominant today, such a belief was itself a construction of modern history. Mori Arinori's argument sheds light on the hidden history of the ideology of language in modern Japan.

The identification of *nihongo,* the Japanese language, as *kokugo,* the national language of Japan, became implicit in linguistic consciousness in modern Japan, and at the same time became the ideological goal to which this modern linguistic consciousness was directed. It was also the unquestionable moral and ethical imperative that the Japanese language be identified as "the national language of Japan." Mori's argument, however, completely lacked such a moral recognition, and this naturally irritated scholars. Although scholars conflicted with each other in their views about *kokugo kokuji mondai,* the issues about national language and script, all considered Mori the common enemy. There were conservatives, such as Yamada and Tokieda, who protected *rekishiteki kanazukai,* the traditional phonetic use of *kana,* and *bungo,* the traditional written language, and there were reformers, such as Hoshina and Hirai, who promoted romanization and *genbun itchi,* the unification of written and spoken languages. But they were all critical of Mori Arinori because Mori's linguistic consciousness was antagonistic and alien to that of late-Meiji intellectuals and because he was an immoral traitor to the Japanese language. This difference in their linguistic consciousness explains why the scholars' criticisms against Mori are colored by their irritation at the incomprehensible and by their outrage against a dangerous view that might corrupt "good" social morale.

Moreover, Mori exposed what they did not want to discuss regarding the linguistic consciousness of modern Japan: Mori boldly defined Japanese as "our meagre language, which can never be of any use outside of our islands." Even while putting up a calm front, the intellectuals in Japan were always haunted by this undeniable fact, which took root among them as a "habit of pessimism towards the mother tongue," as Tanaka Katsuhiko points out (1989, 14–16), or the "Japanese people's subconscious curse against their own language," as

Suzuki Takao puts it (1989, 15). However, such pessimism was supposed to be an unmentionable. Intellectuals have always reacted neurotically against Mori's argument, fearing that it might contain "undesirable truth." After Mori, Japan searched agonizingly for ways to cure its sick linguistic consciousness, or to forcefully deny it. It is possible to suspect that the later scheme for the Greater East Asia Co-Prosperity Sphere was partially motivated by the phantom depicted by Mori Arinori.[4]

I-2. Baba Tatsui's Criticism of Mori Arinori

Mori's argument did not elicit instant reactions in Japan, probably because it was written in English and published abroad. Only Baba Tatsui, who was also abroad, gave an immediate response to it in a series of harsh criticisms. Baba, who later became famous as a prominent warrior in the Liberal Rights Movement, was then a student of law in London.

Baba's criticism was the most thorough, though it only concerned Mori's opinion in his introduction to *Education in Japan;* it did not include in its scope Mori's letter to Whitney in which Mori argued for a simplified English. In contrast to the emotional reactions to Mori from later scholars, Baba attempted to invalidate Mori's perception that Japanese was an insufficient language. Baba did this through elaborate and laborious intellectual work resulting in 1873 in a complete book in English of Japanese grammar—*An Elementary Grammar of the Japanese Language.* Commonly known in Japan as *Nihongo bunten,* it was the first book that systematically described Japanese grammar. Mori Arinori, unintentionally, thus triggered the production of the first grammar book of the Japanese spoken language.

In the introduction to the book, Baba unfolded succinct and pointed criticisms of Mori with the following two purposes: to refute Mori's allegation that Japanese was a meager language and no match for English and to caution against the social inequity that would very likely occur if English became the only official language. As shown in the last section, Mori pointed out that the "poverty" of Japanese was evident in that it could not be used for education or modern communication without depending on Chinese words and sentences. Baba's response to this was as follows:

> Before the introduction of Chinese, we must have had some sort of language, which served as a means of communication. Since we introduced the Chinese classics, literature, &c., we have been obliged to use Chinese words or phrases which we could not express in Japanese, and so it became necessary to teach our language with the aid of Chinese. This is generally the case when one nation

introduces the classical literature of another country: because there are always many words in the latter, for which the language of the former cannot find synonyms or equivalents. (Baba 1873, 7–8)[5]

Baba argued that each language community with different cultural customs forms different concepts, which sometimes cannot be exactly translated into other languages. Such untranslatable words are commonly adopted as loan words not only in Japanese but also in other languages. For example, that the English translation of Roman laws contains many Latin words "does not show the poverty of the English language, but only the difference in their ideas and customs," and therefore, Baba asserted, "the fact that one language is taught with the aid of another, does not prove its poverty" (9). Thus, Baba was far more optimistic than Mori about the Chinese influence on Japanese. However, his point was not to protect the position of Chinese in Japanese, but to criticize Mori's conclusion that Japanese was an inadequate language because of its prevailing use of Chinese characters and words. For that purpose, Baba illustrated the relationship between Chinese and Japanese as being parallel to the relationship between Latin and modern Western languages, especially English, which Mori believed in. I must note here that Baba's argument is substantially different from those in the debate about national script in post-Meiji that defended the position of Chinese as the classic language of the East, equating its status to that of Latin in the West.

It was not that Baba tried to depict the Japanese of his time as a perfect language. His view came from a certain healthy relativism: Every language has strong and weak characteristics; this is also true for English, which Mori insisted should be adopted: "There are perfections and imperfections in both languages." It was only because of a difference in customs and ways of thinking that Japanese might lack equivalents for some English words, but it was not an indication of the unequivocal superiority of English to Japanese (10). Baba even said that Japanese surpasses English in the regularity of its writing and pronunciation systems. (Note that Mori also made the same criticism of English, but Baba did not know that.) However, regardless of their shortcomings, there cannot be any superiority or inferiority between the two languages since each has "words which serve as signs of ideas for the help of memory" (11).[6]

With *Nihongo bunten*, Baba attempted to prove that "certain rules are observed throughout every part of [Japanese] speech; there are eight parts of speech, their subdivisions, tenses, moods or voices of verbs, rules of syntax, and so on." He claimed that Japanese was "sufficiently perfect to teach the elements of common education so far as grammar itself is concerned" (9–10). Baba had a sociolinguistic insight: describing the grammar substantiates the language and best represents the autonomy of the speech community of that language. Moreover, Baba perceived political and social implications in Mori's proposal, which he refuted as follows: there were indeed cases in which people of a nation came to speak another's language, but such cases were a result of the enforcement of the language by a conqueror, not a result of the willingness of the conquered to change language; in this respect, Mori's argument failed in its premise. Mori's attempt to replace the language of one nation was fundamentally unrealistic and unreasonable because "even when one nation was forced to introduce a language by the superior power of the conqueror, the former did not give up their native tongue which they had been accustomed to speak for hundreds of years, and which was consequently most convenient to them" (13).

Baba cautioned that such a forced bilingual system would without doubt bring tragedy to the people; it would create social class divisions based on language:

> Naturally the wealthier classes of people can be free from the daily occupation to which the poorer classes are constantly subjected, and consequently the former can devote more time for learning the language than the latter. If affairs of state, and all affairs of social intercourse are to be transacted through the English language, the lower classes will be shut out from the important questions which concern the whole nation, just as the Patricians in Rome excluded the plebs from *jus sacrum,* Comitia, &c.; the consequence being that there will be an entire separation between the higher class and the lower, and no common sympathies between them; and thus they will be prevented from acting as one, and so the advantages of unity will be entirely lost. These evils appear to be felt in India. . . . These evils will necessarily exist, unless some means are employed to establish the universal instruction of a people through their own language. (13–14)

Whitney, also, pointed out, in commenting on Mori's idea, that the adoption of English might create social distance between a handful of intellectuals and the majority of the people. Nonetheless, he merely pointed out the case of Latin in the Middle Ages as an example of linguistic separation, and contradicted himself in advising Mori to adopt English as "the learned tongue and the classical language" (Whitney 1872, 421). In contrast to Whitney, Baba referred to the political and social problems caused by the enforcement of English and the resulting bilingualism in India, and also in Wales, Ireland, and Scotland, whose Gaelic languages were invaded by English from England. Here, Baba had a more keen and realistic understanding of problems of linguistic hegemony in colonies than the English speaker Whitney.

Insights such as Baba's cannot be found in any of the other critics of Mori; *J* they raised their voices to accuse Mori of slighting the tradition of *kokugo* and of blindly worshipping the West. Baba neither indulged himself in fanatic linguistic chauvinism nor did he charge Mori with destroying tradition as a follower of the West. The basis of Baba's assertion was his resistance to the use of language for controlling society and his hope of linguistic democracy that would support political democracy. As Hagiwara Nobutoshi[7] keenly pointed out, "for Mori, international advantage was the priority, while for Baba, domestic impact was the concern. This debate over the good and evil of adopting English accidentally revealed the choice in Japan's modernization: national authority or civil rights, as seen later in the heated contest between the *hanbatsu seifu,* the government dominated by elites from previously powerful fiefs, and the civil rights movement" (Hagiwara 1967, 42–43).

The debate between Mori and Baba was an earnest dialogue and discussion, which later scholars failed to understand: as represented by Yamada Yoshio, they appreciated Baba only in their own convenient terms. Yamada's *Kokugogakushi yō* (Concise History of *Kokugogaku;* 1935) is the most representative work and is often cited as the classic commendation of Baba in discussions of Baba's epoch-making contribution in *Nihongo bunten* (39). *Bunten* was no doubt "the first systematic study of overall grammar of spoken Japanese" and "an important masterpiece in the history of *kokugo*" (299). However, we must not overlook Yamada's hidden intention behind his praise of Baba as "the great protector of *kokugo*" (300), an intention distinct from the wish to engage in a genuine academic evaluation.

As will be further discussed in a later chapter, Yamada believed that the true tradition of *kokugo* breathes in the classical written language of the past, and not in the current spoken language. It was from this neotraditionalism that he supported the historical use of *kana (rekishiteki kanazukai)* and fervently objected to the restrictions on the use of *kanji.* Furthermore, Yamada made a tight connection between the "unbroken line of special national polity" *(bansei ikkei no kokutai)*[8] and the sacred tradition of "*kokugo.*" For Yamada, the reform of *kokugo* was an unforgivable plot that would lead directly to a change of *kokutai.* As a part of his protest against the reformers who advocated the phonetic use of *kana (hyōonshiki kanazukai)* and the restrictions on *kanji,* Yamada first defined Mori as their forerunner, who had slighted "*kokugo.*" Then Yamada used Baba to strengthen his own camp in opposition to Mori.

Baba's organization of Japanese grammar actually followed that of English grammar. For example, a verb has present, past, and future tenses, and conjugates in agreement with the person and number of its subject. Though Yamada intensely detested the measuring of Japanese against the grammar of

Western languages, he nonetheless applauded Baba for being a "great protector of *kokugo*," only because Baba was critical of Mori.

Though Yamada used Baba as a model patriot of the Japanese language, it was not Baba's central concern that the adoption of English might ruin the tradition of *kokugo*. Baba's fear was that the adoption of English would potentially alienate a majority of the people from education and that education would become accessible only for a handful of elites who could use English. We do not find here any indication that Baba intended to protect the sacred tradition of *kokugo*. Rather, we are convinced that Baba would be, if he were alive, harshly critical of Yamada's ideology of language, which denies linguistic democracy.

I-3. Baba Tatsui's Linguistic Void

Japanese grammar in Baba's time was discussed only in terms of the written language of the past. In contrast, Baba attempted to show the systematic rules of "the Japanese language as it is spoken." His book *Nihongo bunten* was a brave and intuitive attempt at descriptivism, which gained public acceptance in modern linguistics only after his time. Though the sentences he used in the book, such as below, are natural for us today, we must understand that it took Baba much academic courage and commitment to write about such an actual spoken language:

> *Watakushi* [sic] *wa ik-imasu.*
> *Watakusi wa ik-imasita.*
> *Watakusi wa ik-imasho.* (Baba 1873, 28)[9]

While his criticism of Mori was credible, Baba's linguistic practice itself was far from the picture of Japanese he drew in *Nihongo bunten*: Baba never used "Japanese as it is spoken" in his own writings. In fact, all of his writings are in English. The few essays in Japanese are lecture notes, all taken by other people. The books and articles he wrote while studying in London and while he was taking refuge in the United States are all written in English. Even his autobiography, which he started right before he fled to the United States,[10] was written in English, together with most of the diary he wrote in London and even in Japan. Baba was well known among civil rights activists as an exceptionally outstanding and eloquent speaker. Therefore, it is shocking to learn, as Hagiwara pointed out, that "Baba spoke in Japanese but never wrote in Japanese. He used English in his writing" (Hagiwara 1967, 94). Hagiwara explained that one of the reasons for Baba's preference for English was his intellectual background in English studies *(eigaku)*; another might be that, unlike other

Japanese intellectuals at that time, he had never equipped himself for Chinese studies *(kangaku)*.

This reminds us of Mori's argument that the dominant use of Chinese *(kanbun)* signified the "poverty of Japanese." This touched a raw nerve with Baba, and, ironically, his linguistic practice proved Mori was right. On the other hand, Baba's warning of the future social stratification that would be caused by the implementation of English was an apt description of the state of contemporary Japan, where he lived, linguistically dominated by *kanbun*. It can be posited that Baba's exclusion from the world of written Japanese was a result of his never acquiring the Chinese writing style. Baba criticized Mori's idea of adopting English, but he was only able to express criticism in English: indeed, this paradox was symbolic of the linguistic context of Japan at that time. Neither Mori nor Baba was able to stand firm on the foundation of "the Japanese language." More precisely, no firm foundation of the Japanese language existed at that time. Only those who were privileged enough to afford time for studying a language monopolized the *kanbun kundoku tai (kanbun-style Japanese)*, as representative of their class status.

To emancipate the Japanese language from the hegemony of *kanbun* style, *genbun itchi,* the unification of the spoken and written languages, would have been imperative. However, the realization of such an ideal required a reckless and daring linguistic crusade against the tenacity of *kanbun* tradition, which is beyond the imagination of us today. For example, Futabatei Shimei, famous for his demonstration of *genbun itchi* in his novel *Ukigumo* (Floating Clouds), had to write first in Russian to express freely what he had difficulty writing in Japanese, and then translate it back into spoken Japanese. For Baba, the spoken Japanese he illustrated in *Nihongo bunten* was hopelessly separated from *kanbun* style, the official written language. The only solution he found to overcome this linguistic gap was, alas, English, a foreign language. Such was the limitation of the Japanese language, not only for Baba, but also for those in early Meiji in general.

Facing the unresolved state of the Japanese language in early Meiji, Mori and Baba each developed a theory: Mori concluded that the Japanese language was not unified enough to support the modern nation, and he proposed as a remedy adopting English as a national language; Baba refuted Mori, warning that the adoption of English would destroy the unity of the Japanese people. Still, even Baba was not able to overcome the barrier that Mori had pointed out between spoken Japanese and written Japanese. *Kokugo* could have been realized only by coming to terms with this predicament. Or, we should say, *kokugo* was created precisely because of the need to resolve this predicament. In other words, *kokugo* had a two-track mission: to reconcile the written and spoken languages through *genbun itchi* and to seek support for the premise of the unity of *kokugo* in the people's sense of the political nation, in their consciousness of a nation-state nurtured by the ideology of *kokutai*.

The reconciliation between the written and spoken languages was a definite requirement as long as *kokugo* was to be liberated from a handful of cultural elites and defined as a linguistic unity to account for linguistic expression by all people in the nation. In the case of Japan, however, such an awakening to *kokugo* was achieved by the exaltation of the consciousness of the nation-state, the empire. In the background of this unique establishment of consciousness for *kokugo,* there was a historical tide in the Japanese political climate. There was also an initiative taken by a modern linguist, Ueda Kazutoshi, who, quickly responding to this political climate, introduced the modern scientific theory of language into Japan.

Ueda Kazutoshi is the most important key character for our understanding of the ideology of *kokugo.* Various struggles in early Meiji about the Japanese language informed Ueda's thinking, which ultimately led to his giving concrete direction to the course that the language was to take as *kokugo.* I will further discuss Ueda's ideas in part 2, but I will first trace the development of two major problems of the language in part 1: issues of *kokuji* (national script) and *genbun itchi* (unification of spoken and written languages). I will also delineate ideas of *kokugo* before Ueda Kazutoshi.

PART I

Kokugo Issues in Early Meiji

CHAPTER 1

Perspectives on *Kokuji,* the National Script

1-1. The Meaning of Writing and the Representation of Language

From the viewpoint of modern linguistics, the substance of language consists ✓ of sound whereas script is the mere outer covering of language. Just as cosmetics and clothing do not affect the human body itself, the choice of script is an external element irrelevant to the substance of language. Thus, the object of linguistics research has been sounds and the relationship among sounds at each level of phonology, morphology, and syntax.

Why, then, do people become so passionate about the choice of script? If the problems of script are a secondary matter in language, then organizations such as l'Académie Française in France, the Deliberative Council on the National Language (Kokugo Shingikai) in Japan, and the Language Institute and Hangul Association in Korea would be ludicrous and absurd, and wasting tremendous energy on trivial matters.

When it comes to script, people become so emotional that they form irrational but intense likes and dislikes. However, this is not because ordinary people are ignorant of linguistics.[1] In people's consciousness about the language that they speak, not solely in the professional field of linguistics, we find the genius of language. It was once a general premise held by linguists that the essential property of language lay in its "structure" or its "system." I will first refer to Eugenio Coseriu, who challenged this premise.

As opposed to Saussure's *langue* vs. *parole* dichotomy, Coseriu (1952) pro- ✓ posed that language consists of three components: *sistema* (system), *norma* (norm), and *habla* (materialized form).[2] *Sistema* is defined in structural linguistics as a network of relations among distinctive and nonactive units: it determines only what must *not* be represented, rather than what must be represented. In that sense, *sistema* only restricts the possible scope of language. Moreover, Coseriu contends, it is an abstraction constructed by linguists' academic interests and does not immediately determine the reality of language. *Norma,* on the other hand, produces active models of certain *habla.* This does not mean, however, that *norma* is the representation of each utterance itself nor is it the totality of utterances: the role of *norma* is to transform the potentiality in the *sistema* of language into active reality.

Here we must consider Coseriu's term *norma* at two different levels: *norma* as a pattern that actual linguistic behavior conforms to and *norma* as a totality of values that a speaker places on language. In other words, the former is the "model" for actual utterances and the latter is the "representation" of language, that is, how the speaker imagines language. It is this latter definition of *norma,* as the representation of language, that is in speakers' minds when they normally imagine "a language" in their daily life.

Most of the problems regarding script belong to the scope of *norma. Norma* in the first sense (as a "model" or pattern) controls the act of writing. As Walter J. Ong (1982) says, people may *speak* unconsciously, but they cannot *write* unconsciously, since the act of writing requires the writer's maximum control of his or her consciousness. The act of writing is controlled by *norma* in many ways; therefore, its result, "what is written," also has power to create and reinforce *norma.*

On the other hand, the significance of writing in creating *norma* in the second sense (as a representation of language) has often been overlooked. *Norma* in this sense has become more important since the appearance of script, which enabled language to shape itself as a written form. How could people represent the "whole" of a language when they did not have script? As Ong puts it, in the time of a purely vocal culture, language was a stream of short-lived events, and the idea of an abstract and latent whole of language without sound would have been impossible.

This discussion implies that problems of script, that is, the choice of script and how to write with it, are much deeper than mere technical problems of a writing system. Intrinsically the question of script concerns the formation of *norma* of language as representation: the *norma,* which controls the way the language *must* be represented. This is the viewpoint from which we must look at the issues surrounding the constant preoccupation of Japan since Meiji: the so-called *kokuji mondai,* problems in the Japanese national script. The script with which to inscribe Japanese closely involves the question of how the Japanese language should be valued and represented.

1-2. Proposals by Maejima Hisoka to Abolish *Kanji*

The debate about national language and script in modern Japan was ignited by Maejima Hisoka, then a shogunate translator *(kaiseijo hanyakukata),* in his 1866 "Kanji on-haishi no gi" (Proposal for the Abolition of Chinese Characters)[3] to Shogun Tokugawa Yoshinobu (Nishio and Hisamatsu 1969, 17–20). The opening paragraph gives the tenor of the proposal:

> The foundation of a nation is the education of its people. Education must be spread among all people, regardless of their social class and status. For this purpose, we cannot but use the simplest script and sentences possible. The goal of all learning must be to learn truth, and we must reject the belief in cumbersome methods of instruction that a mastery of script is the only way to understanding of all profound academic matters. Hence, I propose that in our country also, as in the Western countries, we adopt the phonetic script *(kana)* in education instead of *kanji.* I propose abolition of the use of *kanji* in ordinary writings for both public and private purposes. (17)

Maejima's argument stems from his practical view of language as instrumental: language and its phonetic symbol, script, are not the object of true learning but mere instruments to convey knowledge. In his view, script must accurately correspond to pronunciation so that the written language allows everyone to pronounce a word in the same way at first glance. True knowledge lies in "things," not in "words"—this realism is the core of Maejima's anti-*kanji* theory, which rejected *kanji* as unsuitable for the acquisition and transmission of modern knowledge.

As motivation to promote his anti-*kanji* theory, we can see Maejima's aspiration to Western civilization and his determination to move away from Chinese civilization. He quoted with empathy what he heard from an American missionary named William: "China was once an empire with vast land and numerous people. But now, withered into stagnation, its people have fallen back into savagery, to a state of contempt for Western countries. This is because China was contaminated by the hieroglyph and its ignorance of the method of common education" (18). Maejima saw that the difference between Western and Eastern civilizations was condensed in the contrast between phonetic and hieroglyphic script.

According to Maejima, the political and cultural stagnation of Japan arose from its "adoption of [Chinese] uninsightful culture together with its impractical and useless hieroglyph, which eventually came into daily use as the national script"; he asserted, however, that Japan fortunately also had its unique script, *kana,* equivalent to the phonetic script of Western countries: "our country possesses its own language unyielding to Western languages, and fifty letters *(kana)* to write it" (17). He thought the phonetic *kana* script could possibly prevent Japan from replicating China's plight and could move the country towards modernization.

While he proposed to abolish *kanji,* Maejima did not go so far as to attempt to abolish *kango,* Japanese words of Chinese origin: "Writing *kango* in *kana,* not in Chinese [*kanji*], is similar to what happened in English and other languages, which adopted Latin-origin words in their own alphabets" (18). Vernacular languages, while nourishing themselves with the Latin heritage, were emancipated from its domination and became languages of modern European nations. This process, Maejima believed, clearly showed the way in which Japanese should deal with Chinese words and sentences. Through the abolition of *kanji* and the consequent simplification of written Japanese, Maejima's ultimate goal was to enforce a common education in order to produce the nation, *kokumin,* the foundation for a modern state, *kokka.*

In 1869 (Meiji 2), shortly after the Meiji Restoration, Maejima presented the "Kokubun kyōiku no gi ni tsuki kengi" (Proposal for Teaching the Japanese Language) to the Meiji government (Yoshida and Inokuchi 1950, 39–43). In its appendix, "Kokubun kyōiku shikō no hōhō" (Administrative Methods for Teaching the Japanese Language),[4] he once again emphasized the need to abolish *kanji* and institute *kana* as the national script in order to establish a modern education for the people and to develop among them a practical education for a strong and wealthy nation. He presented concrete five-stage plans over seven years for language education, including plans for abolishing *kanji.*

In Maejima's proposal we do not find the slightest hint of the reactionism seen in some of the later scholars of Japanese classics. In his first "Proposal for the Abolition of Chinese Characters," Maejima had warned against a return to classical Japanese in instituting the Japanese language and its grammar *(bunten).* He insisted on employing the current and common language. He gave a more detailed explanation of the goals of the first stage in his "Administrative Methods for Teaching the Japanese Language," which even suggests the later *genbun itchi:*

> Select from many districts *(fu, han, ken)* three to five scholars in each of Japanese, Chinese, and Western studies, who shall institute a style of written Japanese determined by national script; they shall select model texts for Japanese language and literature. . . . Note: *The new Japanese national language shall allow foreign words whether Chinese or Western, and the written form shall follow the current vernacular style, not classical grace.* (40; emphasis mine)

In 1873 (Meiji 6), Maejima composed yet another proposal, "Kō kokubun hai kanji no gi" (The Enforcement of Japanese and the Abolishment of *Kanji*),[5] a year after the promulgation of the educational system. Nonetheless, the series of proposals he wrote between the end of the Tokugawa shogunate and early Meiji were mostly ignored, laughed at, or even received with hostility.

It was not until 1899 (Meiji 32) that Maejima's writings were introduced to the public in honor of his pioneering contributions to the reform of national script.[6] That same year, he was appointed head of the Division for National Script Reform (Kokuji Kairyōbu) of the Imperial Board of Education (Teikoku Kyōiku Kai) and the following year, director of the National Language Investigation under the Ministry of Education. However, facing issues beyond his simple utilitarianism, his major role was already over by then.

Besides the series of proposals he wrote to the government, Maejima earnestly practiced what he proposed, as clearly seen in his publication of *Mainichi hirakana shinbunshi* (Daily Hirakana Newspaper), from February 1873 (Meiji 6) through May 1874 (Meiji 7) (Yamamoto M. 1965, 101–103). Following his own proposal, he wrote all of the articles in *hiragana* with a space between words.[7] This all-*hiragana* newspaper was a real innovation (though the sentence style was still classical), considering the fact that numerous announcements by the Meiji government as well as newly appearing newspapers were written in *kanbun kundoku* style, a Chinese-influenced style full of *kango* (including made-in-Japan Chinese words, the number of which suddenly increased in Meiji). It is unfortunate that such an inventive practice, together with his proposals, did not bear fruit at that time with any followers; probably Maejima was simply ahead of his time.

1-3. Proposals by Scholars of the West: *Kana* and *Rōmaji* for National Script

Maejima wanted to abolish *kanji* and institute *kana*, the phonetic symbols similar to the English alphabet, as the national script. It was not surprising that such a wish to slough off Chinese culture triggered discussions about using *rōmaji*, the alphabet itself. Discussions about *kana* and *rōmaji* became the central debate in the academic journal *Meiroku zasshi* (Meiji 6 Magazine), which had been started by a collaboration of eminent *yōgakusha* (scholars of the West), in an endeavor to promote Meiji civilization and enlightenment. In its first issue in 1874 (Meiji 7), Nishi Amane wrote "Yōji o motte kokugo o shosuru no ron" (Writing Japanese in the Western Script) (Nishio and Hisamatsu 1969, 23–28). In this essay, Nishi echoed Maejima in asserting that *kanji* was the biggest obstacle to Japan's cultural development and that a reform of the script was necessary to break the impasse. However, Nishi recommended *rōmaji* over *kana*. He argued that *rōmaji* describes each phonetic element more accurately than *kana,* a syllable that is an inseparable combination of vowel and consonant.

Nishi's enthusiastic proposal for the romanization of Japanese was motivated by his practical belief in Westernization: during the time when Japan was hastily importing European culture and customs, Nishi asked, "Why should we leave alone their script? . . . Why hesitate to adapt the other's strength to our own?" He listed ten concrete advantages of romanizing Japanese, which included the unification of speaking and writing styles (though Nishi did not yet use the word *genbun itchi*); wide dissemination of education and culture; easier access to the study of foreign, that is, Western, languages; and direct employment of Western technical terms in Japanese translation. He even went on to insist that "the establishment of this method [i.e., romanization] will enable us to obtain everything possible in Europe." The early movement for romanization advocated by scholars of Western studies thus stemmed from their ardent wish for assimilation with Western civilization. Nonetheless, Nishi's romanization theory was still rather immature in that it allowed both classical and vernacular pronunciation for one spelling. For example, it allowed the word spelled *omosirosi* (interesting) to be pronounced either /*womoshiroshi*/ [classical way] or /*womoshiroi*/ [vernacular way]. This disparity in pronunciation defeats the alleged advantages of romanization.

Meiroku zasshi also published proposals for *kana* script, such as Shimizu Usaburō's "Hiragana no setsu" (Suggestions for *Hiragana* Script), in its seventh issue in May 1874 (Meiji 7) (Nishio and Hisamatsu 1969, 28–29). According to Shimizu, Western civilization progressed because the dissemination of education was made possible by the fact that "their spoken and written languages were identical." He argued that Japan also had to obtain a writing system identical with its spoken language in order to advance knowledge among its people. The best means to achieve this goal was to write sentences in *hiragana* rather than *rōmaji,* for Japan already had a *hiragana* tradition that was very familiar to common people.

However, the *kana* method unexpectedly betrayed an inherent shortcoming at the opposite extreme from *rōmaji*'s radical Westernism: in all-*hiragana* writing, words and sentence style were still embedded in the classical tradition of *hiragana,* which was fatal for translating Western languages. For example, in 1874 (Meiji 7), before Shimizu published his essay "Suggestions for *Hiragana* Script," he published a translation of an introductory book on chemistry, *Monowari no hashigo* (Steps to the Principles of Things) in *hiragana* (see Yamamoto 1965, 185–189; 1978, 146–148). This was an epochal work dealing with natural science in very early Meiji. However, in addition to its classical Japanese style, Shimizu's translation of technical terms in chemistry into *yamato kotoba* (classical Japanese words) sounded very awkward compared to their current use today. For example, he used a classical word, *ohone*, for today's *genso* (element), *honoke* for *kūki* (air), *suine* for *sanso* (oxygen), *mizune* for *suiso* (hydrogen), and *sumi no su* for *tansan* (carbonic acid). Here, Shimizu's translations clearly contrast with those of Fukuzawa Yukichi, who never used Japanese classical words and instead used *kango* to translate nouns in *Kunmō kyūri zukai* (Introductory Theories with Illustrations), an introductory science book he wrote in 1868 (Meiji 1). Most of these technical terms translated by Fukuzawa are commonly used today in physics and chemistry. This fact tells us that fluctuation in modern Japanese started taking definite shape at this time in history: we who live today no longer have a sense of the *hiragana* spelling of, say, *sanso,* as being the genuine script. Rather, we recognize it only as the *furigana*, the phonetic transcript, of the *kanji* characters for oxygen.

The debate between *rōmaji* and *hiragana* pointed in completely opposite directions: adherents of the former sought assimilation with Western civilization, supporters of the latter, the preservation of Japanese tradition. Nonetheless, they had a common enemy, *kanji,* and both sides shared a strong desire to be emancipated from the mesh of Chinese civilization.

1 4. The *Kokuji* Reform Movement in the Second Decade of Meiji

By the middle of the second decade of Meiji (1877–1886), the movement towards *kokuji* reform had grown more sectarian in nature with the formation of many different organizations. In 1882 (Meiji 15), *kana* advocates organized Kana no Tomo (Friends of Kana), Iroha Kai (Iroha Association), and Irohabun Kai (Iroha-writing Association),[8] all of which were united in July of the following year as Kana no Kai (Association of Kana). As for the *rōmaji* movement, its advocates founded Rōmaji Kai (Rōmaji Association) in January 1885 (Meiji 18).[9]

An example of these reformers is Toyama Masakazu, who was first a member of Kana no Kai and later turned and became the driving force for the formation of Rōmaji Kai. On November 4, 1884 (Meiji 17), Toyama gave a somewhat hyperbolical lecture at a meeting of Kana no Kai, titled "Shintai kanji yaburi" (Dump *Kanji* for a New Style), which was published the following month (Nishio and Hisamatsu 1969, 33-36). "Shintai" reminds us of *Shintai shi shō* (Collection of New-style Poetry), for which Toyama was a coeditor with Yatabe Ryōkichi and Inoue Tetsujirō. Toyama might have intended to promote script reform to follow the reform in poetry. In fact, Yatabe also joined Rōmaji Kai later with Toyama. (Inoue was studying abroad.) In the beginning of "Shintai kanji yaburi" Toyama boasted, "I will join any team—the bigger the better—as long as its goal is to abolish *kanji*. It does not matter a bit to me how we should use *kana*. I would support it whether the team's name is Moon or Snow, whether we advocate *kana* or *rōmaji*. Because there is nothing I detest today more than *kanji*" (33–36). Maejima Hisoka and Nishi Amane also furnished their opinions and theorized from their utilitarian views of language and their longings for Western civilization, but Toyama did so to an extent that was almost ludicrous.

According to Toyama, there are two kinds of knowledge: "true knowledge," which is about things and skills beneficial for society, and "tool knowledge," which is "a mere instrument to convey true knowledge or to exchange ideas among people." Language and script belong to the latter knowledge, and acquisition of such knowledge alone is of no use. Consequently, the tool "doesn't have to be any one language or script. As long as it serves for conveying [true] knowledge and ideas, any language or script would do."

Toyama argued that if the learning of "tool knowledge," such as language or script, takes away our time from learning "true knowledge," such "tool knowledge" must be abandoned. *Kanji* was a form of such tool knowledge. *Kanji* was the evil that was keeping the nation from progress and prosperity, pulling it further away from Western civilization. Said Toyama bitingly,

> If you are not convinced, look at the good example of the China-France War.[10] No matter how many *kanji* characters you learn, you cannot use them for a war.... We cannot keep up with Westerners while using *kanji*: while we are studying *kanji*, they are using electricity; while we are practicing writing *kanji*, they are arming their ships. How ridiculous it is to dare to even talk about a war against Westerners while we are spending enormous amounts of time on things like practicing *kanji*. (Nishio and Hisamatsu 1969, 34)

Toyama concluded his lecture saying, "The abolition of *kanji* is far more urgent than founding the Diet or reforming religions." This was also his indirect criticism of the liberal civil rights movement and the Christian movement of that time. Toyama, as a leading social evolutionist, together with Katō Hiroyuki, his colleague at Tokyo University, advocated the tenet "the stronger prey upon the weaker," and therefore must have felt that he had to criticize the fundamental philosophy of these movements, the natural rights of man. Thus, "Shintai kanji yaburi" was an attempt to promote social evolution in script, with the hidden intention to nip in the bud an evil of social change.

Though he was speaking for the Kana Association, Toyama's article in June of the same year indicated that by that time he had already changed his vote from *kana* to *rōmaji*. The article, titled "Kanji o haishi eigo o sakan ni okosu wa konnichi no kyūmu nari" (Urgent Task Today: Abolition of *Kanji* and Promotion of English) (1884; Meiji 17), suggested that "the best strategy is to use *rōmaji* rather than *kana*" after abolishing *kanji* because *rōmaji* would allow for copying the original Western language. For Toyama, Japan was at the stage where it had no choice but to "eagerly copy" and "learn everything from" Western civilizations: it was time to depart from *kanji,* "the weaker" in the social evolution, and to strengthen "national power" and "national productivity" (Yoshida and Inokuchi 1950, 74–79).

Then how did Toyama himself write sentences in *rōmaji?* The following is an example of his *rōmaji* writing:

NYOSHI NO KYŌIKU TO YASOKYŌ KAIRYŌ NO HŌ
Hito no kengu wo shiran to hossuru mono wa nani yori mo mazu sono haha no kengu wo toubeshi. Kuni no kaika wo susumen to hakaru mono wa yoroshiku mazu sono kuni no fujin wo kairyō suru koto wo tsutomezaru bekarazu.

[EDUCATION FOR WOMEN AND CHILDREN, AND REFORM OF CHRISTIANITY
Those who wish to know the level of a person's intelligence should first inquire about his mother's intelligence. Those who work towards the nation's development must first try cultivating the women of the nation.] (Yamamoto Y. 1965, 314)

Clearly, all Toyama did was transcribe the traditional *kanbun* sentences into *rōmaji.* This was the common tendency among other *rōmaji* advocates of that time. No matter how much they were devoted to radical Westernization, their writing remained in *kanbun* style—a characteristic paradox among Meiji intellectuals (though they did not, at that time, think of it as a paradox).

Kana advocates also had problems in their writing style, though different from those of *rōmaji* advocates: they wrote in the pseudo-classical style, as in the following example.

かなもじにて、ふみ、かゝむには、ひとの、みゝに、いりやすくして、むげに、いやしからぬ、ことばを、えらび、なるべく、かんごを、もちひぬことを、こゝろがくるこそ、かんえうならめ。

Kanamoji nite, fumi, kakam niwa, hito no, mimi ni, iriyasuku shite, muge ni, iya-shikaranu, kotoba wo, erabi, narubeku, kango wo, mochiinu koto wo, kokorogak-uru koso, kan'yō nara me.

[In writing in *kana,* choose the least vulgar words and words that sound easy to the ears. It is important to try not to use *kango.*] (From "Kana no michibiki" [Introduction to *Kana*-writing] by Fujino Nagamasa, 1883; quoted in Yamamoto 1965, 262)

As the above examples show, these inherent problems in Japanese writing styles of that time weakened the impact of Kana no Kai as well as of Rōmaji Kai, and became a target for criticism from other scholars.

Suematsu Kenchō, for example, harshly criticized the writing styles of the above advocates in his 1886 (Meiji 19) book *Nihon bunshōron* (Theory of Japanese Writing). In the chapter "Bunshō no teisai" (Sentence Style), Suematsu asserted the importance of establishing a standard writing style regardless of the kind of script used. "Rōmaji Kai tends too much to copy *kanbun* style; Kana no Kai, on the other hand, seems to adhere to extremely eccentric old language. For those reasons, I do not support either group." He further attacked Kana no Kai for its dream of the "restoration of ancient-style classical studies," calling it impossible because it went against the current of the time (Yamamoto M. 1978, 255–260). According to Suematsu, reform of script was merely a part of the reform of spoken and written language, and the ultimate goal of these reforms should be *genbun itchi.* Thus unsuccessful examples from Kana no Kai and Rōmaji Kai brought to the forefront the urgent need for *genbun itchi,* which had been, until then, only secondary to the script-reform movement.

1-5. *Kokuji* Problems in the Fourth Decade of Meiji

In his essay "Kanji genshōron" (Proposal for Reduction of *Kanji*) (1900; Meiji 33), Hara Takashi,[11] who was then the president of the Osaka *Mainichi shinbun* and was vocal about *kokugo* and *kokuji* issues, proposed a gradual reduction of *kanji* moving towards its total abolition. Hara said that he no longer heard about the current activities of Kana no Kai or Rōmaji Kai, nor had he seen any success by the remaining members of these groups. "I am not a member of either group, so I have no intention of speaking for them. . . . In fact, I can't even remember what they were advocating" (Nishio and Hisamatsu 1969, 92). Times had changed that quickly, within just a few years, as indicated in his remark, and the climate of the time had changed the nature of the debate about a national script towards the fourth decade of Meiji (1897–1906). The change reflected the anti-Chinese sentiment and rise of nationalism caused by the Sino-Japanese War. Therefore it is not surprising to find that even seemingly competing viewpoints about script shared the emotional climate of the time, as seen in opposing proposals by Inoue Tetsujirō and Miyake Setsurei.

Inoue was a front-line advocate of the imperial order *(tennō-sei),* as outlined in his work *Chokugo engi* (Popular Version of the Imperial Rescript) in 1891 (Meiji 24). He urged that *kanji* be replaced by a new national script. In contrast, Miyake, who was promoting nationalism through the publication of the magazine *Nihonjin* (The Japanese),[12] strongly supported *kanji.*

In his lecture "Moji to kyōiku no kankei" (Relation between Script and Education) in April 1894 (Meiji 27), four months before the outbreak of the Sino-Japanese War, Inoue lamented that Westerners could write books of any kind with only twenty-six alphabet letters, while the number of *kanji* was almost infinite, exacerbated by the number of their possible combinations. Therefore, "by the time we have barely learned how to write *kanji*, they are already doing further research to develop knowledge."

As we have seen, Inoue was not the first to articulate such a view of *kanji* as the principal cause of cultural stagnation. However, what Inoue really wanted to say was not limited just to this argument against *kanji*. He continued, maintaining that "as long as Japanese people use the script of China, we are somehow controlled by them, which is really undesirable," and that "it is regrettable for us today to be controlled by the script of a country that we consider inferior." For Inoue, a threat to the independence of script also meant a threat to the independence of the nation and the people's thinking. Inoue firmly believed that departure from *kanji* would allow Japan to break completely free from China. Nevertheless, he did not support the adoption of *rōmaji* or *kana*. Nor did he support the reduction of *kanji*. Though he had once supported *rōmaji*, he realized that he "was very wrong" because *rōmaji* "does not appeal to the sentiment of the Japanese" even though it was arguably practical. It was this very "sentiment of the Japanese," not a rationale, that was the fundamental principle in maintaining *kokutai*, Japan's special national polity. Inoue was appreciative of the *kana* devotees' patriotism, but he considered the lengthiness of *kana* writing as "retrogression." As for the reduction of *kanji*, Inoue regarded it as "ridiculous" to reduce *kanji* while the vocabulary of the time was increasing.[13]

In short, Inoue proposed to extend the spirit of the reformers of *rōmaji* and *kana*: he wanted to improve Japanese script so that it "can express our intention as precisely as possible, as simply as possible, and can be an instrument to state and exchange our ideas as conveniently as possible." Thus he recommended "creating simple script such as *hiragana* which we always had." He believed that the establishment of this new script would enable Japan to "keep up with education in Europe" (Nishio and Hisamatsu 1969, 53–58).

In contrast to Maejima, for whom only Western countries were in a position to patronize China, Inoue did not hesitate to say that now Japan was entitled to "look down on" China. Such an attitude corresponded to the idiosyncratic theory of *kokutai*, which was put forward in Inoue's discussions. In Maejima's time, the institution of national language and script had no relation to the reminiscers' argument used to justify and identify so-called *kokutai*, as clearly referred to in Maejima's "The Enforcement of Japanese and the Abolishment of *Kanji*" in 1873 (Meiji 6) (Yoshida and Inokuchi 1950, 1:59). However, this *kokutai* was now used without hesitation in Inoue's argument as his official justification. Needless to say, Inoue's position reflected the context of that time, which had begun with the promulgation of Dai Nihon Teikoku Kenpō (Great Japan Imperial Constitution) in 1889 (Meiji 22), followed by *Kyōiku chokugo* (Imperial Rescript on Education) in 1890 (Meiji 23). Note here that Inoue was not an antiquitist, and his proposal was based on his "spirit of reform." His *kokutai* was not the retrospective one used by the classicists of early Meiji, but the ideology defined by, and further supportive of, the system of the modern nation-state. In this respect, *kokutai,* the national polity that Inoue used for criticizing *rōmaji,* was a direct continuation of the practical view of script proposed by Nishi and Toyama, *rōmaji* advocates: their view was that script must be an "efficient instrument" to communicate ideas.

In opposition to Inoue, Miyake Setsurei developed a unique theory in defense of *kanji* in his "Kanji ridō setsu" (Beneficial Use of *Kanji*) in 1895 (Meiji 28). While admitting various shortcomings of *kanji,* Miyake contested its abolition. The nationwide project to abolish *kanji* would cost tremendous labor and huge expense. Instead, "it would be more appropriate for the nation to make an effort to take advantage of *kanji,* rather than forcing its abolition." Even though *Kōki jiten* (The Chinese *Kangxi zidian* Dictionary) contained forty-seven thousand *kanji,* five thousand would suffice for a print shop's type, and two to three thousand *kanji* would be sufficient for the knowledge used in daily life. Improvement in teaching methods would reduce difficulties in learning this number of *kanji.* In other words, Miyake argued that the difficulty of learning *kanji* cited by anti-*kanji* people was "not the nature of *kanji* itself, but rather is due to the absence of an orderly method of teaching" (Nishio and Hisamatsu 1969, 79–82).

What, then, was the "benefit of *kanji*" that Miyake supported? It was "to understand ways of thinking in East Asia, which would help our conquest over East Asia and its commerce. This requires learning *kanbun* together with the writing of *kanji.* . . . Knowledge of most *kanji* and the principle of their combinations would enable us to monitor communication in East Asia" (Nishio and Hisamatsu 1969, 81). Furthermore, Miyake believed that China, considering its population and the shape of its society, should be seen as a continent rather than a country such as France or Germany. "In order to learn their ways of thinking and to strengthen our commercial and political strategies, we should be intent on learning the script of this continent." Miyake paid special attention to the fact that *kanji* was the common means of communication that overcame the various dialects in the different regions of China. In other words, Miyake claimed that *kanji* was indispensable as a means for communication in Asia.

Note here that in Miyake's argument, China was no longer a political unit and was replaced by a neutral geographical concept, "a continent." *Kanji* was no longer the script of an enemy country, China, as it was for Inoue. It was simply a script used on the continent that was the target of political and commercial conquest. Inoue and Miyake appeared to be in opposition, but at the same time, they complemented one another: Inoue was focused more inward, while Miyake was focused outward. This is why both arguments, Inoue's "new script" *(shin kokuji)* and Miyake's "reduction of *kanji*," were included in the agenda of Kokugo Chōsa Iinkai (National Language Investigative Committee), which began in 1902 (Meiji 35). The two were appointed as committee members after having served as *kokugo* investigation staff since 1900 (Meiji 33).

Here, a brief mention of the background of the inauguration of the National Language Investigative Committee is in order. The Imperial Board of Education (Teikoku Kyōiku Kai) was established in 1896 (Meiji 29), and the Division for National Script Reform (Kokuji Kairyōbu) was added in October 1899 (Meiji 32), headed by Maejima Hisoka. This division expedited various projects for policy making for *kokugo* education, and the Imperial Board of Education submitted a "Petition regarding Improvements in National Script and Language" (Kokuji kokugo kokubun no kairyō ni kansuru scigansho) to the Diet on January 26, 1900 (Meiji 33) (Nishio and Hisamatsu 1969, 107–109). The petition argued as follows: The Japanese language is in complete disarray without any clear standards in its script, style, and grammar. Because of this, "our students and pupils spend most of their school life on learning this language and script and do not have time for learning other important knowledge." Now that Japan is "a triumphal Empire of the competitive world," it is our urgent task to reform this "chaotic, confusing, disordered, and inconsistent script and language," for "the good or evil of a script and a written language correspond to the active or inactive education of the people, to their open or closed mindedness, their strength or weakness, and their wealth or poverty, and thus seriously correspond to the rise or fall and superiority or inferiority of the nation's power."

Reform of the national script was the first task. Previous proposals for the reduction of *kanji*, the use of *kana*, the use of *rōmaji*, the creation of new script, and so forth, were all in agreement as to discontinuing *kanji* because of its inconvenience and disadvantages. The merits and demerits of these proposals, however, required further investigation. Thus the Imperial Board of Education considered that the reform of the national script and language should be handled through national research and investigation, and it proposed to the cabinet and to each minister, the Ministry of Education, chairs of the House of Peers (Kizokuin) and the House of Representatives (Shūgiin), "that the

government promptly resume research into methods for reform and enforcement of a national script and language."

The Ministry of Education gave an unusually prompt response to this proposal in April of the same year (1900) by appointing seven ministry members
to be *kokugo chōsa iin* (national language investigators); this became an official
government office in March 1902, chaired by Katō Hiroyuki. In August of the
same year, the Ministry of Education also instituted, on revising *Shōgakkōrei*
(Elementary School Order), a limitation of the number of *kanji* to twelve hundred, the phonetic usage of *kana* (so called *bōbiki kanazukai*), and a standardization of *kana* form. These reforms were put into practice in *Jinjō shōgaku
tokuhon* (Normal Elementary Reading), the first language textbook compiled
by the national government.

The brains behind this treatment of language issues belonged to Ueda Kazutoshi, who became a professor of philology at Tokyo Imperial University in
1894 (Meiji 27) on his return from Germany with new knowledge of the modern science of language.[14] Ueda was an active director of the Kokugo Research
Office, which he started at Tokyo Imperial University, and also had served the
Ministry of Education since 1898 as director of the Office of Academic Matters
(Senmon Gakumukyoku) and as councilor *(sanyo kan)*. It was Ueda and people
with his backing who took the actual initiatives in policy making at the Ministry of Education and National Language Investigative Committee.

In his article "Shin kokuji ron" (New National Script) (May 1895; Meiji 28),[15]
Ueda had argued, while acknowledging Inoue's position, that he was against
both "ideographs like Chinese script" and "*shirabikku shisutemu* (a syllabic system) like Japanese *kana*." He further argued that a "*fonechikku shisutem* (phonetic system)[16] like romanization, which distinguishes vowels and consonants"
should be preferentially considered (Ueda 1897, 207). He noted, however, that
such a "new national script" could not be put into effect by anyone without
accurate knowledge of phonology. Thus, with his training in the modern theory of linguistics in Europe as his strength, he was to promote *kokugo* reform as
a determined *rōmaji* advocate.

Ueda will be the topic of part 2 of this book, and here I would like only to
point out the following: Inoue's inward focus on protecting the national polity and Miyake's outward focus on advancing into the Asian continent came
together in Ueda's view. That is, Ueda's ideal of a "national language," *kokugo*,
was born where these two perspectives intersected.

In closing this chapter, I must remark on the fact that the idea of abolishing
kanji, though possibly stemming from anti-Chinese sentiment, was predominant among many intellectuals and bureaucrats in Meiji. Both the "Petition
regarding Improvements in National Script and Language" by the Imperial

Board of Education[17] and the decision by the National Language Investigative Committee[18] were aimed at the ultimate abolition of *kanji.* Ironically, however, it was in this Meiji era that *kango* (vocabulary in *kanji*) was invading every corner of the society: as Yanagita Kunio[19] later lamented, even girls in the countryside spoke unpolished *kango* such as "*kankei* (relation), *reigai* (exception), *zenzen* (absolute), *hantai* (opposition), etc." (Yanagita 1963a, 517). Such dualism [the influx of *kango* against the nation's desire for its abolition] became a haunting problem for the modern Japanese language.

CHAPTER 2

Genbun Itchi and *Kokugo*

2-1. Linguistic Crisis and *Genbun Itchi*

Anyone who set his face towards language reform at the dawn of modern Japan was aware of the extraordinary distance between the spoken and written language. However, people became aware of such distance only when the social order started to disintegrate, the social order that had supported and allowed these two languages to coexist without conflict.

Kanbun kundoku[1] or *kanbun*-style language was the language for cultural and administrative matters among intellectuals and the samurai class throughout the Edo era, but as the Meiji era started, it suddenly became relevant to common people. This was the context:

> Since the Meiji Reform, there were fewer good things, and the government was facing things that are more difficult. The government issued ten times more announcements than in the shogunate time, but their language included too many *kango* and was too difficult for people from the countryside to understand. Even though newspapers were also distributed, people were unable to read them and confused. Nonetheless, they had no choice but to receive them as ordered by the government. (Meiji Bunka Kenkyūkai 1967, 524)

The shogunate-domain system *(bakuhan taisei)*[2] before Meiji had prohibited interactions, both material and nonmaterial, among domains *(han),* that is, among clans or their provinces, a prohibition that resulted in the further splitting of the spoken language into dialects. Furthermore, in each dialect the spoken language had strict distinctions among the four social classes—samurai, peasants, craftsmen, and merchants, as described by Fukuzawa Yukichi in his *Kyū han jō* (Matters of Old Domains) in 1877 (Meiji 10). According to Fukuzawa, there were class distinctions in every aspect of life among upper-class samurai, lower class samurai, merchants, and peasants in the Edo period, from minute manners to various customs in food, clothing, and housing. "Such differences in their cultures were also found in their dialects" (Fukuzawa 1980–1981, 12:49). That is, one could tell a person's class right away on hearing the person speak. Fukuzawa skillfully illustrated this in the following examples (49).

To say	Upper-class samurai	Lower-class samurai	Merchants	Peasants
"Look!" *mite kure yo*	*michi kurei*	*michi kurii*	*mite kurii*	*miche kurii*
"Go!" *ike yo*	*iki nasai*	*iki nahai* or *iki nai*	same as lower-class samurai	same as lower-class samurai or *iki naharii*
"What shall we/I do?" *ikaga sen ka*	*dō shō ka*	*dō shū ka*	*dogei shū ka* or *dō shū ka*	same as merchants

Fukuzawa attempted to write in the "vernacular language people commonly use" in the hope of overcoming such linguistic splits and achieving broad communication among the people. In his first book, *Seiyō jijō* (Matters of the West), Fukuzawa declared that he would "use elaborate sentence style but . . . common language," and write sentences "whose aim is to communicate one's intention" (1980–1981, 1:101). He wrote that "depending on how the context goes, I would not hesitate to use *kango,* or insert *kango* in common language, while using common words replacing *kango*—thus mixing up the classic and common languages, so that by rejecting the sacred *kanbun* world and confusing its grammar, I would simply use as easy and accessible sentences as possible in order to let common people learn about new ideas in civilization" (12:144).

What, then, was the meaning in linguistic terms of the search for communication among the people of Japan in early Meiji? One answer is that in a social situation with geographic and class fragmentation, there was a need to establish a form of expression with style and vocabulary comprehensible to all. This has to do with the problematic reality of the language of that time. At the same time, another problem tended to be overlooked: the problem of representation. As Fukuzawa pointed out, the very fact that one could tell the speaker's social class immediately on hearing the person talk implies that language is constantly splitting into lower social echelons. In such a situation, the idea of a single *kokugo* (national language) was difficult to grasp. Therefore, it became necessary to create an image of the language that was spoken by an anonymous "nation-people," an indefinite "somebody" who could be anyone from the upper or lower class of samurai, merchants, or peasants. For that purpose, it was necessary to represent a linguistic model that was supposed to exist some-where, a pure linguistic model not contaminated by geographical and social variations.

The reality was, however, that such odorless, transparent language could not be found anywhere. When an individual speaks, his or her language is already an idiosyncratic variation. Any language model, however standard it might be, is created through history from certain geographical, social, and stylistic vari-ants. However, the logic of linguistic representation itself formulates criteria for these variants to measure the degree of their variation. Such manipulation was the prerequisite and core of the idea of *kokugo,* and the newly created linguistic form to carry out this idea in Meiji was the *genbun itchi.*

2-2. From Script Reform to *Genbun Itchi:*
Maejima Hisoka, Nishi Amane, and Kanda Takahira

As briefly mentioned in the previous chapter, there was already an orienta-tion towards *genbun itchi* in the proposals for script reform by Maejima and Nishi. Maejima hoped to abolish *kanji* and then to institute a national language and grammar that did not differentiate between the spoken and written modes. However, Maejima sought the standard for this unification in the rather offi-cial language spoken by the samurai class when he made a case for the "use of today's common language [for ending a sentence] such as '*tsukamatsuru*' and '*gozaru*' instead of the classical '*haberu*' and '*kerukana*'" (Nishio and Hisamatsu 1969, 18).

The spoken language that Nishi proposed was also that of public lectures and the notes from them and not of daily conversation. Nishi attempted a kind of *genbun itchi* in such writings as "Yōji o motte kokugo o shosuru no ron" (Writing Japanese in the Western Script) and *Hyaku ichi shin ron* (101 New Theories) (both in 1874; Meiji 7), but they were all question-answer formats in the *gozaru* style of the samurai class. Such attempts by Nishi were of course closely related to the fact that he was also a member of Meirokusha (Meiji 6 Association), the first organization in Japan to advocate public lectures and speeches as a part of the cultural enlightenment movement.

The proposals by Maejima and Nishi were the early foundation of the later arguments over hegemony between *gen* (the spoken) and *bun* (the written) lan-guages: whether the *genbun itchi* should be a compromise, adapting features of the spoken language into the written language, or a reform, by making *bun* correspond to *gen.* The *genbun itchi* we know in history is the latter, but, as I discuss later, in Meiji the former was more prevalent. In either argument, how-ever, the concept of *gen* was still too unharmonious and ambiguous to initiate the movement of *genbun itchi*. There was a need to select a model for *gen*. Thus Maejima chose the language of the samurai class and Nishi public speech as the models for the spoken language. The *kokuji* reformers in early Meiji, represented by Maejima and Nishi, thus were well aware of the need for *genbun itchi*. However, for them the issue was still secondary to that of the script, as exemplified in the practice of Kana no Kai and Rōmaji Kai mentioned in the previous chapter.

Through these struggles, some of the language reformers in Meiji realized that the *genbun itchi* itself was more pressing issue than script reform. Kanda Takahira was one of these reformers, and we must not overlook his 1875 (Meiji 8) article "*Bunshōron* o yomu" (Rereading *Theory of Writing*), the first article that used the term *genbun itchi*, according to Yamamoto Masahide (1965, 39). This term played a significant role in instantly consolidating the spirit of various earlier proposals to bring together the spoken and written languages.

Kanda's article "Rereading *Theory of Writing*" was a critique of Nishimura Shigeki's 1874 (Meiji 7) book *Bunshōron* (Theory of Writing) (see Yoshida and Inokuchi 1964, 169–174). Nishimura argued that the then-current two types of Japanese writing styles, *kanbun* (Chinese style text) and *wabun* (classical Japanese style text), were both extremely troublesome, and he advocated reforming written Japanese in a way suitable for the new era, Meiji. However, his proposal was rather unrealistic: to create a brand new writing system based on an expert knowledge of classical grammar not only of Japanese but also of Chinese, European languages, and even Greek and Latin.

Acknowledging Nishimura's suggestion to discard both *kanbun* and *wabun*, Kanda denied the need for such an extensive knowledge of classical languages as Nishimura claimed. He maintained that one's "knowledge of ordinary, daily language is sufficient" for reform (175–176), for the purpose of the reform was "to unify our spoken language and the written language." *Kanbun*, even with Japanese guiding marks, is a language of a different grammatical structure from Japanese; *kana* sentences [*wabun*] use the language of the past. Writings in *kanbun* and *wabun* are inevitably remote from our daily language. If we wish to eliminate such problems in our written language, we must make our written language comprehensible when it is read aloud. Kanda thus emphasized the need for *genbun itchi*, that is "to use the ordinary language of conversation and to write in that language" (177). Kanda extended his criticism to the script-reform proposals. He asserted that in whichever approach, *rōmaji, kana,* or reduction of *kanji*, the reform of the written language must come before the script. Once the written language was reformed, the use of any script should cause no problem. Reforming the script before reforming the written language was backwards (178).

These proposals by Kanda, as well as by Suematsu as discussed in the previous chapter, promoted the trend towards placing priority on *genbun itchi* before script reform (though none of these proposals was written in the *genbun itchi* style).[3] The desire for *genbun itchi* grew stronger among the members of Kana no Kai and Rōmaji Kai, as represented by Mozume Takami and Basil Hall Chamberlain, who were colleagues at Tokyo University and who each wrote a book titled *Genbun itchi*.

2-3. *Genbun Itchi* by Mozume Takami and B. H. Chamberlain

In 1886 (Meiji 19), Mozume Takami, a scholar of classics and councilor of Kana no Kai, published a book titled *Genbun itchi*. The book was written in the spoken language, consistent with his avowal in his original lectures at Kana no Kai. Mozume illustrated in seven areas the urgency and advantages of *genbun itchi*, which he summarized as follows:

> In general, it would be good to speak in the way that people can easily understand. When you write what you want to say, you should also write it in an intelligible way. Even if we try to write in the way we speak, however, the written language will not be exactly the same as the spoken and so needs extra attention. I would suggest that we write in the way we speak, that is, making the written language as plain and easy as possible. (Yoshida and Inokuchi 1964, 182)

Mozume criticized the written language of his time as mimicry clinging to antiquated rules, as in the saying "the mouth is one's own while the hand is of the dead" (181). He proposed in contrast to use the naturalness and spontaneity of the spoken language: "Stop writing another's words like a parrot. The best way would be to write your own lively words as naturally and spontaneously as you speak them" (186).

As for the polite expressions that abound in Japanese, Mozume advised omitting these expressions in writing one's diary and notes to avoid verbosity (187). Here, Mozume was commenting on dealing with Japanese sentence endings, the very first hurdle in realizing *genbun itchi*: what to do about writing with politeness, which changes kaleidoscopically in spoken Japanese according to the relationship between the speaker and the hearer. Mozume was extremely conscious of this problem in his radical experiment of writing the first half of his book in the formal written style with sentences ending with *de aru* and the latter half with more colloquial sentence endings, *masu* or *de arimasu*. In that sense, Mozume's book marked an epoch in the theory and practice of the *genbun itchi* movement and moved it forward from the stage where the advocates' proposals themselves were still written in pre–*genbun itchi* style.

Another such experiment was "GEM-BUN ITCHI,"[4] an essay by Chamberlain published in May 1887 (Meiji 20) that was written in *rōmaji* with the colloquial *masu*-style sentence endings. This essay was based on his lecture for the members of Rōmaji Kai, where he criticized the unintelligible writing style of their journal *Rōmaji zasshi* and emphasized the need for *genbun itchi,* that is, "writing in the way one speaks" (216). According to Chamberlain, the writing of the *rōmaji* advocates was still in *kanbun* style and otherwise unintelligible unless each word was replaced with *kanji.* Such a reality implied faint hope for the success of the *rōmaji* movement. Similarly, it was not desirable to opt for ancient *yamato kotoba,* as Kana no Kai did. The ultimate direction to take, Chamberlain maintained, was to "simply use the real Japanese language, that is, our daily language as it is used" (219).

While Mozume's emphasis was on the spontaneity of expressions, Chamberlain's was on the social impact of *genbun itchi:* in every advanced country, people wrote in the way they spoke. In China, Korea, Japan, and Vietnam, however, which were dominated by *kanji,* common languages were despised, civilization belonged to only a handful of intellects, and people's education was neglected, just as medieval Europe had been dominated by Latin. Barriers to natural language, that is, a common language, robbed great literature of creativity and fresh expressions. The only way to eliminate such obstacles was to put *genbun itchi* into practice, as had been done in modern European countries. Abolition of the numerous difficult styles of the past would be the best way to improve education and advance people's knowledge in Japan (221). Chamberlain concluded his article urging the immediate practice of *genbun itchi* in *Rōmaji zasshi* and proposing to encourage newspapers to adopt it.

Advocacy by Mozume and Chamberlain exerted a far-reaching influence, as can be seen in the radical style change in the novels of Yamada Bimyō, who together with Futabatei Shimei became the standard-bearers of *genbun itchi* novels. However, this did not mean that the *genbun itchi* movement had all smooth sailing: Mozume himself later turned against and retracted his *genbun itchi* theory. In December 1902 (Meiji 35), sixteen years after the publication of his book *Genbun itchi,* Mozume published an essay in the *Yomiuri shinbun* with the title "Genbun itchi no fukanō" (*Genbun itchi* Is Impossible). In the essay, Mozume said that he had come to realize, through his work of editing a Japanese grammar book, that there were two distinct styles of Japanese text, conversational *(kaiwabun)* and descriptive *(kirokubun),* and that *genbun itchi* was not the right solution. *Kaiwabun* had second-person pronouns, present tense, and polite endings. *Kirokubun,* on the other hand, used third-person pronouns, all of the past, present, and future tenses, but not many polite expressions. It was impossible to apply *genbun itchi* to both of these distinct styles (Yamamoto M.

1979, 485–490). In other words, *genbun itchi* for Mozume was limited to texts that simply copied the actual spoken language of dialogues.

This is an apparent retrogression from his book *Genbun itchi*. His proposal for the distinctive styles, however—*kōgo,* the colloquial style for dialogues, and *bungo,* the literary style for description—was also a reflection of a trend in literature of that time dominated by the style of the novelists of Ken'yūsha.[5] While it embodied the spirit of the age, Mozume's proposal also betrayed a fatal problem in his understanding of the idea of *genbun itchi.* That is, he had mistaken the fundamental idea of *genbun itchi,* "write as spoken," for "copy exactly as spoken." Though Mozume aspired to written language with the spontaneity of spoken language, his theory of *genbun itchi* was not free of problems. For example, towards the end of his book *Genbun itchi,* in explaining "why it cannot be difficult to write as we speak," he showed that the openings of twenty-one classical literary works from *Ise Monogatari* (The Tale of Ise) of the Heian era to *Yoshitsuneki* (Story of Yoshitsune) of the Kamakura era could be easily translated into modern language with only minor revision of tense and conjunctions. Mozume's intention here might have been to give authority to modern language by emphasizing its continuity from classical language. However, it is puzzling that he chose to show the revision of classical language as an example of *genbun itchi* while fervently emphasizing a need for the language "that comes from within one." In the end, Mozume was not daring enough to make the impossible possible.

As for Chamberlain, we have to consider Tatsumi Kojirō's harsh criticism of him in "Baku genbun itchi ron" (Refuting *Genbun itchi*) (1887; Meiji 20) (Yoshida and Inokuchi 1964, 224–233), where Tatsumi asked difficult questions of supporters of *genbun itchi.* Tatsumi began his article with praise for Chamberlain's simple style of writing, which he attributed to the minimum use of *kango* and extensive use of common language. Tatsumi even counted the number of *kanji* and *kango* words *(jukugo)* in Chamberlain's article and made statistical comparisons with writings by other *rōmaji* advocates. Such a meticulous analysis showed that Tatsumi had no objection to Chamberlain's practice of *genbun itchi.* Moreover, he was even critical of the residue of *kanbun* style in Chamberlain's writing—although Tatsumi's writing itself was in the classical written style of a mixture of *kanji* and *kana.*

Tatsumi attacked Chamberlain's *Genbun itchi,* therefore, not on its practice but on its theory. The object of his attack was Chamberlain's proposal that "Rōmaji Kai's goal should be that they use common language as it is actually spoken." Tatsumi attempted to refute this by theorizing about the substantial difference between the spoken and written languages. His argument had two major points: that the government must not interfere in the language issue and that language was to change its style as civilization advanced. As for the first point, Tatsumi argued that the government should not control how people speak even though it could standardize the language in official documents, just as a government of a civilized country entrusts its people with morality even though it governs them with law. He emphasized the fact that the spoken language varied vastly among dialects, demonstrating as an example twenty-four variations in dialects for the sentence ending *de gozaimasu*. Distinct local characteristics and customs were beyond political control. In the same way, he claimed, "it is out of the question" for the government to "interfere and meddle with" the people's spoken language. He said that enforcing Chamberlain's *genbun itchi* could mean forcing people to speak two languages: "the common language of the imperial nation" and "the particular language of the local."

As for the second point [that language is to change its style as civilization advances], Tatsumi explained that spoken language was suitable to "describe things happening under one's eyes," while written language was appropriate for the transmission of cultural tradition. He counterattacked Chamberlain's assertion that European countries exercised *genbun itchi* by pointing out that conversational language and written language in these countries were different. Tatsumi maintained that "barbarians have spoken language but no written language; only civilized people have both spoken and written languages" (Yoshida and Inokuchi 1964, 233), and thus he defended the separation of spoken and written languages from the standpoint of "civilization."

Tatsumi's criticism raised an important contradiction that *genbun itchi* advocates could not avoid confronting: The current *genbun itchi* theory allowed the writing of spoken language as it was, then it would allow writing different and mutually unintelligible dialects also.

2-4. Tokyo Language and *Genbun Itchi*

One who was able to give a clear-cut response to Tatsumi's criticism was Yamada Bimyō, who had already established fame with his novel *Musashino* in *genbun itchi* style in 1887 (Meiji 20). He wrote "Genbun itchi ron gairyaku" (Outline of *Genbun itchi* Theory) in 1888 (Meiji 21) in defense of *genbun itchi*, giving this movement a theoretical foundation (Yoshida and Inokuchi 1964, 234–245).

He first pointed out that there were two schools of *genbun itchi* advocates: the advocates for "so-called *futsūbun*, the standard written style" who "attempted to bring the spoken language close to the written," and those for "so-called *genbun itchi*, or *zokubun,* the vernacular-style," who "attempted to bring the written language close to the spoken" (234). Then, as a member of the latter school, Yamada articulately refuted every criticism by the former, the *futsūbun* advocates.

The central criticism by *futsūbun* advocates was that the use of colloquial language for writing would mean unintelligible communication in many places in Japan. Yamada argued against this as follows: it was not the case that he believed in the use of *any* colloquial language in his writing in *genbun itchi* style. Various expressions particular to each dialect, regardless of their roots in classical language, could not be regarded as "common" usage of the language. Only if we could find and use common language would there be no obstacles to our communication in *genbun itchi* style. Furthermore, Yamada proposed that Tokyo language, upon his careful examination of its characteristics, was the language that met this need, because "the degree of unintelligibility of Tokyo language is much lower than that of Sasshū[6] or Ōshū[7] dialect," and "there is hardly any place where Tokyo language is not at all understood" (235). Thus, Yamada declared that *genbun itchi* should adopt the Tokyo language as its standard.

Yamada then explained the historical reasons why the Tokyo language had gained central status in Japanese. During the Edo period,[8] Tokyo, called Edo at that time, was the center of the government and drew samurais and merchants from various parts of Japan. As a result, "there was a linguistic blend that was only seen in Edo." The current Tokyo language inherited these advantages of the Edo dialect. Furthermore, as the communication network spread in the future, the ripple effect emanating from Tokyo, the capital, would meet no obstacles, and "the language used in Tokyo would become more common in different parts of Japan." Yamada concluded that "if we take our vernacular language as the base and control its development by grammatical restrictions, then we could easily create a perfect written language and a truly appropriate spoken language" (237).

The rest of his article was a series of lucid arguments: that even common language could not avoid linguistic changes over time, that a "control of grammar" would protect vernacular language from drastic changes, that even vernacular language had systematic grammatical rules, and that it was merely nostalgia for today's people to admire the beauty of things in the past, such as classical language.

Yamada's sober response to each of the anti–*genbun itchi* arguments thus defended *genbun itchi* from both social and historical perspectives, and, helped by his fame as a writer, impressed the public with the rightness of *genbun itchi*. It was indeed "the proclamation of advancing *genbun itchi,* the declaration of promoting a new writing style, and the flag of the writing style reform" (Yamamoto M. 1965, 666).[9] We should also note that in contrast to Futabatei's *-da* style,[10] Yamada began writing essays in colloquial -*desu* style,[11] later known as his trademark style.

The very fact that Yamada had to emphasize the standard quality of the Tokyo language indicated the reality of his time that it was not yet established as the model for the written language. For example, in the second edition of *Wa-ei gorin shūsei* (Japanese-English Dictionary) in 1872 (Meiji 5), James Curtis Hepburn mentioned that "the language of Kyoto, the capital where the Emperor and educated people live, is considered as the most authoritative, standard language. However, there are significant differences among dialects, and various local accents and slang abound" (Hepburn 1872, 14). In its third edition in 1886 (Meiji 19), however, Hepburn revised the last sentence as follows: "However, after the Restoration of Imperial Rule *(ōsei fukko)* and the transfer of the capital to Tokyo, the Tokyo dialect has gained ascendancy" (13). It is not a coincidence that the *genbun itchi* movement first peaked during the 1880s, when the Tokyo language was gradually gaining its authority.

In June 1885 (Meiji 18) an article "Tōkyōgo no tsūyō" (Common Use of Tokyo Language) appeared in *Jiyū tō* (Light of Freedom), a newsletter of the Liberal Party (Yamamoto M. 1978, 224). The author, pen-named Asanebō (A Late Riser), began the article saying, "If anybody asks me which one of the local languages of daily use will become a common Japanese, I would readily answer that it would be the Tokyo language." As provinces developed closer communication with the capital after *haihan chiken*—the abolition of domains and institution of prefectures[12]—their people had gradually started using the Tokyo language instead of their dialects and local accents. In the past, people had learned the Edo language through popular books such as *ninjōbon* (love stories), but "nowadays they can so easily learn [the Tokyo language] with *furigana shinbun* (a popular version of a newspaper which provided pronunciation in *kana* of each *kanji*) that cocky students can use it even before they actually visit Tokyo." Here the author was not criticizing the students' cocky behavior. Rather, he was asserting that local elementary education should be conducted exclusively in the Tokyo language, because "in order to standardize the ordinary written language free from extreme division between the spoken and written languages, we must first standardize the spoken languages." We must note that this was an early attempt at connecting *genbun itchi* and the standardization of the language before the institutionalization of the latter.

Another example is the *Yōgaku tokuhon* (Elementary Reader), which was edited in 1887 (Meiji 20) by Nishimura Tei, an executive member of Dai Nihon Kyōiku Kai (Great Japan Education Board). This was an important and pioneering work in that as a textbook it adopted a conversational style for the most part, with the intention of following "the model of the pronunciation of educated people in Tokyo." According to Nishimura, language has a natural tendency to assimilate, and "Tokyo is the goal of assimilation" (Yamamoto M. 1965, 440).[13]

Behind the demand for *genbun itchi* was the reality of the gradual spread of the Tokyo language and the rising awareness that the Tokyo language was gaining hegemony. The novels in *genbun itchi* style were among the main forces circulating the Tokyo language. Most of the novelists of early *genbun itchi,* such as Futabatei Shimei, Yamada Bimyō, Tsubouchi Shōyō, and Ozaki Kōyō, were born in Tokyo. Futabatei, for example, on publishing in 1886 (Meiji 19) his first work of translation, *Tsūzoku Kyomutō Keiki,*[14] wrote in the advertisement for his own book that the book was written in the "elegant Tokyo language" (Yamamoto M. 1965, 492).

In *Seinen* (Young Man) by Mori Ōgai (1910–1911; Meiji 43–44), the main character, Koizumi Jun'ichi, arrives in Tokyo and pays a visit to a novelist, Ōishi Kentarō. Greeted by the maid, "a country boy, Jun'ichi says, '*Ōishi-san ni omenikakari-tai no da ga*' [I would like to meet Mr. Ōishi] in the Tokyo language that he had learned in novels. He carefully pronounces each word, just as one tries to speak an unfamiliar foreign language. And he feels happily relieved when he is able to successfully answer the maid" (Mori Ō. 1978, 54).

This certainly was not an experience of Ōgai himself, since he was, unlike the poor student in his novel, an elite born to a doctor's family that served a lord of the Iwami domain, mastered reading *kanbun* at the age of five, studied Dutch at eight, and moved to Tokyo and studied German at ten. Nonetheless, the reality of many students of his time who came to Tokyo from the provinces must have prompted Ōgai to describe the above scene. The *genbun itchi* style in novels was thus constructed on the Tokyo language and exported the language to the provinces.

Yamada Bimyō emphasized the continuity between the Edo language and the Tokyo language to justify the standard status of the Tokyo language of his time. However, a close examination of Yamada's argument reveals a small flaw. The *genbun itchi,* which had been a highly charged venture, was toned down in Yamada's discussion to become a historical necessity without subjective involvement. That is, Yamada rationalized the shift of the Tokyo language from merely one of many forms to a norm as a logical consequence. However, we must not overlook the discontinuity between the Tokyo language and the Edo dialect: the former was born in Meiji by discarding the latter, the so-called native downtown language *(shitamachi kotoba).*

According to Heibonsha's *Nihongo no rekishi* (History of the Japanese Language), "the native Edo dialect, the daily language of *edokko,* the common natives of Edo, continued to be used after the Edo era as their home tongue which identified them as *edokko* when contacting other dialects. On the other hand, the Tokyo language was a sort of representative of *kokugo*, considered as a formal language for those whose dialect was different from that of Edo" (*Nihongo no rekishi,* 1965, 6:35–36; presumably written by Kamei Takashi).

The Edo language and the Tokyo language thus had been intricately and intermittently related, until the state institutionalized the "standard language" *(hyōjungo)* and forced their separation. When the Tokyo language was redefined as "the language of educated people in Tokyo" (as defined in the *Elementary Reader*) it was reborn as "the standard language." Furthermore, it later became a defining concept, "the language of the middle-class in Tokyo," which was the basis of the prescriptive language that the state attempted to propagate through school education.

2-5. Meiji Standard Written Style and *Genbun Itchi*

Miyake Yonekichi, a member of Kana no Kai, proposed *genbun itchi* as early as 1884 (Meiji 17) in his "Kuniguni no namari kotoba ni tsukite" (About Local Dialects)" (see Yoshida and Inokuchi 1964, 487–497).[15] He discussed *genbun itchi* and linguistic unification from the same perspective. He postulated three plausible methods for linguistic unification: by classical language, by modern language used in a certain city (possibly either Kyoto or Tokyo), or by selecting common elements in all dialects. However, he questioned the practical possibility of all of them. Nor did he believe that it was possible to mold dialects forcefully into the institutionalized frame of a national language. The best method was to let the reform occur naturally by promoting communication among people. Thus, Miyake condemned the idea of artificial unification of the language, including any proposal for a model language.

In his next essay, "Zokugo o iyashimu na" (Don't Despise Vernacular Language), in 1885–1886 (Meiji 18–19) (455–467),[16] Miyake rejected the traditional authority of *kanbun* and classical language and articulately justified the status of vernacular language. The vernacular language Miyake advocated, however, was not dialects or local slang such as *beranmē* or *danbe.*[17] The model language he postulated was "the language used daily by those of the middle class" (458). His exaltation of the vernacular language was unconventional for that time, but notice here that Miyake targeted the language of the middle class, as if he foresaw the later debate about the formulation of the standard language.

Miyake gradually became insistent on assigning a formal and normative quality to spoken language, as seen in his "Genbun itchi no ron" (Theory of *Genbun itchi*), which he wrote in 1888 (Meiji 21) after his return from study abroad. The only way to pull closer the written and spoken languages, Miyake asserted, was to cultivate the rhetoric of the spoken language. For example, he recommended that public speakers must be skillful in choosing words, distinguished intellectuals should have more opportunities to give public speeches, plays must be observed and critiqued by upper-class audiences, and schoolteachers must be careful of the way they speak while correcting their pupils' speech (Yamamoto M. 1978, 498). Such "reform of the spoken language" was, Miyake envisioned, a step towards the unification of spoken and written languages.

There had been two directions in the *genbun itchi* movement from its beginning, as pointed out by Yamada Bimyō: one by advocates of the vernacular style *(zokubunronsha),* who attempted to draw the written language closer to the spoken, the other by advocates of the standard written style *(futsūbunronsha),* who proposed to reconcile the written and the spoken. Here, "standard style" means the style of the written language that began in Meiji, simplifying the traditional *kanbun* style with colloquial elements. In another article, "Tokuhon kyōju no shui" (The Point of the Teaching of Reading), which he wrote at about the same time as the "Theory of *Genbun itchi,"* Miyake overtly spoke from the *futsūbunron* position: "In order to discuss today's elementary education, I cannot but speak as an advocate for reconciling the written and the spoken languages. . . . In fact, we must not teach texts that are written in colloquial style" (Yamamoto M. 1965, 688).

Miyake's changeover from *zokubunron* to *futsūbunron* paralleled the shift of the *genbun itchi* movement from its original upward protest against *kanbun* and classical language to its downward demand for standardization of the spoken language. The imposition of the standard language through teachers' correction of pupils' dialects—which Miyake encouraged—was now to become the compelling force in the effort to prescribe a spoken language.

2-6. Imperialism and *Genbun Itchi*

The Imperial Board of Education (Teikoku Kyōiku Kai) installed the Genbun Itchi Committee in March 1900 (Meiji 33) as a part of its vigorous activities in language policy planning, as already seen by its Division for National Script Reform (Kokuji Kairyōbu). The year 1900 was significant in that there emerged several private organizations, such as the Genbun Itchi Club (Genbun Itchi Kai), established by Hayashi Mikaomi, and the Genbun Itchi Association (Genbun Itchi Kyōkai), founded by Kiryū Yūyū,[18] which espoused research and promotion of *genbun itchi* (Yamamoto M. 1965, 49, 52). It was the year that *genbun itchi* overtook script reform as the most urgent language issue, and it became included in the scope of the state's language policies.

The Genbun Itchi Committee in the Imperial Board of Education, the most influential among all of the above organizations, held two lecture meetings in

1901 (Meiji 34), inviting eminent scholars and educators. Some of the lectures were published for general readers in the *Yomiuri shinbun,* which had been featuring the *genbun itchi* debate for some time. Some of these articles showed how the sentiment about the language of that time acutely reflected the upsurge of nationalism after the Sino-Japanese War.

The first of such articles was "Genbun itchi ni tsuite" (About *Genbun Itchi*) by Inoue Tetsujirō (see Yoshida and Inokuchi 1964, 317–330). He began by saying that "the spoken and written languages are in the most incompatible state in Japan and China." According to Inoue, written Chinese was so difficult and outdated that it had seriously obstructed the development of Chinese thinking; the lack of conjugations or declensions in the Chinese language hindered precision in expression of ideas; therefore "it is impossible, even for intelligent people, to express in written Chinese Western ideas such as logic, economics, and philosophy." On the other hand, Inoue contended, "the Japanese writing system is far more advanced than that of the Chinese; the innovation of adding *kana* to [*kanji*] words contributed to the development and progress of the Japanese people." And Inoue even exaggerated such linguistic devices as "one of the causes that brought the Japanese victory over the Chinese." In other words, for Inoue the superiority of Japanese to Chinese was the justification for adopting *genbun itchi* to further the Japanese superiority in writing style. Here, an advantage in Inoue's view of *genbun itchi,* in addition to its naturalness and intelligibility, was that it was "to greatly strengthen the independence of the national language." Japan had long been "under the dominance of *kango,* which impeded the development of its own language of the nation. Therefore, *genbun itchi* was essential and a most suitable first step for emancipation from China's control over the written language." Inoue continued to list shortcomings and defects of *kanji* and *kango,* and claimed, "Whether in *rōmaji* or *kana, genbun itchi* could bring us there [to the emancipation] within a short stretch." He closed his article with his anticipation that the Genbun Itchi Committee would play a significant role in script reform also, which was another "huge task for the nation's future."

While Inoue compared Japan and China, Shiratori Kurakichi included Korea in his article "Genbun no itchi o yōsuru rekishiteki gen'in" (The Historical Grounds behind the Need for Unification of the Language). Both the Japanese and Korean languages belong to the Altaic language family and show numerous affinities with and influences from the Chinese language. However, Shiratori contended, "Japan had gradually been liberated itself from the Chinese tradition and valued its own language and writing," which led the people to demand *genbun itchi,* but in Korea the written language was still authentic Chinese while the spoken was their own native language. Shiratori accounted for this as follows: "Every language shares its destiny, its rise and fall, with its nation. . . . Korea was heavily influenced, politically and culturally, by the Chinese race, and therefore was never able to gain its firm independence. . . . The country [Korea] did not have independent spirit and thus its language lost its own vitality and fell to subordination." On the other hand, Japan never lost its *kokutai*, "the sense of being the Japanese nation" and "the patriotic pride of being Japanese," and therefore Japan "has maintained its independent status as a nation and never surrendered to China," and nurtured *kokugo* (the national language) "to emancipate itself from the tenacity of *kanbun*." According to Shiratori, the reason *kanbun* was promoted in the Edo era was "because of the motivation for adopting China's advanced merits, and not out of adoration for Chinese people, nor did it mean our subordination to China. . . . The prevalence of *wakan konkōbun*[19] in Meiji was even the sign of victory of *kokugo* over *kanbun*." Furthermore, argued Shiratori, the Sino-Japanese War confirmed that "China is inferior to our country in every aspect of its power and civilization." Now that "Japan had entered the world powers," he urged in conclusion the need for reform in many areas, including abolition of uneconomical *kanbun*, and "writing with the grammar of actual language today to bring great productivity to academics as well as immense profit to our nation" (Yoshida and Inokuchi 1964, 297–312).

Shiratori's argument has some interesting points from the viewpoint of linguistics, in that he contrasts Chinese, which lacks morphological elements, with Japanese, which does have them, though not extensively. Shiratori and Inoue shared a determination to emancipate Japanese from the hegemony of *kanbun*, which reminds us of Antoine de Rivarol's[20] claim in *Discours sur l'universalite de la langue française* (1784) that French is a superior language to Latin in its rationality and clarity. At the same time, however, just as Rivarol fell into arrogant Franco-centrism, the fervent argument by Shiratori and Inoue revealed their ultranationalistic zeal to demonstrate Japan's superiority. While Rivarol's logical basis was universal human "reason," the single authority these two scholars adhered to was the idea of *kokutai*, which could not be held true in any other place but in Japan.

We have to note here, more than the misunderstanding or distortion of facts, that the overall discourse of *genbun itchi* had completely altered. Previously, the reality of disunity of the Japanese language was contrasted with the unity of Western languages. But now, Japan was contrasted to China and Korea in that throughout its history it had undercurrents of linguistic aspiration towards *genbun itchi*. Even though actual *genbun itchi* was still far from its goal, the sense of its progress derived from Japan's confidence in its membership among the world powers. In this regard, the Genbun Itchi Association led by Hayashi Mikaomi was no different. In the association's manifesto, which he wrote, Hayashi declared that "our nation Japan now stands on competitive ground with other powerful nations abroad," and that without *genbun itchi* and script reform, "it would be absolutely impossible for Japan to compete with them in developing and advancing its civilization" (Nishio and Hisamatsu 1969, 117–118).

Japan had entered the state of imperialism. If we consider the time around 1900 as the turning point from Meiji Japan to imperial Japan, as Marius B. Jansen (1956) speculated, it was also at that time that the national sentiment about language as well as language policies turned towards "the language of the Japanese Empire."

In February 1901, the Genbun Itchi Committee in the Imperial Board of Education presented its "Petition for Actions towards *Genbun Itchi*" (Genbun itchi no jikkō ni tsuite no seigan) to the House of Peers (Kizokuin) and the House of Representatives (Shūgiin), and had it approved. The opening sentence of the petition was "We believe that *the independence, dissemination, and advancement of the nation's language is the first step to solidify the unity of the nation-state,* to help the nation expand its power, and to expedite its advancement towards a flourishing future" (emphasis mine). *Genbun itchi* now was believed to be the key to the future of the nation state, its fate and its power, the linguistic weapon to compete with Western powers. The petition continued: European countries liberated themselves three hundred years ago from the domination of the Latin language, and their exercise of *genbun itchi* since then advanced their "civilization and enlightenment" and enabled them to become "wealthy nations with strong military"; on the contrary, Korea, Nuzhen, Qitai,[21] Manchuria, and Mongolia failed to realize *genbun itchi,* and consequently these nations were doomed to wither; currently in Japan, the difficulty in learning its language, script, and styles was distracting people's tremendous energy from "gaining other necessary and useful knowledge"; this was "an extreme waste for Japan, which now is in a race with the world," and "*genbun itchi* must come first and foremost in educational reform." In conclusion, the petition proposed the prompt establishment of a National Language Investigative Board (Kokugo Chōsakai) as a government agency to "*carry out genbun itchi as the nation's task,*" in accordance with the decision by the National Language Investigative Committee (Kokugo Chōsa Iinkai) (Yoshida and Inokuchi 1964, 288–289; emphasis mine).

Upon approval of this petition, the government instituted in March 1902 (Meiji 35) the National Language Investigative Committee (Kokugo Chōsa Iinkai) chaired by Katō Hiroyuki, president of Tokyo University. It was Katō who sent Ueda Kazutoshi, the focus of part 2 of this book, to Germany to bring home the Western science of language.

CHAPTER 3

The Creation of *Kokugo*

3-1. Conception of *Kokugo*

The debates about *genbun itchi* and national script and the linguistic turbulence in the Meiji era became closely tied to consciousness of the "nation-state" and the "empire," triggered by the Sino-Japanese War. The rallying point of these debates was the ideology of *kokugo,* and the central person who promoted it was Ueda Kazutoshi. Before discussing Ueda's philosophy of language in part 2, we will investigate in this chapter how the concept of *kokugo* had developed before his time.

The word *kokugo* itself existed before Meiji. However, *kokugo* with a modern connotation, used in opposition to *kango* in its modern sense, was a child of modernity born out of the intense determination of Meiji Japan. And the process from its conception to its birth must not be overlooked—though tracing its historical origin is a considerable intellectual challenge today when the word *kokugo* is widely accepted as self-explanatory.

Such an intellectual challenge might start with examination of the violent potential in the ideology of *kokugo,* or it might take the form of an academic critique of the field of *kokugogaku* (the study of *kokugo*) as a truism. In fact, both of these approaches are necessary in order to clarify the origin of the ideology of *kokugo* in history because *kokugo* has been not only the political apparatus that controls the nation-state but also the intellectual apparatus that casts a spell over the spirit of modern Japan.

A pioneering work in tracing the historical background of the concept of *kokugo* is Kamei Takashi's essay "*Kokugo* to wa ikanaru kotoba nari ya" (What Kind of Language Is *Kokugo*?). As an example of early sources for the concept of *kokugo* before Meiji, Kamei quoted Kawamoto Kōmin, a scholar of Western learning with an 1855 book on physics, *Kikai kanran kōgi* (Outlook of Nature), who explained why he avoided *kanbun* in his writing: "If I translated [the foregoing] into *kanbun,* it might be misinterpreted. Therefore, I wrote it in '*kokugo*' so that it will be easily understood" (Kamei 1971, 240; emphasis on *"kokugo"* in original. See also Kyōgoku 1986).

Kamei pointed out that *kokugo* here was used obviously as a contrasting concept with *kanbun* (Chinese-style Japanese), but that it also referred to the parts of sentences that were written in *kana* and *jikun, kanji* words in Japanese pronunciation. Kamei suspected that Kawamoto attempted to choose the character 国 [*koku* or *kuni,* meaning a country] over 和 [*wa,* the traditional word for Japan or Japanese] and to shift the focus from the sentential to the lexical level in explaining Japanese. That is, he took a position in his own writing style by choosing neither *wago* [和語, classical Japanese words] nor *kokubun* [国文, Japanese texts], but *kokugo* [国語, Japanese language].

There was another idea of *kokugo* at that time that was completely different from Kawamoto's. It was the Japanese translation of the Dutch word *tale* ("language" in English), which appeared at the opening of *Waran bunten: Zenpen* (Dutch Grammar Book: Volume 1), first published in Dutch in 1842 and translated several times during the late 1850s. In its Japanese edition *(Waran bunten zenpen yakugosen)* in 1855, the word *tale* was translated as 国語 [with no *kana* transcription] and in the 1856 edition *(Waran bunten dokuhō)* as 国語 with *kana* transcription *kuni kotoba* (Yamamoto M. 1965, 71). It is obvious that 国語 here, either as *kokugo* or *kunikotoba,* did not refer to the Japanese language per se, nor to lexical elements opposed to *kanbun,* but were used as a common noun for a nonparticular "language" as a whole.

The characters 国語, however, were not used as a consistent translation of "language." For example, *Kunten Waran bunten* (Dutch Grammar with Japanese Translation, 1857), another Japanese edition of *Waran bunten: Zenpen,* translated *tale* as 国詞, probably read as *kunikotoba* (71). In *Sōyaku Igirisu bunten* in 1867, the translation of *Igirisu bunten* (English Grammar, 1866, published by Kaiseijo[1]), "language" was written as 国言葉 and 国詞 [both probably read as *kunikotoba*] (83). To further complicate the matter, *kunikotoba* was also used, as mentioned before, as *furigana,* the *kana* transcript, of 国語. In other words, it is possible that the *kanji* 国語 were used merely as the *kanji* transcript, say, as *furi-kanji* [as opposed to *furigana*] for the word *kuni kotoba.*

The intricacy of the concept of 国語 can also be found in English-Japanese dictionaries during early Meiji. For example, *Fuon sōzu ei-wa jii* (English-Japanese Dictionary with Pronunciation and Illustrations), the first full-scale English-Japanese dictionary in Japan, edited by Shibata Shōkichi and Koyasu Takashi in 1873, listed the following *kanji* words with *furigana* for the English word "language": 語 *go,* 言葉 *kotoba,* 話 *hanashi,* 国語 *kokugo,* 話法 *hanashi-kata,* and 民 *tami.* At the same time, "speech" was translated as 説話 *hanashi,* 言語 *gengo,* 国語 *kunikotoba,* 言葉 *kotonoha,* 公言 *kōgen,* 演述 *nobetate,* and

口演 *kōjaku*. Thus, the dictionary seemed to distinguish between "language" and "speech" as *kokugo* and *kunikotoba* respectively, the former meaning language as a total system of grammar and lexicon and the latter indicating actual usage and utterances. What complicates the matter is the fact that the very same *kanji* 国語 were used for both meanings. The revised and supplemented edition of the above dictionary by the same editors in 1882 (Meiji 15) listed *kanji* words 語, 言, 話, 言語, 詞, 談, 国語, 話法, 民 for "language" and 説話, 言語, 国語, 公言, 演述, 口演 for "speech," but it did not provide *furigana* for them, and it is no longer clear whether or not 国語 was pronounced differently to distinguish "language" from "speech." Such a practice of reading the *kanji* word 国語 as either *kokugo* or *kunikotoba* continued for quite a long time. This is an important point, though it may appear trivial, in considering the later formation of the concept of *kokugo*—the fact that the stiff *kanji* word *kokugo* eventually drove away the native *Yamato* word *kunikotoba*.

The aforementioned dictionary by Shibata and Koyasu had a model, *An English and Chinese Dictionary* by William Lobscheid, published by Daily Press in Hong Kong 1866–1869. According to Morioka Kenji, 47.2 percent of the entries in Shibata and Koyasu's dictionary had the same translations as Lobscheid's (1969, 95). However, Lobscheid's translations for "language" were only 話 and 語; his book did not contain 国語. This indicates that the *kanji* word 国語 for "language" was a genuine made-in-Japan *kango*. Nonetheless, the word *kokugo* was not in common use at that time, as seen in the fact that even the observant Hepburn did not include the word *kokugo* in the first (1867) or the second (1872) edition of his *Wa-ei gorin shūsei* (Japanese-English Dictionary). It was not till 1886 (Meiji 19) that the word appeared in the third edition.

From the above findings we can gather that in early Meiji *kokugo* was an extremely stylish word for "language" used by Japanese scholars of English and Western learning. In sum, the *kanji* word 国語 in early Meiji had two completely different meanings: one referring to the indigenous language of Japan at the lexical level, as contrasted to Chinese-originated *kango* (and later to Western words also) and as slightly different from *wago* (Japanese classical words), and the other meaning corresponding to English "language," a common noun meaning linguistic expression as a whole and not a particular language. However, this latter usage of 国語 did not gain stability because of the existence of other expressions such as *kunikotoba*.

3-2. Changes in the Concept of *Kokugo* in Early Meiji

As a pioneer in every aspect of language issues in modern Japan, Maejima Hisoka played an important role in forming the concept of *kokugo*. In the aforementioned "Proposal for the Abolition of Chinese Characters" in 1866 (Nishio and Hisamatsu 1969, 17–20), he used 国語 *(kokugo)*, 本邦語 *(honpōgo)*, and 御国語 (presumably pronounced as *mikuni kotoba*), and their meanings can easily be distinguished from the context: *honpōgo* refers to the Japanese language as a whole as opposed to *shinago* (支那語 language of China), *kokugo* to lexical elements in Japanese as opposed to *kango* (Chinese words). Maejima's usage of *kokugo* as lexical elements in a language was not limited to Japanese, as seen in this passage: "England, for example, has adopted in her *kokugo* Latin words as they were." *Mikuni kotoba* (language of the honorable country) must have been used as a rhetorical expression for *kokugo* in the context of his discussion about patriotism and *Yamato damashii* (the Japanese spirit), but not necessarily referring to classical vocabulary.

What is worth more attention in the above proposal is Maejima's awareness of the nation as 国家 *(kokka,* "the nation-state") and 国民 *(kokumin,* "the nation-people"), as declared in the opening: "The foundation of *kokka* is education of its *kokumin*." The word *kokumin* came into common use only later, through the enlightenment movement led by Fukuzawa Yukichi and also through its frequent use in various decrees issued by the new Meiji government. Maejima, through his knowledge of Western civilization, must have already realized the significance of the nation-people as a modern political concept and advocated early on the importance of common education for strengthening the nation-state.

Maejima's awareness of *kokka* and *kokumin* reached full flower in his "Proposal for Teaching the Japanese Language" (Kokubun kyōiku no gi ni tsuki kengi) in 1869 (Meiji 2) (Yoshida and Inokuchi 1964, 39–43), in which *honpōgo* and *mikuni kotoba* disappeared and instead *kokugo* and *kokubun* were used throughout the text, with significant meaning in each. As mentioned in chapter 1, Maejima recommended, as the first stage of the "Administrative Methods for Teaching Japanese Texts" (appendix to the above proposal), to let scholars of Japanese, Chinese, and Western learning "establish a style of Japanese text" and "select models for Japanese language and text." In other words, he liberated *kokugo* and *kokubun* from the sole possession of *wagaku* (later *kokugaku*, "the study of classical Japanese"), as he declared "the new *kokugo* shall include [foreign] words, whether Chinese or Western." For Maejima, *kokugo* had risen above the competition among Japanese, Chinese and Western vocabularies. The "new *kokugo*" indeed depicted Maejima's conviction that *kokugo* must not be preserved in tradition but must be able to respond to the present demand. And that present demand, of course, came from the *kokka* and *kokumin,* which embodied utilitarianism. Such linguistic consciousness led Maejima to propose in his "Kō kokubun hai kanji no gi" (Proposal for Enforcement of *Kokubun* and the Abolition of Chinese Words) in 1873 (Meiji 6) the establishment of the Kokugo Division as a part of the government agency for making language policies (Yoshida and Inokuchi 1950, 51–61)—as though he had foreseen the establishment of the later Kokugo Chōsa Iinkai (National Language Investigative Committee).

In contrast to Maejima's consistency in his use of the word *kokugo,* Nishi Amane was volatile in his use of the term, as seen in his article "Yōji o motte kokugo o shosuru no ron" (Writing Japanese in the Western Script, 1874) (Nishio and Hisamatsu 1969, 23–28). While he used *kokugo* in the title, he switched it with *wago* in the main text, as in *"yōji o motte wago o shosu,"* together with *kokugo* as in "let children learn first *kokugo* and then *kango."* *Wago* in Nishi's use, however, did not refer to so-called *mikuni kotoba* because he was harshly critical of scholars of classical Japanese *(kokugakusha)* who "use classical grammar for pretentious display." Nishi's romanization theory also reflected his vague awareness of *kokugo,* compared to Maejima's, as it allowed both classical and vernacular pronunciations for one spelling as seen in chapter 1. For both Maejima and Nishi, however, *kokugo* was still considered only at the lexical level and not as the entirety of the language.

Incidentally, in the proposal for enforcement Maejima made an express note that the purpose of studying *kokugo* was to develop practical learning, which had nothing to do with "the argument by the conservatives for justifying the national polity and their mission" (Yoshida and Inokuchi 1950, 59). He might have feared the possibility that the expression *kokugo* could be connected to conservatism.

One of the ideologies that supported Meiji reform was the advocacy of *sonō jōi,* the principle of reverence for the emperor and the elimination of foreigners, which originated from *kokugaku,* the study of ancient Japanese thought and culture. Thus the scholars of *kokugaku (kokugakusha)* became active in various political aspects of the new Meiji government, not only in its policy making on religions, which started from the anti-Buddhist movement[2] *(haibutsu kishaku)* and peaked in 1870 with the Imperial Rescript for the Propagation of the Great Doctrine (Taikyō senpu no mikotonori),[3] but also in making various educational and cultural policies. In 1868, the Institute of Imperial Learning (Kōgakusho) was established in Kyoto together with the Institute of Chinese Studies (Kangakusho). In the next year, the *Daigakkō* (Grand School) was founded in Tokyo, restoring Shōheikō[4] and other former shogunate schools. In the Grand School the study of *kokugaku* predominated over *kangaku* to the extent that the head of the Grand School submitted to the government's Legislative Council a blatantly anti-*kangaku* agenda to ban the enthronement and celebration of Confucius or Buddha, to prohibit the practice of reading Chinese texts, and to replace them with those of *kokugaku* (Meiji Bunka Kenkyūkai 1955, 169–172).

The agenda, "Shōhei gakkō e no tasshi" (Advice to Shōhei School) (1869), which contained the Grand School's regulations, had the following passage: "The essential point of literatures of Shinto *(shinten)* and *that of the nation (kokuten)* is to respect the Imperial ways *(kōdō)* and to ascertain National Polity *(kokutai)*." (emphasis mine). According to Kamei Takashi, the word *kokuten* here refers to indigenous Japanese texts (other than Shinto texts) as opposed to Chinese texts. Kamei points out that the establishment of the word *kokugo* had roots in such usage as the word *koku* in *kokuten* (*Nihongo no rekishi* 1965, 6:209).

Another example can be found in *Goi* (Vocabulary), published by the Ministry of Education in 1871. Its explanatory notes in volume 1 contain the words 皇国語 and 皇国言. Since they are contrasted with Chinese pronunciation, they are both supposed to be read [in a classical Japanese way] as *mikuni kotoba*—an example of excessive use of the character 皇 (emperor), which could have been harshly dismissed by Fukuzawa Yukichi as "an invention of a series of words that never existed before" (Fukuzawa 1980–1981, 2:236).[5]

The Meiji government, however, was gradually turning its aim from "imperial restoration" to "civilization and enlightenment," as indicated by "Gakusei kōfu" (Promulgation of the Educational System), in 1872. This helps to explain the background that triggered Maejima's proposal for enforcement in the following year, when he emphasized that *kokugo* had nothing to do with the *kokutai* advocated by the reactionaries.

In fact, scholars of *kokugaku* were pelted with scathing criticism from all directions. Confucian scholars had long scolded them as "those who are extremely illiterate who bark humbug about national learning *(kokugaku)* and imperial learning *(kōgaku)*" (Meiji Bunka Kenkyūkai 1955, 173). Scholars of Western studies were even harsher, as represented by Katō Hiroyuki's *New Theory of National Polity (Kokutai shin ron)* (1874). He railed at the *kokugaku* scholars as "those who have stupid ideas and unsophisticated opinions, and who should be laughed at," and condemned their emperor worship as "absurd exposure of their obsequious souls." Katō then asserted that "it is on its people that the nation-state rests its attention, and it is for them that the monarch and the government exist," and thus he insisted on building a "just and fair national polity" founded on the idea of the natural rights of man (Matsumoto 1967, 263–264). The fact that he believed that "the emperor belongs to the same humankind as people like us" indicates that the word *kokutai* at that time still had elastic meaning. (However, Katō later disclaimed all of these opinions in fear of elevating the democracy movement, which acclaimed the natural rights of man, and in 1881 he announced discontinuation of the publication of the *New Theory of National Polity*).

The above implies that the word *kokugo*, the word formation being rooted in *kokugaku*, carried a nuance that consorted ill with scholars of Chinese and Western learning (Kamei et al. 1965, 6:209). Probably because of that, the word 邦語 *(hōgo)* with the more commonly used character 邦 for Japan was preferred in general use during the early part of the second decade of Meiji, since it was related to familiar words such as 邦人 *(hōjin,* "Japanese person") and 邦国 *(hōkoku,* "Japanese country"). *Hōgo* had established its consistent usage in, for example, Kanda Takahira's "Hōgo o motte kyōju suru daigakkō o setchi subeki setsu" (Need for Instituting Grand Schools for Teaching in Japanese) in 1879 (Meiji 12) (see Yoshida and Inokuchi 1964, 59–62) and Katō Hiroyuki's "Hakugengaku ni kansuru gian" (Bill of Linguistics) in 1880 (Meiji 13), which urged "the need for improving our *hōgo* and establishing its grammar" (63–64). Those progressive Western scholars were not the only ones who used the word *hōgo*. For instance, Motoda Nagazane, the emperor's tutor, used this word when he drafted "Kyōgaku taishi" (Essential Points for Teaching) in 1879 (Meiji 12) as he criticized the trends in contemporary education, which had been carried "to such an extremity that even though one can use Western words one cannot translate them into *hōgo*" (Matsumoto 1967, 263–264; emphasis mine). The fact that this document was published as the emperor's words should attest to the commonality of the word *hōgo*.

Nonetheless, the word *kokugo* itself survived as a common noun for the word "language," while *hōgo* or *nihongo* was used specifically for the Japanese language. For example, Katō Hiroyuki in the above document used *kokugo* as follows: "through the study of linguistics we become familiar with most of the languages, *kokugo*, of both East and West." Other examples can be seen in Yatabe Ryōkichi's use of the word in his "Rōmaji o motte nihongo o tsuzuru no setsu" (Proposal for Writing the Japanese Language in *Rōmaji*) in 1882 (Meiji 15): "a language, *kokugo*, such as Chinese, where one pronunciation corresponds to one word" or "our language, *waga kokugo*, is significantly different" (Nishio and Hisamatsu 1969, 30–32). Thus we may consider that *kokugo* in these writings was used as a common noun. Though the last example, *waga kokugo*, is slightly ambiguous, Yatabe himself used *kokugo* elsewhere referring to the concept, which applied to languages whether English, French, or Chinese, not limited to Japanese, when he said, for example, "a language, *kokugo*, is not born overnight." Such use of the word *kokugo* did not imply any covert intention.

The common noun *kokugo* was also used as an academic term. For example, Chamberlain, who was invited to the Imperial University as professor of linguistics, used the term as follows in the introduction to *Nihon shō bunten* (Concise Japanese Grammar Dictionary) published by the Ministry of Education in 1887 (Meiji 20): "There are many *kokugo* in this world, such as English, French, German and Chinese, each having its own grammar" (Chamberlain 1887, 1). It is obvious that his use of *kokugo* here corresponds to "language."

There was, however, still another word, *kunikotoba,* competing with the common noun *kokugo.* In his article "Nihongogaku no koto ni tsukite" (Regarding the Study of the Japanese Language) in 1890 (Meiji 23), Katō pointed out that "Japanese *(Nihon kotoba)* does not have an appropriate word that corresponds to the original word *language (rangēji),*"[6] and he used *kunikotoba* as the translation "for the use of the word [*language*] as the whole of the language" (Yoshida and Inokuchi 1964, 84–95). In contrast, he used the word *kokugo* as a concept referring to individual words at the lexical level. It is also noteworthy that Kato used *nihongogaku,* not *kokugogaku,* for "the study of the Japanese language" in the same article.

As seen above, the concept of *kokugo* in early Meiji was far from its maturity. Sekine Masanao's essay "Kokugo no hontai narabini sono kachi" (The True Form of *Kokugo* and Its Value) in 1888 (Meiji 21), an important document to be discussed later for changes in the meaning of *kokugo,* begins as follows: "I know that there is a subject called *kokugo* today in elementary and middle schools. However, what is this *kokugo?* When it comes to its substance, nobody seems to know at all" (Yamamoto M. 1978, 405). In other words, the word *kokugo* was not recognized generally as an established concept. Sekine continues, saying that "*kokugo* seems to be used as a translation of *language (rangueji),*"[7] but if that is indeed the case, he suggests the word *koku-bun* be used to make a distinction from *koku-go* because "*-go* is interpreted as individual words" (405). This is a very important statement testifying that the word *kokugo* was generally used as a translation by scholars of English, and that it was a concept at the lexical level and was considered inadequate to refer to the language as a whole. Thus, even after the first decade of Meiji, the word *kokugo* had two separate layers, one as a translation of the English word "language" and the other as Japanese vocabulary as contrasted with *kango* (Chinese words) and *yōgo* (Western words).

3-3. Ōtsuki Fumihiko and the Development of *Kokugo*

The preceding section showed that *kokugo* in early Meiji was too unstable in its meaning and usage to gain any powerful and symbolic significance, as would be seen at a later time. In other words, the concept of *kokugo* was not an urgent topic in early Meiji. However, we will see the growth of the concept of *kokugo* into, ultimately, its uninhibited true nature. The first good example of this change is seen in the transformation of the meaning of *kokugo* in Ōtsuki Fumihiko's works.

Genkai (Sea of Words), compiled solely by Ōtsuki during 1889–1891 (Meiji 22–24), became a model for various later *kokugo* dictionaries. However, *Genkai* was not titled a "*kokugo* dictionary"; its full title was *Nihon jisho genkai* (*Genkai*: Japanese Dictionary). In its preface, "The Objective of This Edition" (1884 Meiji 17), Ōtsuki defined the dictionary as one "of common Japanese language *(Nihon futūgo)*" (Yoshida and Inokuchi 1972, 288–322). In fact, he never used the word *kokugo* in this preface. Instead, he used *nihongo* (the Japanese language), as he said "a Japanese dictionary should be what explains *nihongo* in *nihongo*" (291). This does not mean that Ōtsuki intentionally refused to use the word *kokugo,* but rather that he did not feel any need to use the word in writing his preface.

Ōtsuki's *Kō Nihon bunten* (Current Japanese Grammar), published only six years after *Genkai,* however, showed significant change. In its "Outline" *kokugo* was defined as an academic term as follows:

> Every country of the world has its own language, each different. <u>Kokugo</u> is a language of a country. Accordingly, the grammar of each language is also different. This book describes the grammar of *Nihon kokugo* (the language of Japan), and thus is titled <u>Nihon bunten</u>. (Yoshida and Inokuchi 1973, 249–250; emphasis in original)

The transformation from *Genkai,* which "explains *nihongo,*" to *Kō Nihon bunten,* which "describes the grammar of *Nihon kokugo,*" represented a promotion of the semantic status of *kokugo.*

There was a reason why the longer term *Nihon kokugo* was used instead of the simple *kokugo* in *Kō nihon bunten.* Here, the *kokugo* by itself was used much as Chamberlain used it in his *Nihon shō bunten.* As Ōtsuki explained in *Kō Nihon bunten bekki* (Notation for Current Japanese Grammar), which was published in the same year (1897), *kokugo* was not used as a synonym of *nihongo,* but as an equivalent for the common English noun "language." In fact, in the introduction to *Notation* the word *kokugo* referred to any individual language according to the context, such as English, French, Russian, Chinese, even the language of Native Americans, who did not have their own *koku* (country). Thus, the word *kokugo* was used as a neutral concept referring indiscriminately to any individual language. Further, the reading of the *kanji* 国語 itself was still not uniform, allowing *kunikotoba* as well as *kokugo* (276).

However, the word *kokugo* was then used in a completely different way in the very same introduction. Ōtsuki assumed that the language *(kokugo)* of England

was invaded by many other languages even in its grammar and that "such a formation of the language *(kokugo)* is a shame for an independent country." As for
Japan, on the contrary, blending during a thousand-some years with Korean,
Chinese, Hindu, and Western languages was limited only to nouns, and never
disturbed "the case and sequence of words" in grammatical organization. This,
Ōtsuki declared, was evidence of the unequivocal superiority of "the language
of Japan *(Nihon kokugo),*" and "this did not change for a thousand-some years
in the past and will not change for thousands of years to come. Neither our
national polity *(kokutai)* nor our language *(kokugo)* has ever been invaded by
others, and both have been kept strong and complete, as if protected by divine
power." And he concluded the Introduction with the following exaltation of the
idea of *kokugo:*

> *Kokugo* of a country is the symbol of the race *(minzoku)* towards the outside, and
> it strengthens the public sense of brethren inside. Therefore, the unification of
> *kokugo* is the foundation for independence and the mark of the independence [of
> the country]. The rise and fall of *kokugo* goes with that of the country; whether
> *kokugo* is pure or impure, correct or incorrect, affects the teaching of morality,
> people's vitality, and the nation's prestige *(kokkō).* Thus, why should we not make
> an effort to expand such a divine power [of *kokugo*]? (274–275)

It is possible to interpret *kokugo* in the above passage as a common noun.
However, once the equation between *kokugo* and *kokutai* was made, the new
concept of *kokugo* inevitably infiltrated the Japanese language, and among
all languages only Japanese was given the highest position, deserving of the
name *kokugo.* Through Ōtsuki's writings, *Genkai, Kō Nihon bunten,* and *Kō
Nihon bunten bekki,* we can see the transformation of *kokugo* from its nonex-
istence and its birth to its huge growth, gaining various symbolic meanings,
epitomizing the general process of birth and growth of *kokugo* in modern
Japan.

The growth of the concept of *kokugo* was not a step-by-step escalation of
gradual refinement of its meaning and usage, but a huge jump. Like the changes
in Ōtsuki's writings between his *Genkai* (1884) and *Kō Nihon bunten* (1897),
something happened to the people's consciousness about language during
the time between these two works. It was a reflection of the consciousness
of "nation-state" in the language and the maximization of the symbolic idea
of *kokugo.* It was during this period that the modern concept of *kokugo* in its
genuine sense, which was to cast a spell on linguistic consciousness throughout
modern Japan, was established.

3-4. Creation of the Ideology of *Kokugo*

Plainly put, the ideology of *kokugo* is a product of the ethos of Japan during the third decade of Meiji, peaking with the Sino-Japanese War (1894–1895; Meiji 27–28). Compared to the second decade of Meiji, which was a time of liberal rights movements and Westernization, we can say that the third decade was a time of unification of the nation-people *(kokumin)* by both government and the public and a time of an upsurge of consciousness of the nation-state *(kokka)*. All the power of every social element then was absorbed into one goal: the search for the ideal nation-people for the modern nation-state.

In 1885 (Meiji 18), the *dajōkan* system, the highest government apparatus in early Meiji, came to an end, and the new cabinet began; Itō Hirobumi, the first prime minister, appointed Mori Arinori as minister of education. Mori stated in the cabinet agenda on his inauguration:

> If we wish to join the world powers with competitive rank and dignity as a nation and to strive for a great and steady achievement for a long future, we cannot but make it most essential to nurture and raise the morale of people. Setting standard goals in education can do this. (Ōkubo 1972, 1:344)

In the following year (1886), Mori promulgated the School Ordinance *(Gak-kōrei)*, an attempt to institute a modern educational system that put elementary and middle schools, teachers' schools, and universities under the nation's control. He called this idea for education "education of *kokutai (kokutai kyōiku shugi)*," though his use of the word *kokutai* did not mean at all a revival of the Tennoism *(kōdōshugi)*[8] at the beginning of Meiji. While *kokutai* in the latter sense was rooted in the nationalistic Mito school of *kokugaku*,[9] which kindled a yearning to return to the ancient imperial regime, Mori's *kokutai* was presented as the fundamental principle of a modern nation and not a call for a restoration of ancient times; according to Mori's words, the "people's spirit to protect . . . the permanence of sovereigns of our country . . . is the indispensable source and the vast treasure-house to support the wealth and strength of a nation." Thus, *kokutai* now became a bona fide political ideology. (The importance of the separation from antiquity in the case of *kokugo* will also be discussed later.)

As for the School Ordinance, among many important changes such as instituting an authorization system for textbooks and introducing military training, we must note the change of the middle-school subject name *wa-kan bun* to *kokugo* and *kanbun*, the installation of a new subject, *kokugo*, in teachers' schools, and later in 1889, the replacement of the department name *wa-bun-*

gaku ka in imperial universities with *koku-bungaku ka*. Such changes of subject names were not of small importance; they had significant implications for a fundamental change in people's linguistic awareness, from 和 *wa* to 国 *koku*.

Such a transition in linguistic awareness was demonstrated in the activities of *kokubun* scholars who joined the Nihon Bunshō Kai (Association for Japanese Texts) and Gengo Torishirabesho (Bureau for Investigation of Language), which were both established in 1888 and shared most of the same scholarly members (see Yamamoto M. 1965, 740–762). Among those scholars, Ochiai Naobumi deserves the first mention for his leadership in the new *kokubun* movement.

Ochiai constantly used the words *koku-bun* (Japanese literature), *koku-go* (Japanese language), *koku-shi* (Japanese poetry), *kok(u)-ka* (Japanese verse), and so forth, along with words such as *koku-tai* (national polity), *koku-i* (national authority), *koku-ryoku* (national power), and so on. More surprising was his switching from *waka* to *kok(u)-ka,* as he considered Ki no Tsurayuki[10] "the restorer of *kokubun* and *kok(u)ku*" (*Ochiai* 1968, 10).

Such persistent use of *koku-* in word formation clearly indicates Ochiai's true intention. It was Ochiai's unique view of history that was behind his use of such words. According to his essays, such as "Nihon bungaku no hitsuyo" (The Importance of Japanese Literature) (1889; Meiji 22) and "Narachō no bungaku" (Nara Court Literature) (1890; Meiji 23), the Nara era (A.D. 710–784) was a time when people strove to preserve the "nation's beauty *(koku bi)*" by "breaking the tradition of imitating" Chinese writing and poetry (7). Ochiai went on to say that Nara was a time when people were full of "loyalty [to the emperor] and love for country," which made Japan "the land where the soul of language *(kotodama)* flourished" (9). This led him to declare that "Japanese literature and Japan's nation have always shared their rise and fall" (9–10). That is, literature and nation were in organic codependence, with the emperor system as their medium. By saying "my joy over the golden age of Nara literature and my sorrow over its decline are not merely for the sake of literature," Ochiai meant to say that his joy and sorrow were for the sake of the nation-state.

Ochiai contended that Confucianism and Buddhism were the cause of the decline of Nara civilization, and he found great similarity between the Nara literature in such a state and the literature of his time in Meiji (10). The Meiji Restoration was supported by *kinnō shisō* (loyalty to the emperor), advocated by *kokugaku* scholars, who accused *kangaku* scholars of being "obsequious worshippers of China who know nothing about the imperial line"; it was this *kinnō shisō* that was "the root of Japanese literature" and "the foundation of the nation's civilization"; nonetheless, today's fad of imitating Western culture weakened "our traditional patriotism," "decreased the nation's power day by day," and "made our people frivolous month by month." Ochiai asserted that this was exactly why "we need Japan's own literature," in order to abandon such a superficial culture and to illuminate Japan's own "unshakable *kokutai*," which should become "the basis of our civilization, the guidance for people towards the true civilization" (3–5).

Though it had been *kokugaku* scholars' favorite trick to denounce China *(kan)* and the West *(yō)* and to stress the uniqueness of Japan *(wa)*, Ochiai was not an absurd reactionary, but a promoter of gradual reform grounded in the classical tradition. His activities as a *waka* poet demonstrated this. The *waka* by the "old school" are "all imitation of poets in the past, and none is interesting or intriguing," said Ochiai. He claimed that one should create *waka* freely without being restricted by ancient rules in form and content and, if necessary, should use *kango* or even motifs from Western literature to express "new ideas" (Ochiai, "Kadan no ichi" [The First Topic about *Waka*], Ochiai 1968, 36–39). His idea of *waka* reform was demonstrated in *Shinsen kashū* (New Collection of Classical Poetry) in 1891 (Meiji 24), which he compiled in a rivalry with *Shintai shi shō* (Collection of New-style Poetry).[11]

The transformation from 和 *wa* to 国 *koku*, like that from *wabun* to *kokubun*, was thus supported by two pillars: the intent to promote gradual reforms while grounded in the tradition and the idea that language and literature were organically connected with the nation-state. Such a transformation was evident in work by Sekine Masanao, who was a colleague of Ochiai in the Association for Japanese Texts and Bureau for Investigation of Language. In concert with the School Ordinance of 1886 (Meiji 19), Sekine compiled *Kintai kokubun kyōkasho* (Modern-style *Kokubun* Textbook) in 1889 (Meiji 22), with the following opening notes:

> *Kokubun* penetrates throughout the people giving them the sense of brethren and thus manifests the nation's uniqueness; it works as an ingredient to strengthen the nation's (*kokumin*'s) unity against other countries, and hence it is vital for *kokka*, the nation-state. (*Nihongo no rekishi* 1965, 6:268)

Sekine thus presented the trinity of "*kokubun-kokumin-kokka*." This idea was also substantiated by his awareness of the present:

> There have been several [text]books for the study of *kokubun*, but most of them were modeled after so-called *gabun* (elegant texts), that is *kobun* (classical texts). Therefore, they might do some good for learning how to imitate old styles, but may be extremely inappropriate to express today's language and information for the purpose of daily use. (269)

That is, Sekine divorced the concept of *kokubun* completely from *gabun* or *kobun*. In one sense, this corresponds to Ōtsuki Fumihiko's synchronic viewpoint in distinguishing *katsugen* (living language) and *shigen* (dead language), or his distinction between the *ga* (elegant) and *zoku* (common, vulgar) language based on function and not on historical eras (Yoshida and Inokuchi 1972, 293).

Sekine expressed this idea in 1888 (Meiji 21) in his essay symbolically titled "The True Form of *Kokugo* and Its Value" (see Yamamoto M. 1978, 405–413). There he warned that the country's language was on the brink of ruin: "the so-called *kokugo* used today," which was dominated by *kanbun* style *(kanbun kundokutai)* or direct translation of Western language, "is in disorder and confusion, and too dismantled to call it the language of our country." At the same time, Sekine criticized "those who happened to be eager about *kokugo*" for merely depending on and yearning for the classical language of the early Heian period and for being "ignorant of the fact that language changes through time." He concluded that this was because these people had completely lost sight of "the true form of *kokugo*":

> It is my humble opinion that the language we actually use today should be the true form of *kokugo*. The most important task in the study of *kokugo* should be to investigate the use and style of the common language of today referring to the grammar that is unique to our country's language, and to correct confusing and intangible language, and to write more simple and concrete language according to the regular rules. (405–406)

That is, Sekine discovered the "true form of *kokugo*" in the synchronic mode of the language, and defined *kokugogaku* as the study of this "true form." *Kokugogaku,* then, was not only the study of the use and style of the language but also was responsible for "correcting the language." *Kokugo* defined this way was a brilliantly practical concept.

Sekine further dismissed two common beliefs: that the classical language was elegant *(ga)* and the contemporary language was vulgar *(zoku)* and that *kango (jion no go)* was not our language. As for the first belief, Sekine said that classical words were not necessarily all elegant and that the distinction between *ga* and *zoku* also existed in contemporary language. While this view was similar to Ōtsuki's, seen in *Genkai,* there was a fine difference between Sekine and Ōtsuki: Ōtsuki pointed out that the contrast between elegant and vulgar did not correspond to the contrast between classical and contemporary, and he insisted on an equality between classical and contemporary languages. On the other hand, Sekine explained that the contrast between elegant and vulgar also existed in contemporary language and proposed "to guide today's common language towards refinement (*gasei* = elegant and correct) and to correct its vulgarity *(rizoku)*." That is, Sekine transferred the *ga-zoku* distinction from a diachronic level to a synchronic level, but he did not touch on the criteria for such a distinction. Against the second common belief, that *kango* was not Japanese, Sekine maintained that those numerous *kango* that had become part of the *kokugo* vocabulary through hundreds of years of tradition did not need to be eliminated from Japanese. Such a view led him to say that some technical terms, "whether English, German, or French, may be used when necessary in their original form [in *kokugo* texts]" (406–407).

Through the above argument, Sekine attempted to show that the "true form of *kokugo*" as the "commonly used language of today" was not an exact copy of current spoken or written language disregarding the tradition and that the linguistic norm must be based on the inherited tradition of the Japanese language. Since he considered the current Japanese language to be in disorder and confusion, "the true form of *kokugo*" had to be a reflection of critical ideas. Therefore, it became the task for *kokugogaku* to exercise this critical nature inherent in the idea of *kokugo*. Such a practical nature for *kokugogaku* was revealed in Sekine's definition of "the essential goal of this study [of *kokugo*]" to "improve the usage and style of the common language of today and regulate the refined and correct Japanese text *(kokubun)*" (409–410). This implies that the real goal of *kokugogaku* was to establish the linguistic norm, and objective research was merely a means to achieve this goal.

There was more to the task of *kokugogaku*. Sekine continued: "The major goal of *kokugogaku* is to strengthen the foundation of *kokugo* in order to proudly present the rules of Japanese language to other countries and their people, and to have them recognize the independence of our nation demonstrated in the pure and unique form of language" (410). Thus the establishment of the norm of *kokugo* now became inseparable from the existence of the nation-state.

To summarize, the consciousness of *kokugo* germinated when the nature of the language surfaced through the clatter of *kanbun* and *wabun* or *kobun* with their cumbersome traditions. To form clearer identity for the language, however, the awareness of *kokka* (the nation-state) had to be used as the agency. Thus, *kokugo* was not something latent in the Japanese language but was a value-loaded object created by the desire for a linguistic norm appropriate for a modern nation.

Nevertheless, the works by Ochiai and Sekine did not go beyond a reasonable compromise with the tradition, and they did not reach the perfection of the ideology of *kokugo*. Indeed, the textbooks they compiled were not very different from traditional textbooks written in *wabun*: Ochiai's *Chūtō kyōiku kokubun kihan* (Standard Japanese Literature for Middle School) in 1892 (Meiji 25) sought the standard in the language of the Kamakura era, and Sekine's *Kintai kokubun kyōkasho* (Modern-style *Kokubun* Textbook) in 1888 (Meiji 21) was mostly a collection of writings from the Edo period.

This is because both were *kokubungaku* scholars associated with the Association for Japanese Texts and the Bureau for Investigation of Language, which aimed at the creation of a new *wabun*-style written language that allowed an appropriate mixture of *kango* in *wabun* texts, as opposed to the traditional norm of *kanbun*-style Japanese. Therefore, their practice rejected the core idea of *genbun itchi,* that is, mapping of the written onto the spoken language. In other words, they put *kokugo* [language] secondary to *kokubun* [text]. Even Sekine, who went so far as to assert the "true form of *kokugo*" as "the language commonly used today," found the goal of *kokugogaku* to "regulate the refined and correct *kokubun*" and was not able to recognize a clear distinction between *kokugo* and *kokubun.* The hurdle was not overcome until Ueda Kazutoshi came onto the scene.

PART II

Ueda Kazutoshi and
His Ideas about Language

CHAPTER 4

The Early Period of Ueda Kazutoshi

4-1. From *Kokubun* to *Kokugo*

Ueda Kazutoshi (1867–1937), though a graduate of the Department of Classical Japanese Literature *(wabun-ka)* at Tokyo Imperial University, began his career with a harsh attack on *wagakusha* (scholars of the Japanese classics). In his 1890 (Meiji 23) essay "Ōbeijin no Nihon gengogaku ni taisuru jiseki no ichi ni" (Examples of Westerners' Views about Japanese Linguistics in the Past), which he wrote based on a lecture that he gave right before his departure for Germany at the age of twenty-four, Ueda recognized that more and more people had come to understand recently that *kokugo* and *kokubun* were "vital for maintaining the nation's independence." Pointing to the two schools in the field of Japanese language, *kogakuha* (school of the classic approach) and *kagakuha* (school of the scientific approach), he explained the former as the school of "*kokugaku* scholars of our country since ancient times, who are the people who have studied, or rather, who are trying to study, the language of this country under various strange labels such as *wagaku* (Japanese studies), *kōgaku* (imperial studies), *kotengaku* (classics studies), *kōtengaku* (studies of classics of the imperial nation), and so forth" (*Ochiai* 1968, 184). Such sarcasm clearly showed Ueda's discontent with the tradition of *kokugaku*. In contrast, he justified *kagakuha* as "the latest school in our country" that "promotes approaches with scientific theories" and advocates the research and education of the Japanese language based on the "most current academic theories" of linguistics and education. However, Ueda bemoaned, this new wave of scientific linguists "had not yet drawn enough public attention to gain authority in the academic field" (185).

Indeed, the department of *hakugengaku*[1] was implemented only in 1886 (Meiji 19), shortly after the establishment of [Tokyo] Imperial University.[2] However, since the name *hakugengaku* was unfamiliar to the academics of the time, Ueda explained that it was a translation of English "philology" or German

Sprachwissenschaft and stated its goals as follows: "to widely collect languages of different countries, compare them, classify them, and examine the causal relations among them, and finally to investigate the origin of languages, the types of languages, the stages and rules of development of languages, and so forth" (185). Ueda was intent on overthrowing the authority of old schools using the power of scientific linguistic theories, and on establishing the genuine field of "Japanese linguistics."

The old schools had inherited the tradition of Keichū-Mabuchi-Norinaga[3] and had always been heavily shielded by the *kokugaku* establishment. On the other hand, Ueda's scientific school was built on Western scholars' research on the Japanese language. Ueda introduced excellent works by Western scholars, from *Nihongo jisho* (Japanese Dictionary) and *Nihon bunten* (Japanese Grammar) by missionary Joao Rodriguez to works by Philipp Franz von Siebolt and Johann Joseph Hoffmann. In particular, Ueda praised Hoffmann as "the father of Western scholars of the Japanese language." In closing the article, Ueda reminded readers "that Dr. Aston is the successor of Dr. Hoffmann, and our Dr. Basil Hall Chamberlain is the successor of Dr. Aston" (188).[4] Chamberlain was a professor of linguistics at the Imperial University, and Ueda was so devoted to him that he called him "*my* Dr. Chamberlain" with respect and affection. Ueda must have been confident in considering himself Chamberlain's successor at the frontier of scientific schools and as their representative to introduce and transport the Western science of language into Japan.

Ueda's view is also spelled out in two essays he wrote in 1889 (Meiji 22): "Nihon gengo kenkyūhō" (Methodology for Japanese Linguistics) and "Gengo jō no henka o ronjite kokugo kyōju no koto ni oyobu" (Discussion of Linguistic Changes and the Teaching of *Kokugo*). In the first essay, Ueda stated his concerns that while "a language is most crucial for the history and education of the country. . . . it is lamentable that those who had been concerned with the language in Japan have had only narrow views and inadequate methods" (181). That is, he wanted to emphasize that Japanese scholarship had never treated language as "language as it is." Ueda presented "the most scientific definition of language" as "the whole of what is uttered by a person and heard by another person and what is used as a code by people in society in order to communicate their ideas." That is, he understood language as first and foremost speech sound. Therefore, "a written script is not language but is like a photograph of a person" (181). The language of the present day was the result of the accumulated history of the language, and it was far more profitable to study this current language and trace back the ancient language than merely to "examine the photographs," which seemed to be the only thing that Japanese scholars had been doing. *Hakugengaku* (linguistics) is the study of language as it is, Ueda repeated, and to investigate a country's language we must depend not on photographs, but on linguistics (182).

Ueda's metaphor of the written language as like a photograph of a person reminds us of Ferdinand de Saussure's claim in his *Course in General Linguistics* that the tendency to seek the essence of language in the written text is the same as the belief that "more can be learned about someone by looking at his photograph than by viewing him directly," a perennial delusion (Saussure 1966, 24). Such a metaphor had already been commonly used among Neogrammarians such as Hermann Osthoff and Karl Brugmann in their attack on traditional philology; they charged that traditionalists had only studied language "on paper" and not the living, spoken language. Ueda must have learned about this central issue of nineteenth-century linguistics through Chamberlain, and his belief in the scientific approach through speech sound was to be confirmed through his direct contact with the theories of the Neogrammarians.

Ueda's view that "language can be explained only by scientific linguistics and not by traditional *kokugaku*" is indeed a Japanese version of the view held by nineteenth-century comparative linguists who were critical of classical philology: Linguistics as a science had to be liberated from the prejudice toward classical philology that stemmed from Greek and Roman literary traditions. The real language is spoken, not written, and is sound, not script; linguistic change is governed by rational rules, not by human intentions. Such a discovery by comparative linguists ran directly counter to the humanistic view of language of that time. Traditional philologists scorned the new comparative linguistics as a study of "primitive" languages with no literary traditions. The new linguists, represented most vocally by the Neogrammarians, defended themselves in their search for scientific rules. We must remember that this conflict between linguistics and philology is at the heart of the history of modern linguistics (see Tanaka 1993; see also Newmeyer 1986).

The other article by Ueda, "Discussion of Linguistic Changes and the Teaching of *Kokugo*," showed him as a practitioner rather than a theorist. He began the essay again with criticism of Japan's conservative studies of the language:

> There are very few people in Japan who know what language is, or the characteristics and history of our language, *kokugo*. Therefore, very few people can teach our language in a systematic way. In other words, our reality is that we neglect to explain what our language is and therefore we are not ready to ask the question of how to teach it. (*Ochiai* 1968, 170)

For Ueda, theory and practice had to go together; the true form of *kokugo* can be made clear only when the "language as it is" is explained. In this sense, Ueda shared the concern of Sekine, who lamented that "the true form of *kokugo*" had been lost. However, while Sekine blamed the *kanbun*-style text and the newly spreading literal translation style, Ueda criticized the lack of linguistic research based on scientific theories. Ueda's importation of the Western science of language was motivated not solely by academic reasons but by his belief in the urgent need for scientific theories to identify the reality of *kokugo* and to establish a methodology of teaching it.

In his articulate treatise Ueda made a direct reference to Whitney[5] and explained (from the same point of view as that held by today's field of general linguistics) that language consists of speech sound with meanings, that language is a code used for communication in a society that shares it, that language is an "unconscious product of the whole society" created by "the society's tacit consent" and is therefore inseparable from the society, and that language reflects the history of the social ethos. Ueda's systematic argument in explaining his views about language was thus founded on his broad knowledge of Western linguistics. In other words, his discourse was completely alien to Japanese academic traditions. In fact, Ueda paid no attention in this essay to *kokugaku* scholars; instead, he explained Japanese phonology and semantics all in terms of Western concepts and terminology.

It is interesting that Ueda made a reference to Whitney: he might have learned from Chamberlain that Whitney, in his *Language and Language Study* (1867) and *The Life and Growth of Language* (1875), was the first to criticize the Neogrammarians' physiological and psychological view of language, emphasizing instead that language is, more than anything else, a social institution. It is known today that Whitney's framework of general linguistics reflecting his ideas about language and society provided a great incentive to Saussure, who was seeking to break the deadlock of the comparative linguistics of the nineteenth century (Silverstein 1971). Whitney's work might also have influenced Ueda's tendency to look at language as a social institution. Further, Hoshina Kōichi, Ueda's student, had made his academic debut with *Gengo hattatsuron* (The Growth of Language, 1899), his abridged translation of Whitney's *The Life and Growth of Language*.

I emphasize that Ueda's importation of Western linguistics was not motivated solely by academic reasons. Ueda believed that only the scientific principles of linguistics would make it possible "to give the right direction to *kokugo*, to develop it by enhancing its merit and abolishing its defects, by eliminating inefficiency and pursuing efficiency; hence to create the orderly *kokugo* of our Great Empire of Japan" (*Ochiai* 1968, 179). He contended that the creation of such *kokugo* was out of the hands of *wagaku* scholars who clung to the conventions of *kokugaku*: "How could this be done by today's *wagaku* scholars? They have no idea about what to do since they are not even aware of the distinction between language and literature" (179).

"Distinction between language and literature"—this was what Ueda most wanted to assert. He used the same rhetoric as the comparative linguists in the West who challenged the authority of classical philology in the nineteenth century. Nonetheless, Ueda sensed some radical ideology in modern linguistics—not just a new methodology for language analysis—which would shake the very definition of language. For Ueda, such linguistic ideology was not merely a Western novelty to worship but a matter of deep conviction. His early writings, hardly discussed before, confirm my assumption that such linguistic ideology was the root of his later works.

Ueda was keenly aware of "the present" and sought the authenticity of *kokugo* not in the written texts of the past but in the language spoken currently. This awareness was also directed to *kokubun* (literature), as seen in the peculiar textbook *Kokubungaku* (The Study of Japanese Literature), which Ueda published in 1890 (Meiji 23), right before his departure for Europe. In the introduction to this textbook Ueda wrote that "*kokubungaku* should become a subject in schools, along with *kokugo*, and should be given equal if not greater status with *kanbun* (Chinese literature)" (107). But this does not mean that he ceased his harsh attack on *wagaku* scholars: "I could not easily compromise with today's *wagaku* scholars, and I wish to propose and introduce to education what they have ignored and disregarded" (107). Thus he declared that his textbook drew a clear line of demarcation from traditional textbooks.

The content of the textbook and the method of compilation were indeed unique. He began the first volume (though this was the only volume that was published) with literature of the late Edo to Meiji periods, with the intention of surveying backwards from modern to ancient literature. That is, he completely reversed the normal chronology of literary history. For Ueda, history had to be interpreted synchronically rather than chronologically. He exercised in this textbook his perspective on history, looking back at the past from the "present facts," a method that was indeed a part of the Neogrammarians' theories but was not familiar to scholars in Japan, who focused on the past and saw history as originating from it.

Furthermore, his selection of literature in the textbook was unconventional: he included late Edo literature such as Shikitei Sanba's *kokkei-bon* (comic books), *kyōka* (comic poems), and writings by Yoshida Shōin and Watanabe Kazan,[6] which had seldom appeared in other textbooks. Even more unusual, Ueda included at the beginning the Imperial Oath (*Gokajō no seimon*) and Imperial Rescript for Soldiers (*Gunjin chokuyu*)[7] because he believed that they were "as crucial in literature as they were to the establishment of the Meiji government" (108). (If he had known of the Imperial Rescript on Education [*Kyōiku chokugo*] before its issuance in October of the same year, he certainly would have included it also.) Considering that even Sekine's aforementioned *Kokubun kyōkasho* was limited to essays by Edo literati, we can easily imagine how revolutionary Ueda's textbook was.

In his later essay in 1902 (Meiji 35), "Kokumin kyōiku to kokugo kyōiku" (Education of the People and Teaching *Kokugo*), Ueda argued that, "even when a teacher teaches Heian court literature or Kamakura literature, it is for the development of contemporary literature" (158), and he clearly maintained the "present-ness" *(genzaisei)* carried over from his textbook *Kokubungaku*. His horizon was drawn in the spiritual space between the achievement of the Meiji Restoration and the establishment of the Meiji government. The fact that he considered the Imperial Oath or Imperial Rescript for Soldiers "most important in Japanese literature" demonstrates that his awareness of "the present" was aligned with the Meiji nation-state. His awareness of "the present" gave a shape to the concept of "language as it is," and it was justified by the concept of the "Meiji nation-state"—this is where Ueda's glory and tragedy began.

Ueda matured too young, in a sense: he had already formed his academic foundation under Chamberlain and was only twenty-four years old when he left for Europe in 1890 (Meiji 23) to learn and transplant the scientific study of language. He then brought home the realization of Japan's uniqueness and the determination to establish the field of *kokugogaku,* upon which the ideas about language that he had planted earlier started to flower.[8] Before we discuss Ueda's later work, we shall trace what he saw in Europe.

4-2. The Neogrammarians and the All-German Language Society

It is not unusual for intellectuals, including Ueda and Hoshina, that their experience overseas determined their future direction. What did his three and a half years in Europe mean to Ueda, who later charged head-on towards *kokugo* reform? Some might explain, as Ōno Susumu did, that Ueda was appalled to find Western civilization far more advanced than Japan, felt a compelling need to catch up, and thus was driven to the idea of *kokugo* and script reform (Ōno 1989, 24–25). Though such explanations might have some truth, Ueda's motivation for the reform was not a simple reverence for Western civilization but was founded on his keen observation and understanding of the reality of languages and the state of the field of linguistics in Europe. We will see in the following what was happening in the Germany that he visited.

4-2-1. The Neogrammarians' Revolution from Above

Leaving Japan in September 1890 (Meiji 23), Ueda first studied at Berlin University, where there was a group of distinguished linguists such as Hermann H. Steinthal [1823–1899], Georg von de Gabelentz [1840–1893], and Johannes Schmidt [1843–1901].[9] In 1892, Ueda moved to Leipzig University, which gave the most crucial thrust to the development of his linguistic ideas. Leipzig University at that time was the frontier in the field of linguistics, with major members of the group of scholars called the Neogrammarians (*Junggramma-tiker*), such as August Leskien [1840–1916], Karl Brugmann [1849–1919], and Eduard Sievers [1850–1932]. They were the young linguists who rejected the former comparative methodology and were intent on introducing new scientific principles. Among these scholars, Brugmann and Hermann Osthoff [1847–1909] were the best known as the coauthors of an article on morphology in 1878,[10] which could be seen as the manifesto of the Neogrammarians. The essay argued that all phonetic changes occurred systematically according to "rules without exceptions." Any irregularities were explained by the psychological factor of "analogy." The thesis "no exception in phonetic rules" became the signature that identified the position of the Neogrammarians and triggered flaming debates.[11]

The name of the group, the Neogrammarians (*Junggrammatiker*), came from the fact that its members were a new generation (*Jung*). Brugmann and Osthoff were only in their early thirties when they published the above article. When Ueda arrived at Leipzig, Brugmann was forty-four and Sievers forty-three, in their prime and about twenty years older than Steinthal's contemporaries, ten years older than Gabelentz's. It was no coincidence that Saussure also studied at Berlin and Leipzig universities. He was at Leipzig for two years from the autumn of 1876 and again for half a year from the autumn of 1879. It was a time when the Neogrammarians were on the cutting edge, with youthful passion to refute the older generation's theories. Their eagerness was so intense that sometimes they became competitive among themselves, as seen in an argument between Brugmann and Saussure over the precedence of their work. Ueda arrived in Germany about ten years after this time; by then those former young scholars were already full professors and were the central force in new research at the forefront of linguistics. The encounter with the Neogrammarians not only taught Ueda linguistic methodology founded on strict positivism but also had a profound influence on his view of language itself, as indicated in his later lectures at Tokyo University in 1896 and 1897.[12]

According to Ueda, the field of linguistics was founded by Franz Bopp [1791–1862] and Friedrich Schlegel [1772–1829], though he placed Bopp before

Schlegel: "While scholars like Schlegel discuss language mixed with *literature* and *history*, Bopp explains language *itself* in a *dry but clear* way" (Ueda 1975, 29). That is, Ueda considered Schlegel to be still confined in a humanistic viewpoint and unclear about the distinction between language and literature; in contrast, Bopp directly investigated language as it is, thereby establishing the field of linguistics founded on scientific principles. As for August Schleicher, who was conventionally considered the successor of Bopp in reconstructing proto Indo-European language, Ueda dismissed him and said that "Schleicher's school was already old-fashioned and so was his student Max Müller [1823–1900]." What Ueda considered the most progressive school was the Neogrammarians: "The newest school is represented by Brugmann, Paul, and Osthoff. Some characterize them as *Neo-grammatiker* (young grammarians)... This new school takes a *scientifical* approach based on *phonetics* and *principles of analogy*, and is very progressive as opposed to the classical and conservative old schools" (32).[13]

Ueda believed that it was the Neogrammarians who made linguistics an autonomous field of science in the true sense. Indeed, before the Neogrammarians "there had been only a few genuine linguists and they were mostly from other disciplines." For example, Humboldt and Gabelentz came from law, Grimm[14] from philology, Bopp from Asian studies, and Müller from anthropology. As for Japan, Ueda found *wagaku,* the study of Japanese classics, in a very similar situation, and must have thought that scientific linguistics could supersede it, just as the Neogrammarians had swept away other old schools.

In Ueda's view, the Neogrammarians brought a revolution to the field of linguistics: they attacked old schools, determined to completely change the methodology of Indo-European comparative linguistics. However, from today's standpoint, the Neogrammarians too are simply an extension of the earlier comparative linguistics. In the accepted history of linguistics, the Neogrammarians are commonly discussed within the scope of comparative linguistics in the nineteenth century, and it is Saussure who is considered to have overturned the paradigm of linguistics. Moreover, the Neogrammarians' novelty has been refuted by, among others, Konrad Koerner, who noted that while they advocated the glamorous claim that there was no exception to phonetic rules, their theory, methodology, and research were not too different from their predecessors' (Koerner 1989, 79–100).

Regarding these contradictory views about the Neogrammarians, science historian Olga Amsterdamska (1987)[15] offered an explanation: the revolutionary meaning of the Neogrammarians could be found not in the type of recognition they received in the field, but in their social and institutional impact. From the first appearance of comparative linguistics in the early nineteenth century, linguistics had had a continuous battle with philology, especially the classical philology of Greek and Latin. On the other hand, the linguists sought the framework of Indo-European languages in the grammatical structure of Sanskrit, an Eastern language, and not in Greek or Latin, and they placed as much importance on the research of "primitive" languages with no literary tradition as on research about classical languages. This was enough to go against the grain of the classical philologists, who believed in the humanistic tradition.

The Neogrammarians' call for scientific positivism in linguistics represented their commitment to free linguistics from the dominance of classical philology. Furthermore, they claimed that linguistics would present methodologies that were necessary for all philological studies; that is, they attempted to place linguistics in a higher position than philology.

As a strategy to achieve these goals, Brugmann and his colleagues created a school, the first in the linguistics field, organizing linguists who had tended to be lone wolves before then. "School" here is a concept in social science that refers to a professional group of scholars who are able to evaluate research and contributions in their academic fields. These groups gradually secured their positions in the university system.

After the 1870s, when the Neogrammarians became the mainstream of linguistics, there was a dramatic increase in the publication of academic journals of linguistics, and new faculty positions in studies of nonclassical languages were created in universities.[16] It was the Neogrammarians who initiated this trend and reveled in it. In this sense, Amsterdamska says, the Neogrammarians' "revolution" was a typical "revolution from above" (137–143).

As the Neogrammarians made advances, studies of nonclassical languages gained equal recognition with studies of classical languages. In particular, Germanic philology became indispensable to university courses, and in the 1870s some universities even implemented both classical and modern Germanic philology classes. Needless to say, the national educational politics of Prussia was deeply involved behind the scenes.[17]

Ueda had witnessed this emergent linguistics establishing footholds in one university after another. On his return to Japan, it was one of Ueda's important plans to form his own school. He implemented a Kokugo Research Office at Tokyo Imperial University in 1897 (Meiji 30) and became its director the following year. At the same time, he founded the Gengo Gakkai (Linguistics Association) in 1898 (Meiji 31) with rising scholars, and started the publication of *Gengogaku zasshi* (Linguistics Journal) the next year. This energetic work of Ueda was also "a revolution from above," inspired by the Neogrammarians.

4-2-2. The All-German Language Association and
Its Language-Purification Movement

The contest between classical philology and modern linguistics was not an issue only in academia. Under Prussia's unification of the German nation, whether to teach classical languages (Greek and Latin) or the modern German language became a critical question towards the formation of national identity.

In the first half of the nineteenth century, classicism and humanism were the educational ideal in Germany. Acquisition of Greek and Latin languages and knowledge of their literature were deemed the foundation of holistic education and the first step towards a sublime spirit. Such an ideal was exemplified in Berlin University, founded by Wilhelm von Humboldt in 1801. The university made its philosophy department its core program, not ethics or law as was conventional. The philosophy program integrated mathematics and natural science, and its goal was to cultivate humanity based on universal reason. Classical philology was given the highest attention in that curriculum: developed since the late eighteenth century through rigorous analyses of Greek classics and the Bible, which had been objects of worship and religious belief, classical philology was now gaining its autonomy as an academic field of science. Nonetheless, it continued to maintain Humboldt's humanistic ideals of "building humanity through study of classical philology" (Sasaki 1985, 2:328). Thus, classical philology at that time was considered the ideal academic discipline, for it could cultivate both specific scientism and universal humanism.

Berlin University's humanistic ideals quickly spread to other campuses: in the mid-nineteenth century, people in elite classes such as government officials and politicians, military officers, lawyers, medical doctors, and high-school teachers, as well as philosophers, mathematicians, and even the revolutionary economist Karl Marx had received educations that made them able to "translate Greek poetry, compose prose in Latin, and recite phrases from Euclid's original writings at the age of eighteen" (2:328).

This humanistic education in universities directly influenced the *Gymnasium,* the secondary-school system in Prussia instituted in 1812 according to the provisions for the qualification examination to enter universities. Since the primary objective of the *Gymnasium* was to train students in general subjects before sending them to specialized departments in universities, its curriculum was directly tied to the educational ideals of universities. There was a clear distinction between the *Gymnasium* and secondary schools that did not qualify students for university entrance. The secondary educational system went through several revisions during the nineteenth century, but this distinction persisted tenaciously: the *Gymnasium* with classical-language education for the exclusive privilege to enter universities, and other secondary schools for practical skills.[18]

As Prussia achieved unification of Germany, however, such overemphasis on classical languages in education became a target of criticism and heated debate. One of the issues was whether the *Gymnasium*'s exclusive qualification for universities should be given to other secondary schools. This involved a crucial question about the linguistic identity of the people: were classical languages or the German language required for a creditable citizen of the German nation?

In December 1890,[19] Emperor Wilhelm II opened a school conference on secondary-school education with harsh criticism of the *Gymnasium* for its lack of a nationalistic foundation, and he decreed that "German was to form the basis of the Gymnasium, whose role was to educate nationally-minded Germans, and not young Greeks or Romans" (Townson 1992, 97).[20] His speech was quoted later in Ueda's writings with great empathy.

The debate resulted in Wilhelm II's issuing of an ordinance in 1900 to make the high schools' practical education equal to that of the *Gymnasium*. Furthermore, the instruction hours for the German language in secondary education dramatically increased in inverse proportion to the reduction of class hours for classical languages. Such promotion of the German language was not merely for teaching practical knowledge or the bases for modern science; it was motivated by the belief that "German-ness" or the German race's spirit inhabited the language. In other words, education of the German language was deemed essential to the education of people of the German nation.

As Grimm indicated, the unification of Germany could not depend on politics, economy, or religion, but on making the German language the symbol of national unity. Germany could exist only as a *Sprachnation* (linguistic nation). Therefore, the issues in its educational system as discussed above must be seen in the wider perspective of the ideological history of the formation of national identity. Education in and about the German language was the best way to make German people realize that they were one nation-people. The goal of such education was to Germanize the German people with the German language. As the nineteenth century moved towards its end, however, leaders began to feel insecure about the question of whether or not the German language itself was genuinely German. Wasn't it continuously invaded by foreign words and loanwords? If nothing was done to prevent this, the German spirit itself could fall apart. Thus, in addition to "Germanization" *by* the German language, Germanization *(Eindeutschung* or *Verdeutschung) of* the German language itself became an urgent issue.

An example of the movements towards this goal was the translation of foreign terms in the postal service promoted by Heinrich von Stephan in the Imperial Post Ministry: Stephan translated 760 postal terms of foreign origin into

German. Such efforts towards Germanization were seen in other areas of the society, and a number of "Germanization dictionaries" were published to that end, such as Hermann Dunger's *Wörterbuch von Verdeutschungen entbehrlicher* (Germanization Dictionary for Unnecessary Loanwords; *Fremdwörter* 1882), Daniel Sanders' *Verdeutschungswörterbuch* (Germanization Dictionary; 1884), and Otto Sarrazin's *Verdeutschungswörterbuch* (1886). These efforts eventually resulted in one organization Allgemeine Deutsche Sprachverein (All-German Language Association) led by Hermann Riegel (Kirkness 1975, 369ff.; Townson 1992, 98ff.).[21]

In 1883 Riegel, who was then the curator of the Braunschweig Museum, published an essay, "Ein Hauptstück von unserer Muttersprache" (A Major Part of Our Mother Tongue), in which he expressed his indignation at the flood of foreign words into German and insisted on the government's intervention by establishment of a language academy in order to eliminate such non-German elements from the language. This essay received an enthusiastic public response, which encouraged him to initiate a linguistic-purification movement and to propose in August 1885 the formation of the Allgemeine Deutsche Sprach-verein, with practical and educational objectives, organized centrally with as many branch offices as possible in German-speaking communities.

The first to echo Riegel was Dunger, professor of *Germanistik* at Dresden University. His opening of the first branch in Dresden on September 10, 1885, marked the official start of the Allgemeine Deutsche Sprachverein. In Novem-ber 1886, the first board meeting was held in Berlin, and Riegel was appointed president. And at its first general meeting in Dresden in November 1887, Riegel announced the following objectives of the association:

1. To promote the purification of the German language from unnecessary foreign elements
2. To strive to restore and protect the unique nature and genuine spirit of the German language
3. Thus to strengthen and spread national identity among people in the German nation (quoted in Kirkness 1975, 372)

The association rapidly branched off not only inside Germany but also in German-language communities abroad, as well as among German immigrants in other countries including the United States. The membership, which already counted five hundred from ninety-one branches before the first general meet-ing, increased to over eleven thousand by 1891 and enlarged to forty-five thou-sand right before World War I. The association firmly urged the movement forward, exposing foreign words in every area of people's lives and replacing them with German, not only in the publishing business but also in politics, economy, law, religion, science, the military, transportation, communication, sports, art, and so forth. The major agents of this movement were the *Verdeutschungsbücher* (Germanization dictionaries), which compiled over ten volumes beginning in 1889, and the association's monthly journal. The journal, the title of which was changed to *Muttersprache* (Mother Tongue) in 1925, continues to this day.

The language-purification movement might be defined as the movement to replace foreign elements in a language with elements indigenous to the language. However, the nature of the movement swung between the two poles of the promotion of smooth public communication and antiforeign ultranationalism. Riegel's whole purpose was to eliminate foreign words that had German equivalents, and he had cautioned against extreme fastidiousness and bigoted ultranationalism. However, the movement gradually assumed the nature of a witch hunt of foreign languages.

Behind the explosive success of the Allgemeine Deutsche Sprachverein was the spreading patriotic nationalism through the public after the Prussian-German victory over France and the achievement of the unification of Germany. Thus, it was symbolic that the association's first target of elimination was the loanwords from French, the language that had been considered superior to German for many centuries. The movement implied aspiration for the linguistic as well as the political independence of the German language. At the same time, however, it was the beginning of a dangerous ideology of equating language and nation, as indicated in the association's slogan: "Remember that you are German when you speak German." As seen later, the association's constitution was all too ready to agree with the political ideology of "Germanization" of the Poles by executing those who spoke Polish, and also with the goal of colonialism to include other German-speaking countries under the control of Germany.

The encounter with the Neogrammarians in their prime and the Allgemeine Deutsche Sprachverein at its rise was bound to have profound influence on Ueda's later direction. The two organizations were distinct in their character: the former was an academic movement mainly among universities, while the latter was initiated by an association that also involved public membership. They were sometimes in conflict, too: the intellectuals, including even conservative ones, had serious misgivings about the extreme chauvinistic tendency of the association, misgivings that resulted in a joint statement of criticism in the *Preussische Jahrbücher* (Prussian yearbooks) in 1889. The signatories included such writers as Theodor Fontane and Gustav Freytag, theologian Adolf von Harnack, historian Heinrich von Treitschke, and an influential Neogrammarian, Berthold Delbrück (Kirkness 1975, 386–387, 475).

Ueda was aware of the different nature of each of these movements, as seen in his later work, which took two polar directions: academic and political—rooted in Prussian-German nationalism.[22] What he brought back from Germany was the realization of the inseparable correlation between language and nationalism. Academic research into language and pragmatic policy making about language were two indispensable leading characters on the same stage, called the nation-state.

CHAPTER 5

Kokugo and *Kokka*

5-1. Politicizing *Kokugo*

In June 1894, on his return from three and a half years of study in Europe, Ueda was appointed professor of linguistics at the Imperial University. It was only two months before the outbreak of the Sino-Japanese War.[1] During that year, Ueda gave two public lectures, "Kokugo to kokka to" (The National Language and the Nation-State) in October and "Kokugo kenkyū ni tsuite" (About *Kokugo* Research) in November, that powerfully impressed the audience. Unlike his essays before his study abroad, which were directed to limited groups of scholars of language and literature, these two lectures were meant to appeal to a wider audience, and their written records reveal Ueda's passion for launching the new field of *kokugogaku* based on information from Western linguistics. They were published in his essay collection *Kokugo no tame* (For *Kokugo*) in the following year (1895; Meiji 28), the title indicating that all of his ideas about language were to be condensed into "*kokugo*."

In this chapter and the next I will discuss these two lectures, which opened a new stage of Ueda's activities and represented his ideas about language—"Kokugo to kokka to" in this chapter and "Kokugo kenkyū ni tsuite" in chapter 6.

Ueda's lecture "Kokugo to kokka to" was quite daring because nobody before him had so directly connected the concept of *kokugo* to the nation-state. Though some scholars had emphasized the spiritual sublimity of *kokugo* in relation to the nation, Ueda presented a completely novel idea that justified, in scholarly terms, the internal and organic connection between *kokugo* and *kokka* (Ueda 1897, 1–28; quoted in *Ochiai* 1968, 108–113).

The most crucial difference from the *kokugaku* scholars' viewpoint was that Ueda first postulated the organic connection between *kokugo*, a national language, and *kokka*, a nation-state, as a universal concept, not limited to Japan, and then explained the uniqueness and particularity of Japan. Remarking that he was not a scholar of "nationalism," Ueda opened the lecture saying that *kokugo* itself could not be discussed without considering *kokka* first.

According to Ueda, *kokka,* a nation-state, consists of four pillars or elements: land, race ("ethnicity" in today's terms), unity, and law. The third element, unity, further consists of five subelements: history and customs, political principles, religions, language, and education. Thus, Ueda attempted to define the universal nature of the concept of nation-state and to analyze its attributes, though he presented them as already proven, saying that the first four elements were the determining factors for the rise and fall of a nation-state (108). Ueda must have adapted this argument from the Prussian *Staatslehre* (doctrine of the state), with which he became familiar during his study in Germany. His intention, however, was not to formulate objectively the creation process or the law of development of a nation, but to paint the ideal picture of a nation-state and to convince the audience of how closely Japan matched such an ideal. Because of this intention, Ueda's discourse on *kokka* came to be strangely distorted. (It is still to be learned how much of this distortion emanated from the Prussian *Staatslehre.*)

This distortion is obvious in Ueda's heavy emphasis on race, history, and language as among the basic ingredients of a nation-state: these elements are the least susceptible to human manipulation and most useful for Ueda's intention to show the nation-state as a natural creation. The significance of this lecture was not Ueda's not-so-innovative discussion of the language itself, but the manifestation of his ideology in an effort to turn this most artificial creation, *kokka,* into a natural one.

Ueda contended that extreme multiethnic situations encouraged unpatriotic traits in a nation, citing the Austro-Hungarian Empire as an example of the decline of a nation resulting from discord among many ethnic groups. The Austro-Hungarian Empire would become a frequently used example in later studies of languages and races, especially by Hoshina Kōichi, typically as a negative model for warning of the danger of multiracialism or multilingualism. Ueda already had such a view, which, as we will later discuss, Hoshina loyally folded into his work on language policy. Ueda, nonetheless, did say, "We must not determine that one nation consists solely of one race." Many European countries are multiethnic nations. However, Ueda continued, even in those countries it was not always the case that all of the ethnic groups took part in the formation of their nations. "We can see that when a nation is to be established, one race always takes the central role in it," Ueda said (110). This was obvious in those nations' language policies: languages of ethnic minorities, such as Welsh and Gaelic in England or Basque and Breton in France had never become the official language in their parliaments because "whether to allow these languages or not would involve the nation's honor, order, and fate" (109). Ueda believed that Japan was free from such concerns, for Japan's "nation is an extension of its people who are extensions of one family" (110). According to his analysis, Japan had great advantages over European countries in maintaining the unity of the nation-state by "race" and language.[2]

As for "history," however, Ueda did not dare to prove Japan's superiority to Europe; instead he used Asian countries for comparison: "Look how weak are the Chinese or Koreans in their national spirit. Look how people of our Japan are brave and energetic in carrying out great tasks with ease" (109). Such differences between these two countries "were born out of each country's history and customs." When he referred to "the great tasks," he was already foreseeing the result of the Sino-Japanese War, which had just begun. His gaze was thus fixed on current affairs.

Nevertheless, Ueda's complacent argument proving Japan an ideal nation in every aspect of its race, language, and history was fanatically shrill, probably reflecting his feeling of guilt as a self-proclaimed student of science:

> Facing this national crisis, a critical time for the nation's fate, we as the people of the Japanese nation are able to move and work together. This is because we are the Yamato race with the loyal and patriotic Yamato soul, who have one national language. Our duty is to protect this unity of our language and of our race, together with the history of our empire, and prevent them from any decline or disarray. (110)

Thus his argument identified the worth of the Japanese nation. His next task was to make a connection between the nation and *kokugo,* to redefine language no longer as one part of the elements of a nation but as the integrating element for the formation of people's spiritual life as a whole.

Ueda's view of language reminds us of Humboldt's: a language forms the worldview of the people who speak it. After Humboldt, the stress on the organic and spiritual relation between a people and their language became one of the traditional German views about language. Ueda considered language as "the manifestation of the speakers' thoughts and emotions in their spiritual life" (110), and he emphasized that the essence of the spiritual life and social life of an ethnic group was imprinted in its language. However, such an interpretation, if materialized, would ignore the pitfall that it has validity only at the abstract level of language and thought. This paradox is implicit in Ueda's characterization of the ideology of *kokugo* of modern Japan:

> A language for the people who speak it is the symbol of the spirit of the brethren, just like the blood shared by their bodies. Therefore, the language of the Japanese nation is the spiritual blood of the Japanese people. The *kokutai* of Japan is maintained by this spiritual blood, and the Japanese race is unified by this most

strong and long-preserved tie. Therefore, even when visited by a crisis, as long as they can hear one's voice our forty-million brethren will listen to it, come to help wherever the voice is, and devote their lives to it. On learning good news of victory the celebration song for the emperor *(kimi ga yo)* echoes from Chishima[3] through Okinawa. If one hears this language in a foreign country, it will sound like music, a blessed message from the sky. (110)

Note an ingenious twist in his argument. The historical significance of the view of language in its organic relation to ethnicity was to be attributed to the experience of the language as the manifestation of its speakers' ethnic identity and to resisting a linguistic norm dominated by an external authority, such as Latin. However, Ueda skillfully manipulated this organic view in order to nullify such a possibility for ethnic identity. By comparing language to "blood" for brethren, he defined language as a "naturally given," uncontestable gift, and then identified it with unbroken *kokutai*. Language thus defined was no longer to serve for communication among people; instead it became the "voice" coming from somewhere to "be heard," or the "music" of blessing. The source of such a "voice" was not some individual person but the sacred *kokutai* as symbolized in "Kimi ga yachiyo" (Our Everlasting Sovereign [the celebration song for the emperor]). Therefore, this "voice" was a language of absolute order and submission. An individual could become a speaker of the language only as long as he or she was deeply rooted in this *kokutai*. Such a language was not felt to be forced upon the individual, but to be valued as the language of the inner morality of the person. This was why no Japanese person would ever dare to resist such a "voice" and was able to devote his or her life to it. There was no individual being to be expressed, but the obedient submission to *kokugo* as dictated by *kokutai*.

It was in the organic linguistic theory of Germany that Ueda found the principles for *kokugo* suitable for the Meiji nation-state, not in the *kokugaku* ideas with their long tradition that Ueda paid little attention to and considered as a mere obstacle to be removed by scientific linguistic theories. This organic view was the backbone ideology of linguistics studies, the self-proclaimed avant garde of the humanistic sciences of that time.

5-2. Mother and Homeland

In order to touch people's hearts with the idea of *kokutai*, Ueda was very creative in exploiting the image of "mother," as in the following:

Our language is not a mere sign of *kokutai*, but is an educator, like one's benevolent mother. From the time of our birth, our mother has cuddled us and has warmly taught us the ways we think and feel as a member of the nation. . . . In Germany, there is a word, *"Muttersprache,"* meaning language of the mother, or *"Sprachemutter"* [*sic*], the mother of language. Very well said. (111)

The imperial system of Japan was founded on the central ideology of a "family nation": on one hand the nation's power embraced emotional intimacy and on the other a family was the microcosm of the nation that taught its members authority and submission. Furthermore, the emperor system was amalgamated with the native ancestor worship and each family, *ie,* was placed in the family tree branching from the imperial family; hence the ideology of "family nation" was given religious authenticity also. It is not unique to Japan that a nation is compared to a pseudofamily, and it is not uncommon that a nation in crisis calls for its people's patriotism as one united family. However, the ideology of the Japanese "family nation" was unusual in that it saturated people's simple daily lives. The horizontal relationship among family members was disregarded, and a family was dominated by the vertical parent-child relationship, that is, loyalty and filial piety. This vertical line emanated from the emperor at the top. Furthermore, the pivot of this vertical relationship was not a father who represented authority and order, but a mother who embodied love and benevolence: a mother was the one who could transform a forceful, merciless directive by the nation into an affectionate one full of devotion and benevolence.

The famous story "Suihei no haha" (A Sailor's Mother), published in the second edition of the national textbook *Normal Elementary Reader* (vol. 9) in 1910 (Meiji 43), illustrates the mother's role in the imperial family nation. It is set in the midst of the Sino-Japanese War. A sailor of the warship *Takachiho* (symbolic name of Japan) is sobbing over a letter in a woman's handwriting. A general who is passing by sees him and reprimands him, saying that crying about missing his wife and children is sissy, shameful behavior for an imperial soldier. The sailor replies that he does not have a wife or children and shows the letter to the general. The letter is from the sailor's mother and reads, "I regret that you have not yet distinguished yourself in the war. Remember you went into the war to devote your life to the emperor. Whenever my neighbors in the village act concerned about me, my heart breaks over your uselessness. I pray the day comes soon when you distinguish yourself." On reading this, the general says, "I am deeply moved by your mother's spirit. Now I understand why you are mortified. Our ship has not yet been given an opportunity for engagement, but when we do, we shall both fight bravely in a glorious war. Do tell your mother so and set her at ease" (Kaigo 1963, 150–151).

"Mother" stories like this became one of the central teaching materials in every textbook. Clearly, they also meant to teach girls that a mother's duty is to dedicate her children to the emperor and the country. Thus, these stories that dramatized purification prepared girls to resolve the tragedy of losing their children.

The underlying purpose of "mother" stories was to present the emperor as the personified nation, to explain the emperor's relation to people as the benevolence of a mother, and thus to imprint in the uncritical minds of school-children the foundation of the nation. As this was done via the image of the "mother," the nation took on the appearance of a family, a natural and harmonious community. The emperor system in Japan found the secret of its power in the intimacy of family supported by the mother-child relation, to almost an incestuous degree.

Ueda's "benevolent mother" who "warmly taught one the ways one thinks and feels as a member of the nation" (*Ochiai* 1968, 111) was on her way to becoming the "mother of the militant nation." Ueda juxtaposed "mother" with the image of "home." When he said "language connects you to the precious, unforgettable memories of your life, especially of your innocent childhood," he appealed to every familiar scene of "home" to move the reader's heart: "mother gently singing a lullaby," "stern father," "picking violets *(rengesō)* with friends in the meadow in spring sunshine" (111).

Wrapping the "mother tongue" in the sentiment of "father," "mother," and "home," Ueda created the following *discours:* to discuss the right and wrong of one's own language is like criticizing your own parents or your own home; though you could do it in the light of pure reason, such is not a true love; a true love, like your reverent affection for the imperial family, is not a choice; only with such love can you discuss the language of your country and the protection of it (111). Here, Ueda unblushingly leaped over the logical discretion of a scientist: if he were to discuss "the language of mother" or "language of home" it had to be a native dialect. How on earth could memories of "mother" and "home" arrive at *kokugo* and *kokka,* the nation and its language?

According to Kamishima (1961), a part of the principles in the formation of the modern Japanese ethos was the transformation and expansive reproduction of social authenticity from the first village *(mura)* with natural orders to the second village with fictional orders. Kamishima's examples for the second village were various associations or organizations among the urban middle class. I suspect that *kokka* itself in modern Japan might have been an inflated fictional village, and with a local dialect being the language of the first village, *kokugo* became the language of the second, fictional village. However, once the transformation from the first to second village was considered a natural process of sublimation, the distinction between the two vanished.

To give the authenticity of order to this second village, disguising its fictional makeup, its analogy to "natural village" was constantly reinforced through the affectionate imagery of "mother" and "home," and thus the fictional village overlapped with one's reflections on one's natural village. However, what was reflected was the way one desired the natural village to be, looking from the perspective of the fictional village. "Mother" and "home" had their existence only in one's reflections, like the negative photographic image of modern Japan.

What did these images of "mother" and "home" mean to modern Japan? They were imagined as nature and shelter: nature before modern rationalism and individual wills, and a cozy shelter where one could take refuge from modernization. However, the village and home in affectionate memories also demanded without mercy one's sacrifice, as indicated by the "neighbors in the village" in "A Sailor's Mother." Indeed, these pristine and sentimental images became the hidden weapons for the later imperial fascism—including Marxism—to annihilate modern consciousness. These images were imprinted deep in the subconscious as eternally lasting, neither to be affirmed nor negated by one's reflective consciousness but simply to be accepted. This was the same place where Ueda wished to imprint *kokugo* and *kokutai*.

As it receded from one, and as its destruction proceeded under the emperor system and imperialism, "home" was idealized and glorified. Indeed, this impulsive yearning for home was at the root of Japan's colonialism. A colony for Japan was not a land plundered by force, but a home recovered from one's memories or a projection of one's memories, a projection of distanced desire. "Home" in modern Japan was in itself a colonialistic concept.

5-3. For *Kokugo*

Using a quasi-scientific argument on one hand and a sentimental appeal to preconsciousness on the other, Ueda made an inseparable connection between *kokugo* and *kokka*. All he had to do next was to give the people instructions on how to regard *kokugo*. Ueda proceeded to say that "it is a virtue for the nation to treasure its own language; people of a great nation always treasured the language of their country and never traded it with languages of other countries," citing examples of China, Greece, Rome, and most important, Germany, with admiration: "Look how Germany cherishes its own language, eliminating any foreign elements from it and restoring its goodness!" (*Ochiai* 1968, 111). He must have been thinking of the movement of language purification led by Riegel, mentioned in the previous chapter. What Ueda was most interested in, however, was not only the linguistic aspect of the movement but also its political consequences. His intention was to emphasize that the progress of the movement came from the same roots as the process in which Prussia, led by Bismarck with the support of its "national education," gained unstoppable power through the wars against Austria (1866) and France (1870) and finally became an empire (111). According to Ueda, the confusion of languages caused the weakening of the unity and independence of a nation, and the rise of the German Empire was supported by its education of the language and the people. Therefore, *kokugo* education towards purification of the Japanese language also must be the foundation of the education of the Japanese people. Ueda continued:

> The people of a great nation know this well and therefore cherish their language in their hearts and use their minds to protect and improve it, and hence establish upon it strong education of the nation's people. The goal of national education, unlike humanist education or religious education, is to raise a person to be an excellent member of the ideal nation, and this cannot be achieved without first attending to the nation's language and then to its history. (112)

Ueda lamented, however, that the Japanese language had not met with the cordial reception it deserved. Japanese culture and education were dictated by *kangaku* scholars and English scholars, both of whom looked down on the Japanese language, and people were never reminded that the Japanese language was "the loyal servant of the emperor and the benevolent mother of the people." Excessive use of *kanji* and *kango* kept the Japanese language from its true independence. Now that Japan as a nation was on its way to a truly independent empire through the Sino-Japanese War,[4] Ueda questioned whether any preparation had been made for *kokugo* that could respond to the rise of the nation. It was not that Ueda was intoxicated by the anti-China sentiment of the time, but he believed that *kokugo* and *kokka* were inseparable in the process of autonomy and prosperity, as evident in Germany.

He closed his lecture "Kokugo to kokka to" with the following twelve questions about the state of *kokugo* study:

1. How has the historical study of grammar been done?
2. How has the comparative study of grammar been done?
3. How about the study of pronunciation?
4. How about the history of *kokugo* study?
5. How about the debate about the script?

6. Can the standard for written texts *(futsūbun)*, if we have such a standard, also dictate our actual [spoken] language?

7. How about the study of foreign words and any restriction on their importation?

8. Has there been any study of synonyms?

9. Has there been any study of homonyms?

10. How about dictionaries, both for technical and common words?

11. How about the teaching methods of the Japanese language?

12. How about the methodologies for foreign language study?

Then Ueda proposed that the nation must initiate these studies as soon as possible. Ueda knew he was the only one who could make them happen. All of those directions of study stemmed from the theories of modern linguistics in Europe and could not be sought in the traditional study of the Japanese language. Ueda proposed the establishment of *kokugogaku,* the study of *kokugo,* as a part of the nation's tasks, and its rightful place could be filled only by disconnecting it from traditions. This is central to his ideas of *kokugo.*

Following this last part of his lecture, Ueda elucidated the methodology of *kukogogaku* in the next month's lecture, "Kokugo kenkyu ni tsuite" (About *Kokugo* Research). Though these two lectures were in very different styles— the former was a political statement written in a passionate literary language *(bungo),* and the latter was an academic proposal written in an easy colloquial language *(kōgo)*—we must not fail to notice their inherent connection. For Ueda, science and politics were mutually supportive; the scientific nature of ideology was linked together with the ideological nature of science.

CHAPTER 6

From *Kokugo* Studies to *Kokugo* Politics

6-1. Scheme for *Kokugogaku*

The changed language in the titles of Ueda's lectures, from "Nihon gengo kenkyūhō" (Research Methods for the Japanese Language) before his study abroad to "Kokugo kenkyū ni tsuite" (About *Kokugo* Research) after his return, shows the change in the focus of his interest from *nihongo* to *kokugo*. As we saw in the case of Ōtsuki, such a transition indicated a fundamental and critical change in the views of language at that time. The major objective of his lecture "Kokugo kenkyū ni tsuite," which followed "Kokugo to kokka to," was to outline the mission of *kokugogaku*, the field of *kokugo* studies. The implicit premise was the need of *kokugogaku* for the *kokugo* to exist: *kokugogaku* was necessary to define the still-obscure framework of *kokugo* for its implementation. In other words, the relation between *kokugo* and *kokugogaku* was quite different from that between a normal academic research field and its research objects.

Ueda opened "Kokugo kenkyū ni tsuite" with an appeal: "Let us reclaim the status for *kokugo* that it truly deserves" (*Ochiai* 1968, 114). We may consider this an extension of his arguments in "Kokugo to Kokka to": liberate *kokugo* from the hegemony of *kango* and *kanbun* and raise the status of texts written in the common language to those written in *kanbun* style. In Ueda's mind, the relationship between *kanbun* and *kokugo* was similar to that between Latin and modern languages in Europe—hence his perception that "the Japanese language has reached a new era, just like the early times of Italian, German, and English" (115). Ueda's idea of *kokugo* consisted of these two aspects: the political significance of *kokugo* as argued in "Kokugo to kokka to" and the academic perspectives on *kokugo* as outlined in "Kokugo kenkyū ni tsuite."

Even before his study abroad, Ueda had considered conventional scholars of Japanese "those who cannot distinguish language from literature." He continued his caustic criticism of "scholars of Japanese language up until today" for their preoccupation with ancient language with no attention to the modern and for their neglect of the spoken language while concentrating only on written texts (116). In other words, Ueda upheld the importance of investigating "language itself," that is, the language that is currently spoken. This viewpoint was to develop into a crucial recognition of the idea of *kokugo:* to make a clear distinction between research of *kokubun* (literature) and that of *kokugo* (language). According to Ueda, *kokubungaku* (research of Japanese literature) focused on unique Japanese texts, that is, esthetic or polite literature. On the other hand, he pointed out the direction that *kokugogaku* should take as follows:

> The major object of investigation in *kokugogaku* is the language of Japan, especially the rules of the language. It considers the language of *kokubun* scholars' interest as only one part of the Japanese language and does not favor it over the language of carpenters, daubers, or dialects of Ōshū[1] and Kyūshū. *Kokugo* scholars look into language of the past and present, east and west, and all people, not discriminating between men and women, the rich and the poor, the old and the young, or the wise and the foolish. The ultimate goal of *kokugogaku* is to make all people be able to speak, read, and write natural, clear, and correct language. Any additional refinement of the language beyond this goal will be left to the expertise of *kokubun* scholars. (116)

Ueda pointed out here not only the difference in methods and scope of research between *kokugogaku* and *kokubungaku* but also the difference in their mode of existence. Such a clear awareness of this difference made him refuse to use the common title *kokugo kokubun* that most scholars had used. It was no longer the case that *koku-go* concerned *go* (words) as a part of *koku-bun* (texts). While *kokubun* was always confined to texts that were written for aesthetic purposes, *kokugo* now referred to a global concept that indiscriminately encompassed all forms of linguistic representation, with no restriction among purposes or ways of expression, social status of speakers, or their regional differences.

The basis of Ueda's idea of *kokugo* was his clear awareness of "the present," or "synchronicity," a term in linguistics methodology: the basis of *kokugo* must be sought only in the language that is spoken or written *now,* at this very moment. From this standpoint, Ueda harshly criticized the current state of research and education of *kokugo:* "It is difficult to understand why the rules of ancient language are still dominating the grammar of our fine language of great Meiji sovereignty. However, educators do not seem to have any objection, nor does any question occur to them while they are faithfully using [medieval texts such as] *Tsurezuregusa* or *Jikkinshō*[2] in the *kokugo* classroom" (117). Thus, Ueda had no intention of seeking a model of *kokugo* in classical texts, as Ochiai's *Standard of Japanese Literature for Middle School* (1892) or Ōtsuki's *Current Japanese Grammar*

(1897) did in their efforts to promote *kokugo*.[3] His goal was to unshackle the Japanese language from Chinese words and texts, and he criticized scholars of *kangaku* and Western studies who looked down on the Japanese language. However, this did not mean that he sided with scholars of Japanese classics *(wagaku)*. On the contrary, for Ueda, with his firm awareness of "the present," the classical language worshipped by *wagaku* scholars had to be excluded from *kokugo,* and only "the language and texts that are natural, and easy to learn and to be understood" must become its basis. Such a view of language led Ueda to initiate an appeal for "an effort to establish a standard language for the forty million fellow countrymen, departing from the language of only twenty thousand or two hundred thousand scholars of Japanese classics and poetry" (117).

When *kokugo* was thus separated from *kokubun* and was defined as the entirety of linguistic expression by all speakers who comprised the nation, the problem of "standard language," which had almost never been thought of before, suddenly surfaced with new meaning: the new definition of *kokugo* could not avoid the question of how to select the norm for daily [spoken] language as well as that for written language. At this point, however, Ueda did not yet have a clear suggestion about any standard written style; he merely raised the question at the end of "Kokugo to Kokka to" whether or not "the standard for *futsūbun* (written texts), if there is one, should be able to control actual [spoken] language." In "Kokugo kenkyū ni tsuite" also, though he used the expression *zokugo-tai no bun* (vernacular style sentences), its context was a proposal for instituting new grammar to establish "a standard written style for the great Meiji sovereignty." Thus his view of style at that time was still confined within "standard" style as the written language of Meiji. It was in his 1895 (Meiji 28) lecture "Hyōjungo ni tsukite" (About the Standard Language) that Ueda began to connect standard language and *genbun itchi* within the idea of *kokugo.* This was where Ueda started his new steps towards his 1900 (Meiji 33) lecture "Naichi zakkyo go ni okeru gogaku mondai" (Language Problems after the Opening of Concessions)[4] and the inauguration of Kokugo Chōsa Iinkai (National Language Investigative Committee) in 1902.

6-2. *Hyōjungo* and *Genbun Itchi*

The concept of *hyōjungo* (standard language) was introduced to Japan for the first time in Ueda's 1895 lecture "Hyōjungo ni tsukite" (About the Standard Language) (Yoshida and Inokuchi 1964, 502–508). Ueda defined *hyōjungo* as equivalent to "standard language" in English or *Gemeinsprache* in German, and as that which is "used in a country as a model language" and is, "unlike so-called dialects, understood by most of the people throughout the country"

(502). Though Ueda did not believe Japan had ever had such a language, he suggested that current Tokyo language could be the standard, as the language spoken in the capital of the great empire, and therefore deserving of such eventual recognition (506).

What did he mean by the "current Tokyo language"? As seen in part 1 of this book, the language spoken in Tokyo had already gained a certain privilege in the early third decade of Meiji through *genbun itchi* novels such as those by Futabatei Shimei and Yamada Bimyō, and it was a language on a continuum with the Edo dialect. Ueda, however, wanted to disconnect *hyōjungo* from the Edo dialect: the "Tokyo language" as the basis for *hyōjungo* was not to be a vulgar language like *beranmē,* typical of Edo natives' colloquialism, but a language spoken by educated people in Tokyo (506). Ueda's idea here was the germ for the later official definition of *hyōjungo* as "the language spoken in middle-class society in Tokyo," specified in *Jinjō shōgaku tokuhon hensan shuisho* (Prospectus for Editing Readers for Normal Elementary Schools) in 1904 (Meiji 37).

At the same time, however, Ueda was aware of the need for various "artificial refinements" of some shortcomings in the Tokyo language before making it the *hyōjungo.* He proposed several measures for such "refinement," among which he considered *genbun itchi* literature in the Tokyo language as "the most helpful for instituting *hyōjungo*" (508). For Ueda, *genbun itchi* was thus helpful for the refinement of the Tokyo language, but this did not mean that he sympathized with some extreme advocates of *genbun itchi* who "became the slaves of slang, using it for every word" (507).

Ueda's tone of argument suddenly changed in his "Language Problems after the Opening of Concessions." As if possessed, he began to rush towards establishment of *hyōjungo.*

In 1894 (Meiji 27), through the first *jōyaku kaisei* (revision of unequal treaties with the Western countries) the Meiji government finally succeeded in abolition of extraterritoriality *(ryōji saibanken)* and partial recovery of tariff autonomy *(kanzei jishuken),* both long-pending problems in Japan's foreign affairs. The revised treaties, which became effective in 1899, also included a policy regarding the integration of foreign residents in Japan, which permitted foreigners to live and travel freely. This policy, *naichi zakkyo* (opening of the concessions), caused greater agitation among the general public than the recovery of jurisdiction or tariff autonomy did, sometimes involving excessive emotional resistance and debates coming from various directions.

For example, in his 1899 (Meiji 32) book *Naichi zakkyo go no Nihon* (Japan after the Opening of the Concessions), Yokoyama Gennosuke alerted readers that *naichi zakkyo* was a serious affair, equal to the Sino-Japanese War. He warned that *naichi zakkyo* would bring an influx of foreign capital and have a destructive impact on Japanese labor. His argument in this book was not about *naichi zakkyo* itself, however, and different from that of many other simplistic antiforeign activists, in that he explained the need for a socialist movement, as seen in his analyses of industrial structure and labor movements in Japan. Nonetheless, his nervousness and wariness can be seen in passages like this:

> While the Sino-Japanese War was a forthright war where arms determined victory or defeat, *naichi zakkyo* is a war that would risk people's hearts, morality, industry, business ventures, labor, and technology. It will not be as easy and fast a game as the war with weapons against China was. (Yokoyama 1954, 14)

According to Yokoyama, *naichi zakkyo* was the same as a war between [domestic] peace and Westerners (16).

Naichi zakkyo also prompted Ueda to reverse the order of urgency between the institution of *hyōjungo* and the refinement of *genbun itchi*. He had already expressed in "Kokugo kenkyū ni tsuite" his concerns about the effect of *Naichi zakkyo,* that is, that the future increase in interaction with Westerners might mean that Western languages, instead of *kango,* would become the chief threat to the uniqueness of the Japanese language:

> Especially now that the unequal treaties have been revised and *naichi zakkyo* is about to become effective, do our fellow countrymen have enough confidence or courage to make those Westerners speak our nation's language? If they do, in what way? On the contrary, their [Westerners'] language may gradually spread and put down our nation's language, just as the Chinese language has done to Japanese. Can we guarantee that this will not happen? (*Ochiai* 1968, 115)

His concern—that frequent interaction with Westerners and their language would jeopardize, as Chinese did, the uniqueness of the Japanese language— might seem paranoid to us today, but *naichi zakkyo* was a serious threat for Ueda, who was devoting his energy to establishing *kokugo.* In 1900 (Meiji 33), immediately after the 1899 implementation of the revised treaties, Ueda published the essay "Naichi zakkyo go ni okeru gogaku mondai" (Language Problems after the Opening of Concessions).

What this essay implies is not that Ueda was xenophobic about the approaching threat of Western languages. Rather, he asked a reflective question, whether the Japanese language had enough strength to repel the threat:

> Fellow citizens of our Great Japanese Empire, are you confident that the current state of *kokugo* is satisfactory and ready for the time after *naichi zakkyo* is implemented? Are you confident that our *kokugo* is sufficient for leading the destiny

of our nation? At the same time, will it be an adequate medium for transmitting ideas to Japanize visitors from abroad or foreign residents who are to be naturalized? (Ueda 1900, 131)

The Japanese language had never been questioned in such a framework before Ueda: it had been sufficient to say that the Japanese language was the language spoken by Japanese people, and such a fact did not even have to enter people's consciousness. However, the tension between Japan and other countries after the Sino-Japanese War brought a completely new context to the question of language. Ueda's answers to his own questions were very negative: "Our people of the Japanese Empire are now facing the opening of the concessions, without the least preparation in the nation's language." He held the despairing opinion that Japan's national language, *kokugo,* "in its strict sense," was unable to become a linguistic protective wall for the nation (131).

What Ueda meant by "*kokugo* in its strict sense" was a language that had uniform quality for both speaking and writing, hearing and reading, a language that could be used equally in both conversation and written texts. That is, it was "*kokugo* that could maintain the same spirit through both speaking and writing of it" (131). The reality of the Japanese language, according to Ueda, seriously split between spoken and written styles, with each in extreme chaos. As for the written language, it was a mix of *wabuntai* (classical Japanese style), *kanbun ōbun chokuyakutai* (literal translation from Chinese or Western sentences), *hōgentai* (dialectal style), and *sōrōbuntai* (official documentation style). Such a state of written language in disarray would not prepare Japan for "its position in Asia towards the twentieth century to enter the keen competition [with the Western countries] in every area" nor for "Japanizing visitors from foreign countries or our future fellows who are to be naturalized." The spoken language was in a similar state: there was no prescribed "standard spoken Japanese." Tokyo language had not yet gained such authority, while the use of dialects in official situations had no penalty. Such realities convinced Ueda that unification of *kokugo* could not possibly be done by voluntary action by the people alone: "the people do not have enough knowledge to recognize the need for unification of the nation's language and writing styles," nor did they "have the knowledge and courage to consciously endorse certain standards for the spoken language" (132).

The only possible way to realize standardization of *kokugo,* Ueda concluded, was its institutionalization "from the top":

Make the Tokyo language *hyōjungo* as soon as possible and determine it as *kokugo* in its strict sense. And let this be the sole institution that will guide description of the grammar and compilation of common dictionaries. Let it be used in elementary schools throughout the country, and at the same time in all reading, writing, speaking, and listening. . . . Thus first establish it as the model language, and then protect it, refine it, and the people will be able to develop it freely. (134)

"First establish it [Tokyo language] as the model language, and then protect it, refine it"—this was the reverse order from what Ueda had proposed in his previous essay, "Hyōjungo ni tsukite" (About *Hyōjungo*), that is, the Tokyo language had been expected to elevate its status to *hyōjungo* only after it received cultural refinement. *Hyōjungo* and *genbun itchi* were now organically connected as principles in the concept of *kokugo*. *Genbun itchi* was no longer merely part of the means for instituting *hyōjungo*, but its practice itself became key for the standardization. This was a natural consequence of Ueda's intention to make "Tokyo language = *hyōjungo*" the sole medium for all linguistic activities. Though Ueda said "the people will be able to develop it [*hyōjungo*] freely," that could happen only after they were taught in school this model language that had already been instituted. The people themselves were not allowed to participate in the formation of *hyōjungo*, but only to receive it. Successful realization of this plan would depend on the establishment of a concrete standard language and on an authority that had the power to disseminate the language through educational institutions. Thus, Ueda proposed the establishment of Kokugo Chōsakai (National Language Investigative Board) inside the Ministry of Education (134)—the first proposal for a language policy-making organ backed up by the national authority.

As if responding to Ueda's proposal, the Kokuji Kairyōbu (Script Reform Section) of Teikoku Kyōiku Kai (Imperial Board of Education) submitted *Kokuji kokugo kokubun no kairyō ni kansuru seigansho* (Petition regarding Improvements in the National Script and Language) to the cabinet in January 1900 (Meiji 33) (Nishio and Hisamatsu 1969, 107–109). Prompted by these proposals, in April of the same year the Ministry of Education commissioned scholars, headed by Maejima Hisoka and including Ueda Kazutoshi, Ōtsuki Fumihiko, Miyake Setsurei, and Tokutomi Sohō, to be *kokugo chōsa iin* (national language investigators). The group started as a nongovernmental agency, but following the houses' approval of the *Genbun itchi no jikkō ni tsuite no seigan* (Petition for Actions towards *Genbun itchi*) submitted by the Imperial Board of Education in February 1901 (Meiji 34) (Yoshida and Inokuchi 1964, 288–289), it became Kokugo Chōsa Iinkai (National Language Investigative Committee), an official governmental committee, in March 1902. The committee, with Katō Hiroyuki as its chair and Ueda the director, announced the following tasks as early as July of the same year:[5]

1. Investigate advantages and disadvantages of *kana* and *rōmaji* for adoption of *phonogram*[6] as the script.
2. Investigate *genbun itchi* style writing for its adoption.
3. Investigate the phonological structure of *kokugo.*
4. Investigate dialects for the selection of standard language *(hyōjungo).*
   (Monbushō 1949, 59)

With the above resolution as a framework, the committee conducted linguistic research on the Japanese language; the research resulted in several important documents such as *Kokugo kokuji kairyō ronsetsu nenpyō* (Chronology of Articles about Reform of *Kokugo* and National Script; 1904), *Hōgen saishūbo* (Collection of Dialects; 1904), *On'in chōsa hōkokusho* (Report of the Phonological Investigation; 1905), *Genkō futsū bunpō kaiteian chōsa hōkoku no ichi* (Survey Report of Suggestions for Revision of the Current Normal Grammar: 1; 1906), and *Kōgohō chōsa hōkokusho* (Investigative Report of the Spoken Language; 1906).

The ultimate goal of the committee was not just to investigate, but also to select *hyōjungo,* that is, to establish the linguistic norm, premised on the spoken language as the base. Item 2 of the resolution was obviously the direct consequence of this premise. For the same reason, item 1 implied far more than mere "investigation": it pointed to a complete abolition of *kanji* in the future, as later confirmed by Hoshina Kōichi in his commentary on the resolution in *Gengogaku zasshi* (Yoshida and Inokuchi 1964, 116). For Ueda, who firmly believed that sound was the essence of language, the ideogram *kanji* that did not represent sound defied this linguistic basis. Therefore, the only remaining choice for Ueda was either a selection between *kana* and *rōmaji* or the introduction of a new script. Ueda himself was a positive advocate for *rōmaji* and the abolition of *kanji,* as he declared, "It is obvious to me that *rōmaji* is far superior to *kanji* or *kana* or any new script, and is most suitable for the national script" (*Taiyō* 1900, 102).

The seemingly academic resolution of items 3 (an investigation of phonological structure) and 4 (an investigation of dialects) was also preparatory work for instituting *hyōjungo.* Ueda was keenly aware of the need for *hyōjungo,* but at the same time, of the inevitable obstacle to its dissemination: the linguistic collision with dialects. The hidden intention of item 4 was an investigation into the actual state of dialects with a view toward their extermination, and item 3 implied preparation for correcting the pronunciation of dialect speakers through teaching them *hyōjungo.*

The above resolution by the committee can be seen as the epitome of Ueda's ideas about language. Such a careful and exact framework for investigation had not been specified in the previous two petitions[7] by Teikoku Kyōiku Kai that prompted the establishment of the committee, and it was brought into the committee by Ueda himself. Within this framework, the linguistic investigation of *kokugo* and the institution of *hyōjungo*, that is, academic description and institutional prescription, two fundamentally opposing courses of action, were connected in wonderful harmony with no contradiction. Ueda made this connection possible with his idea of *kokugo*, and he was to become the actual leader of the committee.

6-3. *Kokugo* Politics and *Kokugogaku*

In 1898 (Meiji 31) Ueda started Gengo Gakkai (Linguistics Association) with eager young linguists and launched its journal, *Gengogaku zasshi*, in February 1900 (Meiji 33). The journal made it mandatory to use *kōgotai* (colloquial style) in its Miscellanies columns and promoted publication of research and reports about *genbun itchi*, many of which were written in *kōgotai*. In fact, it was this journal that coined the word *kōgotai*, replacing *genbun itchitai*.[8] The journal articles faithfully reflected Ueda's ideas about language. For example, Fujioka Katsuji, a student of Ueda at Tokyo University, argued in his 1901 (Meiji 34) article "Genbun itchi ron" (Theory of *Genbun itchi*) as follows:

> *Genbun itchi* does not mean an act of copying all kinds of Japanese expressions in the exact way they are. . . . *Kokugo* must be unified, and towards this goal, we must overcome minor difficulties as long as the standard for unification is quite satisfactory. . . . That is, we must build on one standard language, *hyōjungo*, and translate dialects into this *hyōjungo* in writing. In other words, *genbun itchi* means writing in *hyōjungo*. (Yoshida and Inokuchi 1964, 343–344)

Thus *genbun itchi* now meant a mere means to translate dialects into *hyōjungo*, which was defined as "the language of educated people in Tokyo." Nonetheless, for Fujioka, *genbun itchi* was still considered as one of many writing styles, as indicated in this passage: "to advocate *genbun itchi* means to teach the writing style called *genbun itchitai*" (349).

Hoshina Kōichi, on the other hand, was more radical about this point. As an alternative member of Kokugo Chōsa Iinkai, he contributed a commentary, "Kokugo Chōsa Iinkai ketsugi jikō ni tsuite" (About the Resolutions by the National Language Investigative Committee), to the July 1902 (Meiji 35) issue of *Gengogaku zasshi*. There he argued that it would be extremely unrealistic in the selection of *hyōjungo* to investigate all dialects and to select different styles from them; rather, one must "first set a standard for dialects, manipulate them with finesse, and thus create a fine *hyōjungo*"; the investigation of dialects is a supplement to the project of refining *hyōjungo*; and the best language recommended for *hyōjungo* is the one "that is used today in the middle or upper class in Tokyo" (1902, 112–113).

As for *genbun itchi,* Hoshina contended, "It is not that there exists a writing style called *genbun itchi. Hyōjungo* itself will be the style for *genbun itchi.* Therefore, once *hyōjungo* is established, the style *genbun itchitai* will be accordingly defined" (115). That is, Hoshino reversed the previous relationship between *genbun itchi* and *hyōjungo:* now the establishment of *hyōjungo* became the prerequisite for *genbun itchi,* not the other way around. Thus, *genbun itchi* lost its original spirit of reform and was sucked into the nation's politics of *hyōjungo*— the enterprise of *genbun itchi* was destined to be destroyed in the ideology of *hyōjungo.*

As seen above, it was Ueda's idea of *kokugo* that was the basis of the *kokugo* politics promoted by Kokugo Chōsa Iinkai, the most important of which was the institution of *hyōjungo.* While asserting an inseparable tie between *kokugo* and *kokka,* however, Ueda also repeatedly complained that Japan did not yet have *kokugo* in its true sense. Then the question was, how could something that did not exist be connected to the nation-state? Or what was the goal of *kokugogaku* when the research object did not exist? In order to answer the question, we must realize that *kokugo* was not an already existing reality but a value understood as an ideal. As seen in chapter 5, Ueda believed that the establishment of *kokugogaku* was the nation's duty and that *kokugogaku* was needed not only for the sake of *kokugo* but also for the nation-state. In other words, *kokugogaku* had a direct impact on the nation's language policy, and at the same time it had to constantly construct *kokugo* as a part of the value system to support the nation-state. The primary goal of the academic field of *kokugogaku* was to produce and reproduce the ideological value called *kokugo.* And the nation-state, supported by this indisputable value, was to modify the actual language according to its purposes.

Ueda clearly distinguished *kokugo* from *kokubun,* and grasped *kokugo* as an inclusive concept of the entirety of linguistic expressions. However, there remained one problem: the actual language currently spoken by the people could not, unchanged, become *kokugo.* In "Kokugo kenkyū ni tsuite" (1894; Meiji 27) he stated that the "ultimate goal" of *kokugogaku* was to realize "correct speaking, reading and writing" among the people (*Ochiai* 1968, 116). This clearly indicated that the research goal of *kokugogaku* was not the language itself, but to make real the ideal of *kokugo.* It was a scholarship in which description of the facts was a mere means; the objective was to prescribe norms of the language. Therefore, it could not exist without practicing the education and policies of *kokugo.* For Ueda, *kokugo* education and *kokugo* policies were not merely the applied fields of *kokugogaku: kokugo* as the object of practice had a priority over *kokugo* as an objective research object. To reiterate, *kokugo* could not come into existence by simply speaking or writing it; it was an ideal and practical value that could be maintained only through constant and conscious reminding.

6-4. *Kokugo* to Be Taught

In this section, we will look into the changes in the position of *kokugo* in educational policies. *Chūgakkōrei* (Middle School Ordinance) of 1886 (Meiji 19) provided that the content of a new school subject—*kokugo* and *kanbun*—was to teach "reading, dictation, and composition of [Japanese] texts with a mixture of *kanji* and *kana* as well as of *kanbun,* classical Chinese texts" (Masubuchi 1981, 71). However, with the outbreak of the Sino-Japanese War in 1894 (Meiji 27), the Ministry of Education, under the *kokugo* advocate Minister Inoue Kowashi, ordered the elimination of the dictation and composition of *kanbun,* keeping only its reading, while increasing class meeting time from five to seven hours a week. This revision was based on the ministry's guideline for the teaching of *kokugo* as "a source to nurture patriotism" (Kaigo 1968, 244), and it promoted the superiority of *kokugo* over *kanbun,* placing the latter as only of secondary importance for passive knowledge. This curriculum revision, along with Ueda's "Kokugo to kokka to" in the same year, reflected in educational policy the rise of the ultranationalism of the time.

The most significant change in education was brought about by the revision of *Shōgakkōrei* (Elementary School Order) in August 1900 (Meiji 33):[9] a new subject, *kokugo,* was implemented in the elementary school curriculum; it combined reading, composition, and calligraphy, which had previously been three separate subjects. "Shōgakkōrei shikō kisoku" (Enforcement Regulations for the Elementary School Order) stipulated that the goal of this new subject was to teach "model *kokugo*": "texts for the reader must be written in an easy, model language for *kokugo,* and [the content] must encourage children to be lively and honest" (Masubuchi 1981, 50). The previous common title of the readers, *Kokubun tokuhon,* was replaced by a new title, *Kokugo tokuhon.*

Corresponding to the changes in the elementary school curriculum, "Chūgakkōrei shikō kisoku" (Enforcement Regulations for the Middle School Ordinance) in 1901 (Meiji 34) revised the content of the middle school subject known as *kokugo* and *kanbun,* placing its focus on modern language: "teach reading, mainly current Japanese texts, introduce classical texts as the students advance, and teach students composition in simple and practical language" (73). Thus, educational policy attached increasing importance to the continuity in the education of *kokugo* from elementary to middle schools, and accordingly, classical Chinese and Japanese lost their central position in the school curriculum.

As Ueda developed the theory of *kokugo,* the educational system of the nation, too, shaped the content and objectives of *kokugo.* Starting with the School Ordinance of 1886, educational reform through four and a half decades of Meiji achieved its goal of establishing an educational system for the people to correspond to the modern nation-state. Most notable was the revision of the Elementary School Ordinance, especially the implementation of the school subject *kokugo.* It was not a mere change in the subject's name, but a representation of the desire from various facets of the society to establish the ideal of *kokugo.* The dissemination of the *kokugo* ideal through elementary schools meant institutionalization of *kokugo* as a normative value to be planted in the people's consciousness.

The Revised Elementary School Ordinance of 1900 (Meiji 33) and *Jinjō shōgaku tokuhon* (Normal Elementary School Reader), the first national *kokugo* textbooks in 1904 and 1905 (Meiji 37 and 38), based on the censorship of national textbooks that was implemented in 1903 (Meiji 36), also meant the first step towards the *hyōjungo* policy. The progressive content of the textbooks, such as the reduction in the number of *kanji,* the unified style of *kana* and its phonetic writing system, and the vastly increased use of colloquial language[10] all aimed at the ultimate goal of teaching *hyōjungo.* The "Editorial Prospectus" stated that the textbook was designed "in the effort to bring unity in *kokugo* by teaching its standard, using colloquial style texts and the language of the middle-class in Tokyo" (Yoshida and Inokuchi 1972, 477).

The textbook placed exceedingly explicit emphasis on "correct" pronunciation. The sounds and vocabulary in the first volume were "carefully introduced in order to make correct" distinctions between certain sounds that were confused in particular dialects, such as between /i/ and /e/, or /shi/ and /su/ in Tōhoku dialect, /shi/ and /hi/ in Tokyo dialect, and /d/ and /r/ in Kyushu dialect. For example, the first sounds in the book were /i/, /e/, /su/, and /shi/, with pictures of a twig [for *eda*], a sparrow [for *suzume*], and a rock [for *ishi*] [for students to recognize the correct sound for each word]—an indication of a thorough and rigorous intention to standardize and unify pronunciation, as Hoshina Kōichi said when he took part in the textbook compilation (Yoshida and Inokuchi 1964, 111).[11]

These radical innovations in textbooks, though criticized by conservatives as destruction of the conventions of the Japanese language, were made possible only when *kokugo* was established as the central concept to integrate them.

Various linguistic problems in Meiji history—script reform, *genbun itchi*, standardization of the language, and so forth—were now subsumed in the idea of *kokugo,* each assigned its place in the nation's language policy making via the Kokugo Investigative Committee. The establishment of the ideal of *kokugo* was the most significant event in the linguistic history of Meiji.

6-5. From *Kokugo* to Imperial Language

The "present-ness" in Ueda's linguistic awareness was founded on the Meiji nation-state. His words—"*kokugo* is the guardian of the emperor, and the benevolent mother of the people"[12]—clearly showed what Ueda expected of *kokugo* in Japan. His theory also reflected his attention beyond Japan, and indicated that he was mindful of modern nation-states in Europe as models. This is why, unlike his predecessors in the field of Japanese language, he was able to begin with a daring argument about the organic relation between *kokugo* and the nation. Another of Ueda's striking ideas was the "Japanization of foreigners in Japan." Unlike the well-worn argument to protect *kokugo* against a threat from Chinese and Western languages, the policy for ethnic assimilation through *kokugo* education could never have been thought of from the traditional view of the Japanese language. Ueda was well aware of the necessity for the assimilation and unification of the people with a national language in order to establish a modern nation-state.

Such identification of the language with the nation took on a new aspect that could have never been imagined in the conventional sense of language supported by literary tradition: advancement of *kokugo* beyond Japan's borders. Ueda opened his 1894 (Meiji 27) lecture "Kokugo kenkyū ni tsuite" (About the Research of *Kokugo*) declaring that the mission of his Kokugo Kenkyūshitsu (Kokugo Research Office) would go beyond just researching the Japanese language of past and present:

> We are committed to improvement and refinement of our language in order not only to create a common language for the entire country, but also to make it the language common for all of Asia, the language that all people must know, as long as they are engaged in Asian affairs of scholarship, politics, and business, whether they are Koreans, Chinese, Europeans, or Americans. (*Ochiai* 1968, 114)

Previously, Miyake Setsurei had recommended taking advantage of "*kanji* as the script of Asia" in order for Japan to control the region, but no one before had ever thought of making the Japanese language the common language for all of Asia. Behind Ueda's idea of *kokugo* as the future common language of

Asia was not the Japanese cultural tradition, but the Meiji nation-state, which was striving for modernization modeled after that of Western countries. That is why an expansion of *kokugo*, an external affair, was considered as a continuing process of the institution of *hyōjungo*, a domestic affair, as clearly stated in Ueda's 1902 (Meiji 35) article "Kokumin kyōiku to kokugo kyōiku" (Education of the People and Teaching *Kokugo*):

> Now we have entered an era when we must work together efficiently and harmoniously at home, and must actively venture abroad, as in the development of China. It will be us, the Japanese people, who will resolve any critical problems in future Asia. . . . It will be worth considering, once we succeed in unifying *kokugo*, its expansion into China, Korea, and India. . . . I think it is our responsibility to seek methods, in whatever country we bring our language and script, to let their people use them. . . . This is an important issue not only for the education of our own people, but further, for the expansion of the language of Japan into the Asian continent. (154–155)

For Japan, a late-player in the competition with the Western powers when they were already at the last stage of dividing their colonies, Asia was the only external land to acquire, the realization of which inspired Japan to seek autonomy from the West and leadership in Asia. When we consider *kokugo* in such a climate, Ueda's concept, in terms of both the unification of the people and overseas expansion, was a masterpiece, born from the core of his idea of *kokugo*, not from political opportunism. This is shown in the following passage, taken from the introduction Ueda wrote for Ōya Tōru's *Kokugo no sogen* (The Origin of *Kokugo*):

> Responding to the Taiwan government-general's invitation, Mr. Ōya is about to devote his energy to the teaching of *kokugo* there. I sincerely wish for him that, with the scholarship and zeal that produced this book, he would transform the current teaching methods in that island. One thing we, the *kokugo* scholars in Meiji, can boast about to those in the Tokugawa era is that we are honored to transplant our sacred *kokugo* onto our new territories. (168–169)

This is an astounding statement. It is not that he was saying that transplanting *kokugo* overseas would be an honor for the nation. He was declaring that it would be an honor for *kokugo* scholarship itself. This indicates that the *kokugogaku*, a newly created scholarship in Meiji, had a political nature from the beginning, not only in its impact on the nation's language policy, but in its theory, method, research objects, and practical goals. This political nature stemmed from the ideology of *kokugo* completed by Ueda, the first realization of which was the *kokugo* education. Therefore, both the standardization of *kokugo* and the language policy for the colonies could coexist under this ideology of *kokugo*. Through *kokugo* education, the tie between *kokugo* and *kokka*, the language and the nation, became accepted in people's linguistic consciousness, and hence a critical dissent never appeared.

In summary, Ueda made a historical contribution in integrating various arguments about language issues in Meiji into an overall framework of *kokugo*. At the same time as his ideology was being constructed, different issues in the standardization and colonization of the language rose to the surface, opening a new stage of *kokugo*. In that sense, Ueda's work came at a historical turning point in the language, from Meiji Japan to imperial Japan. Language issues after this point, therefore, were to take different appearances, raising different arguments about them.

6-6. The Later Years of Ueda Kazutoshi

When Ueda published "Kokugo to kokka to," an epochal article in the history of the concept of *kokugo*, Japan did not yet have a colony. However, the colonization of Taiwan through the Sino-Japanese War and of Korea through annexation meant the end of the era of a one-race family nation, and Japan became a multiethnic nation-state, though not exactly like the Austro-Hungarian Empire, which Ueda had once used as a negative example. How could the Japanese language maintain the status of *kokugo* as "the language of mother," now that it was not the mother tongue of the colonized people? Ueda was put in a sensitive position: one of his main arguments, the equation "*kokugo* = language of mother" was now to come apart.[13] Ueda himself, though, was not very concerned about this equation, as seen in his use of the German word *Muttersprache*, not the Japanese word *bogo* [mother tongue], in his fervent praise of the virtue of the "language of mother." In *Dai Nihon kokugo jiten* (Dictionary of the Japanese National Language, 1915; Taishō 4), which he compiled with Matsui Kanji, there is no entry for *bogo*.[14]

Kokugogaku no jukkō (Ten Lectures about *Kokugogaku*), which Ueda wrote in his later years (1916; Taishō 5), is a very important work in that it explained the methods and objectives of the discipline of *kokugogaku* for general readers, while openly reflecting on how his ideas were concerned with the time. However, we no longer find the same passion he showed in "Kokugo to kokka to": in 1916 he wrote, "It is rather difficult to define the meaning of *kokugo* to respond to every situation." According to Ueda, it was no longer satisfactory to describe *kokugo* as "the language used by the people of one nation" because "there are

Koreans, Ainus, and Taiwan natives in Japan." To justify *kokugo* in relation to their languages, he had to come up with the following explanation:

> The concept of *kokugo* goes with the unified nation, *kokka*. The unified language, *kokugo*, unites spirits of the people and strengthens the fabric of the nation-state. Therefore, *kokugo* has to be the language of the core race among the nation-people, the language that has a power to unite all people. . . . Our Yamato race became the core of the nation in the past and has been maintaining the nation to this day, assimilating different races, and shall continue to do so in the future. . . . Our *kokugo*, over a long time, has adopted and adapted foreign elements, and yet never lost its purity because it never lost the uniting power of the language of the Yamato race, the core race of the country. We cannot stop longing to maintain such uniting power and to preserve the prestigious authority and purity of *kokugo*. (Ueda 1916, 36–38)

This passage implies that Ueda knew very well that the equation "*kokugo* = mother's language" worked only for the Yamato race and that there must be an insuperable divide that separated the ruling race from the ruled. However, such a division was a serious contradiction to Ueda's original intention, as seen in chapter 5, to make language and the nation a natural creation. Bringing consistency to his theory of language while carrying out the demand for colonization and assimilation called for a concept distinct from "*kokugo* = mother's language." This was where Hoshina Kōichi came into play, as will be discussed later, introducing the concept of *kokka-go*, the language of the nation-state—though it did not gain attention at that time.

Regarding the relation between speech sound and script, on the other hand, Ueda's argument remained consistent. "There is no other language in the world like Japanese that has maintained its purity through its speakers even after the nation's opening to the outside world" (21), Ueda affirmed, but he disputed any idea of purity in Japanese script and continued criticizing scholars and writers who valued *kanbun* or those who slighted dialects. He maintained that "the *esprit de corps* of our people comes from the unity of their 'spoken' language" (22) and that "the language lingering in literature is not, other than for scholars, the same *kokugo* as that in the minds of the people" (24). Sound, not script, hence spoken language, not written, was the substance of language. This belief was the backbone of Ueda's idea of language, and it was the basis for his continued rejection of *kanji* and support for *rōmaji*.

> The Japanese language today, even that which is spoken among farmers or vulgar people, is a gift from our ancestors, far more precious than Chinese or Western

words. . . . It would be a most delightful future task for us to support this heritage and spread it to the world as the language of our empire. . . . And it is my wish to abolish *kanji* and treasure *kokugo,* and to present to the world our *kokugo* dressed in *rōmaji.* (185–187)

However, the intellectual climate of that time would not accept such an inventive idea for *kokugo* reform. In spite of his status as the head of the *kokugo* curriculum at Tokyo Imperial University and of the Specialized Academic Office (Senmon gakumukyoku), where he was in a position to initiate *kokugo* policies of the Ministry of Education, his ideas continued to be ignored. Ueda wrote in indignation:

> The Japanese people are extremely indifferent to their own language, which they inherited from their ancestors, received through time, and are themselves using today. In fact, they hardly have any awareness about *kokugo* as members of the nation. (2)

> Even to this day of the Taisho era, Japan's living language is still ignored by its own people, and receives no understanding, protection, or promotion. (5)

According to Ueda, the true form of *kokugo* was the "living language" which was "used currently." But if it received no national awareness, as he lamented, then how could *kokugo* exist? If *kokugo* was only spoken but did not stay in the people's consciousness, it did not deserve its name as the national language. This is why the academic field of *kokugogaku* established by Ueda had to carry out the practical mission to carve out the shape of *kokugo.*

Kokugo no jukkō also shows Ueda's pessimism, resignation, and self-mockery:

> I came back from abroad in Meiji 27, when the war against China began, and the nation's hostility against China was at its peak, creating the best opportunity for an effort to free our language from *kanji* and Chinese studies, and to resolve problems in our language and script. . . . However, this trend turned around at the time of the Russo-Japanese War, especially on our victory, when Japan realized that some Asian products and systems were far superior to those of the West and that Japan should make progress while at the same time guarding these cultures. In other words, the Japanese society and the educational field became reactionary, returning to conservatism. . . . Accordingly, the issues in *kokugo* and script have been overlooked, or rather, have been returned to their state before the Sino-Japanese War, or the time right after the Meiji Restoration. (171–173)

And he concluded the book with a pang of remorse:

> In closing, I would like to add that I was after all a general of the defeated army.
> Or, if "a general" sounds too presumptuous of me, "a soldier" of the defeated. I
> did everything I could do in my time, but society did not always understand my
> approach. I believe, however, that things will be done in the right way in the end.
> I still trust that what I said and did during the fourth and fifth decades of Meiji
> will some day in the future win the battle. (188–189)

What made him call himself "a general of the defeated army"? What did he mean
by the "reactionary" or "conservative" trend? We will look into those questions
through investigating the course of thinking about language after Ueda, especially the direction taken by Hoshina Kōichi, a loyal student of Ueda.

PART III

———

Kokugogaku and Linguistics

CHAPTER 7

Hoshina Kōichi—
a Forgotten Scholar

7-1. From Ueda to Hoshina

In part 2 we saw the effort by Ueda Kazutoshi to build *kokugogaku,* a new academic discipline based on ideas from linguistics, the modern science of language. Ueda's passion and determination produced many brilliant scholars, such as Shinmura Izuru, Ogura Shinpei, Kindaichi Kyōsuke, Hashimoto Shinkichi, Fujioka Katsuji, and Okakura Yoshisaburō. Among them, however, Hoshina Kōichi has been almost forgotten today, in spite of his loyal devotion to carrying on Ueda's achievements in language policy and education.

Let me begin this chapter with a brief chronology of Hoshina's life.

1872 (Meiji 5)   Born in Yonezawa City, Yamagata Prefecture.
1889 (Meiji 22) Entered Dai-ichi Kōtō Gakkō (First High School).[1]
1897 (Meiji 30) Graduated from the Department of Kokubun, Tokyo Imperial University; appointed as an assistant at the Kokugo Research Office founded by Ueda.
1898 (Meiji 31) Contracted as a staff member in the Library Section of the Ministry of Education, engaging in the investigative project for *kokugo kokuji mondai* (issues of *kokugo* and script).
1900 (Meiji 33) Appointed as lecturer at the School of Letters, Tokyo Imperial University.
1901 (Meiji 34) Promoted to assistant professor at the School of Letters, Tokyo Imperial University, and to professor at the Tokyo Teachers' School.
1902 (Meiji 35) Appointed as an alternate member of Kokugo Chōsa Iinkai (National Language Investigative Committee), which started in the same year.
1904 (Meiji 37) Took part in the compilation of the first national textbook by the Ministry of Education.

1911 (Meiji 44)   Assigned to do research abroad about national-language
                  education and language policy in Germany and France for
                  two years.
1913 (Taishō 2)   Returned to Japan in December after Kokugo Chōsa Iinkai
                  was dissolved in June.
1916. (Taishō 5) Appointed as chief of the project Kokugo ni Kansuru Chōsa
                  Shokutaku (Contracted Investigations regarding *Kokugo*)
                  at the Futsū Gakumukyoku (Office of Normal Academic
                  Affairs), Ministry of Education.
1917 (Taishō 6)   Founded and became editor in chief of a monthly journal,
                  Kokugo kyōiku (*Kokugo* Education).[2]
1921 (Taishō 10) Appointed as an executive officer of Rinji Kokugo Chōsakai
                  (Interim Investigative Board for Kokugo), which started in
                  the same year.
1923 (Taishō 12) *Jōyō kanji hyō* (List of Characters for General Use) published.
1924 (Taishō 13) *Kanazukai kaitei an* (Proposal for Revision of *kana* Usage)
                  issued.
1927 (Shōwa 2)   Resigned from Tokyo University.
1930 (Shōwa 5)   Appointed professor at Tōkyō Bunri Daigaku (Tokyo
                  University of Letters and Science); appointed an executive
                  officer of Rinji Rōmaji Chōsakai (Interim Committee for
                  Investigation of Rōmaji), which started in the same year.
1931 (Shōwa 6)   Interim Investigative Board for Kokugo published modi-
                  fied version of *Jōyō kanji hyō* and *Kaitei kanazukai* (Revised
                  Kana Usage).
                  Gave a lecture for the emperor on issues of *kokugo* and
                  script (June 18).
1934 (Shōwa 9)   Appointed as an executive officer of Kokugo Shingikai
                  (Deliberative Council on Kokugo), which started in the
                  same year.
1937 (Shōwa 12)   Ministry of Education promulgated *Rōmaji tsuzuri hyō*
                  (Phonetically Oriented System of Romanization) based on
                  the report from *Rinji Rōmaji Chōsakai*.
                  Kokugo Shingikai published *Kanji jitai seiri an* (Proposed
                  Modifications to the Form of *Kanji*).
1940 (Shōwa 15)   Retired from Tokyo University of Letters and Science;
                  awarded emeritus professorship.
1941 (Shōwa 16)   Appointed chief secretary of Kokugo Shingikai; stayed in
                  the position through World War II.

1942 (Shōwa 17) Kokugo Shingikai published *Hyōjun kanji hyō* (List of Standard *Kanji*), infuriating ultranationalists.
1955 (Shōwa 30) Died.

Hoshina may be remembered today only as someone who proposed *kokugo* reform early on and tried hard to see its institutionalization before World War II, the result of which we see today in *Gendai kanazukai* (Modern *Kana* Usage) and *Tōyō kanji hyō* (List of *Kanji* for Everyday Use). Yoshida Sumio, who had long worked for *kokugo* reform under Hoshina, praised him as one "who devoted his life to the groundwork [for the reform]" (see Yoshida 1975), the groundwork that finally resulted in the realization of *kokugo* reform after World War II.

Beginning with his appointment by the Ministry of Education in 1898, Hoshina consistently advocated the adoption of the phonetic way of writing *kana,* the reduction of *kanji* with a view toward its ultimate abolition, and the use of colloquial language in public sectors. That is, he loyally, even to a fault, adhered to Ueda's wish to put all these measures into practice. Hoshina's persistence enraged the conservatives, who clung to the canonical "tradition of *kokugo,*" which we will discuss later in detail.

We may say that Hoshina represented an archetype of a *kokugo* reformer. Therefore, assessments of Hoshina's work split depending on how the reform was viewed after the war. Proreformers deferentially remembered Hoshina as a "long-term, hard worker at the Kokugo Section of the Ministry of Education, who supported, as chair, all the tasks of the Committee for Investigation of Kokugo" (Ōkubo Tadatoshi 1978, 43). On the other hand, those who viewed the simplification or rationalization of *kokugo* and script as "a destruction of the tradition of our race" labeled Hoshina "a troublemaker, who stayed on in the Ministry of Education trying to railroad unilateral ideas through the national project called *kokugo* reform" (Sugimori 1983, 106). Such a split indicates a serious question in the history of the modern Japanese language: how did the Ministry of Education, which led educational policy before the war, store the seeds for the postwar *kokugo* reform?

As indicated by the title of his memoir published after the war, *Kokugo mondai 50-nen* (Fifty Years of *Kokugo* Issues), Hoshina's work itself chronicled Japan's *kokugo* politics before the war. In reality, however, every one of his works and plans was thwarted in his time. It was only after the war that the *kokugo* reform that Hoshina had been pushing started to move forward. Yet Hoshina seemed fairly content and proud of the fact that his work had ushered in the realization of the reform. He recalled this feeling of satisfaction:

It was my conviction that reduction of *kanji,* revision of the *kana* system, and promotion of the colloquial style were the most important issues in *kokugo,* and that without resolution of these issues it would be impossible to catch up with Western civilizations. Even though I was eager to move towards these goals, I also knew that these problems were too difficult to be resolved in my lifetime. Therefore, it was quite a revelation to me, like a dream, to learn that the new constitution, reflecting dramatic changes in the international situation, was drafted in a colloquial style following the *Tōyō kanji hyō.* . . . The reform had no longer happened only in my dream but in my lifetime, and I was speechless with joy. (Hoshina 1949a, 1–2)

It might be fair to say that Hoshina planted the seeds for democratizing *kokugo,* but that in itself is hardly reason enough to reevaluate the meaning of his work, which was limited by the narrow perspective of the postwar *kokugo* reform.

As noted before, the seeds for the postwar *kokugo* reform had been sown in the Ministry of Education before the war. Therefore, postwar *kokugo* reform was not forced by the occupation army, nor was it necessarily the result of the democratic power that had been suppressed until after the war. It was rather a realization of the plans that the reformists among the bureaucrats had already drawn before the war.

It would be too simplistic to characterize Japan's social order before the end of the war as fascist under the imperial order, since there were various competing powers in the society. In the field of language, also, the conservatives and the reformists were in constant battle regarding the problems and policies of *kokugo.* The conservatives identified *kokugo* with *kokutai* (the national polity) and attacked *kokugo* reform as an antinational scheme. In that sense, they were ultranationalists. It was not these conservatives but the reformists who felt an urgent need for language policies. The first point of conflict had to do with the domestic policy on language. For the conservatives, the central idea of *hyōjungo* came from the traditional written language, and they stubbornly refused to consider *kokugo* at the level of spoken language. The reformists adhered to their claim to make spoken language the *hyōjungo* and insisted that education promote the changeover from dialects to *hyōjungo.* If *kokugo* were found only in the traditional written language, it would have been enough for it to be learned by only a small group of highly educated people. However, if the model was sought in the daily spoken language, it became necessary to develop policies to control various linguistic behaviors of speakers. Thus, the rigorous *hyōjungo* education, symbolized by its "penalty system,"[3] came from the reformists' aggressive attempt to accomplish *kokugo* reform rather than from the conservatives' reverence for *kokutai.*

A more serious contention between the conservatives and reformists occurred around language policies for the colonies. The conservatives did not find such policies necessary. All that mattered to them was to observe tradition in the linguistic forms of the "Japanese race"—though nobody has yet defined this concept—and it was not their concern how other people used the language because such use couldn't affect its essence. For the reformists, on the other hand, the expansion of the Japanese language overseas entailed that non-Japanese people were to learn it; hence, the direction of language policy in the colonies was vitally important for the future of the Japanese language. Thus it was the reformists again, not the conservatives, who took great pains to work on language policies in the colonies. After the war, the conservatives/ultranationalists lost their power almost entirely, but the reformists in the government, represented and led by Hoshina, almost all survived in spite of the military defeat, as expressed in Hoshina's recollections above.

7-2. *Kokugo* and the Colonies

While he was the front man to be challenged by the conservatives regarding domestic language issues, Hoshina was anxiously striving after language policy for the overseas colonies, Manchuria, and the Greater East Asia Co-Prosperity Sphere. He aimed to expand the domination of the Japanese language by assimilating different ethnic groups in the colonies. His argument for this was a typical representation of linguistic colonialism, which will be further discussed later. For Hoshina, domestic *kokugo* reform and language politics overseas were inseparable, or rather, ultimately complementary as prerequisite to each other. We cannot be reminded enough that it was not the conservatives who pressed the "tradition of *kokugo*," but the reformists like Hoshina who asserted and tried to justify the consistency and integrity of the language policy for the colonies. Moreover, it would be one-sided to discuss Hoshina only as a spearhead of postwar *kokugo* reform based merely on the technical aspects of the reform. Such a course of discussion is one of the common symptoms of amnesia that postwar Japan seems to suffer from: Japan, after the war, swept from its memory many truths about its domination of the colonies. In the sphere of language, the major interest in *kokugo* and *kokuji* after the war centered on the use of *kana* and *kanji*, solely at the level of the writing system, as if no other concerns had ever been involved. In that sense, the postwar discussion about these language issues has been more insensitive or even deceptive than before the war. Hoshina seems to have had accurate foresight about the future of the Japanese language, anticipating, for example, the recent sensational "internationalization of the Japanese language." In any case, various issues surrounding Japan's linguistic colonialism, without receiving serious examination, were buried in complete oblivion in the nation's subconscious, together with the memories that could jeopardize the nation's identity—though the memories might still come back once the jeopardy is removed.

In the above chronology, Hoshina might appear as a typical bureaucrat in education politics. He promptly responded to each political situation of the time, working on language policy with every step the Japanese Empire made towards the "annexation" and colonization of Korea, the founding of Manchuria, and the declaration of the Greater East Asia Co-Prosperity Sphere. However, Hoshina's work, in spite of its complete lack of a critical spirit, had some nonpolitical emphases that deserve reevaluation. For the theory of language policy in the field of sociolinguistics, Hoshina is an interesting research object, and some of his works even seem to have predicted the state of today's scholarship in sociolinguistics. His work, under its pedestrian guise, is too complex to be reduced to "typical bureaucratese."

When we consider the above context, the scope of *kokugo* and *kokuji* issues in the conventional sense, which focuses only on *kanji* and *kana* usage, is obviously too narrow. Or rather, it was the people's sense of *kokugo* after the war that limited it. It is more important in order to analyze Hoshina to investigate the linguistic consciousness that shaped those language problems into a whole rather than examining each one separately. Further, we must investigate linguistic consciousness in modern Japan with Hoshina as an agent, placing it in a historical and philosophical perspective. Such an approach is necessary because Hoshina's activities as a language policy maker were closely tied to his work as a *kokugo* scholar. Ueda handed him down two missions: the construction of the science of *kokugogaku* and the solid establishment of *kokugo* policy, with no contradiction between the two. It was the academic mission for *kokugogaku* to christen the language of Japan as *kokugo*, the national language, and to offer scientific prescriptions to resolve its problems. We find here the vector from academics to politics.

At the same time, both Ueda and Hoshina believed it necessary for the establishment of *kokugogaku* to standardize *kokugo* itself. In that sense, the *kokugo* policy was not an applied field of *kokugogaku* after its establishment. Rather, without *kokugo* policy, the academic foundation of *kokugogaku* would be in danger, and the unity of *kokugo* would be only a dream. Thus in this case the vector from politics to academics was at work.

The ideology of *kokugo*, constructed by Ueda and promoted by Hoshina, was born out of the conflict between scholarship and politics, and at its birth it sublimated that very conflict. It created a framework in which scientific *kokugo* scholarship and language policy—that is, the sacred and the civil—were to be tightly interlocked. Therefore, mere understanding of *kokugogaku* only on the plane of academic history or of *kokugo* policy only within political science would distract from comprehension of the ideology of *kokugo*. The ideology of *kokugo* as an academic apparatus and as a concept in language politics will become clear only when we pay close attention to the linguistic consciousness underneath the two. Therefore, in this study I will not discuss them separately, splitting the validity of *kokugo* as scholarship and its political efficiency. That is, I am not questioning Hoshina's academic contribution or the actual effect of his proposals for language policy. Rather, I will reconsider the way Hoshina envisioned the *kokugogaku* for the new era and the way his vision led him to propose certain policies as the expansion of an idea about language. From this perspective we may be able to see a condensed manifestation of the problems in linguistic modernity.

I am interested in Hoshina not just to fill in a blank in research history, nor to celebrate this forgotten scholar for his accomplishment. It would be a difficult job to glorify him as a hero, since his writings lack theoretical strength, scholarly elaboration, and engaging energy, and his style and ideas are extremely undramatic. Perhaps this is why Hoshina has not gained the status he deserves in Japanese academic history.

For me, however, as a foreigner, especially as a Korean, Hoshina's ordinariness is the very reason to be interested in him. This is not a paradox. While Japanese studies in Korea have mainly focused on revealing the evil of "Japan's heroes" or on a small number of "conscientious" thinkers, I myself believe that a society's consciousness that has spread and settled deep is constructed by rather ordinary and inconspicuous people, even though not articulated in words. Only ordinary intellectuals such as Hoshina, who do not have intense philosophical struggles or extraordinary foresight, may be able to actually represent the general, average state of a society. More research like mine may help Korean people see Japan as it is without varnish or exaggeration.

"Ordinariness" here refers to the way Hoshina expressed his ideas, and not to their content. Hoshina repeatedly complained volubly that Japan, though modernized, had no introspection about its own language. In the dominant climate of that time, however, where problems of language were slighted, Hoshina was a lonely and even an extraordinary exception. Japanese people have always been interested in topics such as the origin of the Japanese language, the etymology of words, or that recent critics' favorite, the "internationalization of Japanese." However, it is quite bewildering to me that they have always ignored the dangerous roles that language can play in a society. This is reflected in the fact that scholars in the field have disregarded, without serious research, language politicians like Hoshina because he was not a lofty academic scholar—indicating an unchanging climate in the field of language research in Japan.

Additional Note

The first chair of the Kokugo Department of the School of Letters, Tokyo University, was Ueda Kazutoshi; the second was Hashimoto Shinkichi. It is possible, however, that Hoshina would have succeeded Ueda. Kindaichi Haruhiko reports, based on what his father, Kindaichi Kyōsuke, had heard from Hashimoto, as follows:

> Doctor [Hashimoto Shinkichi] was forty-five years old in Shōwa 2 (1927), after his eighteen years as an assistant [to Ueda]. That was the year of Ueda Kazutoshi's retirement, and Dr. Hashimoto was appointed his successor, became assistant professor on February 12, and started to teach in April. He skipped the rank of lecturer. At that time Hoshina Kōichi was a lecturer[4] above the rank of Dr. Hashimoto, who had thought that Hoshina might succeed Ueda. He said that he was ready to turn in his resignation to Ueda if Hoshina was appointed to assistant professor.[5] (Kindaichi 1983, 307)

Kindaichi judged that "the appointment of Doctor Hashimoto to assistant professor was unexpected, as if Ueda did it on a whim" (310).

Hoshina remembered these events differently:

> Mr. Hashimoto had worked loyally for twenty-three long years as a research assistant, and many colleagues were sympathetic to him and critical of Professor Ueda for not promoting him. Some recommended Mr. Hashimoto to be promoted to be the editor of historical documents, but Professor Ueda did not agree to this and did not seem to plan to promote him from the current assistant position. I had been an adjunct assistant professor since Meiji 35 (1902), and Professor Ueda sometimes mentioned that he did not intend to stay until retirement age and that he would hand over his position to me some day. However, I replied to him that even if I succeeded to his position, I would have only four or five years before my retirement, and that I would rather he appointed Mr. Hashimoto as his successor. I expressed my commitment to work at the Teachers' School on improvement in *kokugo* education and solutions to *kokugo* problems. And I was always glad that that was how things turned out at the end. (Hoshina 1952, 62)

As indicated in Hoshina's memoir, it seems that Ueda had a cold side to his personality and rarely confided his real feelings. Therefore, his true intention [regarding his successor] cannot be known.

CHAPTER 8

The History of *Kokugogaku*

8-1. *Kokugogaku* vs. Linguistics

Hoshina loyally followed Ueda's plan to establish *kokugogaku* on the foundation of modern linguistics theories and to apply it in shaping language policy. Though his work in his later years was focused almost solely on practical aspects of education and policy, this came from his desire to realize his earlier ambition for systematic organization of *kokugogaku*. His language policies, though not necessarily elaborate but faithful to Ueda's intention, were based on his understanding of the theoretical framework of *kokugo*. Therefore, before discussing his *kokugo* politics, his strong suit, we will look into the way Hoshina envisioned *kokugogaku* as a field of scholarship. We will first consider the implications of the fact that Ueda created *kokugogaku* by introducing the modern science of language.

Both *kokugogaku* and linguistics are academic fields concerning language. We naturally expect that there should be exchanges between them of information about methods or results of research. We might also assume that *kokugogaku* is the linguistic study of the Japanese language *(nihongo)* as simply one of many languages. However, this is not the case in reality. Even linguistic research on the Japanese language using, for example, the methodology of structuralism or transformational grammar, would not be considered the result of a *kokugogaku* approach. This is not because structuralism or transformational grammar was not the mainstream methodology in the field of *kokugogaku*, nor is it because of the way academic disciplines are partitioned in universities and the academic world. A deep-rooted fear in the field of *kokugogaku* is that a recognition of *kokugogaku* as a subfield applying linguistics methodology to the Japanese language would threaten the academic identity and justification of *kokugogaku*. Theoretically speaking, *kokugo* scholars must be linguists, and some scholars, though very few, like Kamei Takashi, may even

125

reject *kokugogaku* as scholarship.[1] Nonetheless, in their academic tradition and methodology, and even in their inevitable ideological assumptions, linguistics and *kokugogaku* are in opposition and rivalry. Considering this relationship between the two disciplines, we can imagine that it was quite an event, and also the cause of subsequent problems, that Ueda founded *kokugogaku* modeled upon the field of modern linguistics.

As mentioned before, Ueda had developed excellent scholars who produced conscientious work inspired by what they had learned from him, such as Hashimoto's historical analyses of phonology, Kindaichi's research on the Ainu language, and Shinmura's findings about Western scholarship on the Japanese language. They never stopped looking up to Ueda as their teacher. Though they were all called "*kokugo* scholars," they followed the methodology of modern linguistics in Europe. For example, Shinmura said that he was most inspired by Ueda's lecture about Hermann Paul's *Prinzipien der Sprachphilosophie* (Shinmura 1937). Earlier, he had expressed his view about the relationship between *kokugogaku* and linguistics as follows:

> As for the future direction of linguistics, as seen by us who are Japanese *kokugo* scholars today, it is no longer desirable to pursue the fields that had been developed from the old school with the *kokugaku* tradition or from the *kokugogaku* of the old generation with a Chinese-style historical approach. We cannot expect to start the linguistics field [in Japan] without echoing, directly or indirectly, Western approaches to the studies of national languages or general linguistics. (Shinmura 1933, 8)

After Shinmura's generation, however, Tokieda Motoki, for example, who became the third chair of the Kokugo Department of Tokyo University after Ueda and Hashimoto, reflected on his own academic direction in a different way, in his memoir *Watashi no eranda gakumon* (The Academic Field I Chose):

> When I started my major in *kokugogaku* in the university . . . what I heard and read was that the research methods and topics in [Western] linguistics should be the guiding principles in *kokugogaku*. This must have been the right course of study then considering our seniors in the field, such as Professors Shinmura, Kindaichi, and Hashimoto, who were all trained in linguistics. . . . One of the reasons why I became skeptical about modern linguistics came from the old studies about *kokugo* that I started reading at that time. The nature of those studies and their views about language were radically different, which fascinated me. I think that was the time I began to turn against modern linguistics in general, believ-

ing that European scholarship was not the only and absolute model and that European linguistics cannot necessarily be the guiding principle for *kokugogaku*. (Negoro 1985, 423–427)

The relationship between linguistics and *kokugogaku* not only represented the theoretical conflict between the two scholarly fields, but also symbolized the relation between Japan and Europe, that is, between tradition and modernity, the blight on the consciousness of modern Japan. How, then, did Hoshina try to resolve this problem?

8-2. Hoshina's *Abbreviated History of Kokugogaku*

Hoshina entered Tokyo Imperial University in 1894 (Meiji 27), the year when Ueda was appointed professor of linguistics on his return from Europe and began his energetic work. Hoshina's impression of Ueda's lectures was that they were fresh from Europe and fascinating:

Professor's course was Introduction to the History of the Studies of the Japanese Language, starting from Shaku Keichū.[2] As he lectured about the development of these studies, he criticized each scholar's work, and taught us how we should advance scientific research of *kokugo, based on the theory of linguistics.* He shed light on the future direction of *kokugogaku,* and inspired us to explore new research on *kokugo.* (Hoshina 1949a, 5–6; emphasis mine)

Upon graduating from the university in 1897 (Meiji 30), Hoshina was hired as an assistant in the Kokugo Kenkyūshitsu (Kokugo Research Office), which Ueda had just begun, and was assigned to collecting and cataloguing documents and resources about *kokugo.* "Through reading the original works on linguistics or phonetics at that time, I came to realize the shortcomings in the Japanese scholarship in the past, and became even more anxious to build a new *kokugogaku,*" said Hoshina (6).

Hoshina's early works focused on two missions: introduction of Western linguistics theories and chronological organization of the previous works on *kokugo.* He made his academic debut in 1899 (Meiji 32) with *Gengo hattatsu ron,* his abridged translation of Whitney's *The Life and Growth of Language.* Whitney was mentioned earlier as the linguist who disputed Mori Arinori's suggestion to adopt English as the Japanese national language. He has recently been recognized also as the one who inspired Saussure with the idea of "general linguistics."[3] Whitney maintained that linguistic codes were arbitrary and that language was, before anything else, a social institution or convention, and was constantly changing. His ideas on language had a great impact on Hoshina: if language is a social institution depending on the speakers' conventions, what is essential in linguistic activities is not historical background or tradition, but the actual way the language is currently spoken. This recognition of spoken language was the backbone of Hoshina's works, not only in *kokugogaku*, but also in the education and policy of *kokugo*, the recognition of which brought significant consequences, as will be seen later.

Energetically, Hoshina continued introducing theories and methodologies of modern linguistics through works such as *Gengogaku taii* (Outline of Linguistics) in 1900 (Meiji 33) and *Gengogaku* (Linguistics) in 1902 (Meiji 35). The most notable work of his early years was *Kokugogaku shōshi* (Abbreviated History of *Kokugogaku*) of 1899 (Meiji 32), the first chronicle of *kokugogaku* in Japan. In this book, Hoshina divided *kokugogaku* history into five periods and discussed the works of scholars in each period in chronological order: (1) before Keichū, (2) from Keichū to Motoori Norinaga, (3) from Norinaga to Tachibana Moribe,[4] (4) from the end of the Edo era to Meiji 19 (1886), and (5) after Meiji 19. In spite of its title "Abbreviated History," it was a bulky book of 468 pages, and though his writing sometimes tended to be wordy, he wrote in *genbun itchi* style, which was notable and unusual for an academic writing at that time (*Taiyō* 1899, 257).[5] Moreover, it was undeniably a commendable achievement for Hoshina to position and evaluate studies on *kokugo* in their sequential context for the first time.

Nonetheless, Hoshina was not impartial in writing this book; after all, the backbone of his book was his severe criticism of *kokugogaku* of the past. He did not hesitate to begin the book by saying, "In our past, there were very few works that we could call linguistic research in a genuine sense. Most of the scholars seemed to believe that the main goal of research was to study the classics. . . . In other words, we might say that previous studies on language produced hardly any result that could contribute to linguistics today" (Hoshina 1899b, 3–4).

If the *kokugogaku* in the past had made no contribution to today's scholarship, what did it mean to compile its chronology? Hoshina's answer to this was that "we need first to compare our predecessors' works to realities, in order to compensate for their shortcomings in various areas, and thus to elevate the status of *kokugo*" (10–11). That is, his mission in this book was to locate flaws and defects in previous research in a historical context, and that was exactly what he did: he provided a detailed illustration of the dogmatic theoretical foundation, inadequate methods, and limited scope of subjects in the traditional approaches to *kokugo*.

For Hoshina, the compilation of the history of *kokugogaku* was a negative work; that is, it did not produce any scientific truth. Significantly, though, it revealed the darkness that had been dominating *kokugo* research for centuries, and it offered a beam of hope in scientific linguistics:

> There has hardly been any study that could be considered as truly scientific research on language. . . . Previous scholarship in Japan in general was not scientific, and there has been no academic field relevant to *kokugo,* hence incomplete scholarship on *kokugogaku.* . . . During the thirty years after the Meiji Restoration, there have been many great accomplishments in other academic fields, but the field of *kokugo* remains unchanged. . . . It might be still too soon to expect to see the result we hope for only ten years after the new linguistics department was created at the university in Meiji 19, but it is our responsibility to advance research on our *kokugo* with scientific knowledge. (453–456)

Hoshina noted the creation of the Linguistics Department in 1886 (Meiji 19) because it was the year that modern linguistics in Europe was introduced to Japan; hence the *Merkmal* or marking to separate the fifth period from the fourth in his book. However, Hoshina did not say much about "*kokugogaku* in the fifth period," since it had just begun at that time. (As we will discuss shortly, his reason was different from that of Yamada Yoshio, who also wrote a history of *kokugogaku* but kept silent about *kokugogaku* after Meiji.)

8-3. Systematizing *Kokugogaku*

After his work in introducing modern linguistics and a chronology of *kokugogaku,* Hoshina began systematizing the "new *kokugogaku,*" which bore fruit in the publication of *Kokugogaku seigi* (Exposition of *Kokugogaku*) in 1910 (Meiji 43). Though preceded by Kameda Jirō's *Kokugogaku gairon* (Introduction to *Kokugogaku*) by one year, Hoshina's *Kokugogaku seigi* was one of the earliest introductory books published shortly after the establishment of *kokugogaku.* It was a voluminous book of 754 pages, appropriate to its title, *Exposition.* It is written in a verbose but moderate style, typical of Hoshina and contrasting with Ueda's passionate style.

How did Hoshina envision the "new *kokugogaku*" in this book? Rather than examining each of the concrete problems he raised, I will focus our discussion on the two major contributions of his work: providing *kokugogaku* with academic justification as the proper subject matter of linguistics and in doing so, offering critical evaluations of pre-Meiji *kokugo* studies. *Kokugogaku seigi* consists of five chapters: (1) introduction, (2) discussion of *kokugogaku* in the past, (3) discussion of *kokugogaku* in the present, (4) discussion of *kokugogaku* in the future, and (5) conclusion. Hoshina's objective is clearly indicated in the number of pages he allotted to each chapter: while each of chapters 2 and 3 has only about seventy pages, chapter 4 exceeds five hundred pages. For Hoshina, the establishment of *kokugogaku* in its true sense was still a challenge for the future, and to achieve this goal it was essential to clear out the past and to bring the theories of linguistics into *kokugogaku.*

Hoshina pointed out flaws in the goals, methods, and research subjects of previous *kokugo* studies. He dismissed the traditional *kokugogaku* as the "study of the classics" which "attempts to explain the evolution of humanity using ancient language and literature."

> Linguistics is the study of language itself, and therefore, it inevitably has to deal with the origin or formation of language, and its evolution in history, in addition to various linguistic phenomena and their rules. However, the study of the classics is not concerned with these latter aspects of language. . . . Classical studies in our country have gone beyond explaining the evolution of humanity and have endeavored to express the essence of *kokutai,* the national polity, and thus their goal is very different from that of linguistics. (Hoshina 1910, 14–15)

Previous studies paid attention only to the extralinguistic attire, or layers of meaning, that veiled language itself, but the mission of the new *kokugogaku* as linguistics was, as Ueda had urged before, to strip off layers and reveal the reality of language. Note here that Hoshina at that time considered that "the essence of *kokutai*" had nothing to do with language itself. Even though he ended up later connecting *kokutai* to *kokugo,* as in his 1936 book *Kokugo to Nihon seishin* (*Kokugo* and the Japanese Spirit), he never became a linguistic reactionary; in fact, he became the target of criticism by traditionalists who raised *kokutai* aloft above anything else.

Note also that Hoshina's criticism of traditional *kokugaku* was equivalent to the criticism of classical philology by the rising comparative linguists in nineteenth-century Europe: the discovery of "the reality of language" enabled modern linguistics in Europe, especially comparative linguistics, to emancipate itself from philology and to gain recognition as a modern science (see part 2, chapter 4). It was this ideal of modern linguistics that Hoshina loyally followed and that suggested the methodology *kokugogaku* should adopt:

> Linguistics is an academic field of the scientific research of language, and its principles and rules can be applied to analyze a language of any country. Therefore, knowledge of such general linguistics would be useful for most *kokugo* research, and I do not need to offer any more reasons why we need that knowledge. It

would also be desirable that we [scholars] become familiar with Indo-European linguistics, which developed from the study of Indo-European languages. (Hoshina 1910, 340)

He had already emphasized in earlier work that the most important research methods in Indo-European linguistics were historical and comparative (e.g., Hoshina 1900, 8–10), that is, diachronic description of changes in linguistic elements such as phonemes and morphemes, and genealogical study that compares cognates among languages in the same family: "both diachronic and comparative methods are most important for the scientific research of *kokugo*, and without either one of them it would be impossible to fortify the foundation of *kokugogaku*" (Hoshina 1910, 40). Hoshina especially felt a call for *kokugogaku* to create "comparative linguistics in East Asian languages" comparable to the work that had been done for Indo-European languages (Hoshina 1900, 9–10), and this vision inspired those in the field to explore new research. For example, in 1910 (Meiji 43), the same year Hoshina's *Kokugogaku seigi* was published, Kanazawa Shōzaburō published *Nikkan ryō-kokugo dōkeiron* (The Common Origin of the Japanese and Korean Languages)—a book that was later used to foster the theory that Japan and Korea have a common origin, an ideology used to justify Japan's colonization of Korea.

Hoshina's persistent assertion of the need for diachronic and comparative methods implied his critical view of the traditional *kokugogaku*:

> As seen in the studies of poetry and classics, our *kokugogaku* in the past was content with research into the language of the Heian era and before, and there was no need to study the development of the Japanese language after that period or throughout history. Scholars of the classics sought a model of the Japanese language in the ancient language, spent all their energy studying nothing else but that language, and thus neglected historical research. They regarded the ancient language as the model of Japanese, believed it to be far superior to any other language in the world, and argued that it was the source in this divine country. They could not have even dreamt of comparing our language to other Asian languages to find kinships between them. (Hoshina 1910, 84–85)

Establishment of scientific *kokugogaku* meant uprooting various values held by traditional *kokugogaku*. The diachronic and comparative methods, which treated all language phenomena equally in any time or place, would not give any privilege to Japanese, not to mention to the Japanese language at any particular time in its history. Naturally, this was true for all linguistic variations in Japanese.

The narrow scope of research subjects in traditional *kokugogaku* was the consequence of its methodological deficiency, according to Hoshina:

> Looking at the range of *kokugo* that scholars treated as research subjects in the past, it was very narrow. The range of research subjects in *kokugogaku* must be as broad as possible. We must treat all of language equally, regardless of its kind, the time in history it was used, and the region where it was used. Without doing so it will be impossible to fortify the foundation of *kokugogaku*. (141)

From this standpoint, dialects of various regions in Japan became equally important research subjects for reconstruction of the history of the Japanese language, and Hoshina harshly criticized those who attached only secondary importance to dialects. Since "the distinction between *kokugo* and dialects is merely an artificial one based on the degree [of linguistic variation] . . . it is acceptable to call those languages *hōgen* (dialects) in comparison to certain standards. However, it is a grave mistake to name them *hōgen* in order to treat them as if they were incorrect and vulgar languages" (667–668). Written documents were only one type of traces of the language of the past, while a dialect was a "living language" spoken to this day. Since the mission of *kokugogaku* was to scientifically explore language as it is, "if you ask which is the more appropriate data for *kokugogaku* research between the dead and the living languages, the answer is obviously the living one" (732). Not only were dialects important research data, but their linguistic presence was the reality of the Japanese language. "The Japanese language is a collective body of the dialects, and it is not that there is some other special language called Japanese" (731). The above explanation may lead us to ask if the content of *kokugogaku* according to Hoshina was dialectology. We will come back to this question in chapter 10.

Hoshina thus attempted to overturn the assumptions that had supported previous research in *kokugogaku*. However, his determination to depart from the past was not the sole motivation behind his harsh criticism. He was well aware of the ghosts from the past still haunting and distorting the reality of *kokugo*, and therefore, reform in linguistic research and in the linguistic norm were two sides of the same coin for him. Meanwhile, for his opponents also, the inheritance of a conventional approach in *kokugogaku* and the maintenance of the traditional norm were inseparable tasks. We will examine in the next chapter how each of these two parties connected *kokugogaku* and its norm, and as a preliminary we will take a look at another *kokugogakushi*, or a history of *kokugogaku*, in opposition to Hoshina's, since the ways the history was perceived represent different understandings of the linguistic tradition.

8-4. Yamada Yoshio's *Concise History of Kokugogaku*

The first of Hoshina's opponents was Yamada Yoshio and his *Kokugogakushi yō* (Concise History of *Kokugogaku*) of 1935 (Shōwa 10).Yamada defined *kokugo* as "the standard language *(hyōjungo)* of the Japanese nation *(Nihon kokka)*," with the following qualification:

> What I mean by *hyōjungo* here is the official standard language for governing the nation, and it is different from what is commonly called *hyōjungo* [i.e., the Tokyo dialect]. To call the latter *hyōjungo* is misleading, and it should be better called *chūōgo*, the central language. (Yamada 1935, 2)

The "commonly called *hyōjungo*" here refers to the common concept since the time of Ueda and the Kokugo Chōsa Iinkai that "the language of the middle class in Tokyo" was the standard. For Yamada, *hyōjungo* as the essential form of *kokugo* did not have to be in *genbun itchi,* and he decidedly dismissed the view that the spoken language was the essence of language:

> Some scholars have an erroneous opinion about the language that is currently used today, saying that only the spoken language is the living *kokugo* and attaching only slight importance to the written texts. Such a view is a blunder, ignoring culture, the most important facts, and adopting the vulgar tongue as standard. Such a fallacy would do more harm than good to our civilized people, and should not exist. (3)

Yamada also dismissed the approach, like Hoshina's, that described *kokugogaku* history in accordance with the criteria of modern linguistics: "The history of *kokugogaku* is not just a history of the scholarship, but is a portrayal of our people's reflection on our language" (8), and therefore, "we must refrain from applying today's knowledge to its criteria" (10).[6]

Yamada, who found absolute value in the classics, despised scholars from Ueda's school who used linguistics theory as the guiding concept of *kokugogaku*. His reaction, as noted above, was typical of the hostility that philologists had towards linguistics. Yamada's *Kokugogakushi yō* did not contain the history of *kokugogaku* after Ueda, and did not even mention Ueda's name. While Hoshina was looking to the future of *kokugogaku*, Yamada recounted only the history of *kokugogaku*. This was not because his academic solidarity led him to refrain from historical judgment about contemporary scholarship, but because he considered, as he wrote in the introduction to *Kokugogakushi yō,* that "the current *kokugogaku*" was not authentic since "it aims at the application of Western linguistics theory to *kokugo,* the theory that was imported in mid Meiji" (Yamada 1935, ii). In his later writing, Yamada confessed:

> I wrote a history of *kokugogaku,* but it covered up to around Meiji 20. I stopped there because *kokugogaku* thereafter came from the wrong source. Until we recognized this mistake, we could not continue writing history, and I would not write it. It was not that I stopped writing for no reason. (Yamada 1943b, 31–32)

Meiji 20 (1887) was the year Chamberlain, Ueda's teacher, wrote *Nihon shō bunten* (Concise Japanese Grammar Dictionary) and when scholarship in linguistics research on the Japanese language had just begun.[7] The "wrong source" of *kokugogaku* after Meiji 20 must refer to the introduction of linguistics as the foundation of *kokugogaku.* Thus Yamada's *kokugogaku* history was built upon his rejection of modern linguistics and further, of the *kokugogaku* that was informed by modern linguistics.

8-5. Tokieda Motoki's *History of Kokugogaku*

Another antithesis of Hoshina's view was found in 1940 (Shōwa 15) in Tokieda Motoki's *Kokugogakushi* (The History of *Kokugogaku*). Tokieda defined *kokugo* as "the language that has the characteristics of the Japanese language *(Nihongo teki seikaku o motta gengo)*" (Tokieda 1966, 3). Against the expected objection to this as a circular argument, Tokieda defended his view as follows: In human science, including *kokugogaku,* in contrast to natural science, "the objects for researchers always appear only in obscure outline" (8). If you tried to shape them into a ready-made foreign system or theory, their true nature might get lost. Therefore, "the task of *kokugogaku,* besides analyses and organization of various linguistic elements, is to clearly define these obscure objects, which are accepted as common sense" (7). One must first "discern the truth of the objects," and "work towards the goal of *kokugogaku* through constant improvement of our discernment" (8). Thus, "what we need is not a theory for organization, but an eye to discover [the truth of] *kokugo*" (10).

According to Tokieda, this should be the approach taken when evaluating *kokugo* research in the past: "The importance of the previous research depends on how closely it looked at *kokugo,* not on how theoretically complete it was. . . . The history of *kokugogaku* before Meiji was the evolution of the scholars' consciousness about *kokugo*" (11). The criterion was "the evolution of consciousness," not "theory"; it was impossible to make judgments according to modern linguistics, an external criterion—this was what Tokieda intended to assert.

In the passage below, though without mentioning his name, Tokieda flatly rejected Hoshina's view that held Western linguistics theory as the ultimate:

> Our *kokugogaku* of the past, however, was reconsidered after Meiji only in terms of theoretical criteria and was attacked for its lack of theory and organization and rejected as worthless. Many scholars believed that the *kokugogaku* of the past would be useful today in that they could correct previous mistakes in reference to modern linguistics theory. That is, the history of *kokugogaku* had a raison d'être merely as a corrective for the future. I dismiss such views entirely, and consider the history of *kokugogaku* as that of the evolution of consciousness about *kokugo*. Furthermore, I see it as a foundation stone for future *kokugo*, because I believe that the history of *kokugogaku* in itself is the reflection of phenomena in *kokugo*. (12)

Tokieda's view of *kokugogakushi* as "the evolution of consciousness about *kokugo*" originated with his graduation thesis, "The Evolution of the Views on Language in Japan, and Goals and Methods of Research: Before Meiji." It is said that Tokieda used only Hoshina's *Kokugogaku shōshi* (Abbreviated History of *Kokugogaku*, 1899) and Chō Renkō's *Nihongogakushi* (History of the Studies of the Japanese Language, 1908) as references, since the objective of the thesis was not to analyze primary sources (Negoro 1985, 50). Tokieda, nonetheless, drew conclusions about *kokugogakushi* that were completely opposite Hoshina's. While writing the rejection above, Tokieda must have had Hoshina in mind and his contention that studies on language in Japan in the past produced hardly any result that could contribute to linguistics today.

As indicated in his above comment, Tokieda saw the studies before Meiji as a foundation for future *kokugogaku*. He criticized *kokugogaku* after Meiji for not nurturing "the eye to look at *kokugo*" while blindly following modern linguistics from Europe and hastily importing its methodology, which could never be the foundation of *kokugo*. Therefore, "the new *kokugogaku* must inherit the consciousness about *kokugo* in the past and be built on its theoretical development" (Tokieda 1966, 12–13).

More definitively, Tokieda concluded that the view of language in modern linguistics itself was wrong. Tokieda understood that modern linguistics examined language as a concrete "thing" existing outside human beings, and that therefore language was a tool, like a shovel or a hoe. The only method of research was to break down language into its smallest units and to observe how they fit together. With this understanding, Tokieda persisted in criticizing the instrumentalism and structuralism in modern linguistics, leading him to offer a competing theory, the theory of language as process *(gengo katei setsu).* Here Tokieda describes the complex relationship between linguistics and *kokugogaku:*

> From what we have seen, we can even say that the *kokugogaku* of the past was founded on a more scientific spirit than the post-Meiji *kokugogaku,* which borrowed Western scientific theory. If we blindly fall for Western theory without standing on such a scientific spirit, linguistics can become not only an alarming example, but also even a huge obstacle for the independent development of *kokugogaku.* (13)

For both Yamada and Tokieda, the history of *kokugogaku* was simply a history of the evolution of consciousness about *kokugo.* This does not qualify them as historicists, however, because they failed to understand the Ueda-Hoshina view of *kokugo* within the historical context of the national consciousness and instead unilaterally rejected it as heretical. Yamada and Tokieda, too, used an absolute criterion to judge history; in their case, it was "tradition."

CHAPTER 9

Tradition and Reform
in *Kokugo*

9-1. Linguistics and *Kokugo* Reform

Saussure's posthumous *Cours de linguistique générale* (1916) is widely regarded as providing the revolutionary basis for the science of language in the early twentieth century. Saussure began by surveying the history of linguistics, distinguishing three stages: first, the study to construct "prescriptive grammar" to teach "correct" language; then philology for deciphering documents and interpreting the literature of the past; and finally, nineteenth-century comparative linguistics, which dealt with languages as they are. He proposed, furthermore, advancing linguistics to the study of *langue,* the synchronic state of language, which is free from history and norms. Though it is clear to scientific linguists today that they must eliminate norms from their approaches, up until half a century ago such an idea was extremely radical. Even today, among teachers of standard languages such as *kokugo* or foreign languages, there is strong resistance and even hostility to the science of linguistics that detaches itself from norms.

Concerned about such antipathy among teachers of the English language, Charles C. Fries (1887–1967), an eminent linguist and scholar of English-language education, wrote *Linguistics and Reading* (1963) to "help to dispel the 'image of the linguist' as one who devotes himself primarily to the destruction of all the qualities that make for precise and full expression—an irresponsible speaker of the language for whom 'anything goes'" (Fries 1963, ix). Fries explained that such intolerance for linguists came from a lack of correct knowledge about the field of modern linguistics and that "linguists have abandoned these conventional views *not because of any deliberate purpose on their part to oppose the conventional views* but because their use of the newer methods of language study forced them to conclusions that made the traditional views of language untenable" (37; emphasis mine).

Those who introduced the idea of "modern linguistics" had to play the role of either an agent for enlightenment or an apologist for compromise, as Fries did. For Hoshina, however, the denial of convention was not just a natural consequence of scientific pursuits. He attempted, with "deliberate purpose," to draw a norm from linguistics itself in order to overturn conventional views. It was not because he was involved in language policy, nor was it because of his obligation as an education bureaucrat. It was because the science of linguistics itself had an ideology that even an ordinary scholar like Hoshina was able to infer.

In exercising *genbun itchi* Hoshina was the most stubbornly serious among Ueda's followers who shared the conviction that the language currently spoken was the real form of *kokugo* and who actively used *genbun itchi* style in *Gengogaku zasshi.* His tenacity, however, also exposed the shortcomings of *genbun itchi,* that is, the tendency to be verbose and monotonous. It is this stylistic problem, not the content itself, that made Hoshina's writing, however pioneering it might have been, soporific and lacking in the power to attract people's attention to his ideas.

In addition to the *genbun itchi* style, Hoshina practiced in his writing a very radical phonetic usage of *kana,* which he believed represented most closely the actual pronunciation of the spoken language. The *kana* usage he adopted was not always consistent in his writings, not because of any arbitrary choice of *kana* as he wrote but because he readily adopted the most recent *kana* usage every time it was updated by the committee he belonged to at the time. In that sense, Hoshina's works, in both their content and style, showed the direction *kokugo* reform was taking. For example, the *kana* usage regulated in the Elementary School Order (1900; Meiji 33) was adopted in his *Kokugo kyōjuhō shishin* (Guidelines for Teaching *Kokugo,* 1901; Meiji 34) and *Gengogaku* (Linguistics, 1902; Meiji 35); its revision reported to the Ministry of Education by the Kokugo Chōsa Iinkai (1905; Meiji 38), in his *Kaitei kanazukai yōgi* (Summary of Revised *Kana* Usage, 1907; Meiji 40); and another revision published by the Rinji Kokugo Chōsa Iinkai (Interim National Language Investigative Committee, 1924; Taishō 13) in his *Kokugo to Nihon seishin* (*Kokugo* and the Japanese Spirit) and *Kokugo seisaku* (*Kokugo* Policy) (both 1936; Shōwa 11). However, with each of these publications, Hoshina was attacked by conservatives who obstinately insisted that *rekishiteki kanazukai* (the historical *kana* usage) was the only legitimate usage faithful to the sacred tradition of Japan, and they made Hoshina retreat into the historical *kana* usage in his *Kokugogaku seigi* (Exposition of *Kokugogaku,* 1910; Meiji 43) and *Daitōa kyōeiken to kokugo seisaku* (The Greater East Asia Co-Prosperity Sphere and *Kokugo* Policies, 1942; Shōwa 17). We will come back to this subject later.

The first of the above examples of *kana* usage, adopted in Hoshina's works in 1901 and 1902, was commonly known as *bōbiki kanazukai* because of the peculiar use of the length mark, "–," which was likened to a *bō* (stick) for prolonged vowels. In addition, this system aimed at a radical phonetic usage of *kana,* such as writing palatalized sounds in smaller letters,[1] and the abolition of the differentiation in *kana* between sounds that had lost their distinctive pronunciation. For example, か (/ka/) merged former くわ (/kwa/) and か (/ka/), が (/ga/) merged ぐわ (/gwa/) and が (/ga/), じ (/ji/) merged ぢ (/dzi/) and じ (/ji/), and ず (/zu/) merged づ (/dzu/) and ず (/zu/). This *kana* usage, however, was at that time applied only to the transcription of *on*-reading (Sino-Japanese phonetic reading) of *kanji* and was enforced only in elementary schools. In other words, it was meant to be an educational step for schoolchildren.[2]

Hoshina, however, went ahead and applied this usage to Japanese words even in his technical writings.[3] The preface for *Guidelines for Teaching* Kokugo, though written in a modest tone, showed his determination:

本書わ愚見の存するところに従って、言文一致体お用い、且つ、それ お表音的に表記した。その表記法案わ、新定字音仮字遣の法式お、国 語にまで及ぼしただけで、別に私案わくわえない。

This book is written, with my humble conviction, in *genbun itchi* style using the phonetic system. I extended the new *kana* usage for Sino-Japanese words to Japanese words, but I have no other axes to grind. (Hoshina 1901, 2)

Here he used *wa* (わ) and *o* (お) as phonetically pronounced for the particles that even today's "Modern Usage of *Kana*" distinguishes as *ha* (は) and *wo* (を).[4] As seen in the examples below, his use of the length mark[5] even for native Japanese words was foreign to those who were used to the historical *kana* usage. His phonetic writing of the particles and his use of the length mark appear very peculiar even to us who today use the modern *kana* system:

一体、禁酒禁煙とゆーこと<u>わ</u>出来るが、節酒節煙<u>わ</u>出来ないとおなじ で漢字の節減<u>わ</u>どーも六かしい。従来の障害<u>お</u>、一洗しよーとゆーこ と<u>わ</u>、国語教育百年の大計でない。単に過渡時代における一時の方便 に過ぎないものである。真に国語教育百年の大計<u>お</u>おもーなら、漢字 <u>わ</u>全く廃止してしまわなければならん。

Just as we may "quit" but find it hard to "reduce" drinking and smoking, reduction of *kanji* is a difficult job. The reduction would not succeed as a long-term plan in *kokugo* education to eliminate all the burdens of the past. It is only a makeshift during the period of transition. If we sincerely aspire to a major plan for *kokugo* for the next century, we must abolish *kanji* completely. (134)

言語学 (Science of Language) わ、どーゆー学鐘かとゆーと、それわ言語
とわいかなるものであるかお説明する科学である。それゆゑ、言語学
者わ国語 (a language) お組織する語詞 (words)について、その意義お研究
し、その発達変化等お説明する、任務お有するものである。[6]

To the question, "What kind of scholarship is *gengogaku*, the science of language?" I answer that it is a field of science that explains what language is. Therefore, the task for a linguist is to investigate the meaning of words that comprise a
language, and to explain their development and changes. (Hoshina 1902, 1)

Such an intense drive for reform as Hoshina's moved the Ministry of Educa-
tion to consider extending the application of this phonetic usage of *kana* to
Japanese writing in general, not just to Sino-Japanese words. In February 1905
(Meiji 38), the ministry consulted Kokugo Chōsa Iinkai about the revision of
kana usage, as represented in this statement by the secretary of the Ministry of
Education at that time:

> It is educationally ineffective to limit the phonetic usage of *kana* only to Sino-
> Japanese words and to continue using the old *kana* system for writing native
> words. Therefore, we believe it very reasonable that the educational sectors hope
> to make some revision in the current usage in order to apply it to Japanese native
> words also. (Monbushō 1949, 69)

In response, Kokugo Chōsa Iinkai submitted *Kokugo kanazukai kaitei an* (Proposed Revisions to *Kana* Usage for *Kokugo*) in November of the same year, proposing the adoption of revised *bōbiki kanazukai* for both colloquial and literary
language and extending it to middle school education (73).

The complete phonetic usage of *kana*, which Hoshina had been advocating
for years, was thus about to be realized, and the above proposal was to be put in
practice in elementary schools starting in April 1908 (Meiji 41). Conservative
literati and writers, however, dismissed Hoshina's radical idea and tried to stop
the revision.

9-2. Dispute over the Revision of *Kana* Usage

Because of the conservatives' fierce attacks, the enactment of the proposed revision was postponed one year. To solve the problem, the Ministry of Education
set up the Interim Investigative Committee for *Kana* Usage (Rinji Kanazukai
Chōsa Iinkai) in May 1908 (Meiji 41). Ueda and Hoshina, the most radical
reformists, were not among its members. The ministry's new revision proposal
to the committee included the disuse of the most controversial *bōbiki kanazukai*,

introduced in 1900; overall it fell back on compromise: while it acknowledged the urgent need for a systematic organization of *kana* usage for Japanese words *(kokugo)* as well as for Sino-Japanese words, it "would abstain from enforcing the new usage, allow both old and new usage, and leave them to natural selection" because "the use of *kana* varies depending on the degree of [the user's] education, and should not be rigidly restricted" (Monbushō 1949, 83).

Even this revision was not agreeable to the conservatives, who held the historical *kana* usage to be the only legitimate *kana* usage for *kokugo's* tradition. The above proposal was assented to by a few members of the interim committee, including Ōtsuki Fumihiko and Haga Yaichi, but was savagely opposed by the majority. The best known of the protests was Mori Ōgai's "My Objection to the Revision of *Kana* Usage" (Yoshida and Inokuchi 1964, 553–574), which began, "As you see, I am the only one in this group who is in military uniform." [See Additional Note below.] The committee was not able to arrive at a conclusion, and the ministry withdrew the proposal in September. Consequently, the ministry changed the regulations in the Elementary School Order to disestablish the *bōbiki kanazukai* that had already been in practice in elementary schools and revived the conventional *kana* usage. The committee was disbanded in December of the same year.

This was the context in which Hoshina wrote *Kokugogaku seigi* in 1910 (Meiji 43) in *rekishiteki kanazukai*. Nonetheless, even at such a time, Hoshina continued to argue determinedly against those who had forced him to withdraw the phonetic *kana* usage against his will and practice:

> *Rekishiteki kanazukai* is a rather inconsequential and illogical system in the two-thousand-year-long history of our language. In contrast, the phonetic *kana* usage has been organized according to a rational system as I explained before, and is far more reasonable and simpler than *rekishiteki kanazukai*. Thus it is a far superior system intrinsic to *kana* usage. (Hoshina 1910, 576)

As an executive member of the interim Kokugo Chōsakai and Kokugo Shingikai, Hoshina remained the central figure among the *kokugo* reformists. The revision proposals by those committees continued to show their efforts to promote the principles of phonetic writing, though partly compromising with *rekishiteki kanazukai*. Every proposal, however, was condemned by the conservatives as "a dangerous idea leading to destruction of the history, morality, and tradition of the nation-state" (Takebe 1977, 283). Yet the conservatives' deification of tradition and their incessant attacks could not stop Hoshina from asserting the superiority of the phonetic *kana* usage and his firm conviction derived from modern linguistics theory: "The relationship between language and script is such that language is what is represented by script. Language is the substance and script is its code. Therefore, the essential role of script is to represent language as accurately as possible" (Hoshina 1910, 552).

This view of language naturally led Hoshina to urge the complete abolition of *kanji*, a script that did not represent language as sound and hence violated the basic principle of language. His attitude towards *kanji* is clear in the following passage:

> As we hope for progress in *kokugo* education and the development of the nation, the complete abolition of *kanji* is clearly the most urgent thing to accomplish. Though there are people who oppose this today, I trust that the general drift of affairs will lead us to the complete abolition of *kanji* sometime in the future. (528)

However, as he involved himself in *kanji* issues, he infuriated the conservatives even more than in the case of *kana* usage.

9-3. Yamada Yoshio and the Tradition of *Kokugo*

Ever since Maejima Hisoka had proposed the abolition of *kanji,* problems about *kanji* had been the central issue of debates between the conservatives and the reformists, who both believed that any solution to the problem would determine the future of the modern Japanese language. As mentioned in chapter 6, Kokugo Chōsa Iinkai's decision to "adopt the phonogram" had implied the move towards abolition of *kanji;* most of the proposals for "reduction of *kanji*" before and during the war aimed at ultimate abolition of *kanji,* not at setting guidelines for its maintenance. (In this regard, they were more radical and adventurous than those postwar proposals represented by *Tōyō kanji hyō.*)

The reaction by proponents of *kanji* to such reforms was ultranationalistic or extremely emotional—as it sometimes tends to be even today. Instead of articulating the merits of *kanji*, they rushed to the conclusion that its reduction would imperil the Japanese national polity, the *kokutai.* Such a conflict between the two sides was brought to the boil in June 1942 (Shōwa 17), when Kokugo Shingikai reported its decision to adopt the *Hyōjun kanji hyō.*

The list showed a total of 2,528 *kanji* in three categories: 1,134 *jōyō kanji* (*kanji* of common use), 1,320 *jun-jōyō kanji* (*kanji* of less common use), and 74 *tokubetsu* (special *kanji*). The method of categorization was explained as follows:

> The *jōyō kanji* are those that are most relevant to the people's daily life and have high frequency in general use. The *jun-jōyō kanji* are less relevant than *jōyō*

kanji to the people's daily life, and have lower frequency in general use. The special *kanji* are those used in the texts of the Imperial House Codes, the Imperial Constitution, posthumous names for the emperors, the Imperial Rescript in the national textbooks, the Imperial Rescript for Soldiers in the army and the navy, and the Declaration of War against America and Britain, and they do not belong to the other two categories. (Nishio and Hisamatsu 1969, 308)

When its interim report had been presented three months earlier, Hoshina, who was the chair of Kokugo Shingikai, told the *Asahi shinbun* (April 5, 1942) that the committee intended to reduce the use of *jun-jōyō kanji* gradually with a view towards their eventual elimination.

The conservatives could not possibly accept such a move towards reduction. They were especially enraged by the categorization implying that the emperor's words in rescripts did not belong to *jōyō kanji* and thus were not "most relevant to the people's daily life." Immediately, in July, they sent a petition against the list to the Ministry of Education with twelve signatures including those of Tōyama Mitsuru and Matsuo Sutejirō.[7] Subsequently they gathered not only *kokugogaku* and literary scholars, but also literati from various fields, and formed the Japan Association for Kokugo (Nihon Kokugo Kai) with a showy opening ceremony in October. Overwhelmed by such fanatical opposition, the Ministry of Education published a revised list in December, merging the three categories, increasing the total number of *kanji* to 3,669, and adding an explanatory note that the purpose of the list was not to restrict the use of *kanji*. After that, the Japan Association of Kokugo became inactive, other than its publication of *Kokugo no songen* (The Dignity of *Kokugo*) in 1943 (Shōwa 18), and gradually dissolved (Hirai 1948, 342–359).

Kokugo no songen was a collection of essays that were effusions of rage against the reformists, except for one by Hashimoto Shinkichi, "Kanazukai no honshitsu" (The Nature of *Kana* Usage). For example, Ōnishi Masao's "Nihon kokugo dō" (The Way of Japanese *Kokugo*) criticized the series of *kokugo* reforms since Meiji and glorified "the dignity of *kokugo* as identical with *kokutai*." While he recognized Ueda's assertion of the tie between *kokugo* and the nation-state in *Kokugo no tame* (For *Kokugo*), Ōnishi nonetheless accused Ueda of a "great fallacy in spite of his being a specialist in linguistics and *kokugogaku*" (Nihon Kokugo Kai 1943, 15). For Ōnishi, Ueda's critical view of the state of *kokugo* and his attempt at abolition of *kanji* and adoption of phonetic script were only insults to *kokugo*; the conventions of *kokugo*, its tradition, should not be altered, nay, it was *kokutai* itself that could not be changed. "The reformists' 'regard for *kokugo*,' including Dr. Ueda's, is inclined to be 'disregard of *kokugo*'" (20), and "Mr. Hoshina, the successor of Dr. Ueda" was no exception, wrote Ōnishi, openly attacking Hoshina. "Starting with the Kokugo Chōsa Iinkai of Meiji 33, Ueda-Hoshina theory has been aided by the government for forty-five years through its committees such as Rinji Kokugo Chōsakai and Kokugo Shingi-kai. However, they have borne no fruitful result" (37) because their views of *kokugo* perverted the course of *kokugo-dō,* "the way of *kokugo* with three thousand years of the tradition of the empire." Education in *kokugo,* therefore, must inherit this tradition "as it is." However, "it is undeniable that those committees have indirectly disturbed such truths of education, that is, they were *the disruptive elements in the way of* kokugo, denying 'the way it is' " (54; emphasis mine).

While Ōnishi discussed the external and practical sides of *kokugo* reform regarding *kokugo* policy and education, Yamada Yoshio's essay in the same collection, "Kokugo no dentō" (The Tradition of *Kokugo*), went further and reached the ideological foundation beneath the reform.[8] He begins with the explanation of the root of the problems:

> We must note the following fact. In February of Meiji 13, Katō Hiroyuki, as a member of the Imperial Academy, today's Japan Academy, proposed to *monbukyō* (today's minister of education) the sending of an elite student to Europe to study linguistics, and to have him initiate, on his return, the reform or reorganization, or whatever you may call it, of *kokugo.* This fact cast a shadow over the development of *kokugogaku* in Meiji, and even today. (Yamada 1943b, 8)

Yamada concluded that this exposure to Western linguistics was the source of the problems, a conclusion he reached after tracing the history of *kokugo* reform from the time Ueda initiated Kokugo Chōsakai through the creation of Rinji Kokugo Chōsakai, "which was a joint venture by Mr. Nakahashi [Tokugorō], the minister of education at that time, and his secretary Mr. Minami [Hiroshi], and Mr. Hoshina Kōichi" (12), up to the creation of Kokugo Shingikai, headed by Minami as chair with Hoshina as executive officer. That is, in Yamada's view, "*kokugo* reform" was an unwanted child born of the importation of Western linguistics into Japan. "What Kokugo Shingikai is doing today is not careful investigation of *kokugo,* but is only a continuation of practicing Katō Hiroyuki's proposal for promoting linguistics for what he called the correction or improvement of *kokugo*" (12).

Yamada attempted to disprove completely the ideas inherited from Ueda about *kokugogaku* and *kokugo* policy. That meant he had to refute axioms in two areas: refute in his scholarship the linguistic axiom "Language changes" and disprove in his practice the premise of *kokugo* reform, "Language can be improved." For this purpose, he extracted technical terms in linguistics from their theoretical contexts and used them to suit his argument. For example, he referred to phrases such as the "social significance of language," "historical nature of language," and "objectivity of language" to argue that language should not and could not be altered arbitrarily according to the needs of individuals or of the times in which they lived. Yamada must have misunderstood, or intentionally ignored, what Whitney and Saussure meant by "language is a social institution, or *fait social.*" Such a distorted interpretation of Western linguistics theory fed into the obsession in the *kokugogaku* field with "tradition," the rhetoric that disguised any theoretical inadequacy and contained any contradictions:

> The authenticity of *kokugo* is nothing else but tradition. This is a universal truth in every language in the world. Therefore, the idea of manipulating *kokugo* for convenience, ignoring this tradition, is rooted in an *extremely frightening ideology.* Those who are engaged in such ideas may not be even aware of this, but any loyal citizen of our Great Japanese Empire must not even dream of slighting our tradition, must not he? (26; emphasis mine)

What did he mean by the "frightening ideology"? He meant that disregard of the tradition in *kokugo* could entail denial of the nation-state and, moreover, of *kokutai*. In other words, Yamada saw the scholarship founded on modern linguistics as a "frightening" anarchy, something that must not exist. He had already expressed his concerns a few years before in his *Kokugogakushi yō* (Concise History of *Kokugogaku*):

> Today's *kokugogaku,* since its importation in mid-Meiji from Western scholarship, aims at explaining *kokugo* according to this [foreign] theory. . . . [The scholars'] infatuation with the Western theory led them to focus only on *go,* "language," and to lose their awareness of *koku,* "the nation," of the national language, *kokugo.* Thus, today's academic field of *kokugo* has mostly regressed to a scholarly preoccupation with no reference to the nation. (Yamada 1935, ii–iii; emphasis Yamada's)

Yamada's words in *Kokugo no honshitsu* (The Essence of *Kokugo*) show the dogmatic grounds for his dismissal of this "frightening" linguistics—the dogma that tied the tradition of *kokugo* to the sacred unbroken imperial line that could not be disturbed:

> The true and pure *kokugo* we use in our daily life is believed to have come from the same origin as the nation. (Yamada 1943a, 43)

In short, *kokugo* is one and eternal, and transcends absolute time throughout history. (81)

Kokugo is inhabited with the spirit of the nation, is the treasure-house of the spiritual and cultural heritage our people have shared, and is the only medium through which we bequeath our tradition from past to present and to the future. (52)

The nation's life is eternal and transcends an individual's life, and it dwells in education. (63)

The *kokugo* we have today is the fruit of the history of Japan. Therefore, the spirit of the nation runs through *kokugo*. . . . We become one and together with our ancestors through *kokugo*. (80)

Our ancestors' precious blood runs through *kokugo,* and the people's spirits reside in *kokugo*. Therefore, any modification of *kokugo* means alteration of the Japanese way of thinking and the Japanese people's spirit. Such an attempt deserves to be called madness. . . . [The *kokugo* reform] is a blasphemy to our nation. (83)

Since its origin, through generations without any revolution, our nation and people have never experienced drastic changes in our language. Thus, our authentic *kokugo* is believed to share its origin with that of the nation. (105)

The point is, *kokugo* is a spiritual and cultural inheritance from our ancestors, and it stirs up in our descendants and us the same excitement and inspiration as it did in our ancestors' blood. *Kokugo* has the power to unite people's hearts today, and at the same time to unite their hearts with their ancestors through time. (112)

I could continue with similar citations from Yamada's writings. His logic, though it might sound impartial at first, goes around in circles, reciting the same chanting, like intoning a Shinto prayer: the unity of *kokugo* and *kokutai*.

For conservatives such as Ōnishi and Yamada, Ueda and Hoshina were the radical leaders of those who believed in the "frightening ideology," even though Ueda had advocated the Japanese language as the symbol of the nation and Hoshina had shaped language policy that compromised with the principles of linguistics. Thus, the conflict between the conservatives and the reformers did not come from different degrees of their veneration or devotion to the nation and the emperor. Rather, it was rooted in the ideological differences between *kokugogaku* and linguistics.

Neither should we shrug off Yamada's assertions as merely extreme rhetoric provoked by heated moments during wartime. His reaction came from his intuitive alarm that *kokugogaku* as a branch of linguistics and a *kokugo* policy for reform would feed off each other and move towards defiance of the "tradition of *kokugo*." This intuition was further refined by Tokieda Motoki, who might be called the "emperor of the postwar *kokugo* field."

9-4. Tokieda Motoki and the Theory of Language as Process

Tokieda's view of *kokugo* was not entirely the same as Yamada's, and sometimes even in sharp contrast to it. For example, Yamada insisted that *kokugogaku* was a name for research done only by Japanese people on their own language and did not include foreigners' study of "our *kokugo*" (Yamada 1935, 5). Tokieda argued against this view, asserting that "even if there was a disjunction between research by Japanese scholars and that done by foreigners, it comes from their different approaches, and we cannot say one is *kokugogaku* and the other is not" (Tokieda 1966, 5–6).

Tokieda also criticized Yamada's concept of *kokugo* as "the model language of the Japanese Empire." He maintained that the concept *kokugo* had to be defined based on its internal linguistic characteristics and not on external realities such as nations or races. "*Kokugo* as the object of *kokugogaku* must be considered the synonym of *nihongo*. Our practice of calling it *kokugo* or *kokugogaku* and not *nihongo* or *nihongogaku* is only for the convenience of us who were born in Japan and speak the language. Strictly speaking, we should adopt the terms *nihongo* and *nihongogaku* and save the term *kokugo* for other occasions" (5). But in spite of his own words, Tokieda himself never used this "strict" academic term *nihongogaku* after making the above statement, and used *kokugogaku* without explaining why. My suspicion is that Tokieda was afraid that the use of the term *nihongogaku* would instantly suggest a particular field of linguistics. He adhered to the use of the term *kokugo* as a proper noun, but not because of his individual conviction. Why deny *nihongo* and adhere to *kokugo*? We will come back to this question.

Tokieda was no less critical than Yamada of the application of the methods of Western linguistics to the Japanese language, though his argument was more elaborate than Yamada's and more intrinsic to the nature of language. He dismissed what he called the "constructional view of language," which objectified language as an entity that existed external to human beings, and he maintained that language was not a tangible entity, but a psychological process embedded in the physical activities of speaking, listening, writing, and reading, and the subjective activities of expression and comprehension. This definition of and approach to language was the basis for his famous *gengo katei setsu*, the "language-as-process" theory. The most characteristic claim in this theory was that a "subjective standpoint" was required of linguists who observe language; that is to say, an "objective" observation of language could not explain its essential nature.

All forms of language are subjective activities. Observation and explanation of them will be possible only through reproduction of them in the observer's own subjective activities. It is unacceptable to reverse the subjective and the objective merely for purposes of convenient research. We must grasp and describe this subject as a subjective thing. (1941, 15)

Tokieda affirmed that the sole method in language research was to investigate the speaker's subjective linguistic consciousness. If he was right, then *kokugo* researchers also needed to share the speakers' psychological experience, and then they would be able to "reproduce" the psychological process in *kokugo.* If that was the case, however, how could foreign researchers, who did not live in *kokugo,* investigate *kokugo* according to this language process theory? While acknowledging *nihongo* as a preferable academic term to *kokugo,* his methodology made Tokieda slide into a contradiction and confined *kokugo* and its research to a closed world.

It is well known that Tokieda, in his *Kokugogaku genron* (The Principles of *Kokugogaku,* 1941), harshly criticized Saussure's theory. Though his argument was not entirely relevant because he used an inadequate Japanese translation of *Cours de linguistique générale* and interpreted it arbitrarily, it is nonetheless worthwhile to compare these two linguists. Although both considered "the speaker's consciousness" as central to the investigation of language, they were quite dissimilar.

Saussure paid attention to "the minds of speakers" because he was interested not in the actual content of their minds, but in extracting formal conditions that constituted their state of mind. With this as a starting point, he refined his theory to reach the concept of *langue,* the language as collective symbol, and further, the language as a system of semiological values. In doing this, he had to rule out script, diachrony, and normatism: A linguist "can enter the mind of speakers only by completely suppressing the past. The intervention of history can only falsify his judgment" (Saussure 1966, 81). It was such strict asceticism that led Saussure to discover the synchronic system *langue.*

Tokieda, on the other hand, identified language with the content itself of the process in the speaker's mind, thus including normatism and diachrony in the nature of language. But this process in a speaker's mind does not allow critical analysis, because once the process is objectified for analysis, it needs an "observer's standpoint." Thus, the "subjective standpoint" in Tokieda's terms does not demand a careful, critical view of language, but rather entails a passive acceptance of linguistic conventions and norms.

Tokieda's point of view is most apparent in his position on written language. The modern science of linguistics considered written language secondary to spoken language, or even an obstacle that concealed language itself. Tokieda argued, however, that "the value and art" were the intentional and conscious acts of a linguistic subject and were "the most fundamental elements of language" (Tokieda 1941, 105). The "value" in Tokieda's sense referred to the speaker's judgment about the appropriateness of linguistic expressions, and "art" to the speaker's deliberate practice of selecting or refining them. According to this view, spoken expressions alone did not constitute language; script, which was an intentional expression informed by extralinguistic tradition, was an equally essential element of language. Thus Tokieda's theory incorporated the peculiarity of the written language into the essence of language and legitimized the use of *rekishiteki kanazukai* and *kanji* as the "value and art" that were intrinsic to *kokugo*.

Tokieda's stance was firm even after the war, as seen in his essay "Kokugo kihan ron no kōsō" (Outline of a Normative *Kokugo*) in 1947 (Shōwa 22):

> As the foundation for diachronic analysis of *kokugo,* a lasting issue in *kokugogaku* since Meiji, I strongly feel that an examination of a speaker's sense of norm is the most urgent requirement. At the same time, I have come to believe that various issues regarding *kokugo* policy and education can be included in the organization of *kokugogaku.* (Tokieda 1976, 36)

The idea of the "norm" was one of the pivotal points in Tokieda's theory, as inherent in the process of a subject's expression and comprehension and at the same time as an object for language policy. For Tokieda, the norm was not secondary to language, not something that surfaces for a speaker when he or she consciously refers to a linguistic system that exists a priori. Rather, "the subject's sense of norm is a part of the facts inherent in the *kokugo* system" (37):

> If we consider language simply as an act of expression, the norm consciousness is the subject's consciousness, not *about* language as material, but *in* language as the act of expression itself. Therefore, the norm must be considered as the foundation of language. To put it strongly, without a subject, or without a subject's sense of norm, language cannot exist. (39; emphasis Tokieda's)

Then what was the significance of the "sense of norm" in *kokugo* policy? In his essay "Reimeiki no kokugogaku to kokugo seisakuron to no kōsō" (Relation between *Kokugogaku* and Theories of *Kokugo* Policy in Incunabula) in 1956 (Shōwa 31), Tokieda wrote that "the current state of *kokugo* is a consequence of the practice of the theory of *kokugo* policy since Meiji and is the result of the distorted connection of that with *gengogaku kokugogaku*" (linguistics theory of *kokugogaku*) (1956b, 233). The unfamiliar words *gengogaku koku-gogaku* probably meant *kokugo* research that was informed by the methodology of modern linguistics. According to Tokieda, such *gengogaku kokugogaku* "was determined to eliminate concepts of elegance or value in *kokugo*," while *kokugo* policy "aimed at establishing the norms for *kokugo* for the future," and thus, these two were "incompatible, like fire and water." Nonetheless, "blind reliance on modern linguistics" led people to a false belief that modern linguistics would be able to guide *kokugo* policy (241).

It is not that Tokieda rejected the connection between scholarship of *kokugo* and practical *kokugo* policy. On the contrary, he believed that accurate *kokugo* theory could and should naturally guide *kokugo* policy and that his theory of language as process was such a theory—because it considered the norm consciousness a part of the nature of language and therefore had the "possibility of subsuming various problems in *kokugo* policy and education into the systematic theory of *kokugogaku*" (1976, 36).

However, the criteria for analysis of speakers' norm consciousness must be completely different from those for setting up a norm for the future. How could the possibility of "establishing a theory of the norm in *kokugo*" (37) in an academic field create "a possibility for setting the right direction of *kokugo* for the future" (41)? Here we are reminded of Tokieda's "subjective position," which rejected the "observational position." That is, Tokieda claimed that the consciousness of a linguist who analyzes language must be a continuum with that of the speakers who use the language in their daily lives. If a speaker is conscious of the norm in actual situations, a linguist should also be able to theorize such consciousness. According to Tokieda, "the norm consciousness of the subject" formed the foundation for the act of communication, and at the same time was the "conservative power" (242) needed to maintain the unity of language and to stop changes in language as a part of culture, and thus supported linguistic tradition. Then a theory of language had no choice but to accept this "conservative power." Tokieda went on to say, "It is nothing but a one-sided opinion that a scientific and progressive theory of *kokugo* policy must accommodate language change" (243). He did not stop criticizing the postwar *kokugo* reform represented by "*kanji* reduction" and the "modern use of *kana*," and we must note that this was also simply another form of his criticism based on his "theory of language as process" directed against modern linguistics.

Tokieda became a member of Kokugo Shingikai after the war, but being extremely dissatisfied with the way the committee was led by the reformists, he resigned from it in 1949 (Shōwa 24) upon its reorganization. The committee continued to be a battlefield for the conservatives and reformists, whose differences erupted at its fifth meeting in 1961 (Shōwa 36): five members, including Funabashi Seiichi,[9] suddenly resigned on the grounds that the committee administration was in tacit agreement with the reformists. The media reported this as a scandal, and the committee deadlocked until the Ministry of Education replaced the former members to begin the sixth committee meeting (Sugimori 1983). Tokieda was asked to return to the committee, but he firmly declined.

Prompted by the above incident, in 1962 (Shōwa 37) Tokieda wrote a book, titled *Kokugo mondai no tame ni* (For *Kokugo* Issues), which clearly explained his view of language, combining his criticism of both modern linguistics and *kokugo* reform. His criticism of postwar *kokugo* reform went as follows: The reform was an extension of the proposals by Kokugo Chōsa Iinkai in Meiji, and it always relied on the theory of modern linguistics; the failure of reform theories in both past and present came from the same failure in modern linguistics theory. That is, the theory of *kokugo* reform was rooted in linguistic structuralism, the erroneous assumption of modern linguistics, which viewed language as a tool, or as a mass of tangible units. The reform disregarded literary language and only considered colloquial language, and it employed in its language policy a one-sided methodology of historical linguistics that paid attention only to language change, creating a standard that slighted literary language and severed convention from tradition.

Unlike Yamada or Tokieda, Hoshina refused to create a unity of *kokugo* by conjuring up "tradition." He did not believe that such a conservative "tradition" could be appreciated by the entire nation's people, since it was a tradition agreed upon among the limited class of intellectuals, especially poets and scholars of ancient Japanese culture. The conservative power of tradition as the norm relied on written language, which contradicted Hoshina's conviction that spoken language was the organic heart of language. The norm he envisioned had to be drawn not from conventions of the past but from current usage of language. Then, however, what he actually had to deal with was the disjointed Japanese language in its many different dialects. The most urgent issue for Hoshina, therefore, was the establishment of the *hyōjungo,* the standard language. In other words, Hoshina's fervent appeal for the standardization of Japanese was another expression of his challenge to tradition.

For both *kokugogaku* and *kokugo* policy in modern Japan, one of the most serious questions was how to find a way to bring unity to *kokugo*. Mori Arinori's bitter realization, noted earlier, that there was no solid unity and autonomy in the Japanese language, therefore, haunted the effort to modernize the Japanese language, part of a nightmare that modern Japan struggled to awake from.

Additional Note

There is a sequel to the episode about Mori Ōgai and *kana* reform. Appointed to the chair for the interim Kokugo Chōsakai in 1921 (Taishō 10), Ōgai returned to work on *kokugo* issues, this time with Hoshina, who was an executive committee member. Ōgai died the following year, but the committee continued to advance the project for *kana* reform, and its proposal was approved at its general meeting in December 1924 (Taishō 13). Ōgai had been known as one of the supporters of *rekishiteki kanazukai* when he was on the Rinji Kanazukai Chōsa Iinkai, and therefore the new committee's decision on *kana* reform stirred speculation about his death: he was so passionately opposed to the reform project that his anger might have hastened his death.

Yamada Yoshio, for example, mentioned in his article protesting against the reform (in *Myōjō zasshi,* February 1925) how much Ōgai had "strained himself over the *kokugo* issues." According to Yamada, the interim Kokugo Chōsakai ignored Ōgai's strong objections to the reform and carried out the project anyway, and it was this reform "that Dr. Mori could not stop worrying about, and that prompted his end" (Yamada 1932, 89–92).

On the other hand, Hoshina's version was completely different from Yamada's. According to Hoshina, Ōgai called him in right before his death and, urging him to start this important reform project immediately, gave him volumes of literature on orthography reforms in Europe. Hoshina took this as Ōgai's bequest to him and followed his wishes soon after Ōgai's death. Therefore, he said, the allegation that the *kana* issue prompted Ōgai's death was "an allegation beyond the pale" that "should be ridiculed" (Hoshina 1949b: 162–163). Hoshina suggested that Ōgai became proreform after the death of Yamagata Aritomo.[10] Yamagata, who was a supporter of *rekishiteki kanazukai,* had been a mentor for Ōgai in the army, where Ōgai was somehow alienated because of his dual status as a surgeon and a man of letters. Therefore, out of obligation to Yamagata, Ōgai did not support the *kana* reform until after Yamagata's death, when he became free to assent to it. Hoshina also suspected that Ōgai's objection had been only to modifications in classical language and that he might have always been in agreement with the reform in regard to modern language (Hoshina, 1952, 237–241).

There is great variance between the statements by Yamada and Hoshina, and we are not able to judge their validity without Ōgai's own testimony.

PART IV

Hoshina Kōichi and
His Language Policies

CHAPTER 10

The Ideology of *Hyōjungo*

10-1. *Hyōjungo* and *Kyōtsūgo*

The term *hyōjungo* seems to carry a special emotional connotation. The institution of *hyōjungo* before the end of the war degraded dialect and afflicted its speakers with a sense of inferiority. Dialect was severely suppressed in schools through "penalty" rules, which mandated hanging a humiliating placard around the neck of a student who used dialect.[1]

The word *hyōjungo* implied a crusade against dialect. Its dark connotations lingered even after the war, and even academic discussions about *hyōjungo* today have to be careful not to summon up the public's neurosis about their experience (Sanada 1987, 203–205). Thus the term *hyōjungo* (standard Japanese) was gradually replaced by *kyōtsūgo* (common Japanese) for the transparent reason of obliterating unpleasant memories.

The *Kokugogaku jiten* (*Kokugogaku* Dictionary) of 1955 (Shōwa 30), the first edition after the war, defines *kyōtsūgo* as "the common language, which can be used for exchanging ideas everywhere in a country," and "*hyōjungo*" as "the ideal *kokugo*, constructed by refinement and control of *kyōtsūgo* according to a certain standard." Therefore, strictly speaking, these two terms refer to different concepts. Nonetheless, *kyōtsūgo* was allowed to replace the term *hyōjungo* for the reasons explained below.

Shibata Takeshi maintains that "the term '*kyōtsūgo*' was welcome because the implication of 'control,' which *hyōjungo* had, fell into disfavor" and that this switch "allowed *kokugo* education to achieve its goal more easily, since '*kyōtsūgo*' merely meant the common language used nationwide, and didn't have to be a specially 'refined' or 'ideal' language" (1977, 23–24). If this was the case, the only reason for the changeover was an extremely practical one, to lower the goal for its easier achievement; that is, *kyōtsūgo* was a step down from *hyōjungo*. Moreover, the thorough dissemination of *kyōtsūgo* was a consequence of *hyōjungo* education since Meiji, only stripping away the connotation of control. The new term concealed the continuity of linguistic institutions before and after the end

155

of the war, diverting people's attention from the problem of linguistic hegemony. Therefore, we must reexamine carefully the ideology of *hyōjungo* rather than rejoicing at the spread of *kyōtsūgo.*

As discussed in section 2 of chapter 6, Ueda was probably the first to use the word *hyōjungo* in its official sense in his 1895 (Meiji 28) lecture "Hyōjungo ni tsukite" (About *Hyōjungo*): the language created by artificial refinement on the one "of Tokyo, the capital of the Great Empire," especially the one "spoken by educated people in Tokyo" (Yoshida and Inokuchi 1964, 502–508). This was the first step towards the centralization of *kokugo.* In 1904 (Meiji 37), the Ministry of Education further defined the term and its usage in *Jinjō shōgaku tokuhon hensan shuisho* (Prospectus for Editing Readers for Normal Elementary Schools) as colloquial language "used mainly by middle-class people in Tokyo," and called for schoolchildren "to learn the standard of *kokugo*" and thus eventually "to bring unity" to *kokugo.* Now the goal of *kokugo* education was clearly to teach children "the standard of *kokugo.*"

How, then, would the dissemination of *hyōjungo* affect regional dialects? And what was the relation between *hyōjungo* and dialects in the unity of *kokugo?* Ueda did not discuss these problems and left them for Hoshina to tackle.

10-2. Dialects and the Standard Language

Each of Hoshina's early works on linguistics and *kokugogaku,* such as Hoshina 1900, 1902, and 1910, contains chapters on the relationship between dialects *(hōgen)* and the standard language *(hyōjungo).* His perspective on dialect was founded on the principles of linguistics that all languages are equal in terms of the complexity of inner structure and that no language is better than or superior to any other. As seen in section 3 of chapter 8, Hoshina defined language as the representation of ideas with phonetic segments, and therefore no dialect "is different from an ordinary language in its form and content" (Hoshina 1900, 161). The distinction between the national language and dialects "is merely a matter of degree, and only made artificially. . . . It is a mistake to label them as *hōgen,* 'dialects,' to treat them as if they are incorrect or vulgar languages" (1910, 667–668).

Then did Hoshina have any rationale for considering certain language as *hōgen?* He used the concept of the "confines" *(tsūyō han'i):* The confines "where a dialect can be used for communication of ideas are far more limited than those for a common language." Because "the role of language" is to "expand the confines of communication," a dialect cannot play this essential role because of the limited size of its confine. "There is no reason to degrade *hōgen* in its form and content, but because of the smallness of its confines, dialects will naturally be avoided, moreover, shall be avoided" (1900, 162–163). Then Hoshina clearly explained the relation between *hyōjungo* and *hōgen* as follows:

> I hope that you understand by now how urgent a task it is to overthrow *hōgen* in order to bring unity to *kokugo*. This task may be naturally accomplished to a certain extent as our civilization progresses, but we must accelerate that process with the art of sophistication. What I mean by the "art of sophistication" is the establishment of *hyōjungo* for the extermination of *hōgen*. (164–165)

The above is not a passage from his book on *kokugo* policy, but from his *Gengogaku taii* (Outline of Linguistics) of 1900, a book on linguistics theory. This suggests that Hoshina's explanation of language as objective description became confused with his argument for the prescription of standardization, as also seen in Ueda's works, and indicating the political role linguistics and *kokugogaku* in Meiji had to play.

When Ueda said "artificial sophistication," he applied it only to linguistic elements such as pronunciation, vocabulary, and writing style. The "art of sophistication," Hoshina's term, however, suggested the "creation" of *hyōjungo* and "extermination" of *hōgen*, both radical concepts for language policy. Still, for Hoshina, the extermination was not a reckless policy disregarding linguistic principles. In *Kokugogaku seigi* (Exposition of *Kokugogaku*) of 1910, he listed three major causes for the splitting of a language and a growth in dialects: disunity among individuals, social institutions, and regions.[2] According to Hoshina, these had effective force when the society was not civilized, but they "disappear or weaken as the society and humanity develop, and eventually the language split loses its force." Therefore, it was not policy that would make *hōgen* disappear, but "as language splitting weakens, hundreds of *hōgen* will naturally be united in time" (Hoshina 1910, 694).

In Hoshina's mind the force for standardization existed in the reality, before any policy, of the language at the center of politics, economy, and culture, and therefore it should be the language to influence other *hōgen* (292). Nonetheless, if left to take its natural course, language unification would be slow and imperfect; therefore, the mission of *kokugo* policy was to make obvious and strong the influential power of the central language, to expand its confines, to accelerate unification, and furthermore, to artificially maintain the purity of the standard language, a purity that could be lost if left to the natural course of unification. In this way, the standardization policy had no contradiction with the nature of language in Hoshina's mind, standing with the extension of change and unification, an inherent process in language. Thus, as Hoshina tried to justify it with linguistics theory, the political nature of the standardization was disguised.

Nonetheless, as a faithful linguist, Hoshina admitted that every language was actually a dialect and that the word *hōgen* was a "conventional" but "temporary" term. "The collective body of all these dialects is the Japanese language, and it is not that there exists something special called the Japanese language" (731). If the Japanese language, that is, *kokugo,* was the collective body of *hōgen,* was *kokugogaku* also a collective body of *hōgen-gaku* (dialectology)? This question leads us again to the relevance of *hyōjungo.*

Hoshina, more than any of his contemporaries, insisted on the investigation of *hōgen,* asserting the linguistic value of currently spoken *hōgen,* not of the documents of the past. Nonetheless, the purpose of his "*hōgen* investigation" was not only academic, as seen in the following statement:

> We have not yet completely achieved this goal [of *kokugo* education] today. It is because we are still not clear about correct Japanese, or more precisely speaking, we still do not have a standardized language and writing style. In such a situation, it is also difficult to identify the foundation of *kokugogaku.* Therefore, as I argued before, the standardization of the Japanese language and writing style is an urgent task, allowing no neglect, and the first step towards its achievement is investigation of *hōgen.* (740)

This is a very perplexing statement, making academic as well as practical connections among three very different things: the foundation of *kokugogaku,* the standardization of *kokugo,* and the investigation of *hōgen.* Hoshina's assertion that standardization was necessary for *kokugogaku* foundation might appear to be confusing scholarship and politics, but for Hoshina, who refused to rely on convention and tradition, standardization was a theoretical prerequisite for constructing the discernible object for *kokugogaku.*[3]

10-3. From *Hyōjungo* to Political Issues in *Kokugo*

After his research in Europe (1911–1913), Hoshina came to distinguish two types of problems in a national language: the humanistic ones intrinsic to one language spoken among people of the same ethnicity, and the political ones that arise from conflict among people of different ethnic groups who speak different languages. Hoshina considered that the former did "not bring any political consequence," while the latter could result in a serious political problem endangering the nation-state system in a multiracial nation or colonies (Hoshina 1936a, 7–8). As will be discussed in section 2 of chapter 13, the serious language problems in Europe that triggered violent political conflicts must have led Hoshina to such a distinction. However, these two kinds of problems, humanistic and political, were not unconnected, but rather connected by a line from the former to the latter, that is, by the belief that the language of a country with political and cultural superiority naturally would and should expel other languages.

In *Kokugogaku seigi* (1910), which he wrote before going to Europe, Hoshina had already argued that

> if a nation's language starts to lose its independence, its people also will gradually lose national identity, and the power of the people will naturally decline. There-fore, in terms of [language] policy, it would be best if the conqueror or sovereign made the conquered or subjects quickly give up the language they inherited from their ancestors and force them to use the conqueror's language. . . . Such expan-sion of a national language would result in the expansion of the nation's might— language has just such an incredible power as this. (Hoshina 1910, 361)

And this "incredible power" of language was the weapon for the central lan-guage to drive away dialects, as well as for the conqueror's language to force assimilation of different ethnic groups. If the solution to the humanistic prob-lems was the institution of *hyōjungo*, the solution to the political problems would be the institution of *kokka-go*.

Hoshina was awakened to such language policy beyond domestic educa-tional issues because of his experience in Europe, especially in Posen Province, where he witnessed the linguistic crisis. There he realized the importance of language policy in governing different ethnic groups. After his return to Japan, he repeatedly and volubly complained about Japan's total indifference to lan-guage policy. His frustration was almost that of a child who had witnessed an accident and was trying to describe it to grownups who would not take him seriously. The more Hoshina railed, the more alienated he became in a society that did not believe in any need for a policy on a thing like language.

CHAPTER 11

Korea and Poland

11-1. Korea and Poland: Double Exposure

Hoshina was unique among those who were sent to Europe by the Ministry of Education at that time, as he recalled later:

> The ministry's bylaws did not grant study abroad for those in the fields of *kokugogaku*, Chinese literature, and Japanese history, so I was not supposed to be qualified for this. However, in recognition of my earnest effort in *kokugo* research, they granted me a scholarship as a researcher of linguistics and language pedagogy. (Hoshina 1949b, 58)

On his return two years later (1913; Taishō 2), he was disappointed to find that Kokugo Chōsa Iinkai had been disbanded. Nonetheless, Hoshina began energetically to marshal the committee's documents and to report on the language problems and language education of Europe. For example, within only two years, 1913–1914, he published in the journal *Kokugakuin zasshi* a series of eight articles on language issues overseas, in Germany, Britain, Switzerland, the United States, Albania, and South Africa, and even included the Esperanto movement.[1] These works showed Hoshina's eager commitment to resolution of *kokugo* issues. Realizing that in language education Japan was far behind Europe, Hoshina was moving his focus from *kokugogaku* to *kokugo* education, and in 1917 he started the monthly journal *Kokugo kyōiku* (*Kokugo* Education). He was editor in chief and wrote its foreword every month.

Hoshina was given another mission during his research abroad: the [Japanese] government-general of Korea asked him to investigate political problems regarding languages and language policy in Europe. As he recalled, "the government-general's office keenly felt the importance of *kokugo* policy in ruling Korea at that time" (1949b, 80), the time right after the annexation of Korea (1910; Meiji 43). This concrete proposition for colonial rule of Korea motivated Hoshina to further commitment to research on language policy.

Hoshina eagerly collected resources and diligently investigated language problems in Europe, especially in Posen Province under Prussian-German occupation (today's Poznan, Poland), where he witnessed the reality of the language policy and recognized its serious consequences.

Posen (German pronunciation of Polish "Poznan") had a largely Polish population. Partitioned three times, in 1772, 1793, and 1795, among Russia, Austria, and Prussia, Poland had disappeared from the map. Prussia-Poland was then revived as the Duchy of Warsaw by Napoleon, but after the Napoleonic Wars, the Treaty of Vienna (1809) had Prussia controlling western Warsaw as the Grand Duchy of Posen. Later, Posen became a territory of the North German Confederation in 1867, then of the German Empire in 1871 (Itō S. 1987, 13–15), and thus was put completely under German control until the Treaty of Versailles (1919) after World War I, which made it a province of the Polish Republic.

While under the Prussian-German regime, Posen Province underwent sweeping "Germanization" in every aspect of its politics, economy, and culture. Prussia suppressed any sign of Polish ethnicity and severely repressed the Polish language, the last shred of Posen's ethnicity, almost to annihilation. Posen Province became the front line of *Sprachkampf*, Prussia's language war against Poland.

The historian Itō Sadayoshi, who focused his studies on Germany, illustrated in *Ikyō to kokyo* (Exile and Home) how the Germanization of the Poles was crucial to the existence of the Prussian nation and commented that "the relation between the Poles and German society in imperialism hangs over us, like a double exposure, mirroring the relation between Korea and Japan" (1987, 10). As colonies, both Poland and Korea faced similar problems such as land reform, forced assimilation, imposed name changes, and racial discrimination. The relationship between Germany and Poland resembled that between Japan and Korea (and some of their problems continue to this day).

Hoshina, too, saw this "double exposure" more than half a century before we did. However, his perspective was completely different from ours: he sought in Prussian German policy on Poland the direction Japan should take with Korea. The double exposure of Poland and Korea prompted Hoshina to become the first scholar of language policy in Japan.

11-2. *Kokugo* Education and Assimilation Policy

In 1914 (Taishō 3), less than a year after his return from Europe, Hoshina published *Kokugo kyōiku oyobi kyōju no shinchō* (The New Wave in Education and Teaching of *Kokugo*), a voluminous book of 854 pages, with the objective of introducing advanced Western language pedagogy in order to "greatly improve *kokugo* education in our country" (Hoshina 1914b, iii). The two chapters on Posen were different from the rest of the book in that they focused on language education as the basis for an assimilation policy for the conquered Poles. Hoshina sought there a model for Japan's educational policy for its colonies.

He noted the school textbooks prescribed for Posen, which were quite different from those for Germany. While the latter did not put overt emphasis on moral lessons, numerous textbooks used in Posen contained moral stories, especially stories about the German emperor and the imperial family. For example, a story called *Our Emperor's Family* in a textbook for lower-level elementary schoolchildren begins with the names of the emperors, their birthdays, years of their reigns, and their family members, and ends with the following passage:

> The emperor loves his subjects just as a gentle father loves his own children *(akago)*. He is our nation's father and we are his children. And we, as loyal, good children, are grateful for his generous heart, and as his subjects, we have deep affection and respect for him. (293)[2]

Hoshina's attention was caught by the way these stories were "selected and arranged in order to inspire in the children in the colony the sense of loyalty and patriotism" (299). The above passage has an astonishing correspondence with Japanese textbooks for imperializing subjects—for example, the expression *akago* (child). It is unclear and needs further investigation whether Hoshina interpreted the original text with Japan's situation in mind or introduced Prussia's imperialistic text as a model Japan should follow.

Another characteristic of textbooks for Posen was the way they were used for education about local communities. While textbooks in Germany usually promoted local education and taught schoolchildren to cherish their hometowns, the textbooks used in Posen were "designed to Germanize Polish children," according to Hoshina, asserting that their homeland belonged to Germany. For example, the textbook *Province of Posen* taught that Prussian kings, through generations, had devoted their energy to the development of Posen; that Posen was once in misery, but "changed completely when it was returned to Germany"; and that the partitions of Poland "finally liberated the Poles" (432–434). Another textbook, *The Decline of Poland,* stated that Poland, cities and villages alike, was "in a pitiful state" before the 1772 partition, but the emigration of Germans led by Friedrich the Great in his effort to save Poland started up industry, developed transportation, and founded schools; that "the

Prussian government had been exerting itself for the happiness of the new land" since 1815, when Posen came under Prussia's rule; and that because of the Prussian army, the "turbulence" of 1848 was settled and "peace and order in the province" were regained (425–427; 439–443). All these lessons aimed to teach children that it was natural and appropriate for Posen and the Poles to turn to Germany.

Hoshina made a long list of textbook methods for exalting colonization, noting that they are all based on "the policy to Germanize the Poles" (314). And he recommended that Japan follow the Prussian example in designing the textbooks for its colony Korea, making the following concrete proposal:

> In the *kokugo* textbooks for normal schools in Korea, we should mention the following topics for local education: the ancient relationship between Japan and Korea in the past, the state of transportation in Korea, China's persecution of Korea, people's constant suffering from cruelty and neglect, and Korea's disorderly taxation and exploitation of the people. And we should note that the annexation to Japan brought Korea an excellent regime and the liberation of the people and that the admirable judicial system provides complete protection of their human rights; the nationwide foundation of schools has promoted education, the transportation system has greatly developed, and such progress in humanity has renewed Korea's spirit. By promoting education that cultivates children's understanding of morals and society[3] through such textbooks, we will be able to Japanize their thinking, and gradually replace their anti-Japan sentiment with amicable surrender. (434–435)

The above examples indicate that Hoshina, immediately after the annexation of Korea, envisaged the future *kōminka kyōiku* (education for imperialization). At the same time, we must note that Hoshina had already recommended a similar pedagogy for *hyōjungo* education in Japan: cultivation of children's morals, focus on local materials, and use of direct teaching methods. The above principles of language policy and education had already proved their effectiveness inside Japan, and were to be expanded to its colony Korea.

The textbooks were of course written in Japanese, and classroom instruction also had to be done in Japanese in Korea, just as all Poles in Posen were taught in German. Hoshina recommended that "the new government-general uses a sensitive policy for conciliating the people, while strongly controlling them through *kokugo* education" (312). He did not forget that bilingual instruction in Austria, as will be discussed later, had turned a language problem into a political one that "endangered the foundation of the nation," and so he concluded as follows:

It is urgent that normal education in Korea be done in Japanese. At this transitional stage, we may have to allow some Korean language, but we must plan to integrate all instruction into Japanese as soon as possible. Otherwise, we could incubate irreparable trouble in the future. (321–322)

11-3. Language Policy in German Poland

With Posen as a perfect model, Hoshina's attention had turned towards language education in the colonies. However, his description of Posen in *The New Wave in Education* was subordinate to the general objective of the book, which focused on language education and not on language policy in a broader perspective. It was in his 1921 (Taishō 10) book, *Doitsu zokuryō jidai no Pōrando ni okeru kokugo seisaku* (Language Policy in German Poland), that he discussed the language policy in Posen from a more comprehensive perspective. Here he explained chronologically Prussia's language policy for Posen, carefully following the detailed documents from the first partition of Poland (1772) to the early twentieth century. This book signified the beginning of his academic career in language policy, though it is puzzling why Hoshina, who was a fast writer, had to wait eight long years after his return from Europe to write a book of this kind. We will return to this question in the next section.

In this book, Hoshina meticulously traced the process of Germanization of the Polish language in each of four areas—official, juridical, educational, and military[4]—through four periods: (1) from the three partitions of Poland in the late eighteenth century to the Warsaw Uprising in 1830; (2) from the termination of the Polish Congress in 1832 to the proclamation of the (revised) Prussian Constitution in 1850; (3) from 1850 to the establishment of the German Empire in 1871; and (4) from 1871 to the time after Germanization by Bismarck. Hoshina's observation in this book was very similar to the method of "domain" analysis in today's sociolinguistics. The book was probably also the most detailed research that a non-Westerner had undertaken at that time, and, regardless of Hoshina's typically discursive writing, it is, to this day, a valuable research reference on Prussian-German language policy. It is an intriguing history of Prussia's language policy written from a sociolinguistic viewpoint half a century before H. Glück's theoretically involved *Die preussische-polnische Sprachenpolitik* (The Language Policy in Prussia-Poland, 1979).

Nonetheless, Hoshina's work was not a critically consistent or objective piece of scholarship: his research was biased, though not explicitly, by his interest in the "colonizer's policy" and by his vision for colonial Korea, which overlapped with Poland, as indicated in his introduction:

It goes without saying that colonial rule depends on assimilation. Pointless abuse of force will not be a wise solution in today's international relations, and might invite hostility and undesirable consequences. We must lead the colonized to amenable surrender without force, and the best way to achieve this goal is to assimilate their thinking [into the Japanese way]. And this is where our *kokugo* policy is extremely important, as clearly seen in the way recent European powers have always taken their language policies seriously. (Hoshina 1921, i)

Hoshina was most interested in Bismarck's Germanization of the Poles, which was quite different in nature from previous Prussian policies for elimination of Polish from official and juridical languages: Bismarck attempted not only to eradicate Polish from public life, but also to transform the Poles' ethnic identity through language policy. Hoshina explained: "In a word, the Prussian Government's policy for the Poles was a *Germanisierrung* (Germanization), and was an eager attempt to destroy by every conceivable means Polish ethnic identity and loyalty to their language, to completely change the Poles into the Germans" (14), and he traced the order of the "eager attempts":

In February 1872, "the Prussian government proposed to the congress administrative regulations for schools and Bismarck welcomed this as an opportunity to solve Polish problems." Bismarck expressed his plans to issue "many laws to disseminate the German language" which were "targeting Posen Province," and he "recognized the central importance of language policy in Polish problems" (75).

In November 1872, "the ministerial ordinance mandated that *höhere Schulen* (high schools) in Posen Province use German in religious education, as in other subjects, starting from April 1873" (76).

In July 1873, "the ministerial ordinance ordered the termination of Polish language classes in high schools in Posen Province after October of the next (academic?) year." In the same month, "the governor (of Posen Province) decided that elementary schools in the province must use German as the instructional language in all subjects except lower-level religion and hymns" (78).

In August 1876, the Prussian government "issued a regulation for the official language to be used in every government office and by officers and other political organizations." This regulation "prohibited any use of Polish in public life" (87).

In March 1883, "the Posen government issued an order to all municipal and private elementary schools to use German in instructing middle- and upper-class religion classes after May 1," but because of the Poles' strong protest, "they modified the application of the order in proportion to the number of children who spoke German" (92–93).

Through his careful observation of the process of Germanization of Posen, Hoshina's attention was drawn to the fact that the instructional language was placed above official, juridical, or military language: it was believed that the most effective policy for the assimilation of the thinking of the conquered was to have all the school subjects taught in the conqueror's language, in addition to teaching it as a subject. This was a strategy to plant in children's minds the conqueror's language as inseparable from what they learned. As seen in the above chronology, the Germanization of instructional language spread from high schools to elementary schools through the 1870s and the first half of the 1880s, leaving only religious education, the last shred of Polish, hanging by a single thread.

In addition, Hoshina mentioned that teachers hired for Posen Province were limited to German persons, specifically, German persons who did not know Polish at all. Poles were excluded from teaching jobs "in fear of their provoking anti-German sentiment [among children], and their failing the original goal to educate Polish children in German" (1921, 117). Again, "the most powerful means for Germanization was provided in schools taught in German" (104).

11-4. The School Strike and the March First Movement

While Hoshina saw Prussia's Germanization as an opportune model for the colonization of Korea, he did not blindly applaud it. He was also aware of its failure: the independence of Poland from Prussian Germany in 1916, followed by the incorporation of Posen into the new Polish Republic, made Hoshina raise the alarm in Japan that "statesmen must realize with caution that even this tireless, hundred-year-long Germanization turned ineffectual, and eventually prompted the revival of Poland" (1921, 115). Another of Hoshina's objectives in *Language Policy* was to examine what had failed in Germany's linguistic colonization. He alleged that the critical flaw was "the inconsistency of language policy that hindered its wholesale practice" (i). After Bismarck, the conciliation policy of Chancellor Caprivi moderated the Germanization, allowing the use of Polish in the private teaching of religion, and even attempting to allow Polish in other areas of private education. But the government that followed reinforced complete prohibition of Polish again. Such a course of action convinced Hoshina that "constant changes in policy disturbed the Poles and prompted the furious resistance that produced a series of school riots" (115).

"School riots" here refers to the large-scale school strike in 1906–1907, a series of radical protests throughout Posen Province against Chancellor Bülow's attempt to eliminate Polish from religion classes in elementary schools. According to Itō Sadayoshi, the series of school strikes culminated in the fall of 1906 and continued for more than a year in about sixteen hundred schools with ninety-three thousand students. It was a strong resistance to the threat to their language and religion, the roots of Polish identity. In such a climate, "the strike received Archbishop Stablewski's approval and drew endorsements from journalists and clergymen, and the wider public supported it through protest meetings." The school strike turned out to be "the largest Polish ethnic movement under German imperial rule," and the rulers "recognized the strike as a critical problem to Prussian German rule, a destructive threat to the unification of the German nation" (Itō S. 1987, 261–262).

Hoshina must have shared the fear of those rulers, which may be why he tried to discredit the school strike. He asserted that "this crime of school strike" was committed not by the schoolchildren themselves but by "their parents," instigated by "Catholic priests, journalists, and aristocrats" (Hoshina 1921, 99–100):

> [These instigators] inflamed the poor lower-class people who had no education or desire for independence. Moreover, it was a terrible crime that they used religion for their motivation (100). . . . The strike by the Poles was sparked by their misguided conspiracy to gain their independence (102). . . . In other words, their purpose was not to resist the Prussian emperor or his government. The strike was used as a test of their wild dreams of regaining their old land from Prussia. Therefore, [the strike] indicated that there was a large-scale anti-Germany movement by the Poles. (104)

The shocking memory of the March First Independence Movement by Koreans must have been still vivid in Hoshina's mind as he wrote the above.[5] And it could not have been a coincidence that this book was circulated as a secret document, two years after the March First Movement, in the government-general of Korea, located at 1 Meiji-cho, Keijō-fu [today's Myongdong, Seoul]. In Hoshina's mind, the Poles' resistance in Posen resonated with Koreans who were resisting Japanese rule. In fact, we find in Hoshina 1921 a complete shift from Hoshina 1914b in his opinion about Prussian colonial rule. In 1914 he had written, "It is regrettable that [the Prussian government] forced Bismarck's coercion and provoked the Poles' resistance. . . . If they had moderated their policy and tried placating their people, they would not have had the difficulties in ruling as they do now" (1914b, 321). In contrast, in 1921 Hoshina asserted the ineffectiveness of the conciliation:

> Their effort to conciliate the people in the new colony [Posen] with the placating policy was completely unsuccessful. Even though people were treated gener-

ously in education, they did not appreciate it, and on the contrary, despised the rulers even more, aggressively reclaimed all benefits, and rebelled against the rulers if they were ignored. This is a way of thinking common among people in colonies. . . . I can say that in the relationship of the ruler and the ruled, it is always the case that conciliation ends in failure. (1921, 26)

Hoshina now believed that Prussia failed in ruling Poland not because of Bismarck's coercion, but because of his successors' conciliation, which hindered assimilation. Between his two works, Hoshina had seen the liberation of Poland on one hand and the March First uprising on the other. These two incidents must have impelled him to write his *Language Policy,* sending a warning to the government-general of Korea, which had just experienced the March First Movement: "If we do not put [Korea] under good control now, it could take the same course as Poland against Prussia, or Ireland against Britain" (ii).[6] That is, colonization would fall apart if it allowed any demands by the colonized.

As for the language policy for the colony, Hoshina made the following four points:

1. The meaning of *kokugo* policy: "The language of a country is intimately related to its people. Therefore, *kokugo* policy is very significant in that it separates the colonized from their own language and has them form an intimacy with the ruler's language." However, Hoshina was against eradication of the language of the colonized: "It is too extreme to completely disallow [the colonized] from using their mother tongue, as the Prussian government did to Poles, and such a prohibition is impossible. An attempt to exterminate their own language would be beyond the extreme" (1921, 6). Excessive coercion would only arouse ethnic identity among the colonized, which could endanger colonial rule—the lesson Hoshina learned from Posen. Still, this did not mean that Hoshina suggested moderation of assimilation. The remaining three points were the conclusions he drew from the above.

2. The purpose of *kokugo* policy: "The assimilation of a different race works most peacefully and swiftly through *kokugo* education. Educating the colonized with the ruler's language will lead them naturally to obedience" (7).

3. Need for long-term *kokugo* policy: "It is almost impossible to assimilate the colonized overnight by *kokugo* education. . . . It could take a century, or even centuries in some cases. . . . If we mistakenly push towards assimilation in haste, it will end in failure, which would turn our future into a lasting disaster." The effort to practice language policy in the colony towards assimilation of the people's thinking "must be taken in a peaceful, *'slow and steady'*[7] way" (8–9).

4. Consistency of *kokugo* policy: "The most important requirement in *kokugo* policy is never to modify it once it is established" (9). In the case of

Posen, "in every repression of several uprisings by the Poles, [the government] acquiesced to their demands, which let them arrogantly assume that resistance would force the government to accept every demand." Therefore, in [Japanese] colonies, "we must stand firm on our policy, and once we put it in practice on the colonized, we must never let it change until we achieve the goal of assimilation, even if that takes many centuries" (11–12).

In the course of his writings, Hoshina continued to hold the above opinion about the basic nature of language policy: in ruling a different people, especially in colonies, a long-term and consistent assimilation policy using language would be the most powerful force. *Language Policy in German Poland* was the most important among Hoshina's writings as the declaration of his convictions.

It is not confirmed that Hoshina's *Language Policy* had any effect on the shift from martial to cultural rule in Korea, specifically on the revision of the Korean Education Rescript in 1922 (Taishō 11).[8] Regardless, Hoshina's words about "assimilation through *kokugo* education" came alive in Japan's colonization after this. Stunned by the March First Movement, the government-general of Korea used a soothing slogan, "cultural rule," as an excuse to suppress any ethnic movement, and its assimilation policy became more ingenious and strictly enforced, as will be discussed in the next chapter.

It is also not certain that Hoshina was aware of the reality of the government-general's policy to eradicate the Korean language, but from this point on he repeatedly asserted his pet theory: "The *kokugo* policy for our colony is an extremely peaceful one," and unlike what Germany did in Poland, "we do not force absolute prohibition of the language of the region, and therefore the people there have no discontent in this regard" (Hoshina 1942a, 28–29). Such a view as Hoshina's became a flawed cliché that was, and still is, used in Japan's justification of its colonization.

His recommendation of a peaceful, "slow and steady" language policy did not mean that Hoshina cared about the sustenance of the ethnic language. It was rather that he hoped to frame a solid language order that would make the colonial rule unshakable. With such a linguistic establishment, Hoshina believed, the consistent ruling policy would promote assimilation naturally, and this view gradually directed his attention towards the idea of *kokka-go*.

CHAPTER 12

What Is Assimilation?

We saw in the previous chapter that Hoshina testified to the need for assimilation, especially linguistic assimilation, as the key to colonial policy. However, what exactly did he mean by "assimilation"? Why was language expected to play a central role in assimilation policy? Hoshina did not offer answers to these questions. His writings, while easy to follow, tend to leap to application of a theory, avoiding important questions. In that sense, Hoshina was not a very good theorist. In this chapter, therefore, we will leave Hoshina for a moment and will examine the meaning of "assimilation" in modern Japan.

12-1. Colonization and Assimilation

As the second Sino-Japanese War[1] escalated, Japan's colonial rule culminated in the enforcement of its imperialization *(kōminka)* of the colonized. Japan had already been practicing a drastic assimilation policy in its colonies, justified as "homeland extensionism" *(naichi enchō shugi),* but imperialization took the mission further, seeking to annihilate the ethnic identity of the colonized and to turn them all into "imperial subjects" *(kōkoku shinmin).* Under the slogan *naisen ittai* (unity of homeland and Korea), General Minami Jirō, on taking up his new post as governor-general of Korea in August 1936 (Shōwa 11), announced that his most important goals were to "receive the emperor's honorable visit to Korea and to start military conscription in Korea" (Miyata 1985, 94). Then followed the Special Army Volunteers System in February 1938, the Third Educational Rescript for Korea in March of the same year, and the notorious *sōshi kaimei* (Japanization of names)[2] policy in February 1940.

Such an upsurge of imperialization had been predicted about six months before the Roko Bridge (Lugouqiao) incident by Yanaihara Tadao,[3] who had always been critical of Japan's forcible assimilation in the colonies. In his article "Gunjiteki to dōkateki: Nichi-futsu shokumin seisaku hikaku no ichi ron" (Mil-

170

itarization and Assimilation: A Comparison of Japanese and French Colonization)" (Yanaihara 1963, 4:276–306),[4] Yanaihara demonstrated the similarities
between Japanese colonization and that by France.

Colonization in both countries started with the military occupation of lands
that were geographically adjacent to the home country: Taiwan, Korea, Sakha-
lin, and Manchuria for Japan, and the Maghreb region of northern Africa for
France. Yanaihara criticized French colonization as "being driven by the nation's
conceit and its possessive hunger for colonies promoted by military expansionism," implying the same about Japanese colonization. He further pointed out
that both Japan and France were constructing "a bloc economy to benefit their
own countries," applying to the colonies the homeland-extension policy, which
was directed not only to expansion of the economic sphere to include the colonies, but also to "building up a huge geographical bloc for a military and political regime," motivated by military reasons.

Another significant similarity between these two countries was found in
their extreme policy of assimilation. Yanaihara observed that in its policy to
assimilate the original inhabitants, France ignored the political and economic
"situation unique to its colonies." And the core of this assimilation policy was
language. Yanaihara indicated that "the best means France chose to assimilate
the colonized was education, specifically, education in the French language,"
and that it was a tradition in French colonial policy exemplified in Alibin
Rozet's words: "Northern Africa will truly become a land of France, an extension of France, on the day when its people start speaking French. They will be
feeling and thinking just as the French are." In this respect, Yanaihara remarked,
Japan's assimilation policy was even more thorough than France's: "Japan uses
the assimilation strategy with education, especially with language, as determinedly as, nay, more determinedly than, France. Japanization of the colonized
through teaching them Japanese is deemed most essential in our educational
policy for the colonies" (297).

Yanaihara saw behind French assimilation policy "the philosophy of the
Enlightenment and the ideals of the French Revolution of the end of the eighteenth century." That is, "the French believe that all human beings, regardless
of the differences in their origin and circumstances, are equally rational beings.
Thus they consider that the colonized also have the same natural human rights
as themselves, and, in principle, can be assimilated to become French" (299). It is
very interesting that Yanaihara found a basis for colonial assimilation in Enlightenment philosophy and the French Revolution, which are usually considered as
implying human liberation. According to his view, then, colonialism was not
incidental to or a mere divergence from the formative principles of a nation-
state, but was rooted in them. Indeed, when the French Revolution sought to

create a nation-people, it was the language problem that loomed in its way. The many different dialects in France itself and the languages spoken in regions such as Alsace, Lorraine, Bretagne, Basque, and Corsica were considered hindrances that had to be eliminated in order to create a homogeneous nation-people. In this regard, formation of a nation-state required domestic assimilation first, and for that purpose, those regions of minority languages were considered "domestic colonies"—though Yanaihara did not make this explicit.

Yanaihara then went on to ask, "While French assimilation policy had the philosophical background I mentioned above, what is the philosophical foundation of Japan's assimilation policy?" His answer was that it was the idea of identifying the Japanese language with the Japanese spirit:

> First, teach Japanese to Taiwanese, Koreans, Ainu, and people in the South Sea Islands, and make them possess the Japanese spirit. Only after they speak Japanese and become Japanese with the Japanese spirit will they be allowed to have social and political freedom—this is the fundamental idea of our assimilation policy for the colonized. It is not based on a humanistic view like the French policy, but on the belief in the superiority of the Japanese spirit. In this sense, the Japanese assimilation policy is much more nationalistic and patriotic than that of France, and can be much more readily connected to military rule. (301)

It was as if Yanaihara had foreseen the imperialization that began immediately after he wrote his article. The daily use of *kokugo* was reinforced throughout the colonies, and assimilation was forced into every aspect of the lives of the colonized, as typically seen in the Japanization of names in Korea and the *kokugo*-family movement in Taiwan.[5] And what motivated the imperialization was Japan's military interest, as seen in the fact that especially in Korea, the ultimate goal was the enforcement of conscription.

Characterizing Japanese colonization as above, Yanaihara had serious misgivings about the fact that language assimilation would become the core policy of colonization. That does not mean, however, that he was critical of colonial rule itself. In his 1926 book *Shokumin oyobi shokumin seisaku* (Colonization and Colonial Policies) Yanaihara maintained as follows:

> Dissemination of the homeland language among the colonized is convenient for activities of both the ruler and the ruled, and a powerful means of communication between the two societies. Therefore, there is no reason not to promote it by policies. However, it would be a hasty conclusion to consider the dissemination of the language as assimilation or conformity among different races. Language is merely one form of social living, and its change does not immediately bring

emotional change [in the speakers]. Furthermore, the language of the colonized has its own history, and its oppression may invite resistance. Dissemination of the mainland language should be left to its natural course as much as possible. (1963, 1:326)

That is, Yanaihara maintained that because language was but one form of social life, linguistic assimilation was far from true assimilation; and on the contrary, the suppression of the colony's original language would cause resistance. He must have been aware of what the promotion of the "natural course" in colonization meant: natural expansion of the suzerain's language and suppression of the language of the colonized. We should keep this in mind as we read the following:

> In normal schools in Korea, the Korean language curriculum has been included recently, but instructional language in all subjects except for Korean language classes is expected to be Japanese. However, I once heard a Korean intellectual say that Japanese must not be forced as the national language in elementary education and that Korean must be used in teaching subjects other than *kokugo* until the students understand Japanese. How can we say this is an unreasonable request? (1:326)

Nevertheless, was Yanaihara correct in saying that language was only a form of social life? His view is certainly important for our understanding of the nature of Japanese colonization, but in terms of understanding the nature of language, he did not have a solid enough position from which to criticize Japanese colonialism. Like many other social scientists, Yanaihara saw language as a mere tool of communication. If "language is merely one form of social living, and its change does not immediately bring emotional change," Japanese assimilation was a waste of time, and the effort of the colonized to seek identity in their languages was useless.

12-2. Eradication of the Ethnic Language in Colonized Korea

Japan's linguistic rule in Korea is known as "the eradication policy" of the Korean language or the ethnic language. The term has become a label to emphasize the cruelty and thoroughness of the Japanese colonization, and it triggers a historical memory that drives Koreans today, in both the North and South, to frenzied campaigns for linguistic patriotism and the purification of the Korean language.

Despite its notoriety, however, the realities of this radical eradication policy, its content and legislative measures, have hardly been examined. The phrase "the eradication of the ethnic language" has been used by historians as an accepted cliché, and that has prevented scholarly research into the actualities of the linguistic oppression. The term might remind us of the actual examples of the similar policy in Europe, and suggest some deliberative laws or series of strategies based on consistent principles. Unfortunately, we cannot find in modern Japan any trace of consistency in creating such a policy or organization for the language problems in the colonies. There was no legislation on official language, or language used in courts or schools, in the colonies. As if it were too self-evident to legislate, the Japanese language dominated the colonies with unabashed force. Not language policy but rather language force was closer to the truth. Nonetheless, today in Japan we often hear a justification or defense for Japan's linguistic colonization, denying Japan's eradication of the Korean language (e.g., Kajii 1980, chap. 4). However, the only argument for this position is that normal schools in Korea had Korean Language as a subject, an argument that obstinately obscures the facts.

The Korean Education Rescript of 1911 (Meiji 44) ordered schools to offer Korean Language and *Kanbun*. This title was deceiving, however, because in reality what was taught was only *kanbun,* and Korean only as an aid to interpret *kanbun.* Korean was also used as an aid to teach *kokugo,* as described in item 10 of the rescript: "Korean and *kanbun* must be taught always in relation to *kokugo,* and when necessary [teachers] must make students interpret them in *kokugo*" (Monbushō 1939, 76). In the Revised Korean Education Rescript in 1922 (Taishō 11), a separate subject, Korean Language, was listed. However, the rescript gave even more weight to *kokugo,* instructing that "Korean must be taught in relation to *kokugo,* and when necessary [teachers] must make students speak in *kokugo*" (658).

The revised rescript is said to have symbolized the shifting of Japanese colonization from martial rule to cultural rule, but at the same time it aimed at reinforcement of assimilation: after the issuance of the rescript *naichi jin* (homeland people) was legally defined as "those who always use *kokugo*" and *chōsen jin* (Korean people) as "those who do not always use *kokugo,*" completely ignoring Korean ethnicity. The negative definition, "those who do *not* always use *kokugo,*" implied that *chōsen jin* were negative beings lacking in something essential to be nation-people, and this something essential was *kokugo.*

The words *naichi jin* and *chōsen jin* had been used throughout the drafting stages of the revised rescript and had been printed in the final draft issued by the government-general (Watanabe and Abe 1987–1991, vol. 16). Curiously, however, in that final draft someone wrote corrections by hand, replacing the word *naichi jin* with "those who always use *kokugo*" and *chōsen jin* with "those who do not always use *kokugo*." It is a very intriguing mystery who invented this clever switch and had these new definitions adopted in the published copy.

There seem to have been realistic reasons why the government-general adopted the new definition of Koreans as "those who do not always use *kokugo*." According to *Kokugo fukyū no jōkyō* (The State of the Spread of *Kokugo*), a pamphlet-form report published in 1921 (Taishō 10) by the Academic Bureau of the government-general, as of the end of December 1919 (Taishō 8) the number of Koreans who "can safely carry on normal conversation" in *kokugo* was 108,276 (100,059 men and 8,217 women), and the number of those who "can understand some" *kokugo* was 232,390 (201,353 men and 31,037 women). The percentage of Koreans who understood some *kokugo*, also listed in the report, indicated that the men in the first group above constituted only 0.60 percent of the Korean population; the women in the same group, 0.05 percent; the men in the second group, 1.20 percent; and the women, 0.16 percent. Of Korean men, 98.20 percent could not understand *kokugo;* of Korean women, 99.77 percent (Watanabe and Abe 1987–1991, vol. 17). Disturbed by this tardy progress, the authorities must have tried harder at assimilation through *kokugo* education. This is indicated in "Main Points of the Revision of the Korean Educational System" by the government-general, which explained that the major goal of the Revised Korean Education Rescript was "to gradually turn Korean people into perfect Japanese citizens, and to continue placing importance on teaching *kokugo* in schools" (vol. 16; original text 1–2). The above circumstances might have prompted the disuse of the term *chōsen jin* as opposed to *naichi jin,* under the slogan *isshi dōjin* (treat and cherish all people equally), and the new definition of it as "those who do not always use *kokugo*." And Koreans were now no longer *chōsen jin* and were merely "those who do not always use *kokugo*" but who were to be assimilated. Furthermore, the second revision of the Korean Education Rescript, in 1938 (Shōwa 13), instituted as part of the imperialization policy, eliminated the Korean language from the regular school curriculum and made it only an additional optional subject. This was a step towards abolition of Korean language classes.

As seen above, it was not that Japanese authorities retained the Korean language curriculum for genuinely educational purposes, but rather as an excuse for concealing the forcible oppression of Japanese rule. Even though Korean Language existed as a subject, all classes in schools were conducted in Japanese. The previously mentioned report, *The State of the Spread of Kokugo,* said, "All textbooks in every school, except for Korean language and *kanbun,* are written in *kokugo* (their [Korean] translation may be distributed if necessary), for both pedagogical convenience and promotion of *kokugo*. . . . The language for instruction, though not necessarily fixed, is normally *kokugo* in public schools." Thus, the Japanese language was employed not merely as the direct teaching method of *kokugo*, but as a vessel for all aspects of learning.

Nonetheless, we can see here the slipshod nature of the Japanese language policy, as I mentioned before: none of the three versions of the education rescript officially legislated Japanese as the instructional language in schools. In contrast to multilingual nations such as the Austro-Hungarian Empire that saw fierce disputes or even ethnic conflict, Japan was negligent in legislation about language, indicative of an aspect of Japanese linguistic modernity.

12-3. What Is Assimilation?

What is assimilation? Is it even possible to assimilate a different people? If the goal of assimilation is to implant essential elements of certain "nation-people" into another people, what are these "essential elements"? In order to assimilate "others," "self" must be first established. Without a clear definition of "self," how is it possible to assimilate "others" to "self"? Thus, an assimilation policy for colonies inevitably asks What is the essence of a "nation-people?" What is the basis of a "national identity?"

An intriguing resource for examining characteristics of Japanese assimilation policy may be found in "Kyōka ikensho" (Comments on Cultivation), supposedly drafted by Kumamoto Shigekichi, secretary to the Academic Department of the Korean government, or by his aides (in Watanabe and Abe 1987–1991, vol. 69). Kumamoto, born in 1873 (Meiji 6), graduated from the History Department of Tokyo Imperial University. After holding the posts of library referee and academic inspector in the Ministry of Education, he was appointed secretary to the Academic Department of the Korean government in 1908 (Meiji 41), which continued as the Academic Bureau of the government-general of Korea after the annexation of Korea in 1910 (Meiji 43). He was transferred to the government-general of Taiwan in 1911 (Meiji 44), where he stayed until 1920 (Taishō 9). After returning to Japan, he worked as principal of high schools such as Ōsaka High School and the Sixth High School. He died in 1952 (Shōwa 27). Thus Kumamoto was the epitome of educators who changed their positions from central government bureaucrats to colonial administrators (see Watanabe and Abe 1987–1991, vol. 63: Commentary, 7).

"Comments on Cultivation" was a secret government-general document dated September 8, 1910 (Meiji 43), right after the proclamation of the annexation treaty on August 29. It was presented to Governor-General Terauchi Masatake during the drawing of the Korean Education Rescript. While the rescript presented its goal as "nurturing a loyal nation-people," in the "Comments" there was a glimpse of the real intentions of the government-general that could not be spelled out in a legal document.

The "Comments" began with the statement of the objective: "to discuss whether or not the assimilation of the Korean race will be possible, and to express, in relation to that, [Komamoto's] personal view about a course of cultivation of this race" (Watanabe and Abe 1987–1991, 69:1). Throughout the document, alongside the *kanji* character for the word *dōka* (assimilation) was *katakana* writing *japanizēshon* (Japanization), indicating that Japanization of Koreans was the specific goal. The main text opened with the premise that the Great Japanese Empire was founded on *kokutai* that was peerless in the world. The *kokutai* had been sustained by the "loyalty of the people of the Japanese Empire, who consecrate the emperor with an unbroken line of eternal reign" (3), a loyalty "deeply rooted in ancestry-worship that is unique to the Japanese race" (4). This means that *kokutai* was founded not on a political power relationship between the ruler and the ruled, but on the Japanese native sentiment of "ancestry-worship." Thus, *kokutai* was a concept that preceded a political system "nation-state"; it existed in "nature" beyond human deeds, as declared in the "Comments":

> The relationship between the sovereign and subjects in other countries is merely surrender to power. However, the Japanese race's relationship to its emperor is supported, in addition to obedience, by reverence rooted in its ancestry-worship. While the former relationship lasts only as long as the power lasts, the latter continues forever and is never severed. (5)

This is an authentic interpretation of *kokutai* from the emperor-centered view of history. However, if *kokutai* as such was inherent in the "Japanese race's" natural sentiment, there should not be any need to "educate" people to implant in them the concept of *kokutai*. In fact, the "Comments" stated that the "loyalty of the Japanese race has been, from the beginning of the country, shared by all of the people in their hearts, and it is not something that is cultivated with explanations or lessons" (6).

If this was indeed the concept of *kokutai*, why was it necessary to proclaim an Imperial Rescript on Education and exercise imperialistic education on the people? This is not a captious question. Under the imperialistic educational system, the original concept of education itself would fall apart because the system did not allow inductive exploration of knowledge, but dogmatically demanded assent and obedience to an extrarational emblem. But for now, we will leave this question and continue looking into "Comments."

Before it discussed the direction of the assimilation policy for Korea, "Comments" first traced precedents of assimilation in history. For Japan, it took as an example the assimilation of the naturalized and the surrendered in ancient times, and contended that "this shows that the Japanese race has had great powers of assimilation." However, the number of those people was small, and they "assimilated themselves on their own will," and thus, "Comments" concluded, this example was not a helpful reference for Japanese colonization (7). As for Western countries, the document referred to the United States, France, and Britain. Assimilation in the United States was "superficial and never penetrated inward"; France was "the model promoter of assimilation," which attempted "to transplant French civilization into its new territories as the extension of its land," but had moderated the assimilation after "the failure in Algeria"; Britain's goal of colonization had been motivated by its "economic expansionism," and Britain therefore did not aggressively promote assimilation. Overall, "Comments" judged all these assimilation policies to be failures, largely because of the extreme racial difference between the colonizers and the colonized and because of the individualism characteristic of Western people.

"Comments" also dismissed the cases of Ryukyu [today's Okinawa] and Taiwan as less problematic than the colonization of Korea. It mentioned the German occupation of Elsass-Lothringen [Alsace-Lorraine] and the partitions of Poland by Russia, Prussia, and Austria, but contended that "our annexation of Korea is a far greater enterprise" and that "saying that it was unprecedented in history is no exaggeration" (14). Such self-praise of the colonization of Korea as an epoch-making enterprise in the history not only of Japan but even of the world, however, implies Japan's covert mindfulness of dreadful problems to come in the colonization of Korea. In fact, one of the purposes of the "Comments" was to outline concrete problems facing Japan in its colonization of Korea, and it listed the following four obstacles between the two countries:

1. "The Korean race does not possess the special requirement for Japanization"; that is, they "do not have the same special relationship to our Imperial family (as the Japanese people do), and therefore it would be impossible to make them acquire such splendid loyalty" (16–17).

2. "The Korean race has had, however incomplete it might be, its own country for three thousand years" and has formed a solid ethnic identity; therefore, "they severely lack [any] desire to receive influence from Japan and to incline themselves to assimilate" (17–18).

3. "They clearly identify themselves as the Korean race," and this identity "will be the largest obstacle for assimilating them into the Japanese race" (19).

4. "The population of the Korean race is as large as 12,000,000, or more," and it will be impossible to expect a small number of Japanese emigrants to cultivate or influence them (19–20).

The "Comments" even warned against overestimating the power of politics and education in assimilation.

If nothing could be done about these four problems, what was left to do with the notion that "assimilation equaled Japanization" other than give it up? The "Comments" then suggested a change in the goal of colonization from loyalty to obedience:

> As explained above, it would be an undue expectation to assimilate the Korean race into as completely loyal subjects as the Japanese, and setting it as the goal of cultivation in institutions and administrations would be a vain effort. Then, is there no method other than abandoning the cultivation of the Koreans? Yes, we see one possible way. Even though they cannot be made into loyal subjects of the empire, we believe that they can be made into obedient subjects. This method of Japanization can be called obedience cultivation, as opposed to the more strict loyalty of assimilation. (22–23)

And as for the concrete method for "obedience cultivation," the document proposed active dissemination of the Japanese language, cultivation of knowledge and skills for living, and the engendering of willingness to obey the empire (24–25).

It was not that the "Comments" rejected the assimilation policy for Korea. It proposed that Koreans, while they could not be loyal to the emperor, could be obedient to him. Nevertheless, this document defined the Japanization of Korea in the strict sense as "making them adopt and imitate the language and customs of the Japanese race, and moreover, making them acquire the loyalty and patriotism that the Japanese have," and it declared that "assimilation must essentially point to the internal spirit" (8–9). If that were the case, would not the "obedience cultivation" in Korea suggested above be only superficial, like that found in U.S. assimilation policy, and far from assimilation in its strict sense?

The above argument in "Comments" displayed the contradiction in the modern concepts of Japanese national polity *(kokutai)*, nation-state *(kokka)*, and nation-people *(kokumin)*. The more Japan persisted in the naturalness of the concept *kokutai*, the more impossible it became to justify assimilation of different people. Assimilation of a different "race" meant to artificially implant in them "the essence of the Japanese race." Claiming this was possible, however, proved that the relationship between the nation and the people did not naturally exist but was artificially constructed.

Still, the ideology of the assimilation policy was justified under homeland extensionism *(naichi enchō shugi)*: the relationship between Japan and its colonies was not that of forcible ruler and the ruled, as seen in the West, but a natural expansion of the uniformity of the imperial reign. Thus the assimilation policy had to be retained to justify the colonial rule itself, and the direction Japan took towards that end was a crafty discriminatory assimilation: instead of "Japanizing" the colonized by giving them the same political and social rights as Japanese, Japan kept them in subordination with no such rights. "Comments" stated that "through and through Korea must be managed as a colony for the development of the Japanese race, and Koreans must be subordinated to the Japanese" (28–29). In other words, assimilation by Japan advanced, paradoxically, discrimination.

In such a discriminatory assimilation, language played a powerful role in surmounting the central paradox. Language is not a mere form of social life, but that does not mean it is an exclusively indigenous folkway that cannot be transplanted. Even if Japanese were born with loyalty to the emperor, none of them were born speaking Japanese. And unlike other indigenous folkways, language can be learned by foreigners through education. The intrinsic role of language is to interface interior and exterior, nature and human deeds—the most elaborate and powerful social role. Therefore, it was indeed reasonable that "Comments" proposed dissemination of Japanese as a great aid for "obedience cultivation." The only possible way to overcome the contradiction between the naturalistic concept of "nation" and the possibility of assimilation was language—that is, assimilation through *kokugo*.[6]

Now, returning to Hoshina, what did "assimilation" mean to him? It is notable that he had never made any reference in his voluminous writings to "obedience cultivation" in the sense of arousing in people absolute obedience to the emperor. "Assimilation" in Hoshina's sense was closer to "cultivation" as used in "Comments," but not with secondary importance. The "assimilation in a strict sense" in "Comments" was a peculiar concept that was valid only in Japan, while Hoshina envisioned practicing in Japan the model policy of modern European nations such as Prussia and Austria-Hungary. His assimilation was no more and no less than a policy for the unification of a people in the colonies, and that was why his proposals lacked an imperialistic or ultranationalistic tone (and this must have irritated Yamada Yoshio, who attacked him on every possible occasion).

However, Hoshina's assimilation was a move away from the "naturalness" of *kokugo,* and this was why *kokugo* was needed as policy; that is, Hoshina was trying to draw *kokugo* into the sphere of artificiality, not nature. It was no longer "natural" evidence that the *kokugo* of the Great Japanese Empire was Japanese. It became necessary somehow to legislate the language, and this was the movement from *kokugo* to *kokka-go.*

CHAPTER 13

Manchukuo and the State Language

13-1. The Multiethnic Nation Manchukuo

Hoshina had made concrete suggestions for Japan's language policy when the March First Independence Movement shook the government-general of Korea. About ten years later, Hoshina had another opportunity to contribute to the empire's language policy when the Manchurian Incident of 1931[1] was followed by the establishment of Manchukuo (the Manchurian nation) the next year.

In September 1931 (Showa 6), the Japanese Kwantung army (Kantōgun) staged the so-called Ryūjōko Incident and quickly occupied the northeastern part of China, hastily creating a nation, Manchukuo, in March 1932 (Shōwa 7), only six months after the incident. To justify this fabricated nation, the authorities manipulated various strategies, such as the well-known but hollow slogans *ōdō rakudo* (paradise of the kingly way) and *gozoku kyōwa* (harmony among five races). "Five races" here refers to "the native Chinese, Manchus, and Mongols, as well as Japanese and Koreans" as stated in the Declaration of the Foundation of the [Manchurian] Nation. In the nation of Manchukuo, these five races were to live in harmony and create a utopian "paradise of the kingly way." In the founding of Manchukuo, its ethnic diversity was thus fantasized and given positive meaning.

A multiethnic nation is also a multilingual nation. What kind of status was to be given to the languages of these "five races"? Which language was to be used in government offices, courts, schools, and other public sectors? The authorities of Manchukuo were eager to gloss over Japanese oppression with "harmony among five races," but they did not recognize or pay attention to the linguistic problems that would occur amid such "harmony." As I will discuss later, they never legislated an official language of Manchukuo.

For Hoshina, on the other hand, the multilingual situation of Manchukuo was too serious a problem to ignore. As seen in chapter 11, Hoshina had found in Prussia-Germany's monolingual policy in Poland a model for Japanese language policy in Korea, and he was well aware of the fact that the Austro-Hungarian Empire fell apart because of its multiplicity of ethnicities and languages. Therefore, he was worried that while Japan was trumpeting the birth of Manchukuo, no one was concerned about the ethnic and linguistic multiplicity of the nation. And he sought in the concept of *kokka-go* a solution to prevent this multilingual nation from disintegrating.

13-2. A Multiethnic Nation and Political Language Problems

In 1933 (Shōwa 8), the year after the foundation of Manchukuo, Hoshina published two books: *Kokka-go no mondai ni tsuite* (About the Problems in State Language) in May and *Kokugo seisaku ron* (Theory for *Kokugo* Policy) in October. He wrote them to suggest a direction for language policy in Japanese colonies and the "new Manchuria-Mongolia nation," using the negative example of the Austro-Hungarian Empire. Much of the above two books was also repeated in his *Kokugo seisaku* (*Kokugo* Policy) in 1936 (Shōwa 11).[2] Hoshina's argument might be summarized as follows: Because the nation-state, its people, and its language are organic parts, nourishing and supporting each other, standardization of the language would immediately lead the nation to unity, and the expansion of a nation and its people would naturally coexist with the expansion of its language; the language follows the nation and the nation follows the language; it is the "wonder of *kokugo*" that fortifies the nation-state system and uplifts the people's spirit; the nation must make a consistent policy in order to maximize this power of *kokugo*; nonetheless, the Japanese nation was ignoring this important mission of language policy. Hoshina lamented that "there have been very few people in our country who were concerned about the importance of *kokugo* policy," and he urged that "now that Japan owns Taiwan and Korea, and has closer relationships with Manchuria-Mongolia and China, its urgent task is to institute a solid *kokugo* policy in order to promote and expand the nation's power" (Hoshina 1936a: 1).

Hoshina sorted language problems into two kinds. The first were of a humanistic nature, such as the institution of *hyōjungo*, unification of writing styles, script reform, and regulation of *kana* usage. These problems were about one language of a certain country and "did not entail any political consequences" (7–8). The second were of a political nature: in a nation of multiple ethnicities and languages, each ethnic group would insist on its language rights, and language problems would inevitably become political. "When a nation consists of different ethnic groups, or of people of the same race but using different languages, it will certainly become problematic to decide which language should be used for administering the nation's affairs" (16-17). In other words, the political language problems would inevitably result in instituting *kokka-go/ Staatssprache/*the state language.[3]

Maintaining a uniform linguistic institution in a multilingual nation posed a political problem. Hoshina identified four areas where political language problems occur: official languages, instructional language, court language, and military language. The official languages included "all that are used in public life, from those used in administering the nation's affairs to those in petitions and reports in each local community" (21). The instructional language was used in school classes; the court language in trials, testimony, and courtrooms; and the military language in formulating specialized military terms and commands. *Kokka-go* was a legal concept that controlled the languages of those four areas. Which language was to be allowed or forbidden in those areas could be a question of life or death for each ethnic group. In *Kokugo seisaku* Hoshina discussed concrete examples in different countries, though I will not refer to them here.

The political language problems were not limited to those four areas that coexisted horizontally. The vertical relationship among the state language *(Staatssprache),* the local languages used in each province *(Landessprache),* and the ethnic language *(Volkssprache/Stammsprache)* that was actually spoken by each ethnic group made the political language problems even more complex. This vertical relationship was hierarchical; as Hoshina explained, *kokka-go* was far superior to local or ethnic languages: "The local language is subordinate to *kokka-go,* and the ethnic language to the local language. The local language means the official language used in the supreme government office in each province and also in its upper-level technical schools, local congress and other government offices, as well as by the local governor and in various kinds of local meetings" (1936a, 147). Based on these premises, Hoshina closely examined language problems in multilingual countries such as Switzerland and Belgium, and most important, in the Austro-Hungarian Empire, which was representative of a multiplicity of ethnic groups with serious problems among them.

As mentioned before, Hoshina's academic work was founded on his realization of the overwhelming superiority of the modern science of language in the West to Japanese traditional *kokugogaku.* In his ideas about language policy, too, he was eager to learn from cases in Europe. Even though he did speak of the "Japanese spirit" in the climate of war, his position was fundamentally different from those held by scholars such as Yamada Yoshio who were immersed in the tradition of *kokugogaku.* Unlike the speculations by ultranationalistic *kokugogaku* scholars, Hoshina's theory was informed by the concrete model of the political problems witnessed in Austria-Hungary. In the same way as he discussed language policy in Prussia, Hoshina meticulously traced the history of language problems in Austria-Hungary, which to this day is an informative resource for researchers in the field.

13-3. The State Language Debate in the Austro-Hungarian Empire

According to Hoshina, "The term *kokka-go, Spaatssprache,* used in Austria-Hungary was quite new, and had never been used in law, etc." (1936a, 148). The word was first used in a speech in the [Austrian] Congress of 1848, and again in 1880 by a congressman [of the Austro-Hungarian Imperial Congress] in his proposal "to institute German as *Spaatssprache.*" At that point, "there were many questions as to the concept of *Spaatssprache,* but no one was able to give clear answers" (149). This proposal stirred a debate in the Imperial Congress in 1883 as to what *Spaatssprache* should refer to, but each congressman "made an interpretation that was politically convenient for him, and no one was able to offer a scientifically accurate definition" (150). Hoshina himself attempted to offer his interpretation, adopting a theory of Johann Kaspar Bluntschli (1808–1881), a Swiss political scientist, but arrived at a rather compromising definition of *kokka-go* as the language "used for administering a nation's affairs" (151). This definition, Hoshina maintained, entailed two kinds of state language: one for external use *(äussere Staatssprache)* and one for internal use *(innere Staatssprache).* The former was the language used in international relations, the latter, "in the power relationships between the nation and its people" (151). What Hoshina was most concerned with was this internal *kokka-go,* and "the areas of a nation's affairs where the internal *kokka-go* should be used are government offices, schools, and public community life" (152). Hoshina then discussed in detail the language problems and their historical context in each of the four fields: (1) the official language, which included *Geschäftssprache* (business language), *Amtssprache* (office language), and *Dienstsprache* (service language); (2) the instructional language *(Unterrichtssprache);* (3) the court language *(Gerichtssprache);* and (4) the military language, which included *Kommandosprache* (command language) and *Regimentssprache* (regiment language). Hoshina's organizational method was no different from that used in sociolinguistics today.

Among the concepts of "state language," "local language," and "ethnic language," probably "local language" would be most prone to misunderstanding. The original word *Landessprache* did not mean a dialect or a special ethnic language spoken in a certain region. It referred to the language that was permitted in government offices, congress, schools, courts, and so forth in a certain district (147). That is, the "local language" needed to be recognized by an authority. In that sense, in a more decentralized federal state such as Switzerland, a local language was closer to a miniature state language. Both concepts were born out of the realities in multilingual nations and therefore might not have been accurately understood in the linguistic climate of Japan. Hoshina himself, in fact, confused local language and ethnic language, as he said Korean was the local language in occupied Korea (Hoshina 1933a, 62). If the Korean language of that time had been a local language, Korea should have had a relatively advanced self-governance equivalent to a region of a federal nation.

Hoshina's confusion of terms might have come from his indifference to theoretical definitions of "state language," for his attention was focused on actual struggles among ethnic groups [in Europe] regarding state language. The following is the gist of his argument.

Up until the early nineteenth century, the actual official language of the Austrian Empire under the Habsburg dynasty was German, though the empire did not practice the Germanization policy *(Germanisierungspolitik)* as Prussia did. However, the empire faced waves of resistance in 1848. Hoshina understood these "revolutions of 1848" as ethnic struggles, that is, "the demonstration of protest against the dominance of German, caused by the rise of ethnic awareness among the non-German-speaking races, the purpose of which was to demand that their languages be treated as state languages and be given the same treatment as German" (Hoshina 1936a, 153). The representatives of the non-German-speaking people demanded of the Constitution Committee of the Imperial Congress that "all ethnic groups in Austria receive equal rights *(Gleichberechtigung).*" As a result, the constitution promulgated in March 1849 included an article stating that "all ethnic groups obtain equal rights, and the rights of their ethnic identity and language shall be protected and not be impaired" (155). It also recognized the following ten languages as official languages: German, Italian, Magyar (Hungarian), Czech, Polish, Ruthenian (Ukrainian), Slovene, Serbian, Croatian, and Rumanian. However, in 1851, after only two years, the constitution was abrogated, and the government intensified a program of Germanization. In particular, in the regions where Hungarian, German, and Slavic languages were used, the instructional language at *Gymnasiums* was completely Germanized by the Cabinet Orders of December 1853 and again of January 1855 (157). This rekindled resistance by non-German-speaking people, which exploded in 1860: "In an attempt to dissolve the problems of state language in Austria-Hungary, these people claimed equal protection of all races and all regions, and equal rights and equal obligations *(Gleicher Schutz für alle Stämme und Länder. Gleiches Recht, Gleiche Pflichten),* and they selected a representative from each region, who successfully achieved their ends" (160).

Hoshina continued to detail descriptions of the flaming debates on language in the Austrian Congress from 1861 to 1865. Though I am not including them here, those debates resulted in the incorporation of the following Article 19 into the Austro-Hungarian Imperial Constitution, promulgated in December 1867:

> All ethnic groups in the nation have equal rights. Accordingly, they have a right to have their ethnic identity *(Nationalität)*[4] and their language be protected and not be impaired. The nation recognizes that all local languages have equal rights in schools, government offices, and public life. In the regions where several ethnic groups reside, public schools shall be established, and furthermore, those schools shall offer essential education in one's mother tongue, without forcing students to use a different group's language. (167)

Article 19 provided a resolution of the language problems in Austria-Hungary, but in Hoshina's view, it was the cause of the fall of the empire:

> There could not have been any problem of state language if they had attained the spirit to protect and respect ethnicity and language and equal rights. The idea of a state language itself was totally incompatible with Slavicism, Magyarism, and Germanism, and was destined to conflict with their ethnicity and protection of their languages. In other words, the idea of a state language does not allow development of local or ethnic languages. Seeing the problems that occurred among ethnic groups, the existence of a state language could never be accepted in Austria-Hungary. (168)

Hoshina thus argued that a multilingual nation had to choose one of two options: institution of a state language or recognition of equal rights for all ethnic groups. These two options could not coexist, and if the nation chose the latter, ethnic conflicts would never cease, and those conflicts would endanger the nation's foundation. Therefore, the nation's only option was to institute a state language with clear legislation and reject equal rights for all ethnic groups. This was the lesson Hoshina learned from the Austro-Hungarian Empire.

13-4. The Idea of *Kokka-go*

Hoshina maintained that in a multilingual nation "the state language wouldn't be meaningful unless it was the single language to be used and the use of [more than] two ethnic languages occurred only in unavoidable situations" (Hoshina 1933a, 7). This also applied to the colonies: "The language used in government offices and other public sectors in the colonies must be that of the ruler. This is where the distinction between the ruler and the ruled is indicated" (1936a, 100). In *Kokka-go no mondai ni tsuite,* Hoshina asserted more directly that "since the colonies are part of the [suzerain] nation, they must be controlled by the nation's sole language, and use of the native language must be limited to private lives" (1933a, 62). Thus Hoshina insisted on express legislation of Japanese as the sole *kokka-go* in all areas of official, instructional, legal, and military language in the "multiracial nation" that was the Great Japanese Empire.

Hoshina at that point did not yet assert the same for Manchukuo, however; he merely suggested that "it is most necessary for the people of the new Manchuria-Mongolian nation [Munchukuo] to learn Japanese" and that "it is urgent that the nation maintains harmony and cooperation with our country through Japanese in order to establish national policies" (1936a, 135–136). He might have thought that it would be seen as hasty to demand the institution of *kokka-go* in Manchukuo, which had just been founded. A few years later, however, in his *Daitōa kyōeiken to kokugo seisaku* (The Greater East Asia Co-Prosperity Sphere and *Kokugo* Policy, 1942; Shōwa 17), Hoshina expressed his conviction that "it is most advisable to declare Japanese to be the *kokka-go* of Manchukuo" (255).

However, the majority of the government officials in charge of Manchukuo were of the opinion that "a single *kokka-go*" would be impracticable for the nation. For example, in his essay "Manshūkoku ni okeru Nihongo" (The Japanese Language in Manchukuo), Maruyama Rinpei[5] contended that "Manchukuo is a multiracial nation, and therefore it is obvious that it cannot have a single national language." At the same time, he explained that a constitution in Manchukuo not having been proclaimed, the legal status of *kokugo* could be found only in educational ordinances such as the Outline of the Educational System, School Ordinance, and School Regulations. After examining those laws, Maruyama arrived at the conclusion that "Manchukuo has three national languages: Japanese, Manchurian, and Mongolian," and "Japanese is given the greatest importance among them" (Asahi Shinbunsha 1941–1942, 6:120–136).

A more substantial argument was made by Shigematsu Nobuhiro, a professor at Kenkoku Daigaku (Foundation University, Manchukuo), in his essay "Manshūkoku ni okeru Nihongo no chii" (The Status of Japanese in Manchukuo) (*Bungaku* 1940, 45–56). Though he was aware that Japanese was considered Manchukuo's national language in the Outline of the Educational System and other school regulations, he contended that those regulations were "equivalent to Japanese ministerial ordinances" and did not have "authority commensurate with the constitution." Shigematsu then attempted to explicate the concept of *kokugo* from a scholarly viewpoint, making an intriguing observation: "the concept of *kokugo* cannot be separated from its relation to the nation"; therefore, *kokugo* was not "a simple linguistic concept" but "a kind of political concept"; but the use of the Japanese term *kokugo* confused these two concepts. In order to make the idea of *kokugo* coherent with the multiethnic reality in Manchukuo, Shigematsu offered a definition of *kokugo* as the language used by "the race that played the central role" in the nation and "the nurturing language of the civilization that supports the nation's existence." According to this definition, *kokugo*, as the nation's language, did not have to be a single language: "Every nation in the world has its language that embraces the spirit and culture that is fundamental to the nation and its people. Japan happens to have a single one, while Manchukuo has two (or three) languages." Shigematsu's conclusion was that as long as Manchukuo was founded on the spirit of "cooperation among different native people under Japanese leadership," it would be "inevitable for Manchukuo to live with the duality of *kokugo* (treating all native languages as one, for convenience)," though he acknowledged that these two *kokugo* should not be equal and that Japanese had leading power superior to the rest.

Note that both Maruyama and Shigematsu used the word *kokugo*, not *kokka-go*, as Hoshina did. *Kokka-go* in Hoshina's sense was very different from Yamada Yoshio's definition of *kokugo* as the standard language of *Nihon kokka* (the Japanese nation). Yamada's "standard language of the Japanese nation" referred to the language that had formed Japanese cultural conventions and was based on an ultranationalistic spiritualism connected to the idea of *kokutai* by an unbroken, eternal line *(bansei ikkei no kokutai).*[6] Hoshina's *kokka-go*, on the other hand, was not colored by such ultranationalism. *Kokka-go* in Hoshina's view had to be legislated in law; that is, it was a political concept in a strict sense.

Whenever an attempt was made to introduce a political concept into the sphere of language, however, it was always disguised by the word *kokugo*. The expression *kokugo*, while it referred to a political idea in truth, had and still has the effect of concealing its political nature and making the language seem to be natural, a given. On the other hand, the idea of *kokka-go* revealed and exposed that political nature. The term *kokka-go* was unheard of in Japan at that time and is still an unfamiliar expression today. In the Japanese climate, where language issues tended to be overlooked as self-evident, Hoshina's attempt to introduce the idea of *kokka-go* had no impact.[7]

Some *kokugo* scholars of his time overtly opposed the term *kokka-go*. For example, Andō Masatsugu, implicitly referring to Hoshina as "a scholar who preaches a need to institute *kokka-go*," wrote the following criticism:

> It is reasonable to interpret *"kokka-go"* as the official language used in various sectors, or the language used in the nation's administration. . . . However, instituting

such *"kokka-go"* does not mean creating something from nothing, but determining one of the existing languages in the nation as the official language. Therefore, it is no different from authorizing *kokugo* by the nation. This might appear to be an enforcement of *kokugo* in a sense, but in another sense, it could unfavorably demarcate the influence of *kokugo*. (Asahi Shinbunsha 1941–1942, 1:18–19)

This must have hurt Hoshina. Andō was not Yamada, and Ando and Hoshina had studied together under Ueda and had worked together on various projects in Kokugo Chōsa Iinkai.[8] Moreover, Andō had shared views with Hoshina about *kokugo* policies on *kanji, kana* usage, *hyōjungo*, colloquial styles, and so forth. Andō, after his retirement from Kokugo Chōsa Iinkai, took a position in the government-general of Taiwan and Taipei University and worked hard to establish language policy in the colony. Andō and Hoshina were the two greatest scholars central to the history of Japanese language policy before the end of World War II, and Andō also became a central figure, together with Yamamoto Yūzō,[9] in the Federation of the Kokugo Movement by the People (Kokumin no kokugo undō renmei) after the war.

It is curious that the idea of *kokka-go* was seen as a threat that would weaken the institution of *kokugo*. Perhaps Andō understood *kokka-go* as the language exclusively used in governmental sectors and not outside them, and thought it would shake the power of *kokugo*, which was supposed to be the absolute authority in every area. Andō feared that confining *kokka-go* to the area of politics would only endanger the authority of *kokugo*.

Andō was also critical of another argument by Hoshina (though, again, without directly mentioning his name):

> There is a scholar among us who is of the opinion that problems regarding *kokugo* can be divided into two types, humanistic ones and political ones . . . and that it is the mission of *kokugo* policy to solve both types of problems. . . . This may be one opinion. As for me, however, I believe that so-called political problems become political only when the nation treats them with some political intention, but in essence, they are no different from the so-called humanistic problems of *kokugo*. (Andō 1975, 412–417)

That is, Andō did not recognize that language was in itself of a political nature even before it became the object of the government's policy. While *kokugo* must reside in the sphere of "nature," beyond "artificiality," the idea of *kokka-go* would drag *kokugo* into the sphere of artificiality and politics.

Hoshina, on the other hand, was keenly aware that language has a political power in the real world, even before it becomes an object of policy. He had repeated on many occasions that "there is nothing like language ... that can strongly unite and bond a race together" (Hoshina 1936a, 56), and he was aware that such a racial identity with language existed not only in the ruling race but also in the ruled. As long as an ethnic group survived, it would justly claim its own language rights, and therefore a language war would become inevitable between the ruling and the ruled. That is why Hoshina believed that "political *kokugo* problems are sure to occur sooner or later when a nation contains different races or when it obtains new colonies" (35). And he knew from his observation of the case in Austria-Hungary that the resistance of the ruled could be so stubborn that it could have dreadful results for the ruling race. The idea of *kokka-go* was the resolution he came up with to prevent the languages of the ruled from gaining a higher status. Hoshina had predicted that demand for the status of local languages or the national language could destroy the ruling system, and this is why he resolutely opposed a multilingual system: "If we allow dual language use in Korea, the Korean language spoken by the majority population would overwhelm Japanese, leading to frequent problematic incidents" (108). He also had misgivings about the future when "Korean congressmen, who are already part of politics, will increase their number every year, and while they are now using Japanese, an occasion might happen in the future when they would demand their native tongue. It is then that the issue of *kokka-go* will have to be taken up formally" (Hoshina 1933a, 64).

The state language in the Austro-Hungarian Empire was proposed to solve the political language problems, but Hoshina proposed *kokka-go* to prevent such problems in the now multilingual nation, the Great Japanese Empire. His attempt at a "scientific definition" of *kokka-go* was after all an academic pretense to justify the need for preemptive measures for the Japanese language.

In relation to the issue of *kokka-go,* Hoshina was also concerned about the pan-ethnic movements that had exploded throughout Europe. He saw the clash among pan-Germanism, pan-Slavism, and pan-Magyarism as the ultimate embodiment of racial struggles. Hoshina observed that these movements considered language as the sustenance of the race's vitality, and therefore "the racial struggles accompanied linguistic struggles" (1936a, 125). A "pan-ethnic movement" is usually understood as a movement towards unification of ethnic groups who speak languages of the same family, disregarding the existing borders. However, Hoshina considered it "the movement towards expansion of a race's own power," that is, a movement for the assimilation of different people, regardless of their ethnic or linguistic families, by expanding the territory of the ruler's language. For Hoshina, a race was an organic body, and therefore a racial or linguistic struggle could bring fatal damage; the struggle was not a matter of good or evil, but was born out of the basic nature of race and language:

> Each race and its language strive to protect its own territory, and furthermore try to invade others' territories, resulting in horrendous struggles. Such struggles will probably never stop. Even if the constitution guaranteed, as it did in Austria-Hungary, equal rights among all languages, it would never be satisfactory for any one of these groups, and they would most likely continue to expand their own territories. Therefore, it is quite evident that solid language policy needs to be established [to prevent such struggles]. (70)[10]

In this way, the institution of *kokka-go* could have become a powerful force, a step towards dissemination of the pan-ethnic movement outside Japan. Among the areas of *kokka-go,* the instructional language had the most important mission, for it had the great power "to nurture the healthy spirit and disposition unique to the race, and at the same time, to assimilate other races" (Hoshina 1933a, 34). After illustrating a series of pan-ethnic movements in Europe, Hoshina pointed to the direction that Japan should take: "Transplanting and disseminating our culture and language to other Asian races would be the most urgent and important measures for expanding the power of the Yamato race"[11] (1936a, 130), and for that purpose, Hoshina argued that establishment of Japanese language schools throughout the continent was of the greatest urgency. It was time for the Greater East Asia Co-Prosperity Sphere to be claimed.

Language for the Co-Prosperity Sphere and the Internationalization of the Japanese Language

14-1. Debates on *Kana* Script in Manchukuo

As discussed in the previous chapter, Hoshina tried to make Japanese the state language, *kokka-go,* of Manchukuo, or at least to accord Japanese a status superior to that of other languages. However, it was not that he tried to transplant the Japanese language just as it was. Hoshina persisted again in his determination for *kokugo* reform. He maintained that the most important agenda in building Manchukuo was the dissemination of education, but that "it would be extremely difficult to reeducate the people there in *kanji,*" and therefore "a different strategy must be used, quickly departing from the troublesome *kanji,* in order to spread education." Towards that goal, "the most expedient method is to disseminate Japanese as quickly as possible, using *kana* as their national script, for cultivation of knowledge and development of culture" (Hoshina 1936a, 133). For the ethnic groups who had never used it, *kanji* would be a hindrance to education; and even for those who did use Chinese characters, the use of *kanji* would be an obstacle to communication because the Japanese pronunciation of *kanji* was drastically different from the Chinese one. Thus, Hoshina advised "education with *kana,* rejecting *kanji*" (1932, 231). His idea was not completely unrealistic, and in fact, the authorities of Manchukuo once made an attempt to institute *kana* as the national script.

Kamio Kazuharu, who took the positions of secretary and counselor in the General Affairs Office, Department of National Affairs of Manchukuo, and then became a professor at Foundation University, wrote in his memoir that "there was once a joint movement by translation officers from the Kwantung army, the Japanese embassy, the government offices of Manchukuo, and the Concordia

Association[1] to make *kana* the national script of Manchukuo," demanding the rejection of *kanji*. However, the authorities at the Southern Manchuria Railroad Company[2] strongly objected to this, as Kamio conveyed to the Department of National Affairs. Later, he was called to the department to receive its "resolution not to take up the issue about *kana* script" (Kamio 1983, 102–105)[3]

When did this happen? According to Kaimio's memoir, "Dr. Hattori Shirō,[4] who happened to stop by on the way back from his research trip to Hulun Buir, listened to my story, and showed his concern." Considering that Hattori returned to Japan in February 1936 (Shōwa 11) after two and a half years of linguistic research in Manchukuo, if Kamio's memory was correct the "*kana* script" debate must have happened around that time.

The debate did not come to an end, however. At the First Conference on Provisions of Kokugo (Kokugo Taisaku Kyōgikai) in June 1939 (Shōwa 11), the Manchukuo representative reported that "research on *tōa kana* [East Asian *kana*] has been undertaken in Manchukuo." This was an attempt to create a convenient *kana* system based on Japanese *katakana,* in the hope that "acquisition of one system of phonetic symbols would enable the people to read Japanese, Chinese, and Mongolian" (Manshūkoku Kyōikushi Kenkyūkai 1993, 307–308). This was probably the project that resulted in *'Mango kana' shuisho narabini kaisetsusho* (Prospectus and Manual for Manchurian *Kana*), published by the Kokugo Investigative Committee of [Manchukuo's] Education Department in 1943 (Shōwa 18).[5] The "Manchurian *kana*" was an elaborate system of writing Chinese with Japanese *katakana,* but it was never put into play before Manchukuo collapsed.

Kamio said that "Hattori showed concern" on hearing about the proposal for *kana* script, but judging from Hattori's own work, this does not seem to have been the case.[6] Hattori at that time was of the opinion that "it is absolutely necessary for the Japanese race in the future to abandon *kanji* and adopt phonetic scripts (*rōmaji, kana,* etc.)" (Hattori 1992, 32). "It is a striking fact that *kanji* is impairing the Japanese language," said Hattori. Criticizing the motives of adherents of *kanji* as either emotional or unimportant, Hattori asserted that use of phonetic script would make the language much easier to learn, not only *kokugo* for the Japanese people but also the Japanese language for other races that did not use *kanji.* And he claimed that "only by adopting phonetic script could Japanese gain a status equal to that of other languages in the world" (32–36).

For Hattori, who was well known as an ascetic scholar, not concerning himself with affairs outside his field in linguistics, the above statement was his candid opinion about the state of the Japanese language at that time. This conviction might have been partly responsible for his extraordinary passion for his research on phonology and the introduction of phonology after the war. Questions about script or transcription ultimately arrive at phonological questions about determining the phonemes. These questions led him to write *On'in-ron to seishohō* (Phonology and Orthography) in 1951 (Shōwa 26), which, atypical of his work, contains much social comment.

In the building of Manchukuo and the Greater East Asia Co-Prosperity Sphere, dissemination and promotion of Japanese were always the most urgent projects aimed at expanding Japan's ruling power, and wherever the Japanese military marched, Japanese language teachers followed. At the same time, however, all the questions about what was to be taught were suddenly magnified, needing urgent solutions: what kind of Japanese was to be promoted with regard to pronunciation, accent, use of *kana*, [number of] *kanji*, grammar, vocabulary, word usage, and style? The urgency for the promotion of Japanese into the Co-Prosperity Sphere in return openly presented the question, "What kind of language should Japanese be?"—the question of, so to speak, the "internationalization of the Japanese language."

14-2. The Greater East Asia Co-Prosperity Sphere and *Kokugo* Policy

Most of Hoshina's works had been concerned almost exclusively with language problems in Europe until he published *Daitōa kyōeiken to kokugo seisaku* (The Greater East Asia Co-Prosperity Sphere and *Kokugo* Policy) in October 1942 (Shōwa 17). This was the last book he wrote before the end of the war, integrating his views about language policy. His major argument in this book was as simple and naïve as that in his previous writings: "the spirit of a race runs through the language the race inherited from its ancestry" (1942a, 3), and therefore "the most effective measure for expanding the power of a race is to transplant its language into other races and thus disseminate its culture" (9–10). But now the realities had leaped ahead of him: the Japanese military's "advance" on Southeast Asia in the name of building the Greater East Asia Co-Prosperity Sphere was aimed not only at military occupation but also at transplanting the "Japanese spirit" into the occupied. To achieve the latter, promotion of the Japanese language was considered the most urgent measure, and thus a number of Japanese language schools were set up in the occupied colonies.

Facing this situation, Hoshina asserted that "making Japanese the common language for the Co-Prosperity Sphere is the most urgent requisite for unification of the different races in it and having them esteem the Great Japanese Empire as their leader" (195). Citing the success of *kokugo* policy in the colonies Taiwan and Korea, Hoshina attempted to chart the future direction of *kokugo* policy by gathering information about elements of *kokugo* education, such as school facilities and textbook compilations, in Malaysia, Indonesia, Vietnam, the Philippines, Thailand, Burma, and China.

Why, then, was it Japanese that was to be the "common language in the Co-Prosperity Sphere"? Hoshina attempted an explanation drawn from linguistics theory. First, the language of the group with politically and socially superior status had the power and influence to lead ethnic groups of other languages: "It is a general principle in the history of language that when uncivilized people have contact with civilized people, the former adopt a great part of the latter's language. Now that the Greater East Asia Co-Prosperity Sphere has been formed, our nation, as the leader, has an important mission to guide its sound and solid development" (375). And because this was a general principle in the history of language, "the Japanese language will spread over those people just as water flows from high to low" (376).

Hoshina also argued for a common language in the Co-Prosperity Sphere because different languages were spoken there not only between different ethnic groups, but even among the same group. In addition to forty different languages spoken in the Philippine Islands, Hoshina mentioned the following: "Chamorro, Palauan, and Sangir on Sangiru Island; Tontemboan, Bolaang Mongondow, Gorontaro, Makasar, Toraja, and Buginese on Celebes Island; Dayak, Tidong, Borogan [*sic*],[7] and Tarakan on Borneo Island; Sundanese, Javanese, and Madurese on Java Island; Balinese, Ache, Minangabau, Batak, Mentawe, and Niasu on Sumatra Island; Malay on the Malay Peninsula and Sumatra Island" (197). It would be necessary to have one common language for communication in such a multilingual environment, and Hoshina insisted that that one language be Japanese.

Certainly, some kind of bridging language was necessary for communication,[8] but the choice should be in the hands of the people themselves who engaged in the communication. The claim that Japanese must be the "East Asian common language" for linguistic and cultural reasons was simply an excuse to disguise [Japan's] unjust military and political occupation. Nonetheless, Hoshina repeatedly wrote, "Every language of a superior people has a powerful and universal influence. The language of Japan, the leader of the Co-Prosperity Sphere, obviously qualifies, and therefore there cannot be any dissatisfaction or opposition among other races in the Sphere" (199). Despite Hoshina's academic training this work of his is full of this dogmatic but empty imperialistic tone.

Nonetheless, Hoshina's characteristic pet theory is well represented here. Just as in the domestic case of the institution of *hyōjungo,* he contended that language policy only artificially enforced the influential power that became inherent in a superior language through the course of nature. This grew into a conviction that any interference of authority into *hyōjungo*, *kokka-go*, and *kyōeiken-go* (Co-Prosperity Sphere language) was justified as ultimately consistent with the course of nature. Even Hoshina, who had been sensitive to the political nature of language, was trapped in this illusion throughout his life. Note, however, that his argument was nonetheless free from the fanatic ultra-nationalism that prevailed in publications at that time on similar topics. He did not glorify "the country blessed with *kotodama*,"[9] nor did he mention at all "the tradition in *kokugo*." He continued to rely almost exclusively on the cases in Prussia and Austria-Hungary, and his assertions were full of utilitarianism and culturalism, and lacking in spiritualism. This may be why his theory was able to survive the counterattacks after Japan's defeat in the war.

14-3. The Japanese Language Expanding Worldwide

In *Daitōa kyōeiken to kokugo seisaku*, Hoshina discussed not only language problems in the Greater East Asia Co-Prosperity Sphere, but also the status of Japanese in the world: "Enthusiasm about the Japanese language is a worldwide trend today. This has been brought about by our nation's development" (1942a, 302). Referring to events in Europe, Hoshina argued that a "great effort has already been made during peace gradually to expand [our nation's] power by transplanting our culture into other races through our language. The first such effort was to establish schools to educate children of those races" (138). According to Hoshina, dissemination and education of Japanese among other races, including the colonized or occupied, was already "a policy towards expansion of the race's power" (134) because learning a language meant acquiring the way of thinking of the race inherent in its language; therefore language education, whatever form it took, was the first step towards "assimilation of ways of thinking." Hoshina believed that establishment of Japanese language curricula in overseas universities was evidence of the expansion of Japan's power, and no different from the advancement of Japanese into the Co-Prosperity Sphere. That is, according to his view, the Japanese curricula in London University and the Paris School of Oriental Languages, like those in the *kokumin gakkō* (national schools)[10] in Japan's colonies, played their part in putting *kokugo* policy in force. Hoshina included in his book the entire list of the overseas schools and organizations that teach Japanese culture and language to foreigners, which had been published by the Cultural Affairs Department of the Ministry of Foreign Affairs, and provided the history, faculty composition, course contents, and textbooks of the major institutions on the list. All of these schools, for Hoshina, were indispensable fronts in the promotion of Japanese.

The Cultural Affairs Department was created under special circumstances, explained in a booklet published in 1939 (Shōwa 14) with the title *Sekai ni nobiyuku nihongo* (The Japanese Language Expanding Worldwide): Japan's withdrawal from the League of Nations in 1933 (Shōwa 8) caused some to be concerned that "our country is suffering a great disadvantage, because the great world powers have ignored our empire's rightful pretensions and status without understanding our superior culture" (Gaimushō 1939, 3). The group set up a foundation, Kokusai Bunka Shinkōkai (Society for the Promotion of International Cultural Relations), in April 1934 (Shōwa 9), with Prince Takamatsu as president and Konoe Fumimaro[11] as chair. Responding to this, the Ministry of Foreign Affairs set up a new section in the Cultural Affairs Department in August 1935 (Shōwa 10) to take charge of international cultural relations.[12] One of the major tasks of this section was the promotion of the Japanese language overseas, including the "establishment of and support for curricula of Japanese culture and language in universities and other educational institutions overseas, administration of their instructions and supervision" (5–6). In this connection, Kokugo Kyōkai (Association for Kokugo), which was formed in 1930 (Shōwa 5), also with Konoe Fumimaro as chair, merged Kokugo Aigo Dōmei (Kokugo Protection League) and Gengo Mondai Danwakai (Language Issues Discussion Club), and started a new journal, *Kokugo undō* (The *Kokugo* Movement), in 1937 (Shōwa 12). The journal played a leading role in connecting the "advancement of Japanese" with the "improvement of *kokugo.*"

The booklet *The Japanese Language Expanding Worldwide* listed Japanese curricula that were established overseas, and it openly stated the objective, the promotion of Japanese: while "the advancement of a language overseas is inseparable from expansion of the power of its nation" (72), the promotion of Japanese itself was not the ultimate goal. The most important goal was "to make the Japanese culture and national spirit understood through the Japanese language," and the project for international cultural relations was "a ceaseless war . . . mobilizing cultures and ideas" (75). The authorities of the Ministry of Education at that time, including Hoshina, considered "the promotion of Japanese" as an engineering project, or even "a linguistic war," during a time of peace.

At issue was the weapon for this "linguistic war," the Japanese language. The Cultural Affairs Department must have been insecure about the power and effectiveness of Japanese, for it proposed in the booklet that since it was not easy for foreigners to learn this complex language, "the Japanese language must be reorganized for foreigners," and that research had to be done into "what kind of Japanese should be taught," with the goal of creating something like "basic Japanese" (67–68).

Preceding this development, Doi Mitsutomo, a scholar of English, had already created a systematic "basic Japanese," following Charles K. Ogden's model of "basic English." This system used simplified grammar and a vocabulary limited to a thousand words. "I heard about the great difficulty in teaching Japanese to people in Korea and Taiwan," Doi explained, and one of the reasons he wrote the book was that he feared "another failure through teaching unorganized, raw Japanese" when Japanese needed to be taught in Manchukuo (Doi 1933, 2–3). It was this "basic Japanese" that he brought with him when he was sent to teach Japanese in the Department of Far Eastern Languages and Cultures of London University.

Doi's pioneer work was followed by various research, such as a selection of the minimum "basic vocabulary" necessary for daily life. As Ishiguro Osamu explained, the "basic vocabulary" was born out of "the difficult experience in *kokugo* education in this time of rapid overseas advancement of Japanese," and it would "contribute to domestic improvement as well as to the overseas development of *kokugo*" (1940, 255–256). The problems in dissemination and promotion of Japanese thus arrived back at the problems in *kokugo* reform, as candidly expressed by Yamaguchi Kiichirō after his long experience teaching Japanese in the colonies: "The situation of the current advancement of *kokugo* overseas will prompt improvement and organization of the modern spoken language in Japan, and will bring changes in language teaching methods" (Yamaguchi 1940, 391).

This was exactly what was troubling Hoshino, too. His words were more radical than those of the above-mentioned scholars, and even angry: "In our country there is no distinct standard language, but nobody in the nation realizes it. Such a lack of self-examination and reflection about Japanese is a painful obstruction to promoting the language abroad" (Hoshina 1942a, 454).

14-4. The First Conference on Provisions of *Kokugo*

Hirai Masao said that "the debate about the overseas advancement of Japanese began in Shōwa 11 and 12 (1936–1937) and erupted during Shōwa 14 (1939)" (1948, 322). It was about this time that journalism frequently featured the "overseas advancement of Japanese," and both governmental and private organizations began active projects in making Japanese textbooks, organizing a list of basic vocabulary, and training Japanese language instructors. The most significant development was the First Conference on Provisions of Kokugo (Kokugo Taisaku Kyōgikai) held by the Ministry of Education June 20–22, 1939 (Shōwa 14). The ministry invited relevant participants from the government-generals of Korea and Taiwan, the Kwantung Headquarters, the South Pacific Office, Manchukuo, and the Boards of Development of Asia (Kōain) in northern China, central China, Mongolia, and Amoy. Scholars such as Fujimura Tsukuru, Ogura Shinpei, Hisamatsu Sen'ichi, and Jinbō Kaku were invited. Hoshina attended as one of the representatives of the ministry, though there is no record of his remarks at the conference.

The conference began with an opening address by Minister Araki Sadao: "Our *kokugo* is the spiritual blood that flows in our people . . . and that solidly unites our people" (Manshūkoku Kyōikushi Kenkyūkai 1993, 273). This is exactly the phrase used in Ueda's "Kokugo to kokka to." However, the conference was not as "united" as the sentiment suggested, and it turned into a free-for-all. Other than some self-praising promotion of *kokugo,* most of the remarks at the conference presented concrete problems in Japanese classrooms. With one voice, local representatives complained about the difficulty of teaching Japanese to people of other languages and about the lack of the ministry's understanding of this difficulty. The issues were not limited to the making of textbooks but included teaching methods, selection of teaching materials, training of instructors, and treatment of teachers.

In the debate about textbooks between the Ministry of Education and the overseas people, the former maintained that textbooks used in *naichi* (the homeland) should be the model for those used in *gaichi* (overseas territories), while the latter insisted that textbooks would be more effective if they were compiled in *gaichi.* In this regard, Manchukuo was in a delicate position: its representatives plainly noted that Manchukuo was neither a colony nor a *gaichi,* but "was in a special situation as an independent nation" (470). This remark caused a highly volatile tension between Manchukuo delegates and the ministry.

The textbook issues ultimately arrived at the problems in the Japanese language itself. All of the representatives' remarks vividly indicated their insecurity about what kind of Japanese should be taught. Complaints focused on the fact that there was no standard in any aspect of the language, such as accent, pronunciation, word usage, or vocabulary. Fukui Masaru from Manchukuo, for example, lamented that instructors were often put in a situation "where they had to question the fundamentals of the Japanese language itself" (303). Morita Gorō from the government-general of Korea expressed his dismay at "the lack of uniformity in accent, not of Koreans but of Japanese [teachers] who came to Korea from different regions, including Tōhoku and Kyūshū" (282). He complained that the question of standard language was "the deadlock" they always came to, and that they frequently had to face a situation where they could not tell whether the words they chose to use were standard. Accordingly, he appealed to the Ministry of Education to "use this problem in making textbooks as an opportunity for instituting standard language and its usage" (428–429).

Another controversy at the conference was about *kana* usage in Japanese textbooks. All of the representatives from Korea were dissatisfied with the incoherent practice in Korean elementary schools of teaching a phonetic *kana* system to lower-level students and a historical system to upper-level students. They asserted that Japanese language education overseas must focus on aural and oral skills rather than on reading—that is, on spoken language and not written language—and for that purpose the phonetic *kana* usage would be the best method. The participants from Manchukuo and China agreed. For example, Ichitani Kiyoaki from Manchukuo affirmed that "*kana* usage in *gaichi* must absolutely follow the phonetic system" and further urged the delegates "not to use *kanji,* or to reduce its number as much as possible" (465). The following comment by Sakamoto Ichirō from central China struck at the crux of the matter:

When we look at the Japanese language, we find it necessary to adopt the phonetic *kana* usage, or to make the [current] usage closer to it. How many of us, even those of the older generation, can perfectly and correctly write with the *kana* system used in the national textbooks today? It would be simply impossible to force foreigners to write a language that even the homeland people cannot. (498)

However, the opposing view about *kana* usage was not concerned with technical questions about which system should be used in textbooks. For example, Jinbō Kaku, a representative from the homeland, commented that even if the phonetic *kana* usage were adopted in overseas colonies, it would serve only as pronunciation marks and wouldn't be *kana* usage in a genuine sense (371), implying that historical *kana* usage was the only genuine *kana* system. Such views as his came from Hashimoto Shinkichi's theory of *kana* usage. Hashimoto maintained that the Japanese historical *kana* usage, unlike orthographies of European languages, was based on "the rules for writing words, not just sounds" (Hashimoto 1943, 78). Here, "writing words" in *kana* meant distinguishing homonyms, words with the same pronunciation and different meanings. Therefore, correspondence to sounds was not the essential role of *kana*. On the other hand, "the phonetic *kana* usage is based on sounds, and its principle is to copy the sounds: thus, they are a kind of phonetic symbol" (94); therefore, "the historical *kana* usage and the phonetic one are based on mutually exclusive ideas" (99).

202   Hoshina Kōichi and His Language Policies

The historical usage as the legitimate one, and the phonetic one for convenience for teaching foreigners—this was in fact the thinking that clearly discriminated between "Japanese *(nihongo)* for foreigners" and "*kokugo* for the homeland." It was a last-ditch defense of the contradiction, admitting the need for reform of Japanese for overseas while refusing to extend the reform into the homeland.

Hoshina flatly rejected such a view. He asserted that the most effective method to teach people in the Co-Prosperity Sphere was "using not the classical usage [the historical *kana* system] but the phonetic *kana* system that correctly reflects the modern standard pronunciation" (Hoshina 1942a, 410). Furthermore, he criticized those who "held onto the historical usage and insisted on the use of the phonetic system only as a pronunciation guide in teaching foreigners." He asserted that "it is unreasonable to call the phonetic *kana* usage 'pronunciation marks.' It would be much more advantageous for teaching overseas to openly adopt the phonetic *kana* usage" (411). Hoshina's intention was to bring the overseas reform in line with domestic *kokugo* reform. Most of the overseas representatives at the conference held the same opinion: the core of the problem lay in the state of the Japanese language in the "homeland," and they demanded prompt actualization of *kokugo* reform and systematization of the Japanese language.

At the end of the first day, Library Director Kondō as the chair of the conference expressed his frustration, perhaps epitomizing the feelings of all the participants:

> In conclusion, we who were born into, grew up with, and will die with *kokugo*, the language of Japan, do not have a clear consciousness about this language. . . . Facing today's situation, when we sincerely try to promote Japanese in other places, we inevitably have to challenge the essence of *kokugo* itself as the most fundamental problem. (Manshūkoku Kyōikushi Kenkyūkai 1993, 358–359)

On the final day of the conference, the following was voted as the first of six resolutions:

> 1. Establishment of an institution for investigation and unification of *kokugo:* We found that the organization and unification of Japanese is the most urgent issue for promoting the language overseas, and request that the Ministry of Education newly establish a vigorous institution for investigation and unification of *kokugo* towards a swift solution of *kokugo* problems. (518)

The other five resolutions were about (2) establishing liaison offices for Japanese language teaching, (3) training Japanese language instructors, (4) compiling a dictionary of standard Japanese, (5) selecting Japanese songs and lyrics, and (6) producing music records and talking pictures (518–519).

In response to these resolutions, the Ministry of Education instituted a Kokugo Section in its Library Office in November 1940 (Shōwa 15), and in December, together with the Board of Development of Asia, it assisted in the establishment of Nihongo Kyōiku Shinkōkai (Association for the Promotion of Japanese Language Education).

14-5. The Second Conference on Provisions of *Kokugo*

The Second Conference on Provisions of Kokugo was held January 20–22, 1941 (Shōwa 16), but this fact was not made public until recently. While the record of the first conference was printed and distributed as a secret document of the Ministry of Education, that of the second conference was never printed; rather, the original stenographic copies were left unattended in the ministry. The first day's record and the complete list of participants are missing, so the only participants known are those whose remarks were recorded. I do not know why the record was never printed; nonetheless, it is as important a resource as the first record, especially in that it shows more of what the Japanese teachers really wanted to say.

The theme of the second conference was "The Current State of the Kokugo Investigation and the Compilation of Japanese Textbooks by the Ministry of Education." The ministry, with its new Kokugo Section, expressed its goal to "promote overseas pure and correct Japanese, not a local, distorted, unattractive language, but a standard, correct, and beautiful language" (Monbushō 1941, day 2, 3).[13] As at the first conference, the participants' arguments centered on the problems in *hyōjungo*, accent, basic vocabulary, standards in pronunciation and word usage, and interference of the students' native languages.

Most notable at this conference, unexpectedly, were complaints about the language voiced by Japanese instructors who were supposed to demonstrate model language. For example, Yoneda Kametarō from Taiwan lamented that

in *kokugo* instruction, accurate correction [of the student's language] is most important. However, the instructors in Taiwan come from all over Japan, from Chishima in the north to Shikoku and Kyushu in the south, and while they are not lacking in personal quality and educational background, they lack experience in teaching *kokugo* as a foreign language, and they each have the local accent of their own dialect. In addition, instructors who are native Taiwanese also teach Japanese. Thus, our *kokugo* instruction has not produced a good result. (Day 2, 127–128)

Imai Sakae reported about the situation in Manchukuo:

> A majority of the Japanese emigrants there come from regions west of Nagoya, especially from Kyushu, and the language spoken there is mostly Kansai [western Japan] dialect. Or rather, it is a sort of Japanese with a Kansai flavor, not exactly the "dialect" of Osaka or Kyushu. Such a reality is problematic when the homeland government selected Tokyo dialect as the standard Japanese. . . . The language used by the Japanese people itself has questionable local variations. (Day 2, 223–224, 226)

And a comment by Ōishi Hatsutarō from Kwantung Province was,

> Regarding *kokugo* policy, I believe that a reform in *kokugo* education in the homeland is most essential for renovation in language education for Japanese people on the Continent. . . . The reality of the Japanese language in Kwantung, Manchukuo, or Northern China, however, is a chaotic mixture of various dialects, none of which can be used as the uniform language, being, of course, far from the *hyōjungo*. . . . When we trace the problems in *kokugo* education we arrive at problems in [the lack of] organization and unification of *kokugo,* and that is where we must begin to work. (Day 3, 48–49, 51)

Criticism by Ōtsuka Masaaki from Manchukuo was even harsher, pointing out the need for "retraining of the Japanese people" in order to promote the language. His remark was beyond mere complaint, almost a tirade:

> The language spoken by Japanese people, not only those who already reside in the Continent, but also those who are currently arriving there, is terribly disordered. There is an actual case in northern Manchuria of about two hundred Japanese people who cannot understand each other. At a recent meeting of Japanese language school directors, when they decided to start a Manchurian language course for Japanese instructors, one of the directors requested a Japanese language course for them also. Everybody laughed at this, but I do not think it is a laughing matter. . . . While the effort is made to build up Japanese language in schools, the language itself is being destroyed in social reality, and it is the Japanese people themselves who are the destroyers. This is a hopeless situation. Every one of those who come to the Continent turn out to be incompetent in the Japanese language. (Day 3, 150–152)

The Ministry of Education's goal to promote "pure and correct Japanese" was an empty slogan to those Japanese instructors who spoke out about the realities overseas.

The conference was concluded by Hashimoto Shinkichi, Tokyo University professor of *kokugogaku*, summarizing the fact that the debate about the "promotion of Japanese" ultimately pointed to the *kokugo* problems in the homeland:

> Listening to your comments about Japanese language education, I became convinced that those various difficulties and inefficiencies exist not just in the Japanese language in overseas lands, but actually in *kokugo* education in the homeland. Some of you talked about the difficulties in bilingualism, which, though different in nature and degree, also exist in the homeland. We might say that most of the children in Japan have already learned the language before entering elementary schools, but their language is their dialect. On the other hand, *kokugo* that is taught in schools must not be such a dialect, but must be the language common throughout Japan, that is, *hyōjungo*. The degree of difference between *hyōjungo* and a dialect might vary depending on the region, but children who speak the dialect of their region are taught *hyōjungo*. This does not mean, however, that they do not use their dialect even after learning *hyōjungo* at school. They continue speaking their dialect with their family and friends. This too, then, is bilingualism. . . . This is a very serious problem in the Japanese language itself, in *kokugo* in the homeland. (Day 3, 181–183)

The second conference closed with the following recommendations. Since there is no published record of them, I will cite here the entire text.

1. Promotion of coordination between Japanese programs in the homeland and overseas: It is urgent for founding the new order in East Asia to coordinate the *kokugo* education in the homeland and the colonies and the *nihongo* education in overseas countries. For that reason, we request that the Ministry of Education establish an appropriate liaison office for this coordination and dispatch relevant personnel to Manchukuo and Taiwan and other colonies.
2. Training of Japanese language instructors: For the promotion of a pure and correct Japanese language, it is necessary to produce many excellent language instructors. We therefore request that the Ministry of Education immediately establish a strong program for training Japanese instructors.
3. Expansion and reinforcement of institutions for organizing and unifying *kokugo*: For the promotion of Japanese overseas, it is urgent to bring organization and unity to *kokugo*. It is very fortunate that the Ministry of Education recently established a *Kokugo* Section in the Library Office, in response to the unanimous proposal by the first conference to establish a vigorous institution for the unified investigation of *kokugo* and swift solution of *kokugo* problems.

> Nevertheless, the current developments demand even more immediate solutions of the various problems in *kokugo*. Thus we hope that the ministry will be committed to expansion and reinforcement of institutions to advance the research, organization, and unification of *kokugo*. (Day 3, 196–203)

In response to these proposals, the government announced the Cabinet Decisions on the Organization and Unification of *Kokugo* and *Kokuji* on February 25, 1941 (Shōwa 16):

> The reinforcement of the research, organization, and unification of *kokugo* and *kokuji* is most urgently needed under current conditions in order to raise the spirit of the people, to advance the efficiency of their education, and to promote pure and correct Japanese as the common language of East Asia. Thus, the government has made the following decisions as important national policy:
> 1. The Ministry of Education will promote the research and organization of *kokugo* and *kokuji*, and the cabinet and each ministry shall cooperate with it.
> 2. The results of the above, on approval by the Cabinet Conference, shall be promptly put into action by the cabinet and each ministry. (Monbushō 1949, 195)

14-6. *Kokugo* Reform and the Promotion of *Nihongo*

The significance of Hoshina's *Daitōa kyōeiken to kokugo seisaku* should be understood in the context described above. Even though the Japanese language had spread through the Co-Prosperity Sphere and even worldwide, Hoshina was pessimistic about its effects:

> There may not be any other language that spread as fast within such a short time as Japanese. This is indeed admirable. On the other hand, we cannot deny that many regrettable problems remain. I cannot help but believe that these problems stem not from bad soil but from bad seeds. That is, our *kokugo* is not a language with a clear standard, nor does it have a clear distinction between standard and local languages. On top of that, the writing system is so irregular and complicated that its mastery is said to be extremely difficult even for Japanese people. (Hoshina 1942a, 347)

Hoshina was bitterly aware that obstacles to the overseas advancement of Japanese were inherent in the language itself. Even though he wrote that "the language of Japan, the leader of the Co-Prosperity Sphere, obviously is qualified [to be the language of the Co-Prosperity Sphere]," he was pessimistic about the meagerness of the "qualification." There was no clear model language, no standard for vocabulary or pronunciation; there was a flood of difficult *kanji* and *kango;* the *kana* usage was inconsistent with the pronunciation; there was extreme disparity between the spoken and written languages. Hoshina contended that unless these problems were solved, promotion of Japanese overseas would be impossible. The same problem plagued the language for other peoples in the Greater East Asia Co-Prosperity Sphere, as Hoshina asked, "What kind of Japanese should be taught to the people in the new colonies?" (210). The moment that Japan tried to make Japanese the language for the Co-Prosperity Sphere, the mass of unsolved problems in *kokugo* and *kokuji* resurfaced and became of pressing importance.

The proposals for improvement of Japanese for overseas promotion were not limited to the organization of the language but extended to its simplification. For example, in April 1942 (Shōwa 17), the Kokugo Kyōkai (Kokugo Association) and the Kanamoji Kai (Kana-script Club) jointly submitted to the cabinet a Proposal for Instituting National Policy on *Kokugo* towards the Foundation of Greater East Asia. The proposal argued that "our language has been extremely complex and irregular. Without drastic measures to organize, reform, and simplify it, we could not hope to spread it as the common language of Greater East Asia." The proposal made six concrete suggestions, the entire text of which was quoted approvingly in Hoshina 1942a: (1) the language style be uniformly colloquial; (2) intelligible words be used; (3) pronunciation be uniform; (4) *katakana* be used as the script; (5) *kana* usage, both for *kanji* and Japanese words, be phonetic; (6) writing be horizontal, from left to right, and with space between words (427–435).

This progressive movement was spurred forward, surprisingly, by the army, with its reform of armament terms. As a result of the large increase in mobilization, the average literacy of the soldiers declined to a degree that hindered the operation of weapons.[14] Because of this, the army decided to simplify the armament terms, in a series of reforms: the Regulations concerning Simplification of Armament Names and Technical Terms in February 1940 (Shōwa 15) limited the number of *kanji* to 1,235 so that the soldiers who finished normal elementary schools could read and write them. The Glossary of Armament Terms in May of the same year translated difficult *kanji* terms into familiar words.[15] The Guideline for *Kana* Usage for Armament in March 1941 (Shōwa 16) adopted complete phonetic usage. These reforms, though confined to the army, were in accord with what Hoshina had been hoping for, and he described them at length as encouraging models for the future (38–100).

This sort of thing was an example of what Hoshina (1942a) saw as the necessity for reform and standardization of *kokugo:* the selection of basic vocabulary for public life, uniform pronunciation and accent, phonetic *kana* usage, restriction of number and usage of *kanji,* standardization of spoken language, simple colloquial style, and so forth. In addition, Hoshina devoutly hoped for textbooks suited for direct teaching methods and professional training of language instructors. Hoshina had held this vision of language reform throughout his career, since he joined the Kokugo Chōsa Iinkai in 1901 (Meiji 34), and he did not compromise with the trend of the time towards "overseas advancement." Rather, he must have hoped that the time had finally come to materialize *kokugo* reform, his dream of many years: the plans that had been frustrated by "the tradition" at home would no longer be obstructed overseas. He hoped that the reform overseas would reciprocally influence the homeland's language.

14-7. Counterattack by the Ultranationalists

The *kokugo* reformists had always been the targets of accusations by conservative scholars and literati. A group of ultranationalistic scholars, headed by Yamada Yoshio, protested vehemently the idea of the reform of Japanese for foreigners, calling it blasphemy against the sacred tradition of *kokugo* protected under the *kokutai.* Such fury against "improvement and advancement" was typified in Yamada's article "Iwayuru kokugo mondai no kisū" (The Result of So-called *Kokugo* Problems) in April 1940 (Shōwa 15) in the journal *Bungaku,* which featured "the Japanese language in East Asia."

> There are those who complain that *kokugo* is chaotic or disordered. But who is responsible for that? Largely those who have been supporting the so-called *kokugo* policy or the *kokugo* reform movement after the Meiji Restoration, promoting use of *rōmaji,* disuse of *kanji,* abolition of historical *kana* usage. . . . Therefore, the disorder is not inherent in *kokugo* itself, but was caused by those *kokugo* politicians who tried to test their egotistic ideas only to devastate the nation's education and mar the purity of *kokugo.* Thus what ought to be controlled and stopped is what these people are doing. (Yamada 1940, 3–4)

The implicit target of the above accusation was Hoshina. Yamada affirmed that the reform that ignored "the tradition of *kokugo*" and "the authority of the nation" was "treason by those who fancied themselves as more important than the nation" (5). Yamada's criticism of the reformists was discussed in more detail in part 3, but his new target was the plan "to simplify *kokugo* because it is too hard to learn." Yamada detested the idea, considering it as an idea of "Japanese who whine about their own language being difficult, and servilely curry favor with foreigners," Japanese who "say we should use phonetic *kana* usage while teaching foreigners this difficult language" as Japan advanced into the East Asian continent. "Such an obsequious commonplace must be firmly rejected," he concluded. According to Yamada, to learn Japanese meant nothing short of "unconditional acceptance and inheritance of the tradition in *kokugo*" (6–10).[16] This opposition to the organization and simplification of Japanese was part of the motivation, along with the opposition to the *Hyōjun kanji hyō*, for the formation of Nihon Kokugo Kai (Japan Association for Kokugo) mentioned in chapter 9.

The argument for *kokugo kokuji* reform gradually quieted under the attack by the conservative ultranationalists. However, the call for making Japanese the language of the Greater East Asia Co-Prosperity Sphere did not disappear. The tone of the argument began to take a new direction under ultranationalism and the emperor-centered view of history, demanding loyalty to pure, correct, and traditional Japanese.

Shida Nobuyoshi's *Daitōa gengo kensetsu no kihon* (The Foundation for Constructing the Language of Greater East Asia, 1943; Shōwa 18), published about a year after Hoshina's *Daitōa kyōeiken to kokugo seisaku*, exemplified such ultranationalistic and spiritualistic discourse: the goal of "spreading Japanese over Greater East Asia" was to "make [the people] know the spirit of the creation of our nation, make them feel the bond of the vital membership of Greater East Asia . . . and confirm their commitment to construct a new, correct order under Imperial Japan." This was the most "essential aim," and making Japanese the common language in East Asia was "subordinate to this goal" (Shida 1943, 8). Shida did not deny that the promotion of Japanese "should occur with the resolution of problems in *kokugo* and with rigorous *kokugo* education" (11), but he maintained that the solution would come only from "the reverence for *kokugo* as the language of the country blessed and guided by *kotodama*," and it would "provide an attitude that is necessary for the rightful advancement and education of *kokugo* founded on its tradition" (22). Therefore, "it must be prohibited to mechanically organize *kokugo* for short-sighted convenience, or to pursue its simplification for overseas promotion" (31), and "a forceful, radical, and careless reform insisted upon by those who complain of the difficulties of *kokugo* is probably related to their rejection of tradition" (60). Needless to say, Shida rejected both the restriction of *kanji* and the phonetic *kana* usage that went against "the tradition and the true form of *kokugo*."

The core of Shida's argument shared Yamada's peculiar idea about *kokugo*:

> *Kokugo* protects *kokutai* and educates the nation people, and is in return supported by *kokutai*. "*Kokugo*" means "*wagakuni no kotoba* [the language of our dear country]," and is not "*nihongo*," one of the many languages of the world. The

sense of *"wagakuni"* is not the same as that of *"wareware no kuni* [our country]," which carries a kind of foreign flavor and came into use by a certain group of people.[17] What is meant by the Japanese word *"kotoba"* also is different from a "language" as defined in the science of language. (147)[18]

According to Shida, the concept of *kokugo* rejects the definition of Japanese as one of many languages; it transcends scientific comprehension and hence cannot be included in the objects of linguistics research. This distinction epitomized the ideological contrast between *kokugogaku* (*kokugo* study) and *gengogaku* (linguistics) discussed in part 3. Such an extreme *kokutai* discourse may be unique only to scholars like Yamada and Shida, but the sense that *kokugo* is different from *nihongo* was widely shared at that time.

Let us refer back to the proposal by the Second Conference on Provisions of Kokugo. It used the term *kokugo* education for "homeland and territories" and *nihongo* education for overseas. All the representatives at the conference were keenly aware of this distinction, and the ones from Korea and Taiwan, in particular, adhered to *kokugo* and rejected *nihongo*. Morita Gorō from Korea said, "In Korea we teach *kokugo,* not *nihongo*" (Monbushō 1941, day 2, 18), and Kobayashi Masakazu from Taiwan said, "I am hesitant to use the word *nihongo,* so would like to say *kokugo*" (67). What was the sentiment that led to this distinction?

In this regard, the comment by Terashima Yasushi, another representative from Korea, was very illuminating: "For those of us who have been teaching in Korea for a long time, the word *nihongo* sounds like the language of some other country. We feel uncomfortable if we don't say *kokugo*" (41–42). The word *nihongo* had a foreign ring to it, while *kokugo* conveyed a sense that it was a language that excluded interference from outside and was understood only by insiders. And yet the "inside" was not contradictory of the "outside," or there was no outside that contradicted *kokugo*. Thus, without external restraint, such inclusive *kokugo* was seen to have unlimited potential to expand and enlarge—a vision of grandeur leading to the "spirit of *hakkō ichiu*" (the whole world under one roof).[19]

As long as *kokugo* was seen this way, Hoshina's *kokugo* reform was destined to fail, because the reform was based on his view of Japanese as *nihongo*. Still, even Shida, who opposed the reform, had to spend more than half of his *Foundation* discussing the domestic problems in *kokugo* and its education, and urging the establishment of *hyōjungo*. This indicates the inveterate and entangled nature of the problems Hoshina was tackling, the paradox inherent in the idea of *kokugo* created in modern Japan.

14-8. A Dream of *Kyōeiken-go,*
the Language of the Co-Prosperity Sphere

Hoshina's argument that related the reform of Japanese to its overseas advancement did not come from ultranationalistic thinking, and that was why he did not hesitate to maintain his proposals both throughout the war and after "the defeat." For his ideas about language, the defeat was not a blow that separated prewar from postwar time. In the closing section of *Kokugo mondai 50-nen,* Hoshina, looking back on his fifty-year endeavor for the reform, commented on the overseas promotion of Japanese as follows:

> As a result of the defeat, the Japanese language, which had spread widely, will inevitably lose its dominance with each passing year. Nonetheless, the time will surely come when the Japanese race recovers from the defeat and contributes to world peace and civilization, and when people again want to learn Japanese. The difficulty generally shared by foreigners in their effort to learn Japanese was the fact that there was no solid standard for the language nor for its pronunciation, neither was there any dictionary of *hyōjungo.* . . . In order to promote Japanese, we must first establish *hyōjungo,* and make a dictionary to provide an accessible reference. . . . In conclusion, I emphasize that we need to organize Japanese so that foreigners will be able to learn it with ease. (1949b, 271–272)

Hoshina's numerous proposals as seen above are astonishingly relevant to the issues that are occurring with the "internationalization of *nihongo,*" a popular topic today.[20] For example, the purpose or idea of *kan'yaku nihongo* (simplified Japanese), which was proposed by Nomoto Kikuo and his colleagues a few years ago,[21] is not very far from that in Doi Mitsutomo's *Basic Japanese* or in the Kokugo Association's simplification movement based on its basic vocabulary. The latter two were even more radical in the sense that they aimed not only at overseas promotion but also at domestic reform: who could dare to claim today, as did the Kokugo Association with Hoshina's full support, that "*kanji* will gradually disappear from the people's daily use, and that will be the natural course of progress in *kokugo*"? (Hoshina 1942a, 432).

On the other hand, today's trend towards "internationalization of Japanese" includes a call for "Japanese as a weapon,"[22] which reminds me of Hoshina's dream of "the language for the Co-Prosperity Sphere," and this is not merely a prejudiced overreaction typical of descendants of "the subjects in the Co-Prosperity Sphere."

CHAPTER 15

Conclusion

The coerciveness of *kokugo* policy in modern Japan was a sign not of the strength of *kokugo* but of its weakness, just as the coercion of the Great Japanese Empire indicated Japan's tenuous modernity. Japan was not able to establish a consistent language policy for its colonies, or even for itself. Mori Arinori was not the only one who despaired of the plight of *kokugo*. Shiga Naoya, for example, is also well known for his suggestion after World War II that French be adopted as the national language. And there was Kita Ikki, who had even more radical ideas than these two.[1]

Kita's *Kokka kaizōan genri taikō* (Outline of the Principal Ideas for Nation Reform) of 1919 (Taishō 8; in Kita 1959), a bible for fascists of his time, has a section headed "Eigo o haishite Esuperanto o kashi dai-ni kokugo to su" (Discard English and Adopt Esperanto as the Second National Language; 251), in a chapter titled "Kokumin kyōiku no kenri" (The People's Rights to Education). There Kita explained that there was no need for the Japanese people to learn English because Japan was not a British colony. Then why did he feel the need to choose a second national language? And why Esperanto? The phrase "second national language" indicated that the language was not merely the object of learning but was presumed to have a certain public function, and Kita's proposal was an astoundingly radical one:

> The fact that we have had numerous disputes on script reform, abolition of *kanji*, *genbun itchi*, adoption of *rōmaji*, and so forth, which are not found in other Western countries, indicates that the entire nation has suffered greatly from the extreme inferiority of the Japanese language and script. If we decide to practice *rōmaji*, the most radical script of all, we may be able to diminish some of the inconvenience in writing we have had before. Nevertheless, when we translate English or Chinese [into *rōmaji*], we realize that the Japanese sentence is inverted, that is, the structure for expressing ideas in the [Japanese] language itself goes against the laws of psychology. The problems in *kokugo* are not only

about script or words. The structure of the language must be revolutionized at its foundation. (252)

Kita's complaint about the Japanese language's inferiority to English and Chinese and the "inverted" word order of Japanese might simply indicate his limited view of language and might be regarded as absurd within the discipline of linguistics, which considers all languages equal in their grammatical complexity. What is most notable here, however, is that Kita so despaired of the "inferior" Japanese that he proposed a revolution in the fundamental structure of the language.

> As the Japanese people use Esperanto as a second language in order to avoid the painful inconvenience of *kokugo,* according to the laws of natural selection they will all be using Esperanto as their first national language in fifty years. The Japanese language we are using today will then become a research object for specialists, like Sanskrit or Latin. (253)

Though equating it with such highly esteemed languages as Sanskrit and Latin, Kita was handing the Japanese language off to the specialists as a dead language, that is, predicting its extinction.

Japanese was not the only language Kita wanted to extinguish. In his view, when Japan expanded its territories to Siberia and Australia in the near future, it could not let people there continue using Russian or English, nor could it force them to use Japanese, because "it would be impossible to force our aggravating language, as we did upon the Koreans, upon those Westerners who have relatively better languages" (253). The "inferior" Japanese language might be forced upon the Korean people, but not upon other people, especially Europeans, who had "better" languages. Koreans were the miserable victims of oppression by an "inferior" language. And the language Kita believed that could unite the vast territory of the Japanese Empire was not Japanese, but Esperanto:

> The laws of natural selection, that the superior survives the inferior, will also determine the fate of the Japanese language and Esperanto. Within the next hundred years, languages in Japan's territories, whether in Europe, China, India, or Korea, are to become extinct and be replaced by Esperanto. Vast lands with no uniform language are like a morning glory destined to wither overnight. (253)[2]

By adopting Esperanto as the second national language, the inferior Japanese language was destined for extinction according to the theory of evolution—this was Kita's astounding argument. If things developed as he foresaw, all Japanese people, even the emperor, would be speaking Esperanto, not Japanese, in fifty years. If Yamada had read this, he would certainly have become enraged and labeled Kita "a traitor," as he did Ueda and Hoshina. How did Kita's fascistic followers interpret his argument? Or perhaps language was not even a part of their concern.

We could dismiss Kita's argument as absurd. But we cannot ignore the fact that it arose from Kita's black despair about Japanese and that Ueda and Hoshina shared a similar despair. Ueda and Hoshina also wanted to solve "numerous disputes on script reform, abolition of *kanji, genbun itchi,* adoption of *rōmaji,* and so forth" and attempted to reform "the extreme inferiority of the Japanese language and script," which the entire Japanese nation suffered from. They were also well aware that "the problems in *kokugo* are not only about script or words," and that "the structure of the language must be revolutionized at its foundation." Nevertheless, they took the opposite direction from Mori Arinori or Kita Ikki: they hoped to find in the concept of *kokugo* itself prescriptions for the reform of the Japanese language and script.

Ueda most passionately asserted the tie between *kokugo* and the nation-state, but *kokugo* in his terms could be created only apart from the "tradition" in Yamada's sense, and he lamented the people's severely limited consciousness about *kokugo.* For Ueda, *kokugo* was not the Japanese language as it was, but the idealized language in a certain framework, the framework of the modern science of language.

Hoshina followed Ueda's ideals very loyally throughout his half-century-long striving for establishment of language policy and language education. He is not given much attention, almost forgotten in today's academic climate in Japan, but his ideas do not belong to the taboo subjects of the past. To reiterate, Hoshina's ideas had two seemingly contradictory facets: while on the one hand they were nationalistic and imperialistic regarding the institution of *hyōjungo* for the homeland and promotion of assimilation in the Greater East Asia Co-Prosperity Sphere, on the other hand they favored democratizing *kokugo* through restricting *kanji,* adopting the phonetic *kana* usage, and promoting the colloquial style. His fundamental view of language was consistent for fifty years, from the time he became a member of Kokugo Chōsa Iinkai and throughout the wars: neither the "Great East Asian War"[3] nor "the defeat" made him reverse his position. The duality of his ideas was not a contradiction for him. He did not compromise them, but resolved and reconciled them through the dynamism of the ideals of *kokugo* itself.

Even his aggressive comments about language policies in colonies were drawn from Ueda's ideals and not from any desire to ingratiate himself in the political climate of that time. More than any of his contemporaries, Hoshina was painfully aware of what Mori Arinori meant by the "poverty in Japanese." His eagerness for the "overseas advancement" of *kokugo* came from his desire to vitalize this "poor" Japanese. He believed that a language was inseparable from its people, and he tried to actualize this conviction in both the progress of the language of the empire and the suppression of the languages of the conquered. It was Hoshina's destiny as a bureaucrat and a scholar to be burdened with numerous problems in the Japanese language as it faced modernity, and these problems continue today, still unsolved.

Yamada Yoshio's idea of *kokugo* was indeed a contraposition of Ueda's and Hoshina's: the latter two were never content with the realities of the Japanese language, while Yamada was completely satisfied with his world of *kokugo*, which was protected by the tradition of *kokutai*. This world did not need to compete with anything outside or non-Japanese; it was a delusional closed world that was to expand infinitely, a linguistic view that reminds us of the *hakkō ichiu* ideology. Such an entranced view of *kokugo* as Yamada's probably will never be revived as such. However, praise for the tradition and purity of *kokugo* could possibly enliven today the narrative that justifies the continuity of the cultural tradition and could again condemn *kokugo* reformists as bureaucrats who destroy the tradition.

In contrast, *kokugo* in Ueda's and Hoshina's terms survived "the defeat." Hoshina's effort of many years bore fruit in postwar *kokugo* reform. Moreover, the rise of the internationalization of Japanese since the last decade[4] can be seen as a continuation of their narratives. As seen in this book, most of the debates today on the internationalization of Japanese had been anticipated by Hoshina even before the war ended. In that sense, seemingly unglamorous Hoshina could be called a pioneer for internationalization. Nonetheless, we must also remember his vision about language policy, his ultimate goal to create *kokka-go* and *kyōeiken-go*. Without the realization that language is by nature political, the narrative on the internationalization of Japanese today could lead us back to the ideology of *kokka-go* or *kyōeiken-go*.

The conservatives and the reformists will most likely continue competing for hegemony over *kokugo*, and it is this competition itself that has shaped the representation of linguistic modernity in Japan. The ideology of *kokugo* has been solidified through their competition, because both conservatives and reformists share the same tacit premise: the unshakable homogeneity of the Japanese language. Even though they seemed to resist and did not agree with each other on the levels of that homogeneity, Yamada and Ueda/Hoshina both believed that the Japanese language was a homogeneous entity.

As long as homogeneity is held as the tacit premise, the Japanese language cannot go beyond the limits of *kokugo*: *kokugo* is the horizon confining the world of linguistic awareness of modern Japan. However, very soon, from beyond that horizon, we will hear various amorphous mutterings—much like Isaac Deutsher's phrase "the non-Jewish Jew"—in "non-Japanese Japanese language." Whether or not the idea of *kokugo* will be transformed into the ideology of a state language or a "co-prosperity" language will depend on how seriously we listen to the voices in this "non-Japanese."

Chronology
Major Events and Publications Cited in the Book
(provided by translator)

1855 (Ansei 2) *Kikai kanran kōgi* (Outlook of Nature), by Kawamoto Kōmin.

1866 (Keiō 2) "Kanji on-haishi no gi" (Proposal for the Abolition of Chinese Characters), by Maejima Hisoka.

———*Sōyaku Igirisu bunten*, translation of *Igirisu bunten* (English Dictionary, published by Kaiseijo).

1867 (Keiō 3) *Wa-ei gorin shūsei* (Japanese-English Dictionary), by Hepburn.

1868 (Meiji 1) *Kunmō kyūri zukai* (Introductory Theories with Illustrations), by Fukuzawa Yukichi.

———Institute of Imperial Learning (Kōgaku-sho) established in Kyoto together with the Institute of Chinese Studies (Kangaku-sho).

1869 (Meiji 2) "Kokubun kyōiku no gi ni tsuki kengi" (Proposal for Teaching the Japanese Language), by Mejima Hisoka.

———Daigakkō, the Grand School, founded in Tokyo.

———*Shōhei gakkō e no tasshi* (Advice to Shōhei School).

1870 (Meiji 3) *Taikyō senpu no mikotonori* (Imperial Rescript for the Propagation of the Great Doctrine).

1872 (Meiji 5) Promulgation of the Educational System.

———May: Mori Arinori writes a letter to Whitney about his views of the Japanese language.

——— *Wa-ei gorin shūsei* (Japanese-English Dictionary), 2nd ed., by Hepburn.

1873 (Meiji 6) "Kō kokubun hai kanji no gi" (The Enforcement of Japanese and the Abolishment of *Kanji*), by Maejima Hisoka (not officially submitted).

———Meirokusha (Meiji 6 Society) formed (–1875).

———*Moji no oshie* (Teaching of Script), by Fukuzawa Yukichi.

———*Fuon sōzu eiwa jii* (English-Japanese Dictionary with Pronunciation and Illustrations), the first full-scale English-Japanese dictionary in Japan, edited by Shibata Shōkichi and Koyasu Takashi.

———*Education in Japan,* by Mori Arinori.

———*An Elementary Grammar of the Japanese Language (Nihongo bunten),* by Baba Tatsui.

1874 (Meiji 7) February–May: *Mainichi hirakana shinbun-shi* (Daily *Hirakana* Newspaper), by Maejima.

———*Meiroku zasshi* (Meiji 6 Magazine), first issue.

———"Yōji o motte kokugo o shosuru no ron" (Writing Japanese in the Western Script), by Nishi Amane.

———*Hyaku ichi shin ron* (101 New Theories), by Nishi Amane.

———*Monowari no hashigo* (Steps to the Principles of Things), by Shimizu Usaburō.

———"Hiragana no setsu" (Suggestions for *Hiragana* Script), by Shimizu Usaburō.

———*Kokutai shinron* (New Theory of National Polity), by Katō Hiroyuki.

———*Bunshōron* (Theory of Writing), by Nishimura Shigeki.

1875 (Meiji 8) "Bunshōron o yomu" (Rereading *Theory of Writing*), by Kanda Takahira.

1877 (Meiji 10) *Kyū han jō* (Matters of Old Domains), by Fukuzawa Yukichi.

1879 (Meiji 12) "Hōgo o motte kyōju suru daigakkō wo setchi subeki setsu" (Need for Instituting Grand Schools for Teaching in Japanese), by Kanda Takahira.

———"Kyōgaku taishi" (Essential Points for Teaching), by Motoda Nagazane.

1880 (Meiji 13) "Hakugengaku ni kansuru gian" (Bill of Linguistics), by Katō Hiroyuki.

1881 (Meiji 14) Katō Hiroyuki announces discontinuation of the publication of his *New Theory of National Polity (Kokutai shin ron)*.

1882 (Meiji 15) *Fuon sōzu eiwa jii* (English-Japanese Dictionary with Pronunciation and Illustrations), rev. and supplemented edition.

———(Meiji 15) "Rōmaji o motte Nihongo o tsuzuru no setsu" (Proposal for Writing the Japanese Language in *Rōmaji*), by Yatabe Ryōkichi.

———*Shintaishi shō* (New-style Poetry), by Yatabe Ryōkichi, Inoue Tetsujirō, and Toyama Masakazu.

1883 (Meiji 16) Kana no Kai (Association of Kana) formed.

1884 (Meiji 17) "Kanji o haishi eigo o sakan ni okosu wa konnichi no kyūmu nari" (Urgent Task Today: Abolition of *Kanji* and Promotion of English), by Toyama Masakazu.

———"Kuniguni no namari kotoba ni tsukite" (About Local Dialects), by Miyake Yonekichi.

———"Honsho hensan no taii" (The Objective of This Edition). Preface for *Genkai*, by Ōtsuki Fumihiko.

———Lecture "Shintai kanji yaburi" (Dump *Kanji* for a New Style), by Toyama Masakazu.

1885 (Meiji 18) Rōmaji Kai (Rōmaji Association) formed.

———Ken'yūsha formed.

———"Tōkyōgo no tsūyō" (Common Use of Tokyo Language), by Asanebō, in *Jiyū tō*.

1885–1886 (Meiji 18–19) "Zokugo o iyashimu na" (Don't Look Down on Vernacular Language) by Miyake Yonekichi.

1886 (Meiji 19) Department of *hakugengaku* (later *gengogaku*, linguistics) implemented.

——*Nihon bunshōron* (Theory of Japanese Writing), by Suematsu Kenchō.

——*Genbun itchi*, by Mozume Takami.

——Promulgation of School Ordinance *(Gakkōrei)* for elementary and middle schools, teacher schools, and imperial universities.

——*Tsūzoku Kyomutō keiki*, translation of Turgenev's *Fathers and Sons*, by Futabatei Shimei.

——*Wa-ei gorin shūsei* (Japanese-English Dictionary), by Hepburn, 3rd ed.

1887 (Meiji 20) "GEM-BUN ITCHI," by B. H. Chamberlain.

——"*Baku genbun itchi ron*" (Refuting *Genbun itchi*), by Tatsumi Kojirō.

——*Musashino*, by Yamada Bimyō.

——*Yōgaku tokuhon* (Elementary Reader), by Nishimura Tei.

——*Jinjō shōgaku tokuhon* (Normal Elementary School Reader), by Ministry of Education.

——*Nihon shō bunten* (Concise Japanese Grammar Dictionary), by Chamberlain.

1888 (Meiji 21) "Genbun itchi ron gairyaku" (Outline of *Genbun itchi* Theory), by Yamada Bimyō.

——"Genbun itchi no ron" (Theory of *Genbun itchi*), by Miyake Yonekichi.

——"Tokuhon kyōju no shui" (The Point of the Teaching of the Reader), by Miyake Yonekichi.

——"Kokugo no hontai narabini sono kachi" (The True Form of *Kokugo* and Its Value), by Sekine Masanao.

——Nihon Bunshō Kai (Association for Japanese Texts) formed.

——Gengo Torishirabe-sho (Bureau for the Investigation of Language) formed.

1889 (Meiji 22) *Kintai kokubun kyōkasho* (Modern-style *Kokubun* Textbook), by Sekine Masanao.

——Promulgation of Dai Nihon Teikoku Kenpō, the Great Japan Imperial Constitution.

——Department name *wa-bungaku ka* in imperial universities changed to *kokubungaku ka*.

——"Nihon bungaku no hitsuyō" (The Importance of Japanese Literature) by Ochiai Naobumi.

——"Nihon gengo kenkyūhō" (Methodology for Japanese Linguistics) and "Gengo jō no henka o ronjite kokugo kyōju no koto ni oyobu" (Discussion of Linguistic Changes and the Teaching of *Kokugo*), by Ueda Kazutoshi.

1889–1891 (Meiji 22–24) *Genkai* (Sea of Words), compiled solely by Ōtsuki Fumihiko.

1890 (Meiji 23) "Narachō no bungaku" (Nara Court Literature), by Ochiai Naobumi.

——*Kokubungaku* (The Study of Japanese Literature), by Ueda Kazutoshi.

——Promulgation of *Kyōiku chokugo* (Imperial Rescript on Education).

——"Nihongogaku no koto ni tsukite" (Regarding the Study of the Japanese Language) by Katō Hiroyuki.

1891 (Meiji 24) *Chokugo engi* (Popular Version of the Imperial Rescript on Education), by Inoue Tetsujirō.

——*Shinsen kashū* (New Collection of Classical Poetry), by Ochiai Naobumi.

1892 (Meiji 25) Chūtō *Kyōiku kokubun kihan* (Standard Japanese Literature for Middle School), by Ochiai Naobumi.

1894 (Meiji 27) April: Lecture "Moji to kyōiku no kankei" (Relation between Script and Education), by Inoue Tetsujirō.

——June: Ueda Kazutoshi appointed professor of philology at Tokyo Imperial University.

——August: Sino-Japanese War (–1895; Meiji 27–28).

——October: Lecture "Kokugo to kokka to" (The National Language and the Nation-state), by Ueda Kazutoshi.

——November: Lecture "Kokugo kenkyū ni tsuite" (About *Kokugo* Research), by Ueda Kazutoshi.

1895 (Meiji 28) *Kokugo no tame* (For *Kokugo*), by Ueda Kazutoshi.

——Lecture "Hyōjungo ni tsukite" (About the Standard Language), by Ueda Kazutoshi.

——"Kanji ridōsetsu" (Beneficial Use of *Kanji*), by Miyake Setsurei.

——May: "Shin kokuji ron" (New National Script), by Ueda Kaszutoshi.

1896 (Meiji 29) Teikoku Kyōiku Kai (Imperial Board of Education) established.

1897 (Meiji 30) *Kō Nihon bunten* (Current Japanese Grammar), by Ōtsuki Fumihiko.

——Kokugo Kenkyūkai (Kokugo Research Office) implemented in Tokyo University by Ueda Kazutoshi.

1898 (Meiji 31) Hoshina Kōichi contracted as a staff member *(shokutaku)* in the Library Section of the Ministry of Education.

——Ueda Kazutoshi starts Gengo Gakkai (Linguistics Association).

1899 (Meiji 32) Kokuji Kairyōbu (National Script Reform Division) set up in the Imperial Board of Education (Teikoku Kyōiku Kai), chaired by Maejima Hisoka.

——*Kokugogaku shōshi* (Abbreviated History of *Kokugogaku*), by Hoshina Kōichi.

——*Gengo hattatsuron* (The Growth of Language), by Hoshina Kōichi.

——"Naichi zakkyo go no Nihon" (Japan after the Opening of the Concessions), by Yokoyama Gennosuke.

1900 (Meiji 33) January: The Imperial Board of Education submitted "Kokuji kokugo kokubun no kairyō ni kansuru seigansho" (Petition Regarding Improvements in the National Script and Language) to the national Diet.

——February: *Gengogaku zasshi* (Journal of Linguistics) started by the Linguistic Association.

——March: The Genbun Itchi Committee installed under the Imperial Board of Education.

——April: Maejima Hisoka appointed as director of national language investigators; Inoue Tetsujirō and Miyake Setsurei appointed as staff members.

———"Kanji genshō ron" (Proposal for Reduction of *Kanji*), by Hara Takashi.

———*Gengogaku Taii* (Outline of Linguistics), by Hoshina Kōichi.

———"Naichi zakkyo go ni okeru gogaku mondai" (Language Problems after the Opening of Concessions), by Ueda Kazutoshi.

———August: Revision of *Shōgakkōrei* (Elementary School Order). *Kokugo* as a new subject implemented in the elementary school curriculum.

1901 (Meiji 34) "Genbun itchi ni tsuite" (About *Genbun Itchi*), by Inoue Tetsujirō.

———"Genbun no itchi o yōsuru rekishiteki gen'in" (The Historical Grounds behind the Need for Unification of the Language), by Shiratori Kurakichi.

———February: Genbun Itchi Committee presents *Genbun itchi no jikkō ni tsuite no seigan* (Petition for Actions towards *Genbun itchi*) to House of Peers (Kizokuin) and House of Representatives (Shūgiin).

———*Kokugo kyōjuhō shishin* (Guidelines for Teaching *Kokugo*), by Hoshina Kōichi.

———"Genbun itchi ron" (Theory of *Genbun itchi*), by Fujioka Katsuji.

———Enforcement Regulations for the Chūgakkōrei revises the content of the middle school subject "*kokugo* and *kanbun*," placing its focus on modern language.

1902 (Meiji 35) March: Kokugo Chōsa Iinkai (National Language Investigative Committee) set up, headed by Katō Hiroyuki.

———July: "Kokugo Chōsa Iinkai ketsugi jikō ni tsuite" (About the Resolutions by the National Language Investigative Committee), by Hoshina Kōichi.

———December: "Genbun itchi no fukanō" (*Genbun Itchi* Is Impossible), by Mozume Takami.

———*Gengogaku* (Linguistics), by Hoshina Kōichi.

———"Kokumin kyōiku to kokugo kyōiku" (Education of the People and Teaching *Kokugo*), by Ueda Kazutoshi.

1903 (Meiji 36) Censorship of national textbooks implemented.

1904 (Meiji 37) *Jinjō shōgaku tokuhon hensan shuisho* (Prospectus for Editing Readers for Normal Elementary Schools). Defined *hyōjungo*.

———*Kokugo kokuji kairyō ronsetsu nenpyō* (Chronology of Articles about Reform of *Kokugo* and *National Script*), by Kokugo Chōsa Iinkai.

———*Hōgen saishūbo* (Collection of Dialects), by Kokugo Chōsa Iinkai.

1905 (Meiji 38) Revision of *kana* usage reported to the Ministry of Education by Kokugo Chōsa Iinkai.

———*On'in chōsa hōkokusho* (Report of the Phonological Investigation), by Kokugo Chōsa Iinkai.

1906 (Meiji 39) *Genkō futsū bunpō kaiteian chōsa hōkoku no ichi* (Survey Report of Suggestions for Revision of the Current Normal Grammar: 1), by Kokugo Chōsa Iinkai.

———*Kōgohō chōsa hōkokusho* (Investigative Report of the Spoken Language), by Kokugo Chōsa Iinkai.

1907 (Meiji 40) *Kaitei kanazukai yōgi* (Summary of Revised *Kana* Usage), by Hoshina Kōichi.

1908 (Meiji 41) May: Rinji Kanazukai Chōsa Iinkai (Interim Investigative Commit-
tee for Kana Usage) set up.
———Ministry of Education revises the proposal for *kana* usage.
———September: Ministry of Education withdraws the revised proposal.
———Changes in the Elementary School Order to disestablish *bōbiki kanazukai;*
revived conventional *kana* usage.
———December: Interim Investigative Committee for Kana Usage disbanded.
1909 (Meiji 42) *Kokugo-gaku gairon* (Introduction to *Kokugogaku*), by Kameda
Jirō.
1910 (Meiji 43) "Suihei no haha" (A Sailor's Mother) in the second edition of the
national textbook *Normal Elementary Reader,* vol. 9.
———*Kokugogaku seigi* (Exposition of *Kokugogaku*), by Hoshina Kōichi.
———*Nikkan ryō-kokugo dōkei ron* (The Common Origin of the Japanese and
Korean Languages), by Kanazawa Shōzaburō.
———August 29: Annexation of Korea.
———September 8: *"Kyōka iensho"* (Comments on Cultivation) by government-
general of Korea.
1910–1911 (Meiji 43–44) *Seinen* (Young Man), by Mori Ōgai.
1911 (Meiji 44) Korean Education Rescript.
1911–1913 (Meiji 44–Taishō 2) Hoshina Kōichi in Europe for research.
1913 Kokugo Chōsa Iinkai dissolved.
1914 (Taishō 3) *Kokugo kyōiku oyobi kyōju no shinchō* (The New Wave in Education
and Teaching of the National Language), by Hoshina Kōichi.
1916 (Taishō 5) *Kokugogaku no jukkō* (Ten Lectures about *Kokugogaku*), by Ueda
Kazutoshi.
1917 (Taishō 6) Hoshina Kōichi starts *Kokugo kyōiku* (*Kokugo* Education).
1918 (Taishō 7) *Gairaigo mondai ni kansuru Doitsu ni okeru kokugo undō* (The
National Language Movements on Problems about Loanwords in Germany),
by Hoshina Kōichi and Andō Masatsugu, published by the Ministry of
Education.
1919 (Taishō 8) *Kokka kaizō an genri taikō* (Outline of the Principal Ideas for
Nation Reform), by Kita Ikki.
1921 (Taishō 10) Rinji Kokugo Chōsakai (Interim Investigative Board for the
National Language) set up, chaired by Mori Ōgai.
———*Doitsu zokuryō jidai no Pōrando ni okeru kokugo seisaku* (Language Policy in
German Poland), by Hoshina Kōichi.
———*Kokugo fukyū no jōkyō* (The State of Spread of *Kokugo*) (in Korea).
1922 (Taishō 11) Revised Korean Education Rescript.
———Mori Ōgai dies.
1923 (Taishō 12) *Jōyō kanji hyō* (List of Characters for General Use) published.
1924 (Taishō 13) December: *Kanazukai kaitei an* (Proposal for Revision of *Kana*
Usage) by Rinji Kokugo Chōsa Iinkai approved.

1926 (Taishō 15) *Shokumin oyobi shokumin seisaku* (Colonization and Colonial Policies), by Yanaihara Tadao.

1927 (Shōwa 2) Hoshina Kōichi resigns from Tokyo University.

1930 (Shōwa 5) Hoshina appointed professor at Tokyo Bunri Daigaku (Tokyo University of Letters and Science); appointed as an executive officer of Rinji *Rōmaji* Chōsakai (Interim Committee for Investigation of *Rōmaji*).

——Kokugo Kyōkai (Association for *Kokugo*) formed.

1931(Shōwa 6) Modified version of *Jōyō kanji hyō* and *Kaitei kanazukai* (Revised *Kana* Usage) published by Rinji Kokugo Chōsakai.

——June 18: Hoshina Kōichi gives a lecture ("Go-shinkō") for the emperor on problems in the Japanese language and script.

——September: Manchurian Incident.

1932 (Shōwa 7) Establishment of Manchukuo.

1933 (Shōwa 8) *Gengogaku gairon* (Introduction to Linguistics), by Shinmura Izuru.

——May: *Kokka-go no mondai ni tsuite* (About the Problems in State Language), by Hoshina Kōichi.

——October: *Kokugo seisaku ron* (Theory for *Kokugo* Policy), by Hoshina Kōichi.

1934 (Shōwa 9) Kokugo Shingikai (Deliberative Council on *Kokugo*) started. Hoshina Kōichi appointed executive officer.

——April: Kokusai Bunka Shinkōkai (Society for the Promotion of International Cultural Relations) formed.

1935 (Shōwa 10) *Kokugogakushi yō* (Concise History of *Kokugo-gaku*), by Yamada Yoshio.

—— August: Ministry of Foreign Affairs sets up a new section in the Cultural Affairs Department.

1936 (Shōwa 11) "Manmō no shominzoku to minzokusei" (Ethnic Groups in Manchuria-Mongolia and their Ethnic Identities), by Hattori Shirō.

——*Kokugo to Nihon seishin* (*Kokugo* and the Japanese Spirit), by Hoshina Kōichi.

——*Kokugo seisaku* (*Kokugo* Policy), by Hoshina Kōichi.

——August: General Minami Jirō appointed governor-general of Korea.

1937 (Shōwa 12) *Rōmaji tsuzuri hyō* (Phonetically Oriented System of Romanization), promulgated by the Ministry of Education based on the report from Rinji Rōmaji Chōsakai.

——*Kanji jitai seiri an* (Proposed Modifications to the Form of *Kanji*), by Kokugo Shingikai.

——*Kokugo Undō* (*Kokugo* Movement) started by Kokugo Kyōkai in Taiwan.

——July: The Second Sino-Japanese War starts.

1938 (Shōwa 13) Second revision of the Educational Rescript in Korea.

——February: Special Army Volunteers System in Korea.

——March: Third revision of the Educational Rescript in Korea.

1939 (Shōwa 14) June: First Conference on Provisions of *Kokugo* (Kokugo Taisaku Kyōgikai).

———"Sekai ni nobiyuku Nihongo" (The Japanese Language Expanding Worldwide), by Ministry of Foreign Affairs.

1940 (Shōwa 15) Hoshina retires from Tokyo University of Letters and Science; awarded emeritus professorship.

———"Manshūkoku ni okeru nihongo no chii" (The Status of Japanese in Manchukuo), by Shigematsu Nobuhiro.

———*Kokugogakushi* (The History of *Kokugogaku*), by Tokieda Motoki.

———"Nihongo no tōsei o kyōka seyo" (Reinforce the Regulation on *Kokugo*), by Hoshina Kōichi.

———January: *Hōgen ronsō* (dispute over dialects) in Okinawa, triggered by Yanagi Muneyoshi.

———February: "Heiki meishō oyobi yōgo no kan'i-ka ni kansuru kitei" (Regulations concerning Simplification of Armament Names and Technical Terms), by the army; *Sōshi kaimei* (Japanization of names) policy in Korea.

———April: "Iwayuru kokugo mondai no kisū" (The Result of So-called *Kokugo* Problems), by Yamada Yoshio.

———May: "Heiki yōgo shū" (Glossary of Armament Terms), by the army.

———November: Institution of *Kokugo* Section in Library Office, Ministry of Education.

———December: Nihongo Kyōiku Shinkō Kai (Association for the Promotion of Japanese Language Education) formed.

1941 (Shōwa 16) January: Second Conference on Provisions of *Kokugo*.

———February: "Kokugo kokuji no seiri tōitsu ni kansuru kakugi mōshiawase jikō" (Cabinet Decisions on Organization and Unification of *Kokugo* and *Kokuji*).

———March: "Heiki ni kansuru kanazukai yōryō" (Guidelines for *Kana* Usage for Armament), by the army.

———Hoshina Kōichi appointed chair of Kokugo Shingikai; stays through World War II.

———*Kokugogaku genron* (The Principles of *Kokugo-gaku*), by Tokieda Motoki.

1942 (Shōwa 17) "Manshūkoku ni okeru nihongo" (The Japanese Language in Manchukuo), by Maruyama Rinpei.

———*Daitōa kyōeiken to kokugo seisaku* (The Greater East Asia Co-Prosperity Sphere and *Kokugo* Policy), by Hoshina Kōichi.

———April: "Daitōa kensetsu ni saishi kokugo kokusaku no kakuritsu ni tsuki kengi" (A Proposal for Instituting National Policy on *Kokugo* towards the Foundation of the Greater East Asia), by Kokugo Kyōkai and Kanamoji Kai.

———June: *Hyōjun kanji hyō* (List of Standard *Kanji*), by Kokugo Shingikai. Infuriates ultranationalists.

———October: Protest against *Hyōjun kanji hyō* by Nihon Kokugo Kai (Japan Association for *Kokugo*).

———December: Revised *Hyōjun kanji hyō,* by Kokugo Shingi Kai.

1943 (Shōwa 18) *Daitōa gengo kensetsu no kihon* (The Foundation for Constructing the Language of Greater East Asia), by Shida Nobuyoshi.

———"Kanazukai no honshitsu" (The Nature of *Kana* Usage), by Hashimoto Shinkichi.

———*Kokugo no honshitsu* (The Essence of *Kokugo*) and *Kokugogakushi* (The History of *Kokugo*), by Yamada Yoshio.

———*Kokugo no songen* (The Dignity of *Kokugo*), by Nihon Kokugo Kai.

———"*Mango kana*" *shuisho narabini kaisetsusho* (Prospectus and Manual for Manchurian *Kana*) (in Manchukuo).

1947 (Shōwa 22) "Kokugo kihanron no kōsō" (Outline of the Theory of Standard *Kokugo*), by Tokieda Motoki.

1951 (Shōwa 26) *On'inron to seishohō* (Phonology and Orthography), by Hattori Shirō.

1955 (Shōwa 30) Hoshina Kōichi dies.

1956 (Shōwa 31) "Reimeiki no kokugogaku to kokugo seisakuron to no kōshō" (Relation between *Kokugogaku* and Theories of *Kokugo* Policy in Incunabula), by Tokieda Motoki.

1961 (Shōwa 36) Kokugo Shingikai, fifth meeting.

1962 (Shōwa 37) *Kokugo mondai no tame ni* (For *Kokugo* Issues), by Tokieda Motoki.

Notes

Translator's Introduction

1. Also called *kanbun yomikudashi* or *kakikudashi*.

2. It only lists Hoshina 1934 and Hoshina 1949b in the bibliography.

3. While the title of the book is *An Encyclopaedia of Nihongo*, and the chapter title is "*Gengo* [language] Policy and Education," the section about policy is titled "*Kokugo* Issues and *kokugo* Policy."

4. On p. 404 in Nomoto Kikuo's "Gengo seisaku" (Language Policy) (Kokugo Gakkai 1995, 399–413), Hoshina is mentioned as the author of a "radical article."

5. http://www.culturalprofiles.net/japan/unit/2258.html. Accessed February 25, 2009.

6. As a language teacher, I am pleased and hopeful about the current movement in the field towards more critical and interdisciplinary approaches to teaching Japanese. Lee's book has been influential in such movements. For example, in *Bunka, kotoba, kyōiku* (Culture, Language, and Education, ed. Sato Shinji and Neriko Doerr, [Tokyo: Akashi Shobō, 2008]), a very recent publication on language education, many of the contributors list Lee's book in their references.

7. Ironically, Haga himself used the English phrase "way of life" in defining *minzoku* as membership by those who share the same language, that is, Japanese.

8. Interestingly, the association's original name in English was the Association for Japanese Linguistics, and this remained unchanged.

9. http://www.jpling.gr.jp/n_hakkan.html. In his inaugural statement as chair, Maeda said that the universities with the old department or major name *(kokugo)* numbered 66 percent in 1992, but by 2002 those with the new name *(nihongo)* increased to over 72 percent; http://www.jpling.gr.jp/aisatu.html.

Prologue

1. (Translator's note) Ordinance of Villers-Cotterêts: King Francis I legislated in 1539 that French would replace Latin as the official language of France. French

Academy: An academic organization established in 1635 with authority in matters related to French literature and language.

2. (Translator's note) *Man'yōshū* (Collection of Ten Thousand Leaves), compiled during the eighth century, is the oldest collection of poetry in Japan.

3. (Translator's note) Yamato is an old name for Japan. *Kojiki* (Records of Ancient Matters), compiled in the early eighth century, is the oldest existing writing about ancient Japanese history.

Introduction: The Japanese Language before *Kokugo*

1. (Translator's note) Archibald Henry Sayce (1846–1933), British philologist and Orientalist.

2. (Translator's note) The writings by Mori and Whitney quoted in this section are all in their original English, not my translation.

3. Mori's comment is prescient: "There are some efforts being made to do away with the use of Chinese characters by reducing them to simple phonetics, but the words familiar through the organ of the eye are so many, that to change them into those of the ear would cause too great an inconvenience, and be quite impracticable" (Mori 1873, 265–266). As we will see in the next chapter, when the *rōmaji* activists who initiated the romanization movement during the late second decade of Meiji used direct romanization of *kanbun*-style texts, their sentences were unintelligible. The movement did not go forward until B. H. Chamberlain, who was invited to the linguistics department of Tokyo University, criticized such practices and pointed out the need for *genbun itchi* as a prerequisite for romanization of Japanese.

4. Florian Coulmas remarks as follows about Mori Arinori in *Sprache und Staat:* "Japan enjoys remarkable homogeneity in its language, very rare in world languages. Therefore, such an audacious proposal as Mori's to abolish Japanese and replace it with a Western language, that is, English, is out of the question" (Coulmas 1985; Japanese translation 1987, 331). However, the "linguistic homogeneity," if such a thing ever exists, was a result of language policies after Meiji, and thus Coulmas's remark is an anachronism, obviously confusing the cause with the result. Such remarks have repeatedly and blindly reinforced assumptions about national language and script. Modern Japanese linguistic consciousness thus had to protect its ground by depicting Mori's argument as absurd. The myth of *kokugo* is so deeply engrained even among foreign scholars that they no longer think to question it.

5. (Translator's note) Baba's writings quoted in this chapter are all in his original English, not my translation.

6. Baba seemed to be profoundly informed by John Locke's theory of language and made frequent reference to Locke's *Essay concerning Human Understanding.* Locke speculated on the arbitrariness of signs and attempted to refute the absolute and universal hegemony of "sacred language." For further discussion about Locke, see Aarsleff 1982.

7. (Translator's note) 1926–2001. Independent historian and a critical biographer. He studied political science at Tokyo University, the University of Pennsylvania, and Oxford.

8. (Translator's note) *Kokutai:* The ideology that taught the Japanese people that the Japanese nation possessed a unique national quality or polity, different from that of any other country.

9. These sentences are in language spoken by Tokyo people but not his own native dialect. The following passage from his autobiography, *The Life of Tatsui Baba,* in an episode about his early days at Keiō University, illustrates Baba's personal struggle and indicates a part of the linguistic problems of his time: "And then he [Tatsui] saw his fellow students, most of whom were much older than he was, and they were thirty in number. He, being thus put among strangers, felt rather helpless and did not understand the speech of his fellow students, as it was so different from his provincial dialect. He often longed to go back to Tosa to see his friends" (Baba 1885/87, 149).

10. (Translator's note) After he returned from England in 1878, he was actively engaged in the Freedom and Human Rights Movement and led the Liberal Party. After resigning from the party over a disagreement, he was prohibited from publicly criticizing politics, and in 1885, he was arrested for possession of illegal explosives. When he was acquitted in 1886, he sought political asylum in the United States, where he continued writing political and personal essays. He died in Philadelphia in 1888.

Chapter 1: Perspectives on *Kokuji,* the National Script

1. In fact, linguists also become passionate about the problems surrounding script. One example is the debate in Korea of whether to use only *hangul* or to allow *kanji* in their writing, which overheated and ended up in a battle with chairs flying.

2. The Japanese translation (1981) of Coseriu 1952 uses *gengo kan'yō* (use of language) for *norma* and *gen* (language, speech) for *habla.* However, I translate the former as *kihan* (norm) and the latter as *jitsugentai* (materialized form) for more clarity.

3. (Translator's note) The title of the proposal in the original characters could be read as *Kanji gohaishi <u>no</u> gi,* as appears, for example, in Christopher Seeley's *History of Writing in Japan* (2000, 138). However, I believe that this honorific prefix in this context should be pronounced as <u>on</u>.

4. (Translator's note) The word *kokubun* today is used mainly as an abbreviation for *kokubungaku* (Japanese literature) or for Japanese language and literature. However, I translate Maejima's use of the word *kokubun* here as "the Japanese language," since this was a time before the word or concept of *kokugo* became clear, and *kokubun* was used for Japanese language, literature, texts, and so forth.

5. This proposal, however, was never officially submitted.

6. Noguchi (1994, 195–196) calls for a need to reexamine whether or not the Proposal for the Abolition of Chinese Characters actually existed in 1866 (Keiō 2). According to Noguchi, who is suspicious about the date of the proposal, this thirty-year-old proposal by Maejima was published [in late Meiji] because of the need to document the starting date of *kokugo* reform as far back as possible. However, I will follow the generally accepted theory here.

7. (Translator's note) Japanese words do not have to be written with a space between them. Here Maejima was following the writing style of Western languages.

8. (Translator's note) *Iroha* (like the English ABCs) is the Japanese *kana* syllabary in the traditional order.

9. For further information about the activities of these two organizations, see Hirai 1948, after 181.

10. 1884–1885, when today's Vietnam became a French colony, Indo-China.

11. Hara later became the first cabinet prime minister, known as "prime minister for the common people."

12. (Translator's note) Started in 1888 (Meiji 21).

13. Here Inoue was confusing the notions of script and vocabulary.

14. In 1900 (Meiji 33) the name of his department was changed from Department of Philology to Department of Linguistics.

15. This article was later printed in Ueda 1879, 202–228. See also Nishio and Hisamatsu 1969, 73–78.

16. (Translator's note) Ueda actually transcribed these technical terms in *katakana*, probably indicating his knowledge of the new European theory of linguistics.

17. "[We are] all in agreement that *kanji* is inconvenient and inefficient and that it should therefore be rejected" (Nishio and Hisamatsu 1969, 109).

18. Katō Hiroyuki's report that the committee voted against the use of the pictograph *(shōkei moji)* (Nishio and Hisamatsu 1969, 125).

19. (Translator's note) Yanagita Kunio (1875–1962), the founder of Japanese folklore *(minzokugaku),* who argued for the importance of local cultures and traditions throughout history. While a bureaucrat in the Ministry of Agriculture and Commerce, he traveled widely in Japan and recorded a vast number of local customs and stories, which he published.

Chapter 2: *Genbun Itchi* and *Kokugo*

1. (Translator's note) The sentence style written in Chinese with diacritics to indicate the reading in Japanese.

2. (Translator's note) *Bakuhan taisei* was the political and social system that was in place by the mid-seventeenth century. It consisted of the Edo shogunate government *(Edo bakufu)* as the central power and domains *(han)* that ruled their own lands but were strictly controlled by the *bakufu*.

3. Fukuchi Gen'ichirō also advocated *genbun itchi* about the same time in several articles he wrote for *Tōkyō nichi-nichi shinbun* (Tokyo Daily Newspaper).

4. (Translator's note) This is the original title, written this way in *rōmaji*.

5. (Translator's note) An association formed in 1885 by realist novelists such as Ozaki Kōyō and Yamada Bimyō, whose styles characteristically combine elements from Edo literature and Western literature.

6. (Translator's note) Today's Kagoshima area in Kyūshū.

7. (Translator's note) Today's Tōhoku region.

8. (Translator's note) 1603–1867, the period under the Tokugawa shogunate's rule.

9. Characterizations by Takamatsu Bōson in his *Meiji bungaku genbun itchi* (Meiji Literature and *Genbun Itchi*) in 1900. Quoted in Yamamoto M. 1965, 666.

10. (Translator's note) The plain-style sentence ending.

11. (Translator's note) The courteous-style sentence ending.

12. (Translator's note) In 1871, three years after the Meiji Restoration, the new government replaced the former *han*s (the domains, or fiefs, that had been given by the shogun to local feudal lords and governed by them) with *ken*s (prefectures), which were governed by the centralized authorities—one of the political reforms by the Meiji government to abolish the former feudal systems.

13. In 1886 (Meiji 19) the school ordinances for elementary and middle-high schools, teachers' colleges, and imperial universities were initiated by Mori Arinori, the first minister of education, who advocated education to develop the national polity. The ordinances were to build the nation's control over education, as seen in its institution of authorization of textbooks or introduction of military exercises into the curriculum. *Jinjō shōgaku tokuhon* (Normal Elementary School Reader), compiled by the Ministry of Education in 1887 (Meiji 20) and based on the school ordinance, referred to the language used in the book as that which "excluded certain dialects and provincial expressions" (Yamamoto 1965, 433); it did not clearly state the government's intention to adopt Tokyo language as the standard. According to Izawa Shūji, who was involved in the compilation, the textbook adopted the neutral colloquial style with the sentence-ending *de arimasu* in order to avoid any dialectal characteristics, including that of Tokyo language. It also used a special way of spelling certain conjugations in order to allow students to pronounce them "according to their local dialect" (436). For example, 取て was allowed to be pronounced either *torite* or *totte*.

14. (Translator's note) A translation of Turgenev's *Fathers and Sons*.

15. The original was written with a space between each word.

16. The original was written with a space between each word.

17. (Translator's note) *Beranmē* and *danbe* are common names for the vulgar speech styles of the natives in the Edo and Tōhoku regions respectively.

18. (Translator's note) Hayashi Mikaomi (1845–1922): *kokugo* scholar and poet; Kiryū Yū Yū (autonym Masaji; 1873–1941): journalist known for his defiant antimilitarism.

19. (Translator's note) Texts in mixtures of Chinese and Japanese styles.

20. (Translator's note) French writer and epigrammatist (1753–1801).

21. (Translator's note) Nuzhen (or Jurchens) and Qitai were among the many competing tribes in Central and Inner Asia before the Mongol Empire.

Chapter 3: The Creation of *Kokugo*

1. (Translator's note) The Institute for Western Learning, begun as Bansho Shirabejo in the late Edo era and renamed Kaiseijo in 1863, where they taught foreign languages and natural science, etc. The predecessor of Tokyo University.

2. (Translator's note) *Haibutsu kishaku* literally means "abolish Buddha and destroy Shakyamuni" (Buddha's given name).

3. (Translator's note) The Meiji government's campaign to promote Shinto, which deified the imperial line, as the state religion.

4. (Translator's note) An educational institution in the Edo era. Its predecessor was started by Hayashi Razan in 1630 and developed through the seventeenth and nineteenth centuries. After its changeover as Daigakkō in 1869, however, because of the rivalry among scholars of *yōgaku, kokugaku,* and *kangaku* the institution was closed down.

5. In *Moji no oshie* (Teaching of Script, 1873), which was written as a reading textbook for children but was also a notable example of Fukuzawa's practice of a new writing style with a reduced number of *kanji.*

6. (Translator's note) Written this way in *rōmaji* in the original.

7. (Translator's note) Written this way in *rōmaji* in the original.

8. (Translator's note) The principle or belief that Japan has been and must be ruled by emperors who embody the divine power that created Japan and has protected the Japanese people.

9. (Translator's note) The Mito school had originally been founded by Tokugawa Mitsukuni (1628–1700), daimyo of Mito domain, through the compilation of *Dai nihonshi* (The History of Great Japan). In its early period, it promoted academic discipline in Neo-Confucianism, but it later advocated and theorized the divine origin of Japan and Japan's prestige and superiority, that is, *kokutai.*

10. (Translator's note) 872?–945? A poet in the late Heian era. Compiled *Kokin waka shū* (Anthology of Japanese Poetry) in 905. The introduction was famous as an early theoretical critique of poetry. He is also important in the history of Japanese literature as the first person who wrote a personal journal, *Tosa nikki,* in *hiragana.* (During the Heian era, men were expected to use *kanji* in their writing. He wrote the jounal "as a woman" in *hiragana.*)

11. (Translator's note) *Shintai shi shō* (1882; Meiji 15), edited by Inoue Tetsujiro, Yatabe Ryōkichi, and Toyama Masakazu, was the first collection of Japanese modern poetry with the aim of transplanting the Western format of "poetry" in order to express ideas and emotions in the modern period.

Chapter 4: The Early Period of Ueda Kazutoshi

1. (Translator's note) Ueda explained that *hakugengaku* is a translation of "philology," but later the term was replaced by *gengogaku* (linguistics) as opposed to *bunkengaku,* which is the translation of "philology" in a traditional sense.

2. (Translator's note) Later Tokyo University.

3. (Translator's note) *Kokugaku* was founded by Keichū (1640–1701) and developed by Kamo no Mabuchi (1697–1769) and Motoori Norinaga (1730–1801).

4. (Translator's note) Joao Rodriguez (1561–1633): Portuguese Jesuit. As a translator served Toyotomi Hideyoshi and Tokugawa Ieyasu until exiled by the latter in 1613. Wrote *Nihon dai-bunten* (1604–1608) and *Nihon shō-bunten* (1620) for the missionaries' language study; they were influential for the later field of Japanese language education. (Nihongo Kyōiku Gakkai 1987, 730).

Philipp Franz von Siebolt (1796–1866): German doctor and scholar of natural history and Japanese studies. Lived in Japan 1823–1828 as a doctor for a Dutch office in Nagasaki and taught Western medicine and natural science. Exiled during the time of the shogunate government's suppression of Western studies, but returned 1859–1862 as an adviser for the Dutch Trading Company (Asao Naohiro et al. 1996, 489).

Johann Joseph Hoffmann (1805–1878): German linguist. Inspired by Siebolt, became a scholar of Japanese and Asian studies. Served Dutch government as a Japanese translator and taught courses on Japan at Leiden University. Wrote many books on Japanese language and culture and contributed to founding Japanese studies in Europe (Nihongo Kyōiku Gakkai 1987, 731).

William George Aston (1841–1911): British diplomat and scholar of Japanese studies. After studying linguistics at Queen's College, came to Japan in 1864 and actively served as a diplomat and translator between the two countries. After his retirement to London, wrote many scholarly books on Japanese language, literature, religion, history, and so forth, notably *A Grammar of the Japanese Written Language* (1872), which was used widely by Western students of Japanese classical language (Nihongo Kyōiku Gakkai 1987, 732).

5. (Translator's note) William Dwight Whitney (1827–1894). Also see the introduction of this book about his correspondence with Mori Arinori.

6. (Translator's note) Shiketei Sanba (1776–1822): Popular novelist in the late Edo era.

Yoshida Shōin (1830–1859): Philosopher at the end of the Edo era who advocated *son'nō shiso* (reverence for the emperor). Many of his students, including Itō Hirobumi, Yamagata Aritomo, and Inoue Kaoru, later became political leaders. Because of his radical political activities against the shogunate government, he was arrested and executed during the *Ansei* purge (*Ansei no taigoku,* 1858–1859).

Watanabe Kazan (1793–1841): Scholar and artist in the late Edo period. Took part in the reform of the domain government. Because of his progressive ideas and protest against the shogunate government's maritime restriction, he was placed under house arrest during the suppression of Western scholars in 1839 *(bansha no goku)* and took his own life.

7. (Translator's note) The Imperial Oath was also called the Charter Oath. Proclamed by the Meiji emperor at his enthronement in 1868. Set forth the principles of the new government, emphasizing the national assembly and public discussion, the unity of people of all classes towards the nation's welfare, departure from old customs, and pursuit of knowledge. The rescript was the code of military ethics issued by the Meiji emperor in 1882. Intended for restructuring the military under the emperor's direct command and for educating soldiers on loyalty to the emperor.

8. Nakauchi discusses Ueda's conversion after the outbreak of the Sino-Japanese War (1985, 158–159). However, I maintain that Ueda was consistent in his ideas about the relationship between *kokugogaku* and linguistics, and accordingly, his plans for *kokugo* policies.

9. According to Tanaka (1989, 251–254), Gabelentz's discussion about Japanese quantifiers in his *Sprachwissenschaft* is possibly based on knowledge he received from Ueda.

10. (Translator's note) Preface to *Morphological Investigations in the Sphere of the Indo-European Languages I* (Leipzig: S. Hirzel).

11. For further discussions about the Neogrammarians' role in the history of linguistics, see, for example, Pederson 1924, Ivic 1965, Kazama 1978, and Robins 1968.

12. This account of Ueda 1975 is based on the notes of these lectures taken by Shinmura Izuru.

13. (Translator's note) Italicized words in these quotations are in English in Ueda's text.

14. (Translator's note) Wilhelm von Humboldt (1767–1835). Jakob Grimm (1785–1863).

15. See especially chapters 4 and 5.

16. According to Amsterdamska (1987),

Beginning in 1860 the number of students in German universities grew at an unprecedented pace. There were twice as many students in 1881 as in 1861. . . . In Leipzig during the same period, student enrollment in this [philosophy] faculty quintupled. . . . Between 1864 and 1880 the number of *Ordinarien* teaching in German universities grew by 30 percent . . . [and] the number of philological chairs grew 53 percent. . . . The increase in all other philological areas was enormous. In 1880 there were eighty-two full professors of nonclassical philology, compared with forty-seven in 1864 (a 74 percent increase). By 1890, another eleven professorships had been added. (130)

The increase in the number of philological journals was fifteen in 1850, twenty in 1870, thirty-two in 1875, and forty-four in 1880 (134).

17. According to Amsterdamska, the Neogrammarians renounced their early goal, inherited from Schleicher, of reconstructing the original language.

> Instead of trying to discover the hypothetical *original* roots and the origins of inflection, the goal of reconstruction should be to arrive at the *oldest* attestable form of Indo-European and to trace its phonetic and analogical transformations through the history of individual languages. The question asked by the Neogrammarians was no longer "What is the original form and how did it decay?" but "What is the oldest form we can reconstruct and how did it change?" (98)

In other words, the Neogrammarians' interest was no longer in legendary "origins" but in a "past" that could be positively verified. This change in the Neogrammarians' direction was juxtaposed with the fact that the Prussian state renounced the mythical *Grossdeutschtum* and shifted to *Kleindeutschtum*.

18. For further discussion, see Umene 1977, chap. 4. About *Gymnasium* in Prussia, see 12–15. The following discussion is greatly indebted to Umene (1967) and Townson (1992).

19. Ueda was already in Berlin by this time.

20. The original speech in German is quoted in Townson 1992, 116 fn. 70.

21. About the history and activities of the All-German Association, Hoshina and Andō 1918 and Kamo 1944 are still helpful references, as well as Koelwel and Ludwig 1969 and Polenz 1970.

22. I think it is important to reexamine the significance of the Neogrammarians in the history of Prussian-German ethos.

Chapter 5: *Kokugo* and *Kokka*

1. The Sino-Japanese War began August 1, 1894.

2. Even though Ueda said Japan did not consist of "one race," the "race" in his mind did not at all mean the Ainu race. His concept of race inherited the distinctions among imperial, divinitive, and immigrant linkages, recorded in the *Shinsen shōjiroku* [Translator's note: New Record of Names, 815; compilation of genealogy of 1,182 clan families around Kyoto area; thirty volumes and one volume of index]. Such stratification of ancient clans according to their distance from the imperial family had been confused with the idea of ethnicity *(minzoku)* and used as the proof of Japan as a multiethnic nation before World War II. And this had been used as the justification for the history of colonization and assimilation. See Oguma 1995 for further discussion.

3. (Translator's note) Kuril Islands today. Northernmost part of Japan at that time.

4. "We conquered Pyongyang yesterday, and today we triumphed on the islands. China is no longer of our military concern and notice" (*Ochiai* 1968, 113).

Chapter 6: From *Kokugo* Studies to *Kokugo* Politics

1. (Translator's note) Old name for the northern part of the mainland of Japan: today's Fukushima, Iwate, Aomori, and part of Akita prefectures.

2. (Translator's note) *Tsurezuegusa* (Essays in Idleness): A collection of essays on nature, life, and society, written by Yoshida Kenkō, a monk and poet, in the late Kamakura period. *Jikkinshō* (A Miscellany of Ten Maxims): A collection of instructive tales for children, written in the mid-Kamakura period. Authors unknown.

3. Though both Ochiai and Ōtsuki used the word *chūko* (medieval) texts, the former referred to the literature of the Kamakura period, the latter, of early Heian.

4. (Translator's note) *Naichi zakkyo* (Opening of the Concessions): the policy that permitted integration of Japanese and foreign residents in Japan, allowing foreigners to live, travel, own lands, and do business freely in Japan. The policy was proposed in 1889 as a part of the revision of unequal treaties with Western nations; it became effective in 1899 after much objection and protest.

5. In the July 4 issue of the government's gazette.

6. (Translator's note) In the original the word "phonogram" is spelled in *kata-kana* as *fonoguramu.*

7. Petition regarding Improvements in National Script and Language (1900) and Petition for Actions towards *Genbun Itchi* (1901).

8. For further discussion about the roles of Ueda and *Gengogaku zasshi* in the *genbun itchi* movement, see "Ueda Kazutoshi no kōgo buntai seiritsu jō no kōseki" (Ueda Kazutoshi's Contributions to the Establishment of Colloquial Style; in Yamamoto M. 1981, 424–451).

9. In April of the same year, the Ministry of Education appointed national language investigators.

10. The sentence-ending style *de arimasu,* which had been commonly used, was replaced by the formal *desu* or the informal *da.*

11. The textbook introduced *otōsan* [father], *okāsan* [mother], *nīsan* [older brother], and *nēsan* [older sister], and made these kinship terms universal; they are in familiar use today. Thus the "family" was embraced into the nation-state system through language as a symbolic institution. Preceding this textbook, the Civil Law issued in 1898 (Meiji 31) had already enforced the feudalistic samurai-like family law among common people.

12. This well-known phrase appeared in the opening page of Ueda's *Kokugo no tame* (For *Kokugo*), but is not included in *Ochiai* 1968.

13. Tokieda (1942) also discussed this question. For further discussion, see Shi (1993, 138–142) and Kawamura (1994, 236–247).

14. This does not mean that the word *bogo* was unfamiliar at that time. For example, *Dai genkai* (Expanded Sea of Words), a major Japanese dictionary by Ōtsuki (revision completed 1932–1937; Shōwa 7–12), has an entry *bogo* with an explanation "the translation of the English word 'mother tongue.'"

Chapter 7: Hoshina Kōichi—a Forgotten Scholar

1. (Translator's note) One of the predecessors of Tokyo Imperial University.
2. The journal continued until 1940 (Shōwa 15).
3. (Translator's note) Known as the *batsufuda* (penalty placard) system: the punishment method started in Okinawa to prohibit students from speaking their native dialect. A student who spoke his own dialect at school was made to hang a placard around his neck as a warning example to others.
4. Error for "assistant professor."
5. Error for "professor."

Chapter 8: The History of *Kokugogaku*

1. The first volume of Kamei's essay collection is titled *Nihongogaku no tameni* (For the Study of the Japanese Language).
2. (Translator's note) Shaku Keichū (1640–1701): A Tendai-sect Buddhist monk and scholar of literature in the early Edo era. His empirical approach to classical texts gave a foundation to the early stage of *kokugaku* and greatly influenced Motoori Norinaga.
3. See Roman Jacobson's intriguing introduction to Silverstein 1971.
4. (Translator's note) Tachibana Moribe (1781–1849): A *kokugaku* scholar in the late Edo era. Developed unique ideas against Norinaga's theories.
5. Hasegawa Tenkei, a literary critic, also took notice of Hoshina's *Kokugogaku shōshi* in his newspaper article "Genbun itchi to wa nan zoya" (What Is *Genbun itchi?*), *Mainichi shinbun* (the Mainichi Newspaper), January, 31, 1900. (In Yamamoto M. 1979, 209–212).
6. Yamada's position here may appear to be historicism, but it is not the case, as we discuss in the next chapter.
7. Chamberlain's *Nihon shō bunten* was published by the Editorial Office of the Ministry of Education and was an officially acknowledged grammar book. However, as we will see later, Yamada considered that *kokugogaku,* the research of the Japanese language, could be carried out only by the Japanese people, and therefore he must have been irritated that Chamberlain, a foreigner, had written a book on Japanese grammar and that a Japanese government office had published it.

Chapter 9: Tradition and Reform in *Kokugo*

1. (Translator's note) For example, /kya/, formerly written as きや, was changed to きゃ.
2. In addition, in the Elementary School Order of 1900, the number of *kanji* was limited to twelve hundred.

3. (Translator's note) I inserted the original texts in Japanese for the following three examples to illustrate the way Hoshina adopted the new *kana* usage.

4. (Translator's note) I underlined the particles in question.

5. (Translator's note) "—." This mark is used today only for Western loanwords, such as in ボール (*bōru*, "ball").

6. (Translator's note) The English words provided here are in Hoshina's original text.

7. (Translator's note) Tōyama Mitsuru (1855–1944): Ultranationalist leader; promoted pan-Asianism and nationalism as a power broker. Matsuo Sutejirō (1875–1948): *Kokugo* scholar; successor to Yamada Yoshio.

8. Yamada's essay was first published in *Bungei shunjū* (September 1942) and is the same as his essay with a different title, "Kokugo no honshitsu" (The Essence of *Kokugo*), in his book of the same title, *Kokugo no honshitsu*, 1943 (Shōwa 18). The book also contains "Kokugo to wa nan zo ya" (What Is *Kokugo?*), "Kokugo kokubun no honshi to kyōiku" (The Principal Object and Teaching of *Kokugo* and *Kokubun*), and "Kokugo to sono kyōiku" (Teaching *Kokugo*).

9. (Translator's note) 1904–1976. Novelist and playwright.

10. (Translator's note) Yamagata Aritomo (1838–1922): Japanese military leader and politician. Prime minister of Japan (1889–1891; 1898–1900). Built and led the newly modernized Imperial Army.

Chapter 10: The Ideology of *Hyōjungo*

1. The well-known *hōgen ronsō* (dispute over dialects) in Okinawa in 1940, which was triggered by Yanagi Muneyoshi's remark, was an extreme example of such suppression. See, for example, Hokama 1971, 85–93; 1981, 331–338.

(Translator's note) Along with the nationalistic climate of the time, the strict enforcement of *hyōjungo* escalated in Okinawa also. In January 1940, the Association of Mingei Artists, led by Yanagi, visited Okinawa and criticized the local government's extreme suppression as humiliating for the native speakers of the Okinawa language, a language they regarded as a valuable subject of academic research. The local government dismissed this protest, however, and their enforcement of *hyōjungo* upon the Okinawan people became even more intense.

2. Hoshina (1900) listed eight causes, but the content was almost the same.

3. Yanagita Kunio harshly criticized such an "ideology of *hyōjungo*" in his writings (see Yanagita 1963a, b). While he did not entirely reject the concept of *hyōjungo*, his view differed from that of Ueda and Hoshina at two points: Yanagita considered *hyōjungo* at the level of vocabulary and not as an entirety of the language; and such *hyōjungo* would be established through "voluntary selection," not by "artificial standardization." Though I do not discuss his work here, Yanagita's ideas about language deserve serious consideration.

Chapter 11: Korea and Poland

1. The eight articles are "Doitsu ni okeru kokugo kokuji kairyō mondai no sūsei" [Trend of Issues in the National Language and Script in Germany] (April 1913), "Sekai-go ni taisuru ni-dai-gengogakusha no hihyō" [Comments by the Two Great Linguists about Esperanto] (May 1913), "Gengo chiri-gaku ni tsuite" [About Linguistic Geography] (November 1913), "Eikoku ni okeru tsuzuriji kairyō undō no genjō" [The Present State of the Spelling Reform in England] (December 1913), "Arubania ni okeru saikin no kokuji kokugo mondai" [Recent Problems in the National Language and Script in Albania] (April 1914), "Hokubei gasshūkoku ni okeru tsuzuri kairyō saikin no undō" [Recent Movement in Spelling Reform in the United States] (June 1914), "Suisu ni okeru kokugo mondai to seiji mondai to no kankei" [The Relation between the National Language and Political Problems in Switzerland] (August 1914), and "Nan-a no kokugo mondai ni tsuite" [About the Problems of the National Language in South Africa] (December 1914).

2. (Translator's note) This passage is my translation of Hoshina's quotation in Japanese of the original German text.

3. (Translator's note): Hoshina used the word *chokkan kyōju*, which referred to the educational philosophy and methods advocated by Johann Heinrich Pestalozzis (1746–1827), which were very influential on Japanese education in Meiji as well as in Europe and the United States.

4. In his later work, Hoshina proposed the term *kokka-go* (state language) as a general concept that determined the use of language in these four areas. In Hoshina 1921, however, his use of the word *kokka-go* did not yet have such a particular meaning.

5. (Translator's note) The March First Movement, or the Samil Independence Movement. On March 1, 1919, representatives of religious organizations in Korea jointly declared Korea's independence in Keijōfu. Students and intellectuals who had been inspired by the rising "self-determinism" of the time readily joined them, together with a crowd in the city, and a huge protest march ensued, which quickly echoed throughout the country. The Japanese brutally suppressed the movement, resulting in seventy-five hundred dead, sixteen thousand injured, and forty-seven thousand imprisoned.

6. Hoshina wrote in the same part of the introduction that "the recent situation in Korea closely resembles what happened in Prussian Poland from 1830 through 1850" (i–ii), that is, from Prussia's annexation of Posen in 1830 through the explosions of ethnic movements in 1848 to the proclamation of the Prussian Constitution in 1850. Hoshina was comparing this process of stabilization with the colonization of Korea. For Hoshina, it would have been highly undesirable for the March First Movement to have taken the same course as "the school strike" which "prompted the rebuilding of Poland."

7. (Translator's note) Written in English in Hoshina's original text.

8. At its revision, the Research Office of Korean Education in the Academic Affairs Department of the government-general published a special issue (vol. 6, no. 6) of its journal *Chōsen kyōiku* (Korean Education). This "Special Issue for the Revision of the Educational Rescript" was meant to explain and promote the revised rescript. However, there was no mention of Hoshina in the journal. This was not unreasonable, because his book was circulated as a "secret document."

Chapter 12: What Is Assimilation?

1. (Translator's note) *Nitchū sensō,* Japan's full-scale invasion into China, started July 7, 1937, and escalated into World War II in December 1941.

2. (Translator's note) Literally, "creation of one's family name, and changing one's given name." Japan forced Korean people to change their names into Japanese.

3. (Translator's note) The Roko Bridge Incident is also known as the Marco Polo Bridge Incident. Several bullets were fired against Japanese troops on night maneuvers at the Roko Bridge on July 7, 1937, and one Japanese soldier went missing. Japan used this as an excuse to attack the Chinese army; this skirmish eventually escalated into the second Sino-Japanese War.

Yanaihara, a devout Christian and pacifist, was a professor of economics at Tokyo Imperial University from 1923 to 1937. His article "The Ideals of the Nation," which criticized Japanese colonial policies and the war against China, was banned by the government, and he was pressured into resigning from Tokyo University in 1937. (He returned to Tokyo University in 1945 and served as president from 1951 to 1957.)

4. This article first appeared in the journal *Kokka gakkai zasshi* (Journal of the Association for National Studies), February 1937.

5. (Translator's note) As a part of the imperialization in Taiwan, the Japanese government enforced the movement for Taiwanese to speak Japanese even at home among family members.

6. Komagome's discussion (1996, chap. 2) offers interesting analyses, though very different from mine in perspective. He interprets "Comments," from the historical viewpoint of educational policy, as reflecting Japanese emigrants' desire for short-term and direct profit (92). From the point of view of intellectual history, I, on the other hand, think "Comments" is a key to understanding the concept of assimilation in modern Japan.

Chapter 13: Manchukuo and the State Language

1. (Translator's note) Also known as the Ryūjōko Incident, the Mukden Incident, and the September 18 Incident. On September 18, 1931, the Japanese Kwantung army blew up the South Manchurian Railroad near Mukden, and using this as a signal, attacked the Chinese army in the north. The Japanese army blamed the Chinese army for the explosion and used this as the justification for invading Manchuria.

2. Repetitious content was characteristic of Hoshina's writings throughout his academic life.

3. Though he sorted language problems into these two categories, Hoshina believed they were a continuum and affected each other. We will return to this point in the next chapter.

4. Here Hoshina translated *Nationalität* as *kokuminsei* (national identity), though I think *minzokusei* (ethnic identity) is a better translation.

5. (Translator's note) Maruyama Rinpei (1891–1974): educator and teacher of *kokugo*.

6. (Translator's note) "The special national polity protected by the unbroken line of imperial succession through eternal generations," the ultranationalistic slogan that supported the Japanese Empire.

7. An example to illustrate how unfamiliar the word *Staatssprache* has become after a century: When Tanaka Katsuhiko once used the word [in his writing], W. A. Grotaers, a Belgian linguist, protested that Tanaka possibly created the word "since *Staatssprache* does not appear in *Lexikon der Germanischen Linguistik* (1973) by Max Miemeyer, or any other similar dictionaries" (Gurōtāsu 1978, 86–87).

8. For example, Hoshina and Andō coauthored a booklet titled *Gairaigo mondai ni kansuru Doitsu ni okeru kokugo undō* (The National Language Movements in Germany against Loanwords), which was published by the Ministry of Education in 1918 (Taishō 7).

9. (Translator's note) Yamamoto Yūzō (1887–1974): playwright and novelist who contributed to *kokugo* issues, promoting an easy-to-understand writing style.

10. In those remarks by Hoshina, we find expressions indicative of the influence of social Darwinism and the Nazi view of the history of racial struggles, current among Japanese intellectuals since Meiji. Given that one of the sources of Nazi ideology was the pan-Germanism movement in Austria, Hoshina's attention to pan-ethnic movements is very intriguing. In a sense, Hoshina was promoting a "pan-Japanism movement" modeled after such movements in Europe.

11. (Translator's note) "Yamato race" [*Yamato minzoku*] is the ultranationalistic term for "the Japanese people."

Chapter 14: Language for the Co-Prosperity Sphere

1. (Translator's note) The (Manchukuo) Concordia Association (Manshūkoku kyōwakai) (1932–1941): an organization whose objective was to assimilate and "imperialize" the people in Manchukuo through activities in the name of welfare and patronage.

2. (Translator's note) Commonly known as Mantetsu. The semiofficial railroad company, which controlled the railroad transportation all over Manchuria. Its operations extended to coal mining, iron manufacturing, commercial business, and even to school management.

3. Kamio (1983) mentions that after this *kana*-script proposal failed, there was also a plan for "Mongolian script reform":

The Kōansō district [today's Inner Mongolia] office proposed a reform of Mongolian script, and I set up a committee with Kikutake and Sato, who were my senior colleagues and graduates of the Mongolian Language Department of Tokyo Foreign Language University, and appointed a few administrators and linguists of Mongolian. About that time, the Soviet had instructed Outer Mongolia to create a phonetic script that resembled Russian, and promoted publications of books in the new script on socialist economy and industry. [Japan's reform of the Mongolian script] must have been a proposed countermeasure against it. However, before the proposal was finalized, we lost the war, and the plan never materialized. (105)

4. (Translator's note) Hattori Shirō (1908–1995): Linguist and a professor emeritus of Tokyo University. Well known and respected for his meticulous empirical research on Japanese, Ryukyuan, Ainu, Korean, Altaic, and Mongolian languages, and on Chinese, English, Russian, and Japanese dialects.

5. See Toyota 1964, 318–321, for the summary.

6. (Translator's note) Kamio's original sentence, "Dr. Hattori, on listening to my story [about the debate], showed his concerns," is ambiguous: one reading is that Hattori was concerned about the movement to promote *kana;* another is that he was concerned about the fact that the movement was rejected. The author's interpretation seems to be the former, but if the latter was the case, Hattori's writings cited here are consistent with his "concerns."

7. Hoshina wrote this word as *borogan-go* in *rōmaji.* However, I was not able to find the original name of the language in any linguistics dictionaries that are available today. The name of the language might have changed over time, or Hoshina might have copied it incorrectly. *Gengogakudai jiten* (Linguistics Dictionary), published by Sanseidō in 1988–1992, has a detailed description about languages on Borneo Island (3:1187–1193), but *borogan* is not mentioned. It lists Baram Kayan, which could sound close to *borogan,* but I was not able to confirm. (Translator's note: This footnote is not included in the original book but I added it, with the author's permission, based on her reply to my question about the original word for the language.)

8. It was, in fact, a serious agenda for Southeast Asian countries to form a unified "national language" when they became independent after the war.

9. (Translator's note) *Kotodama:* Spiritual power believed to inhabit words. A belief in Shintoism.

10. (Translator's note) In 1941, the name for the previous elementary schools *(shōgakkō)* was changed to national schools *(kokumin gakkō)* with eight years of compulsory curriculum in order to educate *kōkokumin* (imperial subjects). In 1947

the educational reform after the war changed the schools back to *shōgakkō* with the six-year curriculum.

11. (Translator's note) Konoe Fumimaro (1891–1945): Politician and later prime minister (1937–1939, 1940–1941). Aggressively built up a war regime and worsened the Japan-U.S. relationship. After the end of the war, he was named as a war criminal and committed suicide.

12. The newly created section was Section 3, which was merged into Section 2 in December 1938 (Shōwa 13).

13. Each day of the conference kept separate stenographic records. I numbered the first sixty-five pages of the second-day record since the original does not have page numbers.

14. (Translator's note) Because soldiers were not able to read or understand the special armament terms written in *kanji*.

15. The glossary also allowed the use of a large number of loanwords, which were supposed to have been forbidden as "the enemy's language."

16. This special issue of *Bungaku* also included Hoshina's article titled "Reinforce the regulation on *kokugo*," a completely opposite argument from Yamada's. The issue turned out to be a battlefield for these sworn enemies.

17. (Translator's note) *Waga* is a possessive "my, our" in the classical language, while *wareware no* came into use as a translation of the foreign equivalent "our."

18. The writing styles of Hoshina and Shida in their original Japanese are very contrastive. Hoshina writes as though talking to readers in plain language, while Shida's writing is hyperbolic and convoluted with many *kango*. In *Daitōa kyōeiken*, Hoshina displayed as a bad example a newspaper report that was drenched in literary style: "The publicized successful results of the navies throughout the numerous battles have immersed the people of our nation in a novel flush, and could not help but amaze the ears and eyes of the entire world" (1942a, 420–421). He considered sentences like this, which cannot be easily understood, ill formed. Shida's writing such as the following was even worse than this example:

> The spirit of the creation of the nation and the realization of the great deeds by generations of emperors are the historic emergence of the essential life of the universe, and it is the source of the force of the historic construction of Imperial Japan, which provides mankind of the world with what they desire, and which fulfills co-prosperity among all nations and human welfare. That is, the essence of mankind can be grasped and constructed only historically, and therefore, the position of the unique nation that observes the Imperial Way is the only position in the history and mankind. (Shida 1943, 5)

This is almost completely unintelligible, like an incantation or delirium. The contrast between their styles itself is indicative of the difference in their viewpoints. Hoshina's writing style might have been what enabled his viewpoint to survive after the war.

19. [Translator's note] Taken from *Nihon shoki* (A.D. 720), where it meant "to make the whole world one house," the phrase that was used as a slogan during wartime (1931–1945) to justify Japan's domination of Asia.

20. Asahi Shinbunsha's *Kokugo bunka kōza* (Series on *Kokugo* Culture), vol. 6 (1942), is titled *Kokugo shinshutsu hen* (The Advancement of *Kokugo*), and taking Fujimura Tsukuru's view that "today's problem in advancement of *kokugo* is part of current affairs" (2), it discussed not only Japanese language education in the colonies, Manchuria, and occupied lands, but also included Japanese language teaching in the West, for foreign students in Japan, and for the second generation of Japanese immigrants. It even indicated concerns about the language of those Japanese children who came back from abroad, in today's term *kikoku shijo,* "the returnees." Except for "the current affairs" of that time, they all resemble today's concerns about the Japanese language.

21. In 1988, the National Language Research Institute initiated a project, under a proposal by Director Nomoto Kikuo, to drastically simplify Japanese in both its grammar and vocabulary. For example, in this "simplified Japanese" all sentences end in *desu/masu* style, the verbs have only one conjugation, and basic vocabulary is limited to a thousand words, and thus expressions that are unnatural for today's Japanese were allowed. The proposal and project stirred up a public debate.

22. (Translator's note) The author might be alluding here to the book by Suzuki Takao, one of the leading *kokugo* scholars today, with a rather provocative title, *Buki to shite no kotoba: Nihon no gengo senryaku o kangaeru* (Language as a Weapon: Linguistic Strategy for Japan).

Chapter 15: Conclusion

1. (Translator's note) Shiga Naoya (1883–1971): Novelist. One of the representative "I-novel" writers, he influenced many later novelists, including Akutagawa Ryūnosuke, and his direct writing style drew many fans who called him *shōsetsu no kamisama* (god of fiction).

Kita Ikki (1883–1937): Social nationalist and influential theorist for the fascist movements in Japan.

2. Okamoto Kōji (1996) attempts to situate Kita's language theory within the entirety of his thinking (chap. 6), which is an important approach. Nonetheless, Okamoto's attention is only on Kita's "adoption of Esperanto," and not much on his despair at Japanese. Kita's theory of language would make sense only if it were situated in the context of development of the *kokugo* ideology after Meiji.

3. (Translator's note) Japanese name for the war between Japan and the Allied Forces during World War II. It was changed to the Pacific War afterwards, and more recently has been called the Asian-Pacific War.

4. (Translator's note) Since the late 1980s.

Bibliography

References for Translator's Notes and Introduction

Asao Naohiro et al., eds. 1996. *Shinpan Nihonshi jiten* [Dictionary of Japanese History—New Edition]. Tokyo: Kadokawa shoten.

Crystal, David. 2001. *A Dictionary of Language*. 2nd ed. Chicago: University of Chicago Press.

Gottlieb, Nanette. 1995. *Kanji Politics: Language Policy and Japanese Script.* New York: Kegan Paul International.

————. 2005. *Language and Society in Japan.* Cambridge, UK; New York: Cambridge University Press.

Haga Yasushi. 2004. *Nihonjin rashisa no kōzō* [The Structure of "Japaneseness"]. Tokyo: Taishukan.

Jankowsky, Kurt R. 1972. *The Neogrammarians: A Re-evaluation of Their Place in the Development of Linguistic Science.* The Hague: Mouton and Co.

Kindaichi Haruhiko, Hayashi Ōki, and Shibata Takeshi, eds. 1990. *Nihongo hyakka daijiten* [An Encyclopaedia of the Japanese Language]. Tokyo: Taishūkan.

Kokugo Gakkai, ed. 1995. *Kokugogaku no 50-nen* [Fifty Years of Studies in *Kokugo*]. Tokyo: Musashino Shoin.

Koyasu Nobukuni. 1994. "Kokugo wa shishite nihongo wa umaretaka" [Did *Kokugo* Die and Has *Nihongo* Been Born?]. *Gendai shisō (Revue de la pense e d'aujourd'hui),* 22, no. 9:45–57.

Miller, Roy A. 1967. *The Japanese Language.* Chicago: University of Chicago Press.

Nihon kokugo daijiten [Grand Dictionary of the Japanese Language]. 2nd ed., 2000–2003. Vols. 5, 11, and 13. Tokyo: Shōgakkan.

Nihongo Kyōiku Gakkai, ed. 1987. *Nihongo kyōiku jiten* [Dictionary for Japanese Language Education]. Tokyo: Taishūkan.

Sakai, Naoki. 1992. *Voices of the Past: The Status of Language in Eighteenth-Century Japanese Discourse.* Ithaca, N.Y.: Cornell University Press.

————. 1996. *Shizan sareru nihongo: "Nihon" no rekishi, chisei-teki haichi* [Stillbirth of Japanese as an Ethnos and as a Language (English title by the author)]. Tokyo: Shinyōsha.

Schieffelin, Bambi, et al. 1998. *Language Ideologies: Practice and Theory.* New York: Oxford University Press.

Seelye, Christopher. 2000. *A History of Writing in Japan.* Honolulu: University of Hawai'i Press.

Shibata Takeshi. 1976. "Sekai no naka no nihongo" [*Nihongo* in the World]. In *Nihongo to kokugogaku* [*Nihongo* and *Kokugogaku*], 1–29. Iwanami kōza: Nihongo 1 [Iwanami Series: The Japanese Language, vol. 1]. Tokyo: Iwanami Shoten.

Unger, Marshall. 2000. "*Kokugo to iu shisō: Kindai Nihon no gengo ninshiki* [The Idea of *Kokugo:* Language Consciousness in Modern Japan], by Lee Yeoun-suk." *Social Science Japan Journal* 3, no. 1: 147–151.

Yasuda Toshiaki. 1997a. Review of "Kokugo to iu shisō." *Minpaku tsūshin* [Newsletter of the Museum of Ethnology] (Osaka), 46–51.

———. 1997b. *Teikoku Nihon no gengo hensei* [Linguistic Formation in Imperial Japan]. Yokohama: Seori Shobō.

References for the Text

Note: The translator used the original sources in English whenever they are available for the author's quotations in Japanese translation used in the original book.

Aarsleff, Hans. 1982. *From Locke to Saussure.* Minneapolis: University of Minnesota Press.

Amsterdamska, Olga. 1987. *Schools of Thought: The Development of Linguistics from Bopp to Saussure.* Dordrecht: D. Reidel.

Anderson, Benedict. 1983. *Imagined Communities: Reflections on the Origin and Spread of Nationalism.* London: Verso. Japanese translation by Shiraishi Takashi and Shiraishi Saya: *Sōzō no kyōdōtai: Nashonarizumu no kigen to ryūkō.* Tokyo: Riburopōto, 1987.

Andō Masatsugu. 1975. *Andō Masatsugu chosaku shū.* [Collection of Writings by Andō Masatsugu]. Vol 6: *Kokugo seisaku ronkō* [Essays on *Kokugo* Policy]. Tokyo: Yūzankaku.

Asahi Shinbunsha, ed. 1941–1942. *Kokugo bunka kōza* [Series on *Kokugo* Culture]. Vol. 1: *Kokugo mondai hen* [Problems in *Kokugo*]. Vol. 2: *Kokugo gairon hen* [Outline of *Kokugo*]. Vol. 3: *Kokugo kyōiku hen* [*Kokugo* Education]. Vol. 6: *Kokugo shinshutsu hen* [Advancement of *Kokugo*]. Tokyo: Asahi Shinbun-sha.

Asao Naohiro et al., eds. 1993–1996. *Iwanami kōza Nihon tsūshi 19 Kindai 4.* [Iwanami Series: Overview of Japanese History, vol. 19, part 4]. Tokyo: Iwanami Shoten.

Baba, Tatsui. 1873. *An Elementary Grammar of the Japanese Language, with Easy Progressive Exercises.* London: Trübner and Co. In *Baba Tatsui zenshū* [Complete Works of Baba Tatsui], 3–109. Tokyo: Iwanami Shoten, 1987.

———. 1885–1888. "The Life of Tatsui Baba." In *Baba Tatsui zenshū* [Complete Works of Baba Tatsui], 3: 135–175. Tokyo: Iwanami Shoten, 1988.

———. 1987–1988. *Baba Tatsui zenshū* [Complete Works of Baba Tatsui]. Vols. 1–4. Tokyo: Iwanami Shoten.

Bungaku. 1940. Special issue: *Tōa ni okeru nihongo* [The Japanese Language in East Asia].

Chamberlain, B. H. 1887. *Nihon shō bunten* [Concise Japanese Grammar Dictionary]. Tokyo: Monbushō Henshūkyoku [Editorial Office, Ministry of Education].

Coseriu, Eugenio. 1952. "Sistema, norma y habla." Japanese translation by Hara Makoto and Ueda Hiroto: "Gengo taikei, gengo kanyō, gen." In *Koseriu gengogaku senshū*, vol. 2 [Selected Essays on Linguistics by Coseriu, vol. 2]. Tokyo: Sanshūsha, 1981.

Coulmas, Florian. 1985. *Sprache und Staat. Studien über Sprachplanung und Sprachpolitik.* Berlin: De Gruyther. Japanese translation by Yamashita Kimiko: *Gengo to kokka: Gengo keikaku narabini gengo seisaku no kenkyū* [Language and Nation: Studies on Language Planning and Language Policies]. Tokyo: Iwanami Shoten, 1987.

Doi Mitsutomo. 1933. *Kiso nihongo* [Basic Japanese]. Tokyo: Rokuseikan.

Fries, Charles C. 1963. *Linguistics and Reading.* Chicago: Holt, Rinehart and Winston. Japanese translation by Okitsu Tatsurō: *Kindai gengogaku no hattatsu* [The Evolution of Modern Linguistics]. Tokyo: Kenkyūsha, 1968.

Fukuzawa Yukichi. 1980–1981. *Fukuzawa Yukichi senshū* [Selected Writings by Fukuzawa Yukichi]. Vols. 1, 2, and 12. Tokyo: Iwanami Shoten.

Gaimushō [Ministry of Foreign Affairs]. 1939. *Sekai ni nobiyuku Nihongo* [The Japanese Language Expanding Worldwide]. Tokyo: Bunka Jigyōbu [Department of Cultural Affairs].

Glück, Helmut. 1979. *Die preussische-polnische Sprachenpolitik.* [The Prussian-Polish Language Policy] Hamburg: Buske.

Gurōtāsu (Grotaers, W. A.). 1978. "Kokugo to nihonjin" [*Kokugo* and the Japanese People]. *Gengo seikatsu* [Linguistic Life] (March).

Hagiwara Nobutoshi. 1967. *Baba Tatsui.* Tokyo: Chūōkōronsha.

Hall, Ivan. 1972a. "*Eibun shiryō ni tsuite*" [About Mori's Writings in English]. In Ōkubo Toshiaki, 1972, 3: 3–33.

———. 1972b. "Hoittonii-ate shokan—Mori no ronjutsu [The Letter to Whitney—Mori's Statement]. In Ōkubo Toshiaki 1972, 1: 93–95.

Hashikawa Bunzō. 1978. *Nashonarizumu* [Nationalism]. Tokyo: Kinokuniya shoten.

Hashimoto Shinkichi. 1943. "Kanazukai no honshitsu" [The Nature of *Kana* Usage]. In Nihon Kokugo Kai, ed., 1943.

Hatano Kanji et al., eds. 1975. *Gendai nihongo no kensetsu ni kurō shita hitobito* [People Who Strove for the Modern Japanese Language]. Shin nihongo kōza 9 [New Series on the Japanese Language 9]. Tokyo: Sekibunsha.

Hattori Shirō. 1935. "Manmō no shominzoku to minzokusei" [Ethnic Groups in Manchuria-Mongolia and Their Ethnic Identities]. *Dorumen* 4, no. 5. Also reprinted in Hattori 1992.

———. [1951] 1979. *On'inron to seishohō* [Phonology and Orthography]. Tokyo: Taishūkan.

———. 1992. *Ichi gengo gakusha no zuisō* [Random Thoughts of a Linguist]. Tokyo: Kyūko Shoin.

Hepburn, James Curtis. 1872. *Wa-ei gorin shūsei* [Japanese-English Vocabulary Collection]. 2nd ed. Shanghai: Meihua Shuyuan.

———. 1886. *Wa-ei gorin shūsei*. 3rd ed. Tokyo: Maruzen Shōsha Shoten.

Hirai Masao. 1948. *Kokugo kokuji mondai no rekishi.* [History of Issues in *Kokugo* and National Script]. Tokyo: Shōrinsha.

Hokama Shuzen. 1971. *Okinawa no gengoshi* [History of the Language of Okinawa]. Tokyo: Hōsei Daigaku Shuppankyoku.

———. 1981. *Nihongo no sekai* [The World of the Japanese Language]. Vol. 9: *Okinawa no kotoba* [The Language in Okinawa]. Tokyo: Chūōkōronsha.

Hoshina Kōichi. 1899a. *Gengo hattatsu ron* [The Growth of Language]. Tokyo: Toyamabō.

———. 1899b. *Kokugogaku shōshi* [Abbreviated History of *Kokugogaku*]. Tokyo: Dai-Nihon Tosho.

———. 1900. *Gengogaku taii* [Outline of Linguistics]. Tokyo: Kokugo Denshūsho.

———. 1901. *Kokugo kyōjuhō shishin* [Guidelines for Teaching *Kokugo*]. Tokyo: Hōeikan Shoten.

———. 1902. *Gengogaku* [Linguistics]. Tokyo: Waseda Daigaku Shuppan-bu.

———. 1907a. *Kaitei kanazukai yōgi* [Summary of the Revised *Kana* Usage]. Tokyo: Kōdōkan.

———. 1907b. *Kokugogakushi* [The History of *Kokugogaku*]. Tokyo: Waseda Daigaku Shuppan-bu.

———. 1910. *Kokugogaku seigi* [Exposition of *Kokugogaku*]. Tokyo: Dōbunkan.

———. 1911. *Nihon kōgohō* [The Grammar of Spoken Japanese]. Tokyo: Dōbunkan.

———. 1914a. *Kokugo kokuji kokubun kairyō shosetsu kōgai* [Outline of Various Theories for Improvement of *Kokugo, Kokuji,* and *Kokubun*]. Tokyo: Kyōiku Chōsakai.

———. 1914b. *Kokugo kyōiku oyobi kyōju no shinchō* [The New Wave in Education and Teaching of *Kokugo*]. Tokyo: Kōdōkan.

———. 1915. *Saikin kokugo kyōju jō no shomondai* [Recent Issues in *Kokugo* Teaching]. Tokyo: Kyōiku Shinchō Kenkyūkai.

———. 1916. *Kokugo kyōjuhō seigi* [Exposition of Methods of Teaching *Kokugo*]. Tokyo: Ikuei Shoin.

———. 1917. *Jitsuyō kōgohō* [The Grammar of Practical Spoken Language]. Tokyo: Ikuei Shoin.

———. 1918. *Taishō Nihon bunpō* [Taisho Japanese Grammar]. Tokyo: Ikuei Shoin.

———. 1921. *Doitsu zokuryō jidai no Pōrando ni okeru kokugo seisaku* [Language Policy in German Poland]. Gyeongseong: Chōsen Sōtokufu [Government-General of Korea].

———. 1927. *Kunren kōza kokugo* [Practice Series for *Kokugo*]. Tokyo: Shakai Kyōikukai.

———. 1932. *Kokugo kyōiku o kataru* [About *Kokugo* Education]. Tokyo: Ikuei Shoin.

———. 1933a. "Kokka-go no mondai ni tsuite" [About the Problems in State Language]. *Tōkyō Bunrika Daigaku Kiyō* [Bulletin of Tokyo University of Literature and Science], vol. 6.

———. 1933b. *Kokugo seisaku ron* [Theory for *Kokugo* Policy]. Tokyo: Meiji Shoin.

———. 1933c. *Shin kyōjuhō to waga kokugo kyōiku* [New Method of Teaching Our Japanese]. Tokyo: Yūzankaku.

———. 1934. *Shintai kokugogaku shi* [The History of *Kokugogaku* in the New Style]. Tokyo: Kenbunkan.

———. 1936a. *Kokugo seisaku* [*Kokugo* Policy]. Tokyo: Kōtō Shoin.

———. 1936b. *Kokugo to Nihon seishin* [*Kokugo* and the Japanese Spirit]. Tokyo: Jitsugyō-no-Nihon-sha.

———. 1939. *Kyōshi no tame no bungohō* [The Grammar of Written Japanese for Teachers]. Tokyo: Ikuei Shoin.

———. 1942a. *Daitōa kyōeiken to kokugo seisaku* [The Greater East Asia Co-Prosperity Sphere and *Kokugo* Policy]. Tokyo: Tōseisha.

———. 1942b. *Waji shōranshō to kanazukai mondai* [The Correct Usage of Classical Japanese Script and Problems in *Kana* Usage.] Tokyo: Nihon Hōsō Shuppan Kyōkai.

———. 1949a. *Kokugo binran: Tōyō kanji, gendai kanazukai kaisetsu* [*Kokugo* Manual: Commentary on Tōyō Kanji and Modern *Kana* Usage]. Tokyo Kyōiku Tosho Kenkyūkai.

———. 1949b. *Kokugo mondai 50-nen* [Fifty Years of *Kokugo* Issues]. Tokyo: Sanyō Shobō.

———. 1952. *Aru kokugo gakusha no kaisō* [Memoir of a *Kokugo* Scholar]. Tokyo: Asahi Shinbunsha.

Hoshina Kōichi and Andō Masatsugu. 1918. *Gairaigo mondai ni kansuru Doitsu ni okeru kokugo undō* [The National Language Movements in Germany against Loanwords]. Tokyo: Monbushō.

Ishiguro Osamu. 1940. "Kiso goi no chōsa" [Investigation of Basic Vocabulary]. In Kokugo Kyōiku Gakkai 1940.

Ishiguro Rohei. 1944. *Hyōjungo no mondai* [The Problems in the Standard Japanese Language]. Tokyo: Sanseidō.

Itō Mikiharu. 1982. *Kazoku-kokka kan no jinruigaku* [Anthropology of the Family-Nation Ideology]. Tokyo: Mineruva Shobō.

Itō Sadayoshi. 1987. *Ikyō to kokyō* [Exile and Home]. Tokyo: Tōkyō Daigaku Shuppan-kai.

Ivic, Milka. 1965. *Janua Linguarum*. [The Gateway to Languages] Japanese translation by Hayata Teruhiro and Inoue Fumio: *Gengogaku no nagare* [Trends in Linguistics]. Tokyo: Misuzu Shobō, 1974.

Iwahori Yukihiro. 1995. *Ei-wa, wa-ei jiten no tanjō* [The Birth of English-Japanese and Japanese-English Dictionaries]. Tokyo: Tosho Shuppansha.

Jansen, Marius B., ed. 1956. *Changing Japanese Attitudes towards Modernization*. Princeton, N.J.: Princeton University Press. Japanese translation by Hosoya Chiharu: *Nihon ni okeru kindai-ka no mondai* [Problems in Modernization in Japan]. Tokyo: Iwanami Shoten, 1968.

Jinbō Kaku. 1941. *Hyōjungo kenkyū* [A Study of the Standard Language]. Tokyo: Nihon Hōsō Kyōkai.

Joseph, John Earl. 1987. *Eloquence and Power: The Rise of Language Standards and Standard Languages*. London: Frances Printer.

Kaigo Tokiomi, ed. 1963. *Nihon kyōkasho taikei: Kindai hen* [Compendium of Japanese Textbooks: Modern Era]. Vol. 7. Tokyo: Kōdansha.

———. 1968. *Inoue Kowashi no kyōiku seisaku* [Inoue Kowashi's Educational Policy]. Tokyo: Tōkyō Daigaku Shuppankai.

Kajii Noboru. 1980. *Chōsengo o kangaeru* [Concerning the Korean Language]. Tokyo: Ryūkei Shosha.

Kamei Takashi. 1971. "Kokugo to wa ikanaru kotoba nari ya" [What Kind of Language Is *Kokugo?*]. In *Kamei Takashi ronbun shū* [Collection of Kamei Takeshi's Essays]. Vol. 1: *Nihongo no tame ni* [For the Japanese Language]. Tokyo: Yoshikawa Kōbunkan.

Kamei Takashi et al., eds. 1965. *Nihongo no rekishi* [History of the Japanese Language]. Vols. 6–7. Tokyo: Heibonsha.

Kamio Kazuharu. 1983. *Maboroshi no manshūkoku* [Manchukuo, the Phantom Nation]. Tokyo: Nitchū Shuppan.

Kamishima Jirō. 1961. *Kindai Nihon no seishin kōzō* [Structure of the Ethos of Modern Japan]. Tokyo: Iwanami Shoten.

Kamo Masakazu. 1944. *Doitsu no kokugo junka* [The Purification of the National Language in Germany]. Tokyo Nichi-Doku Bunka Kyōkai.

Kawamura Minato. 1994. *Umi o watatta nihongo* [The Japanese Language Overseas]. Tokyo: Seidosha.

Kazama Kiyozō. 1978. *Gengogaku no tanjō* [Birth of Linguistics]. Tokyo: Iwanami Shoten.

Kimura Muneo, ed. 1991. *Kōza: Nihongo to Nihongo kyōiku* [The Japanese Language and Its Teaching]. Vol. 15: *Nihongo kyōiku no rekishi* [The History of Japanese Language Teaching]. Tokyo: Meiji Shoin.

Kindaichi Haruhiko. 1983. *Nihongo seminā* [Seminar of the Japanese Language]. Vol. 5: *Nihongo no ayumi* [Footsteps in the Japanese Language]. Tokyo: Chikuma Shobō.

Kirkness, Alan. 1975. *Zur Sprachreinigung im Deutschen 1789–1871. Eine historische Dokumentation* [On Cleansing the German Language 1789–1871.

A Historical Documentation]. Teil 1. Tübingen: TBL Verlag Gunter Narr.

Kita Ikki. 1959. *Kita Ikki chosakushū* [Collection of Kita Ikki's Writings]. Vol. 2. Tokyo: Misuzu Shobō.

Koelwel, Eduard, and Helmut Ludwig. 1969. *Gepflegte Deutsch.* 4th ed. Japanese translation by Otomasa Jun: *Senren sareta Doitsugo: Sono ikusei no ayumi* [Sophisticated German: The History of Its Development]. Tokyo: Hakusuisha, 1977.

Koerner, Konrad. 1973. *Ferdinand de Saussure.* Japanese translation by Yamanaka Keiichi: *Soshūru no gengoron.* Tokyo: Taishūkan, 1982.

———. 1989. *Practicing Linguistic Histography.* Amsterdam: John Benjamin.

Kohn, Hans. 1961. *The Habsburg Empire.* Japanese translation by Ineno Tsuyoshi et al.: *Hapusuburuku teikokushi nyūmon.* Tokyo: Kōbunsha, 1982.

Kokugo Gakkai, ed. 1955. *Kokugogaku jiten* [*Kokugogaku* Dictionary]. Tokyo: Tōkyōdō.

Kokugo Kyōiku Gakkai, ed. 1940. *Hyōjungo to kokugo kyōiku* [*Hyōjungo* and *Kokugo* Education]. Tokyo: Iwanami Shoten.

Komagome Takeshi. 1996. *Shokuminchi teikoku Nihon no bunka tōgō* [Cultural Unification in the Colonial Japanese Empire]. Tokyo: Iwanami Shoten.

Kugimoto Hisaharu. 1944. *Sensō to nihongo* [Wars and the Japanese Language]. Tokyo: Ryūbun Shokyoku.

Kyōgoku Koichi. 1986 "Kokugo, hōgo, nihongo ni tsuite" [About *Kokugo, Hōgo,* and *Nihongo*]. *Kokugogaku* 146.

Lobscheid, William. 1866–1869. *English and Chinese Dictionary.* Hong Kong: Daily Press.

Manshūkoku Kyōikushi Kenkyūkai, ed. 1993. *Manshū, manshūkoku kyōiku shiryō shūsei* [Compilation of Educational Resources of Manchuria and Manchukuo]. Vol. 10: *Kyōiku naiyō, hōhō* [Content and Methods of Education]. Tokyo: Emutii Shuppan.

Maruya Saiichi, ed. 1983. *Nihongo no sekai* [The World of the Japanese Language]. Vol. 16: *Kokugo kaikaku o hihan suru* [Critique of *Kokugo* Reform]. Tokyo: Chūōkōronsha.

Masubuchi Tsunekichi, ed. 1981. *Kokugo kyōiku-shi shiryō* [Source Book of History of *Kokugo* Education]. Vol. 5: *Kyouiku katei-shi* [History of Curriculum]. Tokyo: Tōkyō Hōrei Shuppan.

Matsumoto Sannosuke, ed. 1967. *Kindai Nihon shisō taikei* [Compendia of Modern Thinking]. Vol. 30: *Meiji shisō shū* [Collection of Meiji Thinkers' Writings].

Matsuzaka Tadanori. 1962. *Kokugo kokuji ronsō: Fukko shugi e no hanron* [The Debate about *Kokugo* and *Kokuji*: An Argument against Reactionalism]. Tokyo: Shinkō Shuppansha.

Meiji Bunka Kenkyūkai, ed. [1928] 1955. *Meiji bunka zenshū* [Meiji Culture Library]. Vol. 1. Tokyo: Nihon Hyōronsha.

———. [1929] 1967. *Meiji bunka zenshū* [Meiji Culture Library]. Vol. 24. Tokyo: Nihon Hyōronsha.

Miyata Setsuko. 1985. *Chōsen minshū to "kōmin-ka" seisaku* [The Korean People and the "Imperialization" Policy]. Tokyo: Miraisha.

Monbushō. 1939. *Meiji ikō kyōiku seido hattatsu-shi 10* [Progress in the Educational System after Meiji, vol. 10]. Comp. Kyōiku-shi Hensan-kai [Editorial Board for Educational History]. Tokyo: Ryūginsha.

———. 1941. Second Conference on the Provisions of *Kokugo.* Stenograph record.

———. 1949. *Kokugo chōsa enkaku shiryō* [Record of the History of *Kokugo* Investigation]. Comp. Kyōkasho-kyoku Kokugo-ka [Kokugo Office of Textbook Department].

Mori Arinori. 1872. "Letter Addressed to Whitney." In Ōkubo Toshiaki, 1:305–310.

———. 1873. "Education in Japan." In Ōkubo Toshiaki, 3:213–267.

———. 1972. *Mori Arinori zenshū* [Complete Works of Mori Arinori]. Vols. 1–3. Tokyo: Senbundō Shoten.

Mori Ōgai. 1978. *Ōgai senshū.* [Selected Writings by Mori Ōgai]. Vol. 2. Tokyo: Iwanami Shoten.

Morioka Kenji. 1969. *Kindai-go no seiritsu: Meijiki goi hen* [Establishment of the Modern Language: Vocabulary in the Meiji Period]. Tokyo: Meiji Shoin.

Nakauchi Toshio, ed. 1969. *Nashonarisumu to kyōiku* [Nationalism and Education]. Tokyo: Kokudosha.

———, 1985. *Nihon kyōiku no nashonarizumu* [Nationalism in Japanese Education]. Tokyo: Daisan Bunmeisha.

———. 1988. *Gunkoku bidan to kyōkasho* [Admirable Stories and Textbooks in Wartime]. Tokyo: Iwanami Shoten.

Negoro Tsukasa. 1985. *Tokieda Motoki kenkyū: Gengo katei setsu* [Study about Tokieda Motoki: The Theory of "Language as Process"]. Tokyo: Meiji Shoin.

———. 1988. *Tokieda Motoki kenkyū: Kokugo kyōiku* [Study about Tokieda Motoki: Kokugo Education]. Tokyo: Meiji Shoin.

Newmeyer, Frederick J. 1986. *The Politics of Linguistics.* Chicago: University of Chicago Press. Japanese translation by Baba Akira and Nishina Hiroyuki: *Kōsōsuru gengogaku.* Tokyo: Iwanami Shoten, 1994.

Nihon Gengo Gakkai. 1995. "Hattori Shirō hakase ryaku nenpyō" [Abbreviated Chronology of Dr. Shiro Hattori's Works]. In *Gengo kenkyū* [Research of Language] (November).

Nihon Kokugo Kai, ed. 1943. *Kokugo no songen* [The Dignity of *Kokugo*]. Tokyo: Kokumin Hyōronsha.

Nihongo no rekishi [History of the Japanese Language]. 1965. Vol. 6: *Atarashii kokugo e no ayumi* [Footsteps towards New *Kokugo*]. Vol. 7: *Sekai no naka no nihongo* [The Japanese Language in the World]. Tokyo: Heibonsha.

Nishio Minoru and Hisamatsu Sen'ichi, eds. 1969. *Kokugo kokuji kyōiku shiryō sōran.* [Summary of Resources about the Educational History of *Kokugo* and the National Script]. Tokyo: Kokugo Kyōiku Kenkyūkai.

Noguchi Takehiko. 1994. *Sannin-shō no hakken made.* [The Path to the Discovery of Third-Person Pronouns]. Tokyo: Chikuma Shobō.

Nomura Masaaki. 1988. *Kanji no mirai* [The Future of *Kanji*]. Tokyo: Chikuma Shobō.

Ochiai Naobumi, Ueda Kazutoshi, Haga Yaichi, Fujioka Sakutarō.1968. Meiji bungaku zenshū 44 [Complete Collection of Meiji Literature 44]. Tokyo: Chikuma Shobō.

Oguma Eiji. 1995. *Tan'itsu minzoku shinwa no kigenn* [The Origin of the Myth of a Single Race]. Tokyo: Shin'yōsha.

Okamoto Kōji. 1996. *Kita Ikki: Tenkanki no shisō kōzō* [Kita Ikki: The Structure of the Ideology in Crisis]. Tokyo: Mineruva Shobō.

Ōkubo Tadatoshi. 1978. *Ichi-oku-nin no kokugo kokuji mondai* [*Kokugo Kokuji* Issues for All Japanese (literally, a hundred million people)]. Tokyo: Sanseidō.

Ōkubo Toshiaki. ed. 1972. *Mori Arinori zenshū* [Complete Works of Mori Arinori]. Vols. 1–3. Tokyo: Senbundō Shoten.

Ong, Walter J. 1982. *Orality and Literacy: The Technologizing of the Word.* New York: Methuen. Japanese translation by Sakurai Naobumi et al.: *Koe no bunka to moji no bunka.* Tokyo: Fujiwara Shoten, 1991.

Ōno Susumu. 1983. "Kokugo kaikaku no rekishi (Sen-zen)" [History of *Kokugo* Reform (Prewar Time)]. In Maruya, ed , 5–94.

———. 1989. *Nihongo to sekai* [The Japanese Language and the World]. Tokyo: Kōdansha.

Ōtski Fumihiko et al. 1932–1937. *Daigenkai* [Expanded Sea of Words] Tokyo: Toyamabō.

Paul, Hermann. 1880. *Prinzipien der Sprachphilosophie* [Principles of the Philosophy of Language] Japanese translation by Fukumoto Yoshinosuke: *Gengoshi genri* [Principles of the History of Language]. Tokyo: Kōdansha, 1976.

Pedersen, Holgar. 1924. *Sprogvidenskaben i det nittende Aarhundrede.* Copenhagen: Gyldendal, Nordisk forlag. Japanese translation by Itō Tadamasa: *Gengogakushi* [The History of Linguistics]. Tokyo: Kobian Shobō, 1974.

von Polenz, Peter. 1970. *Geschichte der deutschen Sprache.* Berlin: de Gruyter. Japanese translation by Iwasaki Eijirō et al.: *Doitsugo-shi* [The History of the German Language]. Tokyo Hakusuisha, 1974.

Robins, Robert Henry. 1968. *A Short History of Linguistics.* Bloomington: Indiana University Press. Japanese translation by Nakamura Tamotsu and Gotō Hitoshi: *Gengogakushi.* Tokyo: Kenkyūsha, 1992.

Sakuma Kanae. 1942. *Nihongo no tameni* [For the Japanese Language]. Tokyo: Kōseikaku.

Sanada Shinji. 1987. *Hyōjungo no seiritsu jijō* [The Background of the Establishment of Standard Japanese]. Tokyo: PHP Kenkyūjo.

Sasaki Chikara. 1985. *Kagaku kakumei no rekishi kōzō* [Historical Structure of Scientific Revolutions]. Vols. 1 and 2. Tokyo: Iwanami Shoten.

Saussure, Ferdinand de. [1916] 1966. *Cours de linguistique générale.* English translation by Wade Baskin: *Course in General Linguistics.* New York: McGraw-Hill, 1966. Japanese translation by Kobayashi Hideo: *Ippan gengogaku kōgi.* Tokyo: Iwanami Shoten, 1972.

Scaglione, Aldo, ed. 1984. *The Emergence of National Languages.* Ravenna: Longo.

Seton-Watson, Hugh. 1981. *Language and National Consciousness.* London: The British Academy.

Shi Gang. 1993. *Shokuminchi shihai to nihongo* [Colonization and the Japanese Language]. Tokyo: Sangensha.

Shibata Shōkichi and Koyasu Takashi. 1873. *Fuon sōzu eiwa jii* [English-Japanese Dictionary with Pronunciation and Illustrations]. Tokyo: Nisshūsha.

———. 1882. *Zōho teisei ei-wa jii. Dai ni-han.* [Expanded and Revised English-Japanese Dictionary. Second Edition] Tokyo: Nisshūsha.

Shibata Takeshi. 1977. "Hyōjungo, kyōtsūgo, hōgen" [The Standard Language, the Common Language, and Dialects]. In Bunkachō, ed., "Kotoba" Shiriizu 6 ["Language" Series 6]: *Hyōjungo to hōgen* [The Standard Language and Dialects]. Tokyo: Ōkurashō Insatsukyoku.

Shida Nobuyoshi. 1943. *Daitōa gengo kensetsu no kihon* [The Foundation for Constructing the Language of Greater East Asia]. Tokyo: Unebi Shobō.

Shiga Naoya. 1974. *Shiga Naoya zenshū.* [Complete Works of Shiga Naoya]. Vol. 7. Tokyo: Iwanami Shoten.

Shioda Norikazu. 1973. *Nihon no gengo seisaku no kenkyū* [A Study of Japanese Language Policy]. Tokyo: Kuroshio Shuppan.

Shinmura Izuru. 1933. "Gengogaku gairon" [Introduction to Linguistics]. In *Iwanami kōza Nihon bungaku* [Iwanami Series of Japanese Literature]. Vol. 2. Tokyo: Iwanami Shoten.

———. 1937. "Ueda sensei o shinobu" [In Memory of Professor Ueda]. *Kokugo to kokubungaku* [*Kokugo* and Japanese Literature] (December). Also in *Ochiai* 1968, 402–404.

Silverstein, Michael, ed. 1971. *Whitney on Language: Selected Writings of William Dwight Whitney.* Cambridge: MIT Press.

Sugimori Hisahide. 1983. "Kokugo kaikaku no rekishi—sengo" [The History of *Kokugo* Reform—After the War]. In Maruya, ed., 95–167.

Sugimoto Tsutomu. 1981. *Kindai nihongo* [Modern Japanese]. Tokyo: Kinokuniya Shoten.

Suzuki Shizuo and Yokoyama Michiyoshi, eds. 1984. *Shinsei kokka Nihon to ajia* [The Divine Nation Japan and Asia]. Tokyo: Keisō Shobō.

Suzuki Takao. 1989. "Nihongo kokusai-ka e no shōgai" [Obstacles for Internationalization of Japanese]. In Nihon Mirai Gakkai, ed., *Nihongo wa kokusai-go ni naru ka* [Will Japanese Become an International Language?]. Tokyo: TBS Britannica.

Suzuki Yasuyuki. 1977. *Kokugo kokuji mondai no riron* [Theories for *Kokugo* and *Kokuji* Issues]. Tokyo: Mugi Shobō.

Taiyō. 1899. Vol. 5, no. 22.

———. 1900. Vol. 6, no. 6.

Takamori Kuniaki. 1979. *Kindai kokugo kyōikushi* [The History of *Kokugo* Education in Modern Japan]. Tokyo: Hato-no-mori Shobō.

Takebe Yoshiaki. 1977. "Kokugo kokuji mondai no yurai" [The Root of Issues on *Kokugo* and National Script]. In Iwanami kōza nihongo 3 [Iwanami Series on the Japanese Language, vol. 3]: *Kokugo kokuji mondai* [The Issues on *Kokugo* and the National Script]. Tokyo: Iwanami Shoten.

Tanaka Katsuhiko. 1975. *Gengo no shisō* [Ideology of Language]. Tokyo: Nihon Hōsō Kyōkai.

———. 1978. *Gengo kara mita minzoku to kokka* [Ethnicity and the Nation-State Seen through Languages]. Tokyo: Iwanami Shoten.

———. 1981. *Kotoba to kokka* [Language and the Nation-State]. Tokyo: Iwanami Shoten.

———. 1989. *Kokka-go o koete* [Beyond a State Language]. Tokyo: Chikuma Shobō.

———. 1993. *Gengogaku to wa nanika* [What Is Linguistics?]. Tokyo: Iwanami Shoten.

Taylor, Alan John Percivale. 1948. *The Habsburg Monarchy, 1809–1918: A History of the Austrian Empire and Austria-Hungary*. Japanese translation by Kurata Minoru: *Hapusuburuku teikoku 1809–1918*. Tokyo: Chikuma Shobō, 1987.

Thomas, George. 1991. *Linguistic Purism*. London: Longman.

Tokieda Motoki. 1941. *Kokugogaku genron* [The Principles of *Kokugogaku*]. Tokyo: Iwanami Shoten.

———. 1942. "Chōsen ni okeru kokugo seisaku oyobi kokugo kyōiku no shōrai" [*Kokugo* Policies for Korea and the Future of *Kokugo* Education]. *Nihongo* [The Japanese Language], August: 54–63.

———. 1947. "Kokugo kihan ron no kōsō" [Outline of a Normative *Kokugo*]. In Tokieda 1976.

———. 1955. *Kokugogaku genron: Zokuhen* [The Principles of *Kokugogaku*: A Sequel]. Tokyo: Iwanami Shoten.

———. 1956a. *Gendai no kokugogaku* [*Kokugogaku* Today]. Tokyo: Yūseidō.

———. 1956b. "Reimeiki no kokugogaku to kokugo seisakuron to no kōshō" [Relation between *Kokugogaku* and Theories of *Kokugo* Policy in Incunabula.] In Tokieda 1976.

———. 1961. *Kokugo mondai to kokugo kyōiku (zōteiban)* [*Kokugo* Issues and *Kokugo* Education (Revised Edition)]. Tokyo: Chūkyō Shuppan.

———. 1962. *Kokugo mondai no tame ni: Kokugo mondai hakusho* [For *Kokugo* Issues: White Paper on *Kokugo* Issues]. Tokyo: Tōkyō Daigaku Shuppan-kai.

———. [1940] 1966. *Kokugogaku shi* [History of *Kokugogaku*]. Tokyo: Iwanami Shoten.

———. 1973. *Gengo honshitsuron* [Essential Qualities of Language]. Tokyo: Iwanami Shoten.

———. 1976. *Gengo seikatsu ron* [Theory of Linguistic Life]. Tokyo: Iwanami Shoten.

Townson, Michael. 1992. *Mother-tongue and Fatherland: Language and Politics in German.* Manchester: Manchester University Press.

Toyoda Kunio. 1964. *Minzoku to gengo no mondai: Gengo seisaku no kadai to sono kōsatsu* [Problems in Ethnicity and Language: Issues in Language Policy and Their Examination]. Tokyo: Kinseisha.

Tsai Mao-Feng. 1989. *Taiwan ni okeru nihongo kyōiku no shiteki kenkyū* [A Historical Study of Japanese Language Education in Taiwan]. Taipei: Soochow University.

Ueda Kazutoshi. 1890. *Kokubungaku* [Japanese Literature]. Tokyo: Sōsōkan.

———. [1895] 1897. *Kokugo no tame.* [For *Kokugo*]. Tokyo: Toyamabō.

———. 1903. *Kokugo no tame. Dai-ni* [For *Kokugo*. No. 2]. Tokyo: Toyamabō.

———. 1916. *Kokugogaku no jukkō* [Ten Lectures about *Kokugogaku*]. Tokyo: Kyōkadō.

———. 1975. *Gengogaku* [Linguistics]. Tokyo: Kyōiku shuppan.

———. [1896 and 1897] 1975. *Gengogaku* [Linguistics]. Lecture notes by Shinmura Izuru; edited by Shibata Takeshi. Tokyo: Kyōiku Shuppan.

———. 1981. *Kokugogaku-shi* [The History of *Kokugogaku*]. Lecture notes by Shinmura Izuru; edited by Furuta Tōsaku. Tokyo: Kyōiku Shuppan.

Ueda Kazutoshi and Matsui Kanji, eds. 1915. *Dai Nihon kokugo jiten* [Dictionary of the Japanese National Language]. Tokyo: Toyamabō.

Umene Satoru. 1967. *Kindai kokka to minshū kyōiku: Puroisen minshū kyōiku seisakushi* [Modern Nations and Public Education: A History of Public Educational Policies in Prussia]. Tokyo: Seibundō Shinkōsha.

———, ed. 1975. *Chōsen kyōikushi.* [Educational History in Korea]. Vol. 5 of *Sekai kyōikushi taikei* [Compendium of World History of Education]. Tokyo: Kōdansha.

———, ed. 1977. *Doitsu kyōikushi II* [Educational History in Germany 2]. Vol. 12 of *Sekai kyōikushi taikei* [Compendium of World History of Education 12]. Tokyo: Kōdansha.

Watanabe Manabu and Hiroshi Abe. 1987–1991. *Nihon shokuminchi kyōiku seisaku shiryō shūsei: Chōsen-hen* [Compilation of Historical Resource on Educational Policy in Japanese Colonies: Korea]. Vols. 16, 17, 63, 69. Tokyō: Ryūkei Shosha.

Whitney, W. D. 1872. "On the Adoption of the English Language in Japan." In Ōkubo Toshiaki 1972, 3:414–423.

———. [1875] 1979. *The Life and Growth of Language.* New York: Dover.

Yamada Yoshio. 1932. *Kokugo seisaku no konpon mondai* [The Fundamental Problems in *Kokugo* Policy]. Tokyo: Hōbunkan.

———. 1935. *Kokugogakushi yō* [Concise History of *Kokugogaku*]. Tokyo: Iwanami Shoten.

———. 1938. *Kokugo sonchō no konpongi* [The Essential Meaning of Respect for *Kokugo*]. Tokyo: Hakusuisha.

———. 1940. "Iwayuru kokugo mondai no kisū" [The Result of So-called *Kokugo* Problems]. *Bungaku* (April).

———. 1943a. *Kokugo no honshitsu* [The Essence of *Kokugo*]. Tokyo: Hakusuisha.

———. 1943b. *Kokugogakushi* [The History of *Kokugogaku*]. Tokyo: Hōbunkan.

Yamaguchi Kiichirō. 1940. "Kaigai ni okeru nihongo kyōiku" [Japanese Language Education Overseas]. In Kokugo Kyōiku Gakkai 1940.

Yamamoto Masahide. 1965. *Kindai buntai hassei no shiteki kenkyū* [Historical Study about the Emergence of the Modern Writing Style]. Tokyo: Iwanami Shoten.

———, ed. 1978. *Kindai buntai keisei shiryō shūsei: Hassei-hen* [Collection of Historical Resources for the Formation of the Modern Writing Style: Emergence]. Tokyo: Ōfū-sha.

———, ed. 1979. *Kindai buntai keisei shiryō shūsei: Seiritsu-hen* [Collection of Historical Resources for the Formation of the Modern Writing Style: Establishment]. Tokyo: Ōfū-sha.

———. 1981. *Genbun itchi no rekishi ronkō. Zoku-hen* [A Study of the History of *Genbun itchi*: Sequel]. Tokyo: Ōfū-sha

Yamamoto Yūzō, ed. 1995. *"Manshūkoku" no kenkyū* [A Study of "Manchukuo"]. Tokyo: Ryokuin Shobō.

Yamamuro Shin'ichi. 1993. *Kimera: Manshūkoku no shōzō* [Chimera: A Portrait of Manchukuo]. Tokyo: Chūkō Shinsho.

Yanagita Kunio. 1963a. *Hyōjungo to hōgen* [Standard Japanese and Dialects]. In *Tei-hon Yanagita Kunio shū* [Vulgate Collection of Works by Yanagita Kunio]. Vol. 18. Tokyo: Chikuma Shobō.

———. 1963b. *Kokugo no shōrai* [The Future of *Kokugo*]. In *Teihon Yanagita Kunio shū* [Vulgate Collection of Works by Yanagita Kunio]. Vol. 19. Tokyo: Chikuma Shobō.

Yanaihara Tadao. 1963. *Yanaihara Tadao zenshū* [Complete Works of Yanaihara Tadao]. Vols. 1 and 4. Tokyo: Iwanami Shoten.

Yokoyama Gennosuke. 1954. *Naichi zakkyo go no Nihon* [Japan after the Opening of the Concessions]. Tokyo: Iwanami Shoten.

Yoshida Sumio. 1975. "Dodai zukuri ni shūshi shita Hoshina Kōichi" [Hoshina Kōichi, Who Devoted His Life on Groundwork]. In Hatano et al., eds., 205–216.

———. 1964. *Meiji ikō kokugo mondai ron-shū* [Essays on *Kokugo* Issues after Meiji]. Tokyo: Kazama Shobō.

———. 1972. *Meiji ikō kokugo mondai shoan shūsei* [Collection of Proposals for *Kokugo* Issues after Meiji]. Vol 1: *Goi, yōgo, jiten, kokugo mondai to kyōiku hen* [Vocabulary, Technical Terms, Dictionaries, and Problems in *Kokugo* and Education]. Tokyo: Kazama Shobō.

————. 1973. *Meiji ikō kokugo mondai shoan shūsei* [Collection of Proposals for *Kokugo* Issues after Meiji]. Vol 2: *Buntai, gohō, on'in, hōgen hen* [Styles, Word Usage, Phonology, Dialects]. Tokyo: Kazama Shobō.

Yoshida Sumio and Inokuchi Yūichi, eds. 1950. *Kokuji mondai ron-shū* [Essays on *Kokuji* Issues]. Vol. 1. Tokyo: Toyamabō.

Index

About the Author and Translator

Lee Yeounsuk is professor at the Graduate School of Language and Society, Hitotsubashi University, Tokyo. The original Japanese edition of *The Ideology of Kokugo (Kokugo to iu shisō)* was awarded the 1997 Prize for Social Sciences and Humanities, Literary and Art Criticism category, by the Suntory Foundation.

Maki Hirano Hubbard is associate professor of Japanese in the Department of East Asian Languages and Literatures, Smith College.

Production Notes for Lee & Hubbard / THE IDEOLOGY OF *KOKUGO*

Interior designed by University of Hawai'i Press production staff with text in Minion Pro and display in ITC Stone Sans.

Composition by Lucille C. Aono

Printing and binding by Edwards Brothers, Inc.